AN HISTORICAL GEOGRAPHY OF IRAN

MODERN CLASSICS IN
NEAR EASTERN STUDIES

GENERAL EDITORS:

CHARLES ISSAWI

AND

BERNARD LEWIS

AN HISTORICAL GEOGRAPHY OF IRAN

W. BARTHOLD

TRANSLATED BY
SVAT SOUCEK

EDITED WITH AN INTRODUCTION BY
C. E. BOSWORTH

PRINCETON UNIVERSITY PRESS
PRINCETON, NEW JERSEY

Published by Princeton University Press,
41 William Street, Princeton, New Jersey 08540
In the United Kingdom:
Princeton University Press, Guildford, Surrey

Library of Congress Cataloging in Publication Data
will be found on the last printed page of this book
ISBN 0-691-05418-5

Publication of this book has been aided by a grant from
The Andrew W. Mellon Foundation

This book has been composed in Linotron Baskerville
Clothbound editions of Princeton University Press books
are printed on acid-free paper, and binding materials
are chosen for strength and durability.

Printed in the United States of America by
Princeton University Press, Princeton, New Jersey

Translated from the Russian *Istoriko-geograficheskii obzor Irana* (Moscow, 1971).
The translation of this volume was made possible through a grant from
the translation program of the National Endowment for the Humanities,
to which we would like to express our deep appreciation.

CONTENTS

LIST OF ABBREVIATIONS

AA	*Archäologischer Anzeiger*
AGWG	*Abhandlungen der Königlichen Gesellschaft der Wissenschaften zu Göttingen, phil.-hist. Kl.*
AI	*Athār-é Irān*
AJA	*American Journal of Archaeology*
AMI	*Archaeologische Mitteilungen aus Iran*
AN	Akademiia Nauk
ANVA	*Avhandlinger utgivet av Det Norske Videnskaps-Akademi, Oslo*
AO	*Acta Orientalia*
AOHung	*Acta Orientalia Hungarica*
AOr	*Archív Orientální*
APAW	*Abhandlungen der Preussischen Akademie der Wissenschaften, phil.-hist. Kl.*
BGA	*Bibliotheca Geographorum Arabicorum*
BSO[A]S	*Bulletin of the School of Oriental [and African] Studies*
CAJ	*Central Asiatic Journal*
EI[1]	*Encyclopaedia of Islam,* 1st edition
EI[2]	*Encyclopaedia of Islam,* 2nd edition
EW	*East and West*
Farhang	*Farhang-i jughrāfiyā-yi Īrān*
GAL	C. Brockelmann, *Geschichte der arabischen Literatur*
GIPh	W. Geiger and E. Kuhn, eds., *Grundriss der iranischen Philologie*
GJ	*Geographical Journal*
GMS	Gibb Memorial Series
HJAS	*Harvard Journal of Asiatic Studies*
HOr	*Handbuch der Orientalistik*
İA	*İslâm Ansiklopedisi*
IIJ	*Indo-Iranian Journal*
IJMES	*International Journal of Middle East Studies*
IQ	*Islamic Quarterly*
Iran, JBIPS	*Iran, Journal of the British Institute of Persian Studies*
Isl.	*Der Islam*
IUTAKÈ	*Trudy Iuzhno-Turkmenistanskoi arkheologicheskoi kompleksnoi èkspeditsii*

JA	*Journal Asiatique*
JASB	*Journal of the Asiatic Society of Bengal*
JAOS	*Journal of the American Oriental Society*
JESHO	*Journal of the Economic and Social History of the Orient*
JNES	*Journal of Near Eastern Studies*
JRAS	*Journal of the Royal Asiatic Society*
JRCAS	*Journal of the Royal Central Asian Society*
JSFOu	*Journal de la Société Finno-Ougrienne*
JSS	*Journal of Semitic Studies*
MO	*Le Monde Oriental*
NGWG	*Nachrichten von der Königlichen Gesellschaft der Wissenschaften zu Göttingen*
NTS	*Norsk Tidsskrift for Sprogvidenskap*
OLZ	*Orientalistische Literaturzeitung*
OON	*Otdelenie obshchestvennykh nauk*
PRGS	*Proceedings of the Royal Geographical Society*
PW	Pauly-Wissowa, *Real-Encyclopädie der classischen Altertumswissenschaft*
REI	*Revue des Études Islamiques*
RMM	*Revue du Monde Musulman*
SA	*Sovetskaia Arkheologiia*
SBAW Berlin	*Sitzungsberichte der Königlich. Preussischen Akademie der Wissenschaften, Berlin, phil.-hist. Kl.*
SBWAW	*Sitzungsberichte der Kaiserlichen Akademie der Wissenschaften zu Wien, phil.-hist. Kl.*
SB Bayr. AW	*Sitzungsberichte der Königlichen Akademie der Wissenschaften zu München, phil.-hist. Kl.*
Soch.	V. V. Bartol'd, *Sochineniia*, Moscow, 1963-1977. 9 vols.
SON	*Seriia obshchestvennykh nauk*
Survey of Persian Art	A. U. Pope and P. A. Ackermann, eds. *A Survey of Persian Art from Prehistoric Times to the Present*. 6 vols. London and New York, 1938-1939.
TPS	*Transactions of the Philological Society*
ZA	*Zeitschrift für Assyriologie*
ZDMG	*Zeitschrift der Deutschen Morgenländischen Gesellschaft*
ZII	*Zeitschrift für Indologie und Iranistik, Leipzig*
ZVORAO	*Zapiski Vostochnogo Otdeleniia Russkogo Arkheologicheskogo Obshchestva*

MAPS

CAUCASUS MOUNTAINS
Kura
Tiflis
Shakī
Aras
Erivan
Ganja
(Kirovabad)
Kura
Bākū
MT. ARARAT
ARMENIA
USSR
IRAN
Aras
MŪQĀN STEPPE
TURKEY
IRAN
AZERBAIJAN
CASPIAN SEA
Tabrīz
Ardabīl
LAKE URMIYA
TURKEY
IRAQ
Marāgha
Miyāna
Bandar Anzalī
Rasht
GĪLĀN
MĀZANDARĀN
Safīd Rūd
Qazwīn
USSR
IRAN
Atrak
GURGĀN
Bandar Shāh
Astarābād
MOUNTAINS
KHURĀ
Mosul
IRAN
ELBURZ
Tehran
Ray
Dāmghān
Sabzawār
Nishāpūr
Simnān
QŪMIS
Warāmīn
Tigris
IRAQ
MESOPOTAMIA
Hamadān
KURDISTĀN
Kirmānshāhān
Qum
Arak
Kāshān
DASHT-I KAWĪR
(desert)
Baghdad
Karkha
Diz
Gulpāyagān
LURISTĀN
QŪHISTĀN
KŪH-I ZARD
Iṣfahān
Dizfūl
Zāyinda Rūd
Kārūn
Yazd
DASHT-I LŪT
(desert)
Euphrates
Kārūn
Ahvāz
KHŪZISTĀN
ZAGROS MOUNTAINS
Baṣra
SHAṬṬ AL-ʿARAB
Ābādān
IRAQ
KUWAIT
Rafsanjān
FĀRS
Kirmān
Shīrāz
KIRMĀN
PERSIAN GULF
Bandar ʿAbbās
MAKRĀ
QISHM
ST. OF HURMUZ
IRAN
miles
0 50 100 150
0 km 150
OMAN
GULF
Masqaṭ

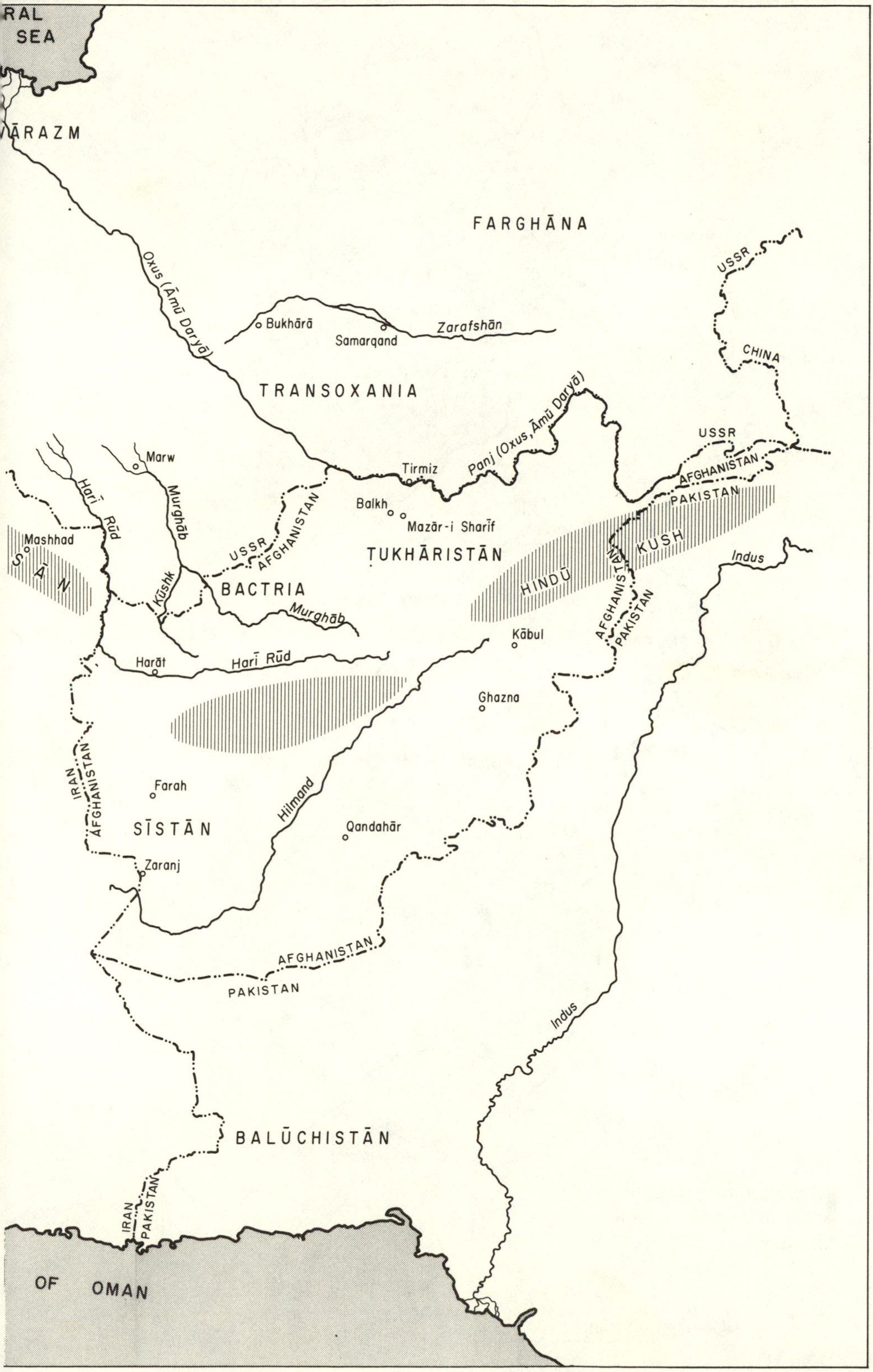

RAL
SEA
ĀRAZM
FARGHĀNA
Oxus (Āmū Daryā)
Bukhārā
Samarqand
Zarafshān
TRANSOXANIA
Panj (Oxus, Āmū Daryā)
USSR
CHINA
USSR
AFGHANISTAN
PAKISTAN
Marw
Harī Rūd
Murghāb
Tirmiz
Balkh
Mazār-i Sharīf
Mashhad
USSR
AFGHANISTAN
ṬUKHĀRISTĀN
HINDŪ KUSH
Indus
Kūshk
BACTRIA
Murghāb
AFGHANISTAN
PAKISTAN
Kābul
Harāt
Harī Rūd
Ghazna
IRAN
AFGHANISTAN
Farah
Hilmand
SĪSTĀN
Qandahār
Zaranj
AFGHANISTAN
PAKISTAN
Indus
BALŪCHISTĀN
IRAN
PAKISTAN
OF OMAN

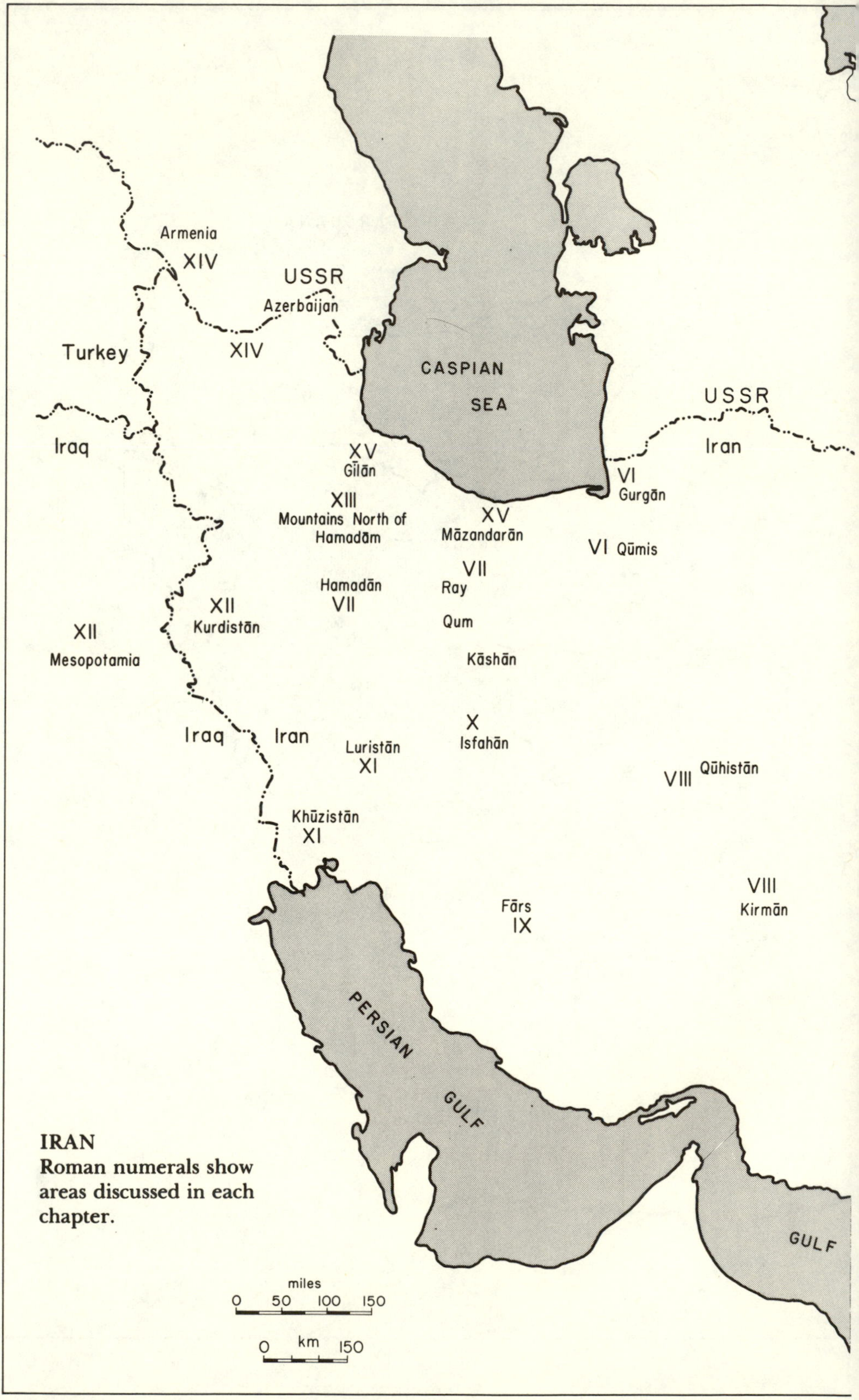

IRAN
Roman numerals show areas discussed in each chapter.

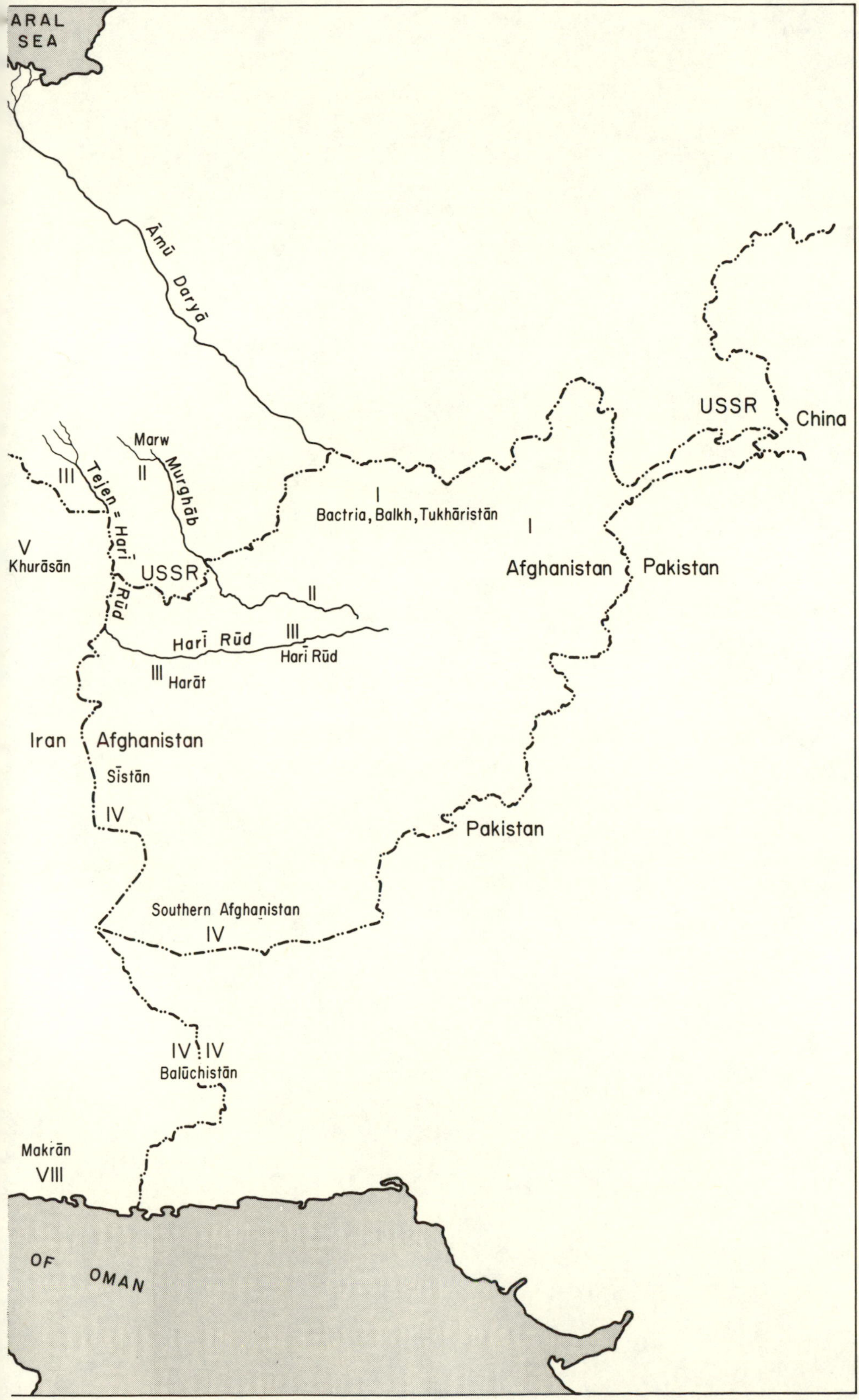
ARAL SEA
Āmū Daryā
Marw
Murghāb
III
Tejen = Harī Rūd
II
I
Bactria, Balkh, Tukhāristān
I
Afghanistan
Pakistan
USSR
China
V
Khurāsān
USSR
II
Harī Rūd
III
Harī Rūd
III
Harāt
Iran
Afghanistan
Sīstān
IV
Pakistan
Southern Afghanistan
IV
IV
IV
Balūchistān
Makrān
VIII
OF OMAN

EDITOR'S INTRODUCTION

No historian of the eastern Islamic world is unfamiliar with the works of Vasilii Vladimirovich Bartol'd (1869-1930), or Wilhelm Barthold, as his name was orginally rendered in the Germano-Russian milieu into which he was born. His magnum opus, the work based on his St. Petersburg doctoral thesis, *Turkestan down to the Mongol Invasion,* appeared in English in the Gibb Memorial Series in 1928, and with an extra, hitherto unpublished chapter, again in 1968. The late Professor V. and Mrs. T. Minorsky performed a valuable service in 1958-1962 by translating as *Four Studies on the History of Central Asia* (in fact, five studies) Barthold's *A Short History of Turkestan, History of the Semirechyé, Ulugh-Beg, Mīr ʿAlī Shīr,* and *A History of the Turkman People.*The lectures that Barthold gave in Turkish at Istanbul in 1926 are available in both German and French versions (*Zwölf Vorlesungen über die Geschichte der Türken Mittelasiens,* 1935, and *Histoire des Turcs d'Asie Centrale,* 1945). A general work on Asian exploration and the evolution of oriental studies appeared in French in 1947, *La découverte de l'Asie, histoire de l'orientalisme en Europe et en Russie.* Various other lesser works have been translated into western languages and into Arabic, Persian, and Turkish; Barthold wrote certain of his articles in the language of his family background, German; and the large number of articles that he wrote for the first edition of the *Encyclopaedia of Islam* (many of them now updated and included in the new edition) are also widely available to the non-Russophone reader. But although the work of translation has gone on steadily in the half-century since Barthold's death, these works still represent only a small part of his total oeuvre, extending over some forty years; the *Collected Works (Sochineniia)* that appeared at Moscow between 1963 and 1977 (comprising ten parts in nine volumes) amount to over 7,000 large pages.

The stature of the man emerges from these bare statistics and the recounting of titles. The lands of eastern Islam, from Iran to Afghanistan and Central Asia, were Barthold's particular sphere of interest, and above all the latter, for the Russian advance into Central Asia during the later nineteenth century opened up for Russian scholars exciting possibilities of historical and archaeological investigation, whereas earlier European travelers to places like Khiva, Bukhara, and Samarqand had had to contend with capricious and barbaric local potentates who hardly observed the international conventions of behavior toward accredited diplomats, let alone toward free-lance travelers and researchers, figures of suspicion at the best of times. Barthold realized early in his scholarly career at the University of St. Petersburg, where he lectured from 1896 onward, that the investigation of the history, topography, and antiquities of Central Asia offered a field similar to that opened up in the Indian subcontinent in the late eighteenth century for British scholars. Barthold made almost annual field trips to Central Asia starting in 1893, undeterred by the fact that in that first year, on a journey to Semirechye, he broke his leg and had to return to Tashkent for medical treatment. In the 1920s, he was much in demand by the various Soviet republics that had by 1924 emerged in Central Asia after the final extinguishing of nationalist and separatist aspirations there, to write local histories and accounts of the different Turkish peoples of the republics. Both in the Tsarist period and after, Barthold was insistent that Russian officials, traders, soldiers, and so on working in Central Asia should busy themselves in their spare time with the study of the region, recognizing how much invaluable work had been done for our knowledge of Indian geography, society, and history by successive generations of devoted British administrators and soldiers.

Central Asia has always been at the receiving end of religious, cultural, and other influences, rather than being a spontaneously creative region, and it is this receptiveness to an assortment of outside civilizations—including those of China, India, the Middle East—that makes the study of Central Asia and the interaction of these strands such a fascinating one. It does, however, make stringent demands on the scholar who would devote himself to Inner Asia, not least in the matter of linguistic equipment; hence the rarity of the multilingual Marquarts and Pelliots. Barthold's concern was more particularly Islamic Central Asia, and his skills lay chiefly in the sphere of the three great Islamic languages, Arabic, Persian, and Turkish. He was an exacting philologist, fully cognizant of the truism not always appreciated today that without philological expertise the would-be specialist in the Middle East, or for that matter, in any part of Asia, is as sounding brass or a tinkling cymbal. Accompanying his *Turkestan* when it appeared in 1898-1900 was a volume of texts, most of them edited for the first time by Barthold from manuscripts bristling with linguistic problems and difficulties of interpretation; many of these texts, such as Gardīzī's *Zayn al-akhbār*, ʿAwfī's *Jawāmiʿ al-ḥikāyāt*, and Isfizārī's *Rawḍāt al-jannāt*, have since been published, but here, as in so many spheres, Barthold was the pioneer.

One of those great civilizations that have profoundly affected Central Asia is the Iranian, for out of Iran such faiths as Zoroastrianism, Manicheism, Nestorian Christianity, and most recently Islam have been mediated to the Asian heartland. If only because a knowledge of Iranian civilization was a necessary adjunct to the understanding of Central Asia, Barthold was bound to be attracted to the study of Iran, a land with which Russia had already long been in intimate political, military, and commercial contact. Two of his major works, indeed, deal with it, the one translated here, and *Iran, a Historical Survey*, and both will now be available in English (a translation of the latter appeared at Bombay in about 1939).

Barthold's basic attitude to history was, as Professor Yuri Bregel has pointed out in a percipient study that should be read in conjunction with this present Introduction,[1] that of nineteenth-century German positivist historiography, with the evolution of mankind viewed as a convergence of originally distinct human societies through the diffusion of culturally more advanced societies to the less advanced. It was in the light of this process that he viewed such diverse phenomena as religion, the growth of world empires, the development of urban life, and the spread of international trade, and that he viewed with favor the *missions civilisatrices* of the imperial powers of his time, whether Britain in India and Africa or Russia in Central Asia, Siberia, and the Caucasus. It was, indeed, Barthold's intellectual support for the Imperial Russian mission in Central Asia (one whose positive achievements were appreciated at the time by outside observers such as Schuyler and Curzon) that eventually contributed to a fuller rehabilitation of his work in post-Stalinist Soviet Russia. For although Barthold, as a Russian patriot, had stayed on in Russia after the Bolshevik Revolution, he gave no assent to Communism and regarded Marx as an unhistorical, unscientific figure whose ideas had no relevance for oriental studies; he had never become a nonperson in Soviet scholarship, but his works had been somewhat neglected or cited only selectively and misleadingly in some quarters, above all in the Central Asian Soviet Republics.

The *Historical Geography of Iran* is essentially an analytical and

[1] "Barthold and Modern Oriental Studies," *IJMES*, XII (1980), 385-403.

descriptive work rather than an attempt at synthesis. Barthold was conscious of the backwardness of oriental studies in the identification and evaluation of the basic sources, compared with long-established disciplines such as classical studies and European literature and history. He held that the critical study of these basic sources was necessary before any meaningful grand syntheses could be made. Iran, with its successive great empires—those of the Achaemenids, Parthians, Sāsānids, and Muslims—its diverse faiths and its fine literary and artistic achievements, was already much more sharply focussed for the scholar than was Central Asia, but the historical geography of Iran, apart from groundwork done by such scholars as Tomaschek, had been hardly explored. As it happened, while Barthold was working on his book, two German scholars were also putting together outstanding contributions to this very subject, though from very different angles. Josef Marquart (a scholar whom Barthold felt to be to some extent a rival to himself, with their overlapping interests, and one whose wide-ranging speculations, even at times lucubrations, Barthold felt were often not sufficiently firmly grounded in reality) in his *Ērānšahr nach der Geographie des Ps. Moses Xorenacʿi* (1901) gave a translation of a brief and jejune Armenian geographical work enriched by a commentary of amazing erudition; and Paul Schwarz was embarking on his *Iran in Mittelalter* (1896-1936), a patient synthesis of all the information available in the medieval Islamic geographers but without any attempt at interpretation. These works Barthold was able to draw upon substantially only for his additional notes, but his own book stands as a parallel, though completely independent achievement, and has the additional advantage of providing a successful blend of classical, medieval Islamic, and modern European information on his subject.

For sources, Barthold accordingly drew upon the results of a patient sifting by earlier Iranists of the classical—above all Greek—sources on Iran; and then, for the earlier Islamic centuries, upon the corpus of ninth- and tenth-century Arabic geographical texts collected by M. J. de Goeje in his *Bibliotheca Geographorum Arabicorum* (1870-1894), supplemented by Yāqūt's *Muʿjam al-buldān*. For the period of the Saljuqs, Mongols, Tīmūrids, and so on, he had texts by authors such as Nasawī, Juwaynī, ʿAbd al-Razzāq Samarqandī, and Ḥāfiẓ-i Abrū, in the exploitation of which Barthold was often a trailblazer. For the period up to the present, for which primary historical sources in Persian or Arabic become sparser, he utilized fully the many European travelers, diplomatic envoys, merchants, members of religious orders, and so on who traveled within Iran, being thereby able, through the citation of such recent observers as I. N. Berezin, E. G. Browne, the Hon. G. N. Curzon, and A. V. Williams Jackson, to make his survey entirely up to date. It is not surprising that Barthold is particularly full on Khurāsān and the northeastern fringes of Iran, for Russian travelers and scholars had done much valuable spadework here for him; but the breadth of his treatment of other provinces such as Fārs and Azerbaijan shows that his mastery of the source material extended to the whole of historic Iran, including Mesopotamia, that at various epochs has formed part of the empires of Iran.

The basic sources for the medieval Islamic period have not been greatly enlarged since Barthold's time. Since it was only in 1922 that A.Z.V. Togan discovered at Mashhad a manuscript of the Arab traveler Abū Dulaf al-Khazrajī's second *risāla* on his travels in northern and western Iran, Barthold was not able to draw upon this, although he was of course aware of the numerous citations from this work in Yāqūt; I have therefore added the relevant references to Minorsky's 1955 edition and translation of the *risāla*. Also, Barthold naturally knew of the anonymous Persian geographical work from the late tenth century, the *Ḥudūd al-ʿālam*, acquired by Captain A. G. Tumanskii at Bukhara in 1893, and whose text he was later to edit and to have published posthumously (1930). But in the earlier period, he was only able to quote to a limited extent from a photographic copy, so that ampler references to the English translation and monumental commentary of Minorsky (1937) have been added by Livshits.

Finally, one should mention that a Persian translation of the *Historical Geography of Iran* was published at Tehran in 1930 by Sardādwar; it is now very hard to find,[2] and it may be fairly claimed that the present translation will for the first time make available to western readers one of the masterworks of a giant of oriental studies.

The translation has been made by Dr. Svat Soucek from the text of the *Istoriko-geograficheskii obzor Irana* given in Vol. VII of Barthold's *Sochineniia* (Moscow, 1971), pp. 31-225, a volume provided with a lengthy Introduction (pp. 5-28) by Dr. V. A. Livshits. Barthold's original text is liberally sprinkled with quotations from Ar-

[2] My colleague, Mr. Mohsen Ashtiany, tells me that it has, however, recently been reprinted in Iran.

abic, Persian, and Turkish sources given in the original Arabic script. These also have been translated; citations from classical Greek authors have been left in the original script.

The notes are an exceedingly valuable feature of this 1971 edition, but as translated in this present work they represent a palimpsest, as it were, of different layers by different hands. Barthold's original notes, given with the 1903 original text, were brief and largely confined to the citation of oriental texts used for the work. But as was his custom with other major works, over the years Barthold accumulated, out of his own reading and in some instances his closer personal acquaintance with the actual terrain, a rich collection of further references. Facsimile examples of Barthold's notes are given by Livshits at pp. 22-26 of his Introduction. Livshits has integrated these with the notes of the original edition (leaving them, in many cases, in their terse, elliptical, notelike form), and in the present translation, these are not otherwise distinguished; anyone who wishes to disentangle the 1903 notes from the subsequent ones can easily do so from the *Sochineniia* text. Livshits has, however, vastly increased the value of the latter text by adding his own extensive annotation, comprising in the main relevant works that appeared during the years 1930-1967. In the present translation, these are marked off by angle brackets, thus: ⟨⟨. . .⟩⟩. The final layer is that of my own notes, references to works that have either appeared since 1967 or that were published earlier but were apparently not available to Livshits in the Soviet Union. Furthermore, references to translations of texts into western European languages, for example to Yule's translation of Marco Polo and to Le Strange's one of Clavijo's *Embassy to Tamerlane*, have been given where Barthold cited only Russian translations. These additions of my own have been placed within square brackets, thus: ⟦. . .⟧ when they represent insertions within or additions to existing notes. Where a few notes have been inserted at fresh points in Barthold's text, these are indicated by letters, thus: a, b, c, etc. In general, however, I have sought not to overload still further an already substantial weight of annotation.

The bibliography given at the end of this book is a select one. Volume VII of the *Sochineniia* contains a bibliography of truly gargantuan dimensions (87 pages), although this also refers, it is true, to the other contents of the volume (*Iran, a Historical Survey,* some review articles and shorter articles, and some *Encyclopaedia of Islam* articles). The system that I have adopted within the body of the translation is to give the full title and bibliographical details when the work in question does not appear in the bibliography. The naturally very numerous Russian works cited by Barthold are usually given by short title only and without full bibliographical details. Sergei Shuiskii has assembled a bibliography of Russian works that gives the full references; this follows the main bibliography.

For measurements and distances, Barthold wisely did not attempt to reduce the figures given in his sources to a common denominator; hence one finds metric measurements side-by-side with, for example, English miles and the traditional Russian units. The reader may therefore find it useful to note that a verst is approximately a kilometer or 3,500 English feet in length, an arshin 28 inches in length, and a desiatina 2.7 acres in area.

C. E. Bosworth
December 1981

AN HISTORICAL GEOGRAPHY OF IRAN

INTRODUCTION

THE purpose of this work is to present a brief survey of the geography of Iran, to dwell in greater detail on the sites that were at various historical periods the centers of life, and to determine, as far as possible, the degree of dependence of this life on geographical circumstances.

"Iran" as a geographical term denotes an elevated plateau, bordering on the north and northeast the basins of the Caspian and Aral seas, and on the west, south, and southeast, the basin of the Indian ocean. The country is one of the so-called interior, landlocked basins, whose characteristic peculiarities have been best described by F. Richthofen in his book on China.[1] The main difference between these basins and the ocean-drained or peripheral ones is that in the former, all the products of mechanical or chemical decomposition (through the action of water, wind, and so on) remain within the region, whereas in the latter they are carried away into the sea; in the former the accumulation of such deposits gradually effaces the unevenness of the soil and is instrumental in its leveling, whereas in the latter the deposits pile up along the coasts and further the formation of deltas and the raising of sea bottoms; the waters that pass through a country on the way to the sea erode the soil more and more, and the unevenness of the latter becomes ever more sharply pronounced. This is, then, how in closed basins the compartmentalization of the surface gradually diminishes, whereas in the peripheral ones it increases. Lack of moisture in landlocked basins, however, allows only a minor part of the country's surface to be cultivated, and this hinders a solid and lasting development of culture and civilization; for these reasons landlocked basins sharply differ from the peripheral ones not only in geography but also in history.

The Iranian plateau is one of such interior basins with an extremely dry climate.[2] Except in a few mountain areas, agriculture

[1] ⟨⟨F. Fr. von Richthofen, *China. Ergebnisse eigener Reisen und darauf gegründeter Studien* (Berlin, 1877), 1. Theil, 6-21.⟩⟩

[2] For the absence of change in the climate during the last millennium, cf. W. Tomaschek, "Zur historischen Topographie, II," pp. 561-62; Polybius, X, 28, 3 cited by L. S. Berg, "Ob izmeneniiakh klimata v istoricheskuiu epokhu," *Zemlevedenie* (1911), book III, p. 80.

is possible here only through irrigation; for this reason all the rivers, except for the most important ones, are divided up into irrigation canals as soon as they leave the mountains. Their remaining waters disappear in the sands. Civilization is of necessity concentrated along the fringes of the mountains that cut through the plateau. For these same reasons, the geographical borders of Iran could not coincide with the political and ethnic ones. The fact that almost the entire interior of the country is unsuitable for sedentary civilization could not but force the Iranians to settle areas neighboring the oceanic and Aralo-Caspian basins. The easternmost branch of the Iranians, the Afghans, now live chiefly in the basin of the Indus, whereas the westernmost one, the Kurds, live in that of the Tigris.[3] These were the approximate limits within which lived the historical Iranians,[4] as a result of which F. Spiegel, the author of a voluminous (now already somewhat dated) work on Iran, considered it possible to give his book the following title: *Érân, das Land zwischen dem Indus und Tigris*.

In the ethnic sense, the term "Iranians," as is well known, denotes that branch of the Aryans who are closely related to those of India. The oldest monuments of Indian and Iranian literatures are linguistically so similar that an attempt has even been made to reconstruct, in general terms, the language spoken by the proto-historical common ancestors of the Iranians and Indians. H. Oldenberg in his book *Aus Indien und Iran* remarks that "we can trace down to individual details the processes through which that language, not a single word of which has been preserved by history, developed to the southeast of the Hindu Kush into the dialect of the Vedas, and to the southwest of these same mountains into that of the Avesta."[5] Of the two branches of the Asian Aryans—the Indians and Iranians—the Indians received their ethnic characteristics, it would seem, only in the country on that side of the Hindu Kush: there are no traces of Indians inhabiting the area to the north of these mountains. On the other hand, the Iranians, in the opinion of today's scholars, had at one time occupied a considerable portion of southern Russia and all of Turkestan, both western, present-day Russian, Turkestan and eastern Turkestan, that is, the Tarim

[3] ⟨⟨For the present-day limits of the spread of the Iranian languages, see Oranskii, *Vvedemie*, p. 288.⟩⟩

[4] In the *Kitāb al-Fihrist*, ed. G. Flügel, I, 18[2], Ṣughd was called Īrān al-Aʿlā, "Upper Iran"; see Ross-Gauthiot, "De l'alphabet soghdien," *JA*, ser. 10, vol. XVII (1911), 532.

[5] ⟨⟨H. Oldenberg, *Aus Indien und Iran* (Berlin, 1899), pp. 137-38.⟩⟩

basin. The languages spoken in this entire area already had the characteristic features of the Iranian idiom, not those of the proto-historical Indo-Iranian tongue. Both this fact and the few historical data available to us—the latter partly set out in F. A. Braun's magisterial dissertation *Razyskaniia v oblasti goto-slavianskikh otnoshenii* ["Researches in the Field of Gotho-Slavic Relations"][6]—make us suppose that the movement of the Iranians, after their separation from the Indians, proceeded from east to west rather than vice versa; the Iranians migrated into present-day Persia, most probably, also from the east,[7] and prior to their irruption there they reached a certain degree of cultural development in regions included today within the borders of Afghanistan. Here, in the basin of the Āmū Daryā and of other rivers that flow from the high mountain ranges that constitute that eastern limit of the Iranian plateau, the conditions of irrigation are somewhat more propitious than in the western part of Iran, for the high snow-clad mountain crests give rise to vigorous rivers. The traveler Ferrier, who in the years 1845-1846 crossed Persia and Afghanistan, states that through the area from Kermanshah, the principal town of Persian Kurdistān, to the Harī Rūd river, which represents the border of Persia and Afghanistan, he had to cross only brooks (*ruisseaux*); the Harī Rūd was the first river "à laquelle on puisse donner le nom de rivière."[8] According to Ferrier again, the Hilmand is the only water course in the entire area from the Tigris to the Indus that deserves the appellation of a full-fledged river (*fleuve*).[9]

[6] F. A. Braun, *Razyskaniia v oblasti goto-slavianskikh otnoshenii. I. Goty i ikh sosedi do V veka. Pervyi period: Goty na Visle* (Saint Petersburg, 1899), pp. 77, 90, 96 (*Sbornik ORIAS = Otdelenie russkogo iazyka i slovesnosti Imp. Akademii nauk*, vol. XIV, no. 12).

[7] ⟨⟨For the possible routes of the movement of Iranian tribes into the territory of the Iranian plateau, see R. Ghirshman, *L'Iran des origines à l'Islam* (Paris, 1951), pp. 58 ff.; I. D'iakonov, *Istoriia Midii*, pp. 124-125, 1249-50; E. A. Grantovskii, "Drevneiranskoe etnicheskoe nazvanie "Parsava-Parsa," in *Kratkie soobshcheniia Instituta narodov Azii AN SSSR*, fasc. XXX (1961), pp. 3-19; V. I. Abaev, *Skifo-evropeiskie izoglosy na styke Vostoka i Zapada* (Moscow, 1961), pp. 122-24; M. Mayrhofer, *Die Indo-Arier im alten Vorderasien (mit einer analytischen Bibliographie)* (Wiesbaden, 1966); V. M. Masson, *Sredniaia Aziia i Drevnii Vostok* (Moscow and Leningrad, 1964), pp. 395-449.⟩⟩

[8] *Voyages*, I, 269.

[9] For the link between the lack of water and the absence of snow-clad mountains, see letter from A. D. Kalmykov.

CHAPTER I

Bactria, Balkh, and Ṭukhāristān

THE earliest center of Iranian culture known to us, perhaps even the earliest center of Iranian governmental structure, was Baktra, modern Balkh, south of the Āmū Daryā.[1] This primeval civilization was doubtless at a much lower level than the civilization of the peoples living at that time around the Mediterranean sea and in the Euphrates-Tigris basin. Even later, when the eastern part of Iran entered into the framework of the Achaemenid empire founded by the Persians, the customs and habits of the Bactrians and Soghdians were sharply distinct from those of the inhabitants of the western half of the kingdom; according to Strabo, the Soghdians and Bactrians in antiquity, that is (judging by the context) until the time of Alexander the Great, differed little in their way of life and customs from the nomads: τὸ μὲν ὦν παλαιὸν οὐ πολὺ διέφερον τοῖς βίοις καὶ τοῖς ἤρεσι τῶν Νομάδων οἵ τε Σογδιανοὶ καί οἱ Βακτριανοί (Strabo, XI, 11).[2]

Due to the absence of any trustworthy testimony, we cannot decide whether relations with the Near East, that is, with Assyria and Babylonia, or with the Indian Aryans had any influence on the civilization of the Soghdians and Bactrians. Traditions about the campaigns of the Assyrians in Central Asia are not borne out by Assyrian inscriptions, which never mention such distant expeditions. There probably were commercial relations, but even about those we can only make conjectures.[3] These conjectures can be made on the basis of the time of the appearance in the West,

[1] The idea of a Bactrian kingdom is doubtful; a Βάκτριον ἔθνος is mentioned by Herodotus, I, 153. ⟨⟨Information about the existence of a pre-Achaemenid state on the territory of Bactria goes back to Ktesias; in recent years there have been attempts to compare it with achaeological data. See J. von Prášek, *Geschichte der Meder und Perser bis zur makedonischen Eroberung* (Gotha, 1906-1910), I, 50-54; M. D'iakonov, "Slozhenie klassovogo obshchestva"; V. Masson, "Problema drevnei Baktrii"; Frye, *Heritage*, p. 39; *Istoriia tadzhikskogo naroda*, I, 154-59, 510-11; Masson-Romodin, *Istoriia Afganistana*, I, 47-50; P'iankov, *Vostochnye satrapii*, pp. 9-10.⟩⟩

[2] ⟨⟨"In early times the Sogdians and Bactrians did not differ much from the nomads in their modes of life and customs." *The Geography of Strabo*, with an English translation by H. L. Jones (London, 1966-1970), V, 281.⟩⟩

[3] ⟨⟨Cf. I. D'iakonov, "Assiro-vavilonskie istochniki," p. 356.⟩⟩

especially in the ruins of ancient towns, of Central Asian minerals, plants, and animals; for example, we find the Bactrian (two-humped) camel depicted on the obelisk of the Assyrian king Shalmaneser II erected in 842 B.C.; two-humped camels[4] are mentioned here as part of the tribute sent by one of the rulers of what later became Armenia;[5] certain scholars (such as Hommel) even point out the similarity of the headdress of the camel drivers to that of the Kazakhs.[6] Central Asia, moreover, is considered to be the original home of the horse. Horses are not depicted on Egyptian monuments of the first fourteen dynasties; they appear only from the time of the Hyksos invasion, which probably goes back to the third millennium B.C. (a more precise establishment of the chronology of Egyptian dynasties is still a matter of debate).[7] From among the minerals, one can point to lapis lazuli, which beyond doubt was mined in Central Asia; according to G. Maspero, lapis lazuli was already among the objects obtained from Central Asia by the pharaohs of the XII dynasty.[8] From lapis lazuli was made the blue color for decoration that we find on the walls of the palace of the Assyrian king Ashshurnasirpal, who reigned in the first half of the ninth century B.C.[9]

[4] In Greek terminology, "Bactrian" in contrast to "Arab" camels: P. Bolchert, *Aristoteles' Erdkunde von Asien und Libiyen* (Berlin, 1908), p. 20. Cf. the Persian expression *shutur-i bakhtī*.

[5] ⟨⟨The term designating the two-humped camels (Akkadian *udru*) becomes common in Assyrian sources from the time of Tiglatpileser III (745-727 B.C.); this allows us to date the establishment of close relations of the Near Eastern countries with the tribes of eastern Media (and through the intermediary of the Medes with Eastern Iran) to the eighth century B.C. Cf. W. Eilers, "Der Name Demawend," *AOr*, XXII (1954), 329; I. B. Iankovskaia, "Nekotorye voprosy ekonomiki assiriĭskoĭ derzhavy," *Vestnik Drevneĭ Istorii* (Moscow), pp. 39-40; I. D'iakonov, *Istoriia Midii*, p. 192.⟩⟩ ⟦The two-humped camel is in fact depicted on a Mesopotamian cylinder seal of 1800-1400 B.C., and a rations list from Alalakh in northern Syria (eighteenth century B.C.) records fodder for camels; also, the *udru* appears in Assyrian usage as early as the reign of Assurbelkala (1074-1057 B.C.), who bought two-humped camels from merchants trading with the East. See the references in R. W. Bulliet, *The Camel and the Wheel* (Cambridge, Mass., 1975), pp. 36, 62-64, 156-60.⟧

[6] F. Hommel, *Die Namen der Säugethiere bei den südsemitischen Völkern* (Leipzig, 1879), p. 218 n. 3. ⟦Barthold's text has here "Kirghiz," but he normally means by this term "Kazakh," following the Russian and East European usage of the term "Kirghiz-Kazakh" to distinguish the Turkish Kazakhs of Central Asia from the Slavic ones or Cossacks; see V. Barthold and G. Hazai, *EI*², art. "Ḳazaḳ," and *eidem*, "Ḳirgiz."⟧

[7] ⟨⟨For the horse in the Near East and the time of its appearance in Egypt, see I. D'iakonov, *Istoriia Midii*, pp. 122-25.⟩⟩

[8] *Histoire ancienne des peuples de l'Orient classique* (Paris, 1895-1899), I, 470.

[9] F. Justi, *Geschichte der orientalischen Völker im Althertum* (Berlin, 1884), p. 264.

Also controversial is the question of whether there are traces of the influence of more civilized nations in the teachings of Zoroaster, teachings that became the national religion of the Iranians. The person of Zoroaster,[10] as well as that of the founders of other religions, later became the subject of fantastic legends; nonetheless, the oldest elements of the Avesta, whose genuineness is proved by linguistic evidence,[11] give us, according to H. Oldenberg, a possibility of forming a general idea about the identity and teachings of the prophet.

Oldenberg considers as historical not only Zoroaster but also the Bactrian king Vishtaspa[12] addressed by the prophet; mentioned

[10] Uncertainty of the name Zoroaster; cf. the article by A. Hoffmann-Kutschke, "Nachtrag zu ⟨⟨Persische Eigennamen⟩⟩," *OLZ*, IX (1906), no. 11, 604; Zohrovastra; according to F. C. Andreas and J. Wackernagel, *Die vierte Gāthā des Zuraˣthušthro,* in *NGWG*, 1911: Zuraˣthušthro.

[11] Linguistic reasons given by P. Tedesco ("Ostiranische Nominalflexion," *ZII*, IV [1926], 129): in Soghdian, Saka, and Afghan there are traces of transition *-ah and *-āh to -i and -ē, whereas in Avestan instead of that there is -ō and -å (that is, -o and -ō); for him there remains only the northwest, because in the southwest there are -a and -ā; "this kind of localization of the Avestan language is supported by a number of other characteristics" (cf. Tedesco, "Dialektologie der westiranischen Turfantexte," *MO*, XV (1921), "Dialektologische Zusammenfassung η," pp. 255-57).

[12] For Zoroaster, see A.V.W. Jackson, *Zoroaster the Prophet of Ancient Iran* (New York, 1899), as well as his article, "Die iranische Religion," in *GIPh*, II, 612-708. Cf. C. Bartholomae's opinion about Zoroaster as the actual author of the Gathas (*Die Gatha's des Awesta. Zarathuschtra's Vorpredigten* [Strassburg, 1905]; *Altiranisches Wörterbuch* [Strassburg, 1904], p. 1,675). For Zoroaster and Gistasp, see Barthold, "K istorii persidskogo eposa," *Soch.* VII, 390. For questions concerning the country of Airan-Vej (J. Marquart's opinion: *Ērānšahr nach der Geographie des Ps. Moses Xorenacʿi, in AGWG*, III/2 [Berlin, 1901], 155, and Nöldeke's objections, *ZDMG*, LVI [1902], 434 ff.), see K. A. Inostrantsev, "O do-musul'manskoi kul'ture," pp. 312-16, and his "Reka Īrān-Vādzha." ⟨⟨Barthold, *EI*¹, art. "Khwārizm," *Soch.* III, 544; E. Benveniste, "L'Ērān-Vēž et l'origine légendaire des Iraniens," *BSOS*, VII (1934), 266-71; E. Herzfeld, *Zoroaster and His World* (Princeton, 1947), II, 688-703.⟩⟩ Hostile attitude of Zoroaster toward Karpan and Kavay; their condemnation to death: *Yasna*, V, 15 (Bartholomae, *Die Gatha's*, p. 31). For Bartholomae, Vishtaspa is an "eastern Iranian prince." Cf. Oldenberg's opinion (*Aus Indien und Iran. Gesammelte Aufsätze* (Berlin, 1899), p. 143: "das östliche Iran, etwa die Landschaft Baktra ⟨⟨der vornehmste oder ein vornehmster Schauplatz des alten Zarathustrism gewesen ist⟩⟩," and p. 147 about the "realm" of Vishtaspa: "dies Bauernkönigthum ist dem Ort nach und wie ich meine auch der Zeit nach von der Welt der Achämeniden weit entfernt." Marquart's arguments in favor of an influence of events of the life of Vologas I (A.D. 52-77) on the legend about Vishtasp especially "Beiträge zur Geschichte und Sage von Erān," *ZDMG*, XLIX (1895), 635 ff.; cf. Strabo, XI, 9, 3, after Poseidonios, concerning the council of the nobility among the Parthians. Under Vologas I, there were for the first time Pahlavi inscriptions together with the

along with Vishtaspa is Queen Khutaosa and two associates of the king.[13] This king is by no means surrounded by pomp comparable to that which later surrounded the Achaemenids, and appears not as the head of a military state but as the representative of a people who are agriculturists and cattle breeders. Zoroaster deals with him and his kinsfolk as with his own friends, patrons, and protectors of his doctrine. As is known, the basic teaching of this doctrine was the existence of two principles, good and evil; a struggle goes on between them, struggle in which both humans and animals take part. Such a doctrine developed quite naturally in places with a sharp contrast between lifeless desert and blossoming oases, areas where man had to strive to use every drop of water for irrigation of his fields, where successes won by civilization needed constant protection both from the sands of the desert and from "the steppe horsemen who kill men, drive away the cattle and lead into captivity women and children," as one of the hymns says. On the other hand, work is richly rewarded: wherever the industrious agriculturist is protected from plunder by the nomads he has almost no reason to fear adverse weather conditions. This is why the evolution of the primeval Aryan cult of nature acquired here a totally different character from that in India. As Oldenberg points out, "in the land of Zoroaster there were no philosophers, no deep metaphysical thought, no desire to escape the woes of this world. There was, however, a vigorous people, filled with a healthy joy of life, accustomed to build and to defend its existence in work and battle." Naturally, the concept of good and its struggle with evil in the absence of "deep metaphysical thought" could not have that ele-

---

Greek ones on coins (A. von Gutschmid, *Geschichte Irans und seiner Nachbarländer von Alexander dem Grossen bis zum Untergang der Arsaciden* [Tübingen, 1888] p. 125). According to C. P. Tiele, *Geschichte der Religionen im Altertum bis auf Alexander den Grossen* (Gotha, 1896-1903), II, 106, Vishtaspa was a "König . . . nur im Reich des Geistes, *magahya khšathra"; kava*, in the strict sense of the word, meant only "seer, wise man"; according to Bartholomae's dictionary (*Altiranisches Wörterbuch*, p. 442) it was a "Bezeichnung der Fürsten."

[13] ⟨⟨For Zoroaster, his name, the place and time of his preaching, as well as for linguistic data concerning the localization of the Avesta, see: W. B. Henning, "The Disintegration of the Avestic Studies," *TPS* (1942), pp. 40-56; *idem, Zoroaster, Politician or Witch-doctor?* (London, 1951); I. D'iakonov, *Istoriia Midii*, pp. 45-56, 371-403; J. Duchesne-Guillemin, *The Western Response to Zoroaster* (Oxford, 1958); *idem, La religion de l'Iran ancien* (Paris, 1962), pp. 135-46, 165-223, 384-99; M. D'iakonov, *Ocherk*, pp. 58-65, 343-45, 360-63; *Istoriia tadzhikskogo naroda*, I, 137-39, 150-54, 168-76, 504, 510, 512-14, as well as the bibliographies to these works.⟩⟩ ⟦M. Boyce, *A History of Zoroastrianism, Handbuch der Orientalistik* (Leiden, 1975); *idem, Zoroastrians, their Religious Beliefs and Practices* (London, 1979).⟧

vated character which it acquired later. For the worshipers of Zoroaster good is identical with usefulness, evil with harm, while no distinction is made between work for the common good and striving for personal comfort. Good is served by him who has a wife and children, works the field, guards his livestock and other possessions, as well as by him who builds roads and bridges or exterminates harmful animals. Struggle against evil and those who are evil is also understood in the literal sense, in contrast to the Christian doctrine of nonresistance to evil and love of enemies; according to the Avesta, he who does good to evil is himself evil, while he who harms it with thought or act is applauded by Ormuzd. Struggle between good and evil also takes place in the animal kingdom. The representatives of good are the dog, which is, as is known, especially glorified in the Avesta; the rooster, which announces the arrival of the day and summons people to rise, to glorify good, and to struggle against evil; and other useful animals. The representatives of evil—creatures of the evil Ahriman—are snakes, ants, mice, wolves, and so on. Extermination of harmful animals represents one of the obligations of the faithful. For the struggle against evil and purification from it man must also perform, in addition to such practical activities, a number of superstitious rituals.

Good and evil are personified by the supreme deities Ormuzd (more exactly Ahuramazda), the radiant god of heaven, and Ahriman (Angramainyush), the spirit of darkness and death, creator and protector of everything harmful, of all miseries, sufferings, and defects. The existence of good, luminous spirits on the one hand, and of evil, dark spirits on the other, is also recognized in primeval nature cults. In one passage of the *Iliad* the Lord of the Underworld is called Ζεὺς καταχθόνιος (IX, 457); this dualism appears even more sharply in the story about the sacrifice during the agreement under oath between the Greeks and the Trojans before the duel between Menelaus and Paris; a white sheep is brought in honor of the sun and a black one in honor of the earth (III, 103-104). However, in the primeval religion of the Aryans in both India and Greece there was not yet an identification of light with good and of darkness with evil. Even to luminous deities are ascribed selfish, sometimes lowly aspirations; the concept itself of the "envy of the gods" shows that even a human with a clear conscience had to experience, before the gods, a feeling of fear above all. The development of the concept of morality was bound to provoke a negative attitude toward such deities. Just as for a Buddhist a human who has reached holiness stands above the gods of the Indian pantheon, so also in the Avesta the word *daēva* (*dīw* in New Persian), which is identical with Sanskrit *deva*, where it denotes "god," serves only to designate the evil spirits. Among the luminous deities, Ormuzd, creator of the heaven and the earth, appears only as the first among the seven "holy immortals" (*amesha spenta*), although in the most ancient hymns the latter appear as personifications of separate attributes of God rather than as independent deities. Here belongs also Asha, a concept that corresponds to the Sanskrit *rita* and that appears to be a personification of the world order, the strengthening and spreading of which constitutes the goal of the struggle between good and evil. Aside from that, the teaching of Zoroaster did not suppress the cult of certain ancient Iranian deities such as Mithra, god of the sun, and Tishtiria, the rain god, who fights against the demon of drought.

We have no information as to when and from where the Aryans came to Bactria and founded the town of Baktra (later called Balkh). The choice of the place was determined by the unusual fertility of the oasis created by the river Baktros (now Balkh Āb) at its exit from the mountains; its fertility surpasses that of all the other oases in the area. When it became the principal town of this area, Baktra,[14] exactly like Balkh later, became the center of trade with India, although some other oases are linked with the Indus basin through more convenient routes; contacts between Balkh and India, as we shall see below, took place primarily along the valley of the Khulm and not of the Balkh Āb. All the rivers that flow out of the northern spurs of Hindū Kush set out in the direction of the Āmū Daryā, but only a few reach it. The Balkh Āb does not reach it, either; even at the time of the Arab geographers it disappeared in the sands. If we can believe classical authors, the Baktros did at that time reach the Āmū Daryā, and even served for the transportation of Indian goods; this information, however, like other reports of classical authors about local rivers, is doubtful in the extreme. According to Ammianus Marcellinus (XXIII, 6, 69), ships from as far away as Harāt (Herat) could reach the Caspian sea. It is hardly likely that conditions of irrigation could have changed so radically in the course of the 1,000 years that separated the Greek geographers from the Arab ones, while they changed so little during the following 1,000 years that separate the Arab geographers from

[14] Bāxtriš in ancient Persian inscriptions (a third-century A.D. Syriac inscription still has the form *bh̲trt'*, "Bactrian women"), Bāxδiš in the Avesta (a reconstruction; cf. Marquart, *Ērānšahr*, p. 88).

us. Most probably, merchandise was brought to Baktra only by caravans and not on waterways. The political and commercial significance of Balkh may also have been enhanced by its position in the center of the eastern Iranian world. The ninth-century geographer Yaʿqūbī asserts—though not quite correctly—that Balkh was situated at an equal distance from Farghāna, Ray, Sīstān, Kābul, Qandahār, Kashmīr, Khwārazm, and Multān.[15]

We do not have a detailed description of the town of Baktra; we only know that it was situated in a plain where the river leaves the mountains, at a distance of three days' march south of the Āmū Daryā, and that the citadel stood on an elevation.[16]

Much more detailed data are provided by Arab geographers, according to whom the distance between Balkh and the bank of the Āmū Daryā could be covered in two days. This distance is defined as two farsakhs, a measure that existed in Persia in remote antiquity, but whose dimension was not clearly determined; a comparison of the distances indicated by the Arab geographers with the modern ones makes one conclude that, in their time, a farsakh most often corresponded to six versts [that is, four miles].[17]

The town was situated in a plain at a distance of four farsakhs from the nearest mountains.[18] A citadel (*quhandiz*) is not yet mentioned in this period.[19] As in the case of other large towns such as

[15] *Kitāb al-Buldān*, ed. M. J. de Goeje (Leiden, 1891), pp. 287-88.

[16] W. Tomaschek, *PW*, art. "Baktra," p. 2,804. ⟨⟨For excavations of the city of Baktra—now an archaeological site in the Mazār-i Sharīf province—see: D. Schlumberger, "La prospection archéologique de Bactres," *Syria*, XXVI (1949), 173-90; J.-C. Gardin, *Céramiques de Bactres* (Paris, 1957); R. S. Young, "The South Walls of Balkh-Bactra," *AJA*, LIX (1955), 267-76; A.M. Mandel'shtam, "O nekotorykh rezul'tatakh," pp. 415-24; Masson-Romodin, I, 73-74, 122-23, 169.⟩⟩ ⟦A. S. Melikan-Chirvani, "L'Évocation littéraire du Buddhisme dans l'Iran musulman," *Le monde iranien et l'Islam* II (1974), 1-72; *ibid.*, "Recherches sur l'architecture de l'Iran bouddhique, I," *Le monde Iranien et l'Islam*, III (1975), 1-61, and the bibliography in both articles. And especially for Khorasan, but relevant here: J. Aubin, "Réseau pastoral et réseau caravanier. Les grand' routes du Khurasan à l'époque mongole," *Le monde iranien et l'Islam*, I (1971), 105-30; and in general this periodical for Iran.⟧

[17] ⟨⟨Cf. *Soch.* III, 119, n. 81.⟩⟩

[18] Balkh was rebuilt by the Arabs in 107/725-726, cf. below, p. 20.

[19] For the existence of the *quhandiz-i Balkh*, see Yāqūt, *Muʿjam al-buldān*, ed. F. Wüstenfeld (Leipzig, 1866-1873), s.v. "Quhandiz." The term *ark*: ref. in Vullers' *Lexicon Persico-Latinum*, s.v., to the dictionary *Burhān-i qāṭiʿ* (1062/1652) about the *ark* as "center of the *qalʿa*" and to Mīrkhwānd about the *ark* as a city in Sīstān. Iṣṭakhrī, *Kitāb al-Masālik wa 'l-mamālik*, ed. M. J. de Goeje (Leiden, 1870), p. 241, about the *ark* in his description of Zaranj: "a very large building called *ark* [= citadel], it served as a treasure house; ʿAmr b. al-Layth had built it." Also Ibn Ḥawqal, *Kitāb Ṣūrat al-arḍ*, ed. M. J. de Goeje (Leiden, 1870), p. 298. In Yāqūt,

Samarqand and Bukhārā, the entire Balkh oasis was at one time surrounded by long walls for protection from nomads; the length of the walls in each case—Balkh among them—is indicated as twelve farsakhs in circumference.[20] At the time of the Arab domination, these walls did not exist any more, and the settled area was divided, like other large towns, into the town itself, the *madīna* (Persian *shahristān*), and the suburb, *rabaḍ*; the Persian term *bīrūn* is not used by the geographers.[21] In all large towns, the inner part, the *shahristān*, was surrounded by a special wall; *rabaḍ* was the term applied to the area between this wall and the outer wall of the town. The word *rabaḍ* itself originally seemed to denote this outer wall, and was often used in this denotation. The few data we have concerning the history of the individual cities, especially the relatively detailed information of Narshakhī, a tenth-century author, about the topography of Bukhārā, show that the *shahristān* was the earliest part, having originated at the time of the exclusive domination of the landed aristocracy, while the representatives of the merchant and artisan classes lived in the *rabaḍ*, where the markets were also concentrated. As the landed aristocracy declined and the merchant-artisan class rose, life shifted more and more from the *shahristān* to the *rabaḍ*.

Arab geographers give us less detailed and precise information about Balkh than about Bukhārā and Samarqand. The dimensions of the city itself in terms of farsakhs are reported variously, and the number of gates varies as well: according to Yaʿqūbī, there were four gates of the *rabaḍ*; according to the tenth-century geographers, seven. Analogy with other large towns makes one assume that despite Yaʿqūbī, the former number, four, should be applied not to the gates of the *rabaḍ* but to those of the *shahristān*. The names of the gates are mentioned. Among these was the "gates of the Indians" (*bāb-i Hindūwān*) and the "gate of the Jews" (*bāb-i Yahūdān*);[22] clearly these appellations point to quarters inhabited by Indian and Jewish merchants. Even now, despite the total decline

Muʿjam, I, 210, s.v. "Ark," the following passage is added: "then it became the seat of the government and a fortress, and it is now called by this name." ⟨⟨See also Barthold, "Persidskoe ark," *Soch.* VII, 413 ff.⟩⟩

[20] Yaʿqūbī, *Kitāb al-Buldān*, p. 288.

[21] Barthold, *Turkestan down to the Mongol Invasion* (London, 1978), p. 78.

[22] Report about seven gates in Maqdisī, *Aḥsan al-taqāsīm*, ed. M. J. de Goeje (Leiden, 1877), p. 302; and about the *rabaḍ* after manuscript C. Iṣṭakhrī, p. 278, names seven gates; the area is half a farsakh long and wide. Cf. Barthold, *Turkestan* (Eng. tr.), p. 78; among the gates is the *bāb al-Nawbahār*.

of the commercial importance of Balkh, there is a considerable Jewish colony in the town, located in a special quarter; there are also Indian shopkeepers.[23] The houses were built, as in all towns of Persia and Central Asia, of clay; the bazaars were located, according to the Arab geographers, primarily in the *shahristān*. On the other hand, the anonymous tenth-century Persian geographer, the manuscript of whose work was discovered in Bukhārā, giving very detailed information about Central Asia, states that many bazaars were located in the *rabaḍ*.[24]

Among the buildings of the town, there is mentioned, besides the Friday mosque, a construction from pre-Islamic times, the Nawbahār. In the tenth century, this building was already in ruins. The Persian geographer says that it had been built by ancient Persian kings,[25] but Arab geographers are more correct in their statement that Nawbahār had been a temple of people of the same faith as Chinese emperors and the shāh of Kābul, that is, Buddhists (Nawbahār = *nava vihāra*). Ibn al-Faqīh gives a similar although somewhat fantastic description of the temple.[26] According to this description, the structure consisted of a dome whose radius was one hundred ells in length, encircled by a round portico; the building was surrounded by three hundred cells for temple servants, and each of these performed his duty only once a year. The temple already existed in the seventh century and was described by the Buddhist pilgrim Hsüan-tsang; in the notes of this traveler, the temple was situated southeast of the town,[27] whereas in his biography it is mentioned as having been situated southwest of it.[28] Arab geographers only say that the temple was in the *rabaḍ* [29] and

[23] C. E. Yate, *Northern Afghanistan or Letters from the Afghan Boundary Commission* (Edinburgh and London, 1888), p. 256.

[24] ⟨⟨*Ḥudūd al-ʿālam*, fol. 21a. Cf. Vavilov-Bukinich, *Zemledel'cheskii Afghanistan*, p. 504.⟩⟩

[25] ⟨⟨*Ḥudūd al-ʿālam*, fol. 21a, where there is mention of Khusrawān. Cf. Barthold, "Die persische Šuʿūbīja und die moderne Wissenschaft," *ZA*, XXVI (1912), 249-66, *Soch*. VII, 367 n. 41, and *Ḥudūd al-ʿālam*, tr. V. Minorsky (London, 1937), pp. 108, 337.⟩⟩

[26] Ibn al-Faqīh, *Mukhtaṣar Kitāb al-Buldān*, ed. M. J. de Goeje (Leiden, 1885), pp. 322-24; tr., pp. 382-85.

[27] Hsüan-tsang, *Mémoires sur les contrées occidentales*, tr. S. Julien (Paris, 1857-1858), I, 30.

[28] *Histoire de la vie de Hiouen-thsang*, tr. S. Julien (Paris, 1863), p. 64.

[29] Cf. Ṭabarī, *Ta'rīkh al-rusul wa 'l-mulūk* (Leiden, 1879-1901), II, 1490: "between the city and Nawbahār [the distance] is two *ghalwas*." For *ghalwa* see Ibn Rusta, *al-Aʿlāq al-nafīsa*, ed. M. J. de Goeje (Leiden, 1892), p. 22 (one twenty-fourth of a farsakh, a little over a quarter of a kilometer; a *ghalwa* is 500 *dhirāʿs*).

that the river of the Balkh Āb[30] had its course past the gate of Nawbahār, most probably entering the city.[31] This supposition is supported by the seventeenth-century Bukhāran historian Maḥmūd b. Walī, who states that the gate of Nawbahār was situated on the southern side of the town, and that in his time it was called the gate of Khwāja Sulṭān Aḥmad.[32] From the Chinese description, one can see that in the temple there were several Buddhist sanctuaries; to the north of it there was a stupa, that is, a structure for the keeping of holy relics, two hundred feet high; to the southwest there was yet another temple, considered to be very ancient. All in all, in Hsüan-tsang's time there were in Balkh up to one hundred Buddhist monasteries and up to three thousand monks.[a]

Thus the city in which the teachings of Zoroaster had first been accepted became one of the principal centers of Buddhism. This fact can be explained through historical events, which after the destruction of the Achaemenid kingdom by Alexander the Great separated Bactria from the rest of Iran and established a close link between it and India.[33]

The Graeco-Bactrian kingdom extended westward to the Harī Rūd, which even today serves for a considerable part of its course as the border between Persia and Afghanistan, and further downstream between Persia and Russia. In the southeast, the Graeco-Bactrian kings subjugated the area beyond the Hindū Kush, which at that time was considered part of India; just as the area along the upper Hilmand, a region whose chief city today is Qandahār, was sometimes also considered part of India. This region was known to classical authors by the name of Arachosia (Harakhushti in the Avesta);[34] in Isidore of Charax's description of the Parthian prov-

[30] Cf. *Dahās* "ten mills" (name of the Balkh river in Iṣṭakhrī, p. 278, and Ibn Ḥawqal, p. 326).

[31] Iṣṭakhrī, p. 278: "it flows through its *rabaḍ* by the Nawbahār gate"; Ibn Ḥawqal, p. 326: "passing by the Nawbahār gate."

[32] *Baḥr al-asrār*, ms. India Office Library 1496, fol. 317a.

[a] On Buddhism in these eastern fringes of the Iranian world, see A. S. Melikian-Chirvani, "L'évocation littéraire du bouddhisme dans l'Iran musulman," *Le monde iranien et l'Islam*, II (1974), 1-72, and *idem*, "Recherches sur l'architecture de l'Iran bouddhique. I. Essai sur les origines et le symbolisme du stūpa iranien," *ibid*, III (1975), 1-61.

[33] The Greeks in Bactria; Aristobulos concerning the route by water. Stasanor of Cyprus; story about the events of 315. The campaign of Demodamas between 312 and 306. The uprising of Diodotos in the reign of Antiochos II (261-246 B.C.). Euthydemos of Magnesia.

[34] ⟨⟨The Avestan form of the name of the region was *Harax^{v}aitī-*. the early Persian form was *Harahuvatī-*.⟩⟩

inces, Arachosia is called "White India." The peak of the Graeco-Bactrian state's might was in the first quarter of the second century B.C. Euthydemos and his son Dimitrios subjugated the regions along the Indus all the way to the sea, and in the northeast they seized mountainous regions up to the domains of the Serai, that is, the Chinese, and of the Fauns, in whom Gutschmid sees one of the Tibetan peoples;[35] Tomaschek, seemingly with considerable justification, considers them to be Huns, the Hsiung-nu of the Chinese chronicles.[36] Gutschmid assumes that the purpose of these campaigns was to establish regular commercial relations with China, which is hardly plausible, since the Chinese had no information about the "western region" before the embassy of Chang Ch'ien.[37]

For an evaluation of the cultural significance of the Graeco-Bactrian kingdom, more basic archaeological and linguistic research is still necessary; linguistic research should make it possible to determine which cultural terms in oriental languages were borrowed from Greek, and would thus indicate Greek influence. The influence of Greek art must have been especially strong, and indeed, little Greek heads adorn the small earthen coffins in which the Zoroastrians kept the bones of the dead after their separation from the flesh; the numerous terra-cotta statuettes, found mostly in the environs of Samarqand, point equally clearly to the influence of Greek art. Its traces are also noted by historians of Indian art, especially of sculpture. The well-known sinologist F. Hirth sees signs of the influence of Bactrian art even in ancient specimens of Chinese art that go back to the second century B.C.; this connection, however, is rejected by another sinologist, E. Chavannes. As for linguistic evidence, there is the opinion that the Chinese word *pu-tao*, "grape," is the Greek word βότρυς (according to Hirth); in that case wine making was brought to Central Asia by the Greeks, and that was where the Chinese became acquainted with it.[38] On the other hand, the Greeks too must have been influenced by oriental cultural elements, especially by oriental religions, and in particular Buddhism, the propaganda of which began in the third century B.C., at the time of King Aśoka. Already in the first half of the second century we find the picture of a Buddhist stupa on the coin of Agathocles, the Greek ruler of Arachosia; at the end

[35] *Geschichte Irans*, p. 45.

[36] *Zur historischen Topographie von Persien*, I, in *SBWAW*, CII (1883), 205.

[37] *Geschichte Irans*, p. 44. ⟦For Chang Ch'ien, see H. A. Giles, *A Chinese Biographical Dictionary* (Shanghai, 1878), pp. 12-13 no. 29.⟧

[38] ⟨⟨Cf. Barthold, "Greko-baktriiskoe gosudarstvo," *Soch.* II/2, 456.⟩⟩

of the second century, Menander, ruling over a substantial part of India, was a Buddhist, and after his death he was recognized as one of the Buddhist saints.[39]

The Graeco-Bactrian state collapsed after 175 B.C. as a result of internal disorders. The event was to provoke an onslaught of Central Asian nomads, who were most probably related to the sedentary Iranians in origin. As early as 206 B.C., Euthidemos in his struggle with Antiochos the Great of Syria threatened to incite the nomads to invade the country, and Antiochos, impressed by this threat, agreed to conclude peace.[40] The son of Euthidemos, Dimitrios, was driven out of Bactria by Eukratidos, and ruled only in India, that is, the country beyond the Hindū Kush. Eukratidos had to wage war against Euthidemos's descendants in India, against the Greek rulers of the Hilmand basin, and in addition, according to Justin, against the peoples of Aria and Soghdiana; as a result of this, the Parthians, gaining strength at that time under the rule of Mithridates I, were able to take the provinces of Aspiona and Turibia from the Bactrians.[41] In Gutschmid's opinion these regions were a part of Aria.[42] There is a report that Mithridates spread his rule to India, but the invasion of the latter country, as Gutschmid shows, was carried out not by the Parthians but by the Sakas, a people of the Chinese chronicles, who at that time were driven out of Semirechie. This movement is known to have been connected with one of the great migrations of Central Asian history. Almost contemporaneous with the invasion of the Sakas was the conquest of Semirechie by their pursuers, the Yüeh-chih, a circumstance which, according to Gutschmid, explains Justin's words when he lists among the enemies of Eukratidos the Soghdians.[43] From Soghdiana the Yüeh-chih gradually conquered Bactria. Strabo mentions as conquerors of Bactria the Assi, Pasians, Tokharians, and Sakarauks instead of the Yüeh-chih; Pompeius Trogus (whom Justin used as a source) calls them Sarauks and Asians, and one of the lost chapters of Pompeius Trogus had the title "How the Asians Established Themselves as Kings among the Tokharians." Together with the

[39] Gutschmid, *Geschichte Irans*, p. 105.

[40] *Ibid.*, p. 38.

[41] *Ibid.*, p. 49.

[42] ⟨⟨For the history of the Graeco-Bactrian kingdom, see: *Istoriia tadzhikskogo naroda*, I, 290-340, 535-40; Masson-Romodin, I, 102-30; W. W. Tarn, *The Greeks in Bactria and India* (Cambridge, 1951); A. K. Narain, *The Indo-Greeks* (Oxford, 1957); G. Woodcock, *The Greeks in India* (London, 1966).⟩⟩

[43] *Geschichte Irans*, p. 50.

Takhorians or Tokharians, Ptolemy mentions along the Syr Daryā also the Iatians. Gutschmid draws the conclusion that the conquerors of Bactria were Tokharians,[44] and that the "words Asians, Assi, Iatii, and Yüeh-chih were more or less successful attempts to render the probably hard-to-pronounce name of the principal Tokharian orda."[45] There is thus a discrepancy between the Chinese sources that mention only one conquering kingdom in Bactria, and the classical authors who mention also the Sarauks or Sakarauks; Gutschmid explains this discrepancy by the fact that the Sakarauks conquered Margiana, which had earlier been a part of the Bactrian kingdom and which had later been taken away from them by the Parthians. Phraates II, successor of Mithridates I, obtained victory over the Sakarauks, but at the end of his reign these same Sakarauks defeated the Parthian; Phraates himself fell in the battle. The Scythians laid waste the domains of the Parthians and then occupied the region that received from them the name Sakastena, modern Sijistān or Sīstān.

The name of the region of Ṭukhāristān has remained as a memorial of the Tokharians, a term that was used at the time of the Arab geographers in two meanings: in the narrower sense, Ṭukhāristān was understood to be the region south of the Āmū Daryā and east of Balkh,[46] with the capital Ṭālaqān (now Ṭāliqān), and extending eastward to Badakhshān and southward to the Hindū Kush. In the broader sense, however, the term Ṭukhāristān was applied to the whole region along both banks of the Āmū Daryā as far the nearest mountains—primarily to the country east of Balkh, even though the ninth-century geographer Ibn Khurradādhbih in one place mentions as part of Ṭukhāristān also the region to the south of the Āmū Daryā below Balkh, down to the basin of the

[44] *Ibid.*, p. 71.

[45] For the "main Tokharian orda"—the Yüeh-chih—cf. Baron A. von Staël-Holstein's 1914 articles: in *JRAS* (January 1914), pp. 79-88 ("Was There a Kusana Race?") and in *SBAW Berlin* (1914), pp. 643-50 ("KOPANO und Yüeh-shih"). Cf. Kitsi (Getsi) in F.W.K. Müller, *Uigurica*, I, in *APAW* (1908), p. 15 n. 1 (cf. S. M. Malov's preface to the edition of *Suvarṇaprabhāsa*), and Gaču in Sanan Setsen, *Geschichte der Ost-Mongolen und ihres Fürstenhauses*, tr. I. J. Schmidt (St. Petersburg and Leipzig, 1829), p. 16. ⟨⟨See also Barthold, "K voprosu o iazykakh"; for the present-day state of the "Tokharian problem" see A. A. Freiman, "Tokharskii vopros"; *Tokharskie iazyki*, bibliography, p. 217; E. G. Pulleyblank, "Chinese and Indo-Europeans," *JRAS* (1966), pp. 9-39.⟩⟩

[46] Cf. Balādhurī, *Futūḥ al-buldān*, ed. M. J. de Goeje (Leiden, 1879), p. 408: "Balkh, it is the [principal] city of Ṭukhāristān."

Murghāb and to the town of Zamm, now Kerki.[47] The Tokharians seem to have had little influence west of Balkh. We have seen that already in the second century B.C., the Parthians had gained control of the western part of Bactriana; further south in the basin of the Hilmand, a separate Parthian kingdom was subsequently formed, which for some time extended to the estuary of the Indus.

A hundred years after the Yüeh-chih or Tokharians settled in Bactria, the clan of the Kushans became prominent among them; they gradually gained control of a considerable part of India.[48] Their kings called themselves "firm in the law," that is, protectors of Buddhism. Only in the third century A.D. did the expulsion of the Tokharians, or, as the Indian sources call them, the Saka, from India begin; their rulers returned to Balkh, where they came under the political and cultural influence of the Sāsānid dynasty, which had just become established. This influence is noticeable in their titles, such as that of *shāhānshāh*, or in their coins that imitated those of the Sāsānids.[49] In the fifth century begins the rule of the so-called White Huns or Hephthalites, who in the opinion of most scholars were also a branch of the Yüeh-chih or Tokharians.[50] The fifth-century author Priscus calls these Huns Kidarites (Κιδαρῖται). This name, according to the successful explanation of Gutschmid, comes from the name of the founder of the new dynasty, Kidara (Tsi-dolo in Chinese transcription),[51] who founded a new state in Balkh and also conquered the regions south of the Hindū Kush.[52] The state of the Hephthalites lasted until the middle of the sixth century, when it was destroyed by the Sāsānids in alliance with the Turkish khans. The name "Hephthalite" was known to the Arabs in the form of Hayṭal (pl. Hayāṭila), and it exists in this form in

[47] Ibn Khurradādhbih, *Kitāb al-Masālik wa 'l-mamālik*, ed. and tr. M. J. de Goeje (Leiden, 1889), tr., p. 26.

[48] Kuṣānu, gen. pl.; kuṣi, nom. sing.; cf. Staël-Holstein, "KOPANO," pp. 645 ff.

[49] E. Specht, "Du déchiffrement des monnaies Sindo-Ephtalites," *JA*, ser. 9, XVII (1901), 487-523. ⟨⟨For more successful attempts to read the inscriptions on Hephthalite coins see H.F.J. Junker, "Die hephthalitischen Münzeninschriften," *SBAW Berlin*, XXXVII (1930), 641-62; E. Herzfeld, *Kushano-Sasanian Coins* (Calcutta, 1930); R. Ghirshman, *Les Chionites-hephthalites* (Cairo, 1948).⟩⟩ ⟦Staviskii, *Kushanskaia Baktriia.*⟧

[50] ⟨⟨For the ethnic affiliation of the Hephthalites, see *Istoriia tadzhikskogo naroda*, I, 413-20, 552-54; A. J. van Windekens, "Huns blancs et ārçi. Essai sur les appelations du 'tokharien'," *Le Muséon*, LIV (1941), 161-86; Ghirshman, *Les Chionites-hephthalites;* S. Konow, "The White Huns and Tokharian," *ANVA* (1947), 2. Hist.-fil. Kl. pp. 77-82, and the bibliographies to these works.⟩⟩

[51] ⟨⟨Today the accepted transcription is Tsidolo.⟩⟩

[52] *Geschichte Irans*, p. 170.

Yāqūt's geographical dictionary. The Greek transcriptions 'Εφθαλῖται and 'Αβδέλαι, the Syriac transcription Abdel, and the Armenian transcription Heptal all seem to show, as Tomaschek had already pointed out, that instead of Hayṭal and Hayāṭila one should read Habṭal and Habāṭila, with a change in the diacritical marks of the Arabic consonant ductus.[53] The same word, most probably, appears in the form Yafṭal (the name of a village in the mountains of Ṭukhāristān); a village in Badakhshān still has this name now. It seems that the Hephthalites lived primarily to the north of the Āmū Daryā, at least in the area west of Balkh; the Arab geographers state that the Āmū Daryā separated Khurāsān on one side from the Hayṭal on the other, and they even report genealogical traditions about two brothers, Khurāsān and Hayṭal (or Habṭal), grandsons of Sim or Shem, son of Noah.[54] The state of the Hephthalites was destroyed by the Turks. In the seventh century, at the time of Hsüan-tsang's pilgrimage, Ṭukhāristān (in the broad sense of the word) was divided into twenty-seven small domains subjected to the Turks; the Hayṭal nation is still mentioned at the time of the Muslim conquest in the beginning of the eighth century. The rule of the Sāsānids did not have, it would seem, much importance here, and the dominant religion was Buddhism in Balkh and in the dependent regions on both banks of the upper course of the Āmū Daryā down to the Arab conquest.

The conquest of Balkh by the Arabs took place, according to one group of reports, at the time of the caliph ʿUthmān, according to others, at the time of Muʿāwiya; the town, it seems, put up a stubborn resistance, so that it was destroyed and for some time ceased to exist. The new Arab town, Barūqān, was built at a distance of two farsakhs, that is, about twelve versts [or eight miles] from Balkh. The temple of Nawbahār was also destroyed, but the place remained sacred for the natives, and in the eighth century, at the time of Qutayba b. Muslim, the Tokharian princes who rose against Qutayba performed their prayers here.[55] In 727 the governor Asad rebuilt Balkh and resettled here the Arabs of Barūqān, which is henceforth no longer mentioned. The reconstruction of the town was assigned to the famous family of the Barmakids, who had at

[53] *Über die ältesten Nachrichten über den skythischen Norden. I*, in *SBWAW*, CXVI (1888), 751.

[54] Maqdisī, p. 261.

[55] Ṭabarī, II, 1205.

one time administered Nawbahār;[56] under the ʿAbbāsids, the Barmakids, as is well known, became the organizers of the caliphal empire. At the time of the ʿAbbāsids and of the first Persian dynasties—the Ṭāhirids, Ṣaffārids, and Sāmānids—Balkh, together with Ṭukhāristān (in the narrow sense), was governed by a local dynasty, which, because of its insignificance, is barely mentioned in the sources, but which struck coins; the numismatists call this dynasty the Abū Dāwūdids, after the name of Abū Dāwūd Muḥammad b. Aḥmad, who ruled at the end of the ninth century.[57] Balkh remained at this time the entrepôt of trade with India.

Several roads lead from Balkh to India; the most important one always followed the valley of the Khulm river which like the Balkh Āb flows from the Hindū Kush but does not reach the Āmū Daryā. The journey from Balkh to the Khulm river was reckoned to take two days. Today, the last settlement that is irrigated by the water of the Balkh Āb is Gūr-i Mār ("tomb of the serpent"); there is a legend about a combat between ʿAlī and a snake in this place. Further up toward the Khulm river, for a distance of twenty-four English miles, there is no water at all; only recently there appeared half-way up the small settlement of Nā'ibābād, to which the water of a stream from nearby hills has been conducted. Near the place where the Khulm river leaves the mountains, there is now the fortified city of Tāsh-Kurgān, built in the eighteenth century by Aḥmad Shāh, founder of the present-day Afghan state; it is situated at a distance of several versts (two to three English miles) south of old Khulm, from which the inhabitants were moved to the new town. The ruins of old Khulm, judging by Yate's description,[58] offer nothing of interest.[59] Even now the town of Tāsh-Kurgān has commercial importance; all the caravans between Bukhārā and India stop here, and the goods are distributed from here throughout the country.

After Khulm, the road enters a narrow gorge of the river; according to travelers' accounts, there is hardly any room for the

56 ⟨⟨Cf. P. Schwarz, "Bemerkungen zu den arabischen Nachrichten über Balkh," *Oriental Studies in Honour of Cursetji Erachji Pavry* (London, 1933), pp. 434-43.⟩⟩

57 ⟨⟨Cf. *Ḥudūd al-ʿālam*, tr. V. Minorsky, p. 341.⟩⟩ ⟦The Abū Dāwūdids are also sometimes called the Bānījūrids, after an eponymous, possibly legendary ancestor; see C. E. Bosworth, *EI*², Suppl., art. "Bānīdjūrids,"⟧

58 *Northern Afghanistan*, p. 315.

59 ⟨⟨Cf. Masson-Romodin, I, 170.⟩⟩ ⟦For Khulm, see now J. Humlum *et al.*, *La géographie de l'Afghanistan, étude d'un pays aride* (Copenhagen, 1959), p. 155; Bosworth, *EI*², s.v.⟧

little river and the road alongside it between the tall cliffs; at one spot the space between the cliffs narrows to forty feet. The journey from Khulm to Siminjān (Simingān) was reckoned to take two days. The town of Simingān (Khelu-si-min-tsian in Chinese transcription) is mentioned as early as Hsüan-tsang's seventh-century account; it still had this name at the end of the fourteenth century, at the time of Tīmūr's Indian campaign. The history of Tīmūr's campaign also mentions between Khulm and Simingān the village of Ghazniyak, now Gaznigak, fifteen English miles from Khulm, where the gorge widens and takes on the appearance of a somewhat wider valley covered with grass.[60] As for Simingān, its location is doubtless identical with that of the fortress of Haybak, which is located in the widest part of the Khulm valley, and which has a great strategic importance. The surroundings of Haybak are distinguished by their unusual fertility; the whole area is covered with trees and orchards. In the surrounding region there are many monuments from the time of Buddhist domination, in particular, caves dug out by hermits and stupas for keeping holy relics.[61] From Simingān or Haybak, the main road led eastward across the mountains up to its junction with the valley of the next river, the Aq Saray, now also called Āb-i Qunduz after the main town of the region; in the valley of the Aq Saray, two days' journey from Simingān, was the town of Baghlān, which still exists under the same name.[62] In the valley of the Khulm river, in the mountains between Simingān and Baghlān and in the surrounding area, the military encounters between Qutayba and the princes of Ṭukhāristān took place in the eighth century, encounters described in some detail by Ṭabarī.[63] Incidentally, the mountain locality of Ishkamish, which still bears that name, is already mentioned at that time.[64] From Baghlān it took

[60] ⟨⟨Ghiyāth al-Dīn ʿAlī Yazdī, *Rūz-nāma-yi ghazawāt-i Hindūstān*, ed. L. A. Zimin and V. V. Barthold (Petrograd, 1915), p. 198.⟩⟩

[61] ⟨⟨For the monuments in the environs of Haybak, see: *Ḥudūd al-ʿālam*, tr. V. Minorsky, pp. 109, 338; Masson-Romodin, I, 29-30; L. Foucher, *La vieille route de l'Inde, Bactres à Taxila* (Paris, 1942-1947), I, 123-29, 170-71, pl. xxvii; A. Godard, Y. Godard, and J. Hackin, *Les antiquités bouddhiques de Bāmiyān* (Paris, 1928), pp. 65-74.⟩⟩

[62] ⟨⟨For the name Baghlān (Bactrian *vaγlāng* = "sanctuary, temple"), and for excavations of the temple complex in Surkh Kotal, see: W. B. Henning, "Surkh Kotal," *BSOAS*, XVIII (1956), 366-67; Masson-Romodin, I, 190-96; D. Schlumberger, "Le temple de Surkh Kotal en Bactriane (IV)," *JA*, CCLII (1964), pp. 303-26.⟩⟩

[63] Ṭabarī, II, 1219 ff.

[64] ⟨⟨Cf. J. Markwart, *Wehrot und Arang. Untersuchungen zur mythischen und geschichtlichen Landeskunde von Ostiran* (Leiden, 1933), p. 86.⟩⟩

three days to reach Andarāb, which was situated next to the principal ridge of the Hindū Kush, and which had considerable commercial importance. Among the mountain passes that lead to the southern side of the Hindū Kush toward the Indus basin and the valley of the river Banjhīr, now Panjshīr, the most convenient one was, according to L. F. Kostenko, that of Khāwak;[65] in Tīmūr's time a fortress was built there. The valley of the Panjshīr was noted for its silver ores, considered to be the richest in Muslim Central Asia; they still exist today.[66] In the valley of the Panjshīr were the towns of Gārbāya (two days' journey from Andarāb), Banjhīr (one day's trip further down) and Parwān or Farwān (two more days); the last one still has this name today, and is located near the confluence of the Ghūrband with the Panjshīr.[67] At Parwān the road bifurcates; one branch sets out directly southward over Chārīkār and Istālīf to the Kābul valley, the other climbs southwestward along the Ghūrbānd, past a settlement of the same name, which was conquered by the Arabs at the end of the eighth century, to Bāmiyān. There was yet another road to Bāmiyān—through the valley of the Khulm river, which becomes narrower again above Haybak, and through several mountain passes, of which the southernmost one, Aq Rabāṭ, is still considered to be the border between Kābulistān and Afghan Turkestān. The tenth-century geographers only briefly mention this road from Balkh to Bāmiyān, and reckon six days of travel from Balkh to the town of Mādar, and from there four more days to Bāmiyān. The settlement of Mādar still exists, and in its vicinity one can see the ruins of the old town.[b] The mention of Mādar shows that the road in question is the one that leads from the valley of the Balkh Āb into that of the Khulm river,

[65] *Turkestanskii krai*, II, 190. Reference to J. Wood, *A Journey to the Source of the River Oxus* (London, 1872), p. 274, in I. Minaev, *Svedeniia*, p. 125.

[66] For the mining of silver, see Samʿānī, *Kitāb al-Ansāb*, facs. ed. D. S. Margoliouth (London, 1912), fol. 92a, as well as Yāqūt, *Muʿjam al-buldān*, s.v. "Banjhīr."

[67] M. Longworth Dames, *EI*[1], art. "Ghazna," about Parwān as the only place of mint of Sebüktekin's coins. ⟨⟨Cf. R. Frye, *EI*[2], art. "Farwān."⟩⟩ ⟦C. E. Bosworth, *The Ghaznavids, Their Empire in Afghanistan and Eastern Iran 994-1040* (Edinburgh, 1963), pp. 38, 43.⟧

[b] This Mādar was one of the two villages linked together in the sources as Mādar u Mūy (for example, in Ibn Bābā al-Qāshānī and Jūzjānī, cf. *Ḥudūd al-ʿālam*, tr. V. Minorsky, p. 109); it was here that Sebüktigin, founder of the Ghaznawid dynasty, died. See Muḥammad Nāẓim, *The Life and Times of Sulṭān Maḥmūd of Ghazna* (Cambridge, 1931), p. 32, and C. E. Bosworth, *The Later Ghaznavids, Splendour and Decay: the Dynasty in Afghanistan and Northern India 1040-1186* (Edinburgh, 1977), pp. 135, 146.

and not the still more arduous road upstream along the Balkh Āb to its source; on the latter road, a place called Band-i Amīr is noteworthy, for the river is divided by several natural dams formed by rocks into five or six lakes full of all kinds of fish. The place is considered sacred and is visited by pilgrims.[68]

A road from Balkh through Khulm also led eastward to Badakhshān and from there to Tibet, that is, to the upper reaches of the Indus system inhabited by the Tibetans. On this road was the largest city of Ṭukhāristān, Ṭālaqān, which still has the same name (Ṭāliqān). In the tenth century it was one-third the size of Balkh; subsequently its importance declined considerably, and in 1837 Wood counted only three or four hundred houses here. The town is located on one of the tributaries of the Aq Saray; Maqdisī states that the town was cut through by two sleeves, that is, probably by two tributaries of the Āmū Daryā.[69] From Khulm to Ṭālaqān the distance was reckoned to be four days of travel; on this road was situated the town of Warwalīz (also spelled Walwalīz and Walwalīj).[70] There is no doubt that both Ṭālaqān and Warwalīz were situated in the valley of the Aq Saray and its tributaries; in the valley of the Aq Saray is also the road that goes to Andarāb and from there across the Hindū Kush. The modern chief city of the valley, Qunduz, did not yet exist in the tenth century; it is mentioned as the capital of an independent domain at the time of Chingiz Khan's campaigns, that is, in the thirteenth century. In the nineteenth century, Qunduz was the chief town of an extensive Uzbek khanate that controlled several regions on both sides of the Āmū Daryā.[c]

From Ṭālaqān, travelers reached the main city of the region, Badakhshān, in seven days. The town of Badakhshān most probably stood on the site of the modern chief city of the region, Fayḍābād. The Badakshān city of Jurm, which still exists today, is called by the ninth-century geographer Yaʿqūbī "the last of the eastern cities which belong to Balkh in the direction of the land of the Tibetans."[71] Badakhshān, moreover, is situated on the direct road from Balkh eastward across the Pamir to eastern Turkestān. Because of the bend here in the river Panj and the difficulties of the road on the right bank of the river, relations even between the

[68] ⟨⟨Cf. Mukhammed Ali, *Afganistan*, pp. 116 ff.⟩⟩

[69] Maqdisī, p. 303.

[70] ⟨⟨Cf. *Ḥudūd al-ʿālam*, tr. V. Minorsky, p. 340.⟩⟩

[c] ⟦On this place, see now Bosworth, *EI*², art. "Ḳunduz."⟧

[71] *Kitāb al-Buldān*, p. 288.

regions situated on the right bank of the Panj usually took place by way of Badakhshān. As for the importance of the Badakhshān region itself, Yate described it as a cold and poor country, which could never become rich because of the lack of arable land.[72] On the other hand, medieval geographers and travelers extol Badakhshān not only for its ruby and lapis lazuli mines, but also for its beautiful climate, its broad and well-cultivated valleys, and its excellent pastures.[73] Badakhshān was frequently subjected to conquest and changes of dynasty; nevertheless, in the nineteenth century the rulers of Badakhshān, who had the title of *mīr* (that is, *amīr*), still considered themselves to be descendants of Alexander the Great; as proof, they kept certain objects of Graeco-Bactrian culture (coins, silver cups, and so on).[74] Badakhshān was the last of the regions of the left bank of the Panj that in the Middle Ages were under some degree of control by Balkh. Also historically linked with Balkh were the regions on the right side of the Āmū Daryā that now constitute a part of the Bukhārā khanate but that are linked with Balkh by much more adequate roads than those to Samarqand and Bukhārā. Despite the commercial importance of Balkh, the late tenth-century geographer Maqdisī calls it "a dreary town, located aside from the main road," which suggests a certain decline in trade with India.[75]

Balkh acquired a special importance in the eleventh century at the time of the Ghaznawids, when it became one of the capitals of the famous sulṭān Maḥmūd, even though it was subjected in 1006 to a destructive incursion by the Qarakhānids. Before this, the Āmū Daryā, just as now, was declared to be the boundary between the kingdoms of Turkestān and eastern Iran; after his victory over the Qarakhānids, however, Maḥmūd annexed the regions pertaining to Balkh that were on the right bank of the river. In the middle

[72] *Northern Afghanistan*, p. 320. ⟦On the geography of the region, see Humlum, *La géographie de l'Afghanistan*, pp. 110-12; L. Dupree, *Afghanistan* (Princeton, 1973), p. 8.⟧

[73] Barthold, *Turkestan* (Eng. tr.), p. 66. ⟦The lapis lazuli mines of the district were exploited from very early times; in Mesopotamia, lapis lazuli objects are found from the late Ubaid period (mid- and late-fifth millennium B.C.). See Georgina Herrmann, "Lapis Lazuli: the Early Phases of Its Trade," *Iraq*, XXX (1968), 21-57.⟧

[74] ⟨⟨See also: V. V. Barthold, *EI*[1], art. "Bada<u>khsh</u>ān," *Soch.* III, 347 ff., V. V. Barthold, A. Bennigsen, and H. Carrère d'Encausse, *EI*[2], art. Bada<u>khsh</u>ān"; Sang Muḥammad Badakhshī and Faḍl Beg Ḥājjī Surkhafsar, *Ta'rīkh-i Badakhshān*, ed. A. N. Boldyrev (Leningrad, 1959); Kūshkakī; T. G. Abaeva, *Ocherki istorii Badakhshana* (Tashkent, 1964), with bibliography.⟩⟩

[75] Maqdisī, p. 302.

of the eleventh century, Balkh was incorporated into the possession of the Saljuqs, who also subjugated its dependent regions, and the Hindū Kush became the official boundary between the Saljuq and Ghaznawid possessions. When in the twelfth century the mountain nation of the Ghūrids, whom we shall discuss below, rose in prominence, Balkh became one of its possessions. The city was destroyed in the Mongol invasion and remained ruined until the first half of the fourteenth century. Just as in the eleventh century, now too the Āmū Daryā was declared to be the boundary—this time between the possessions of the descendants of Chaghatay and those of Hülegü. This time, too, the boundary was soon violated: the Chaghatay khans firmly established themselves in Balkh and in the neighboring regions in the thirteenth century. The restoration of Balkh is attributed by Muslim historians to the Chaghatay khan Kebek, who died in 1326, but Ibn Baṭṭūṭa, who was there in 1333, still found the city in ruins.[76] In 1368, the amīr Ḥusayn, Tīmūr's predecessor, decided to rebuild the fortress of Hinduwān, the former citadel of the city of Balkh; the inhabitants of the city were forcibly moved to the fortress, so that the former was ruined [again]. After the overthrow of Ḥusayn by Tīmūr in 1370, the fortress was destroyed and the inhabitants were ordered to return to the old city. Tīmūr received the oath of the Chaghatay nobles and commanders in the vicinity of Balkh. In the fifteenth century, the city formed part of Tīmūrid domains, and subsequently it was a bone of contention between the Uzbek khans, the shāhs of Persia, and the Great Mughals of India, whose place was taken by the newly formed Afghan state in the eighteenth century. The Uzbeks became the ethnically dominant element in Balkh and in the regions to the east and west of it. The country from the Murghāb to the border of Badakhshān received the name of Turkestān, and it has kept it to this day, even after its incorporation into Afghanistan; before that, it was alternately under the rule of independent Uzbek rulers and of the khans of Bukhārā. The latter, for understandable reasons, especially valued Balkh, which still belonged to them in the nineteenth century. In the heyday of the Bukhāran khanate, Balkh was an important city and was called, as before, *umm al-bilād* ("mother of cities") and *qubbat al-Islām* ("dome of Islam"). We have a detailed description of the city as it was in the seventeenth century in the work called

[76] Ibn Baṭṭūṭa, *Riḥla*, ed. and tr. C. Defrémery and B. Sanguinetti (Paris, 1853-1858), III, 58-62.

Baḥr al-asrār fī manāqib al-akhyār by Maḥmūd b. Walī.[77] Balkh was joined to Afghanistan in 1850; the final subjugation of the entire Afghan Turkestān took place only in the 1880s.

From among the more recent travelers, Burnes visited Balkh in 1832, Ferrier in 1845, and Yate in 1886. The last-named describes the ruins of the city in great detail and includes a plan.[78] The old wall encompasses an area about six and a half English miles in circumference and has four gates (in Maḥmūd b. Walī's time it had six gates). Contiguous with the city on the northeastern side are the ruins of the fortress, which is situated at a considerably higher level; the citadel itself, fifty feet higher still, is located in the southwestern (according to the plan, southeastern) corner of the fortress. The fortress and the citadel are totally uninhabited; Yate observes that there is absolutely no water in the former, and that it is hard to see from where water could have been brought in the past. The citadel (*quhandiz*) still existed in the seventeenth century, when it was called the *shahr-i darūn* ("inner city") and had four gates.[79] Today only the southern side of the city is inhabited. Visible at the western gate are three tall arches—remnants, according to the inhabitants, of the Friday mosque; at a certain distance to the east one can see the remnants of the *chārsū* (*chahār sū*), that is, the central dome of the bazaar. As in the case of other large cities of Afghanistan, such as Harāt, Balkh was traversed by two main streets, from south to north and from west to east, alongside which were the covered bazaars; at the intersection of these two main streets was the domelike structure. Somewhat further east, one can see the remnants of a high gate. Yate points out that the remnants of the old wall are visible from the southwestern corner of the city, specifically from the tower Burj-i Azarān, all the way to the southwestern corner of the fortress; here, in his opinion, ended the old town, whereas the western part was joined on to it later. From his description, however, one could also draw the opposite conclusion, namely, that the eastern part is more recent than the western. Yate describes two more buildings, without mentioning their location, namely, the "green mosque" (*masjid-i sabz*) with the tomb of a saint, and the ruins of a madrasa built by Subḥān Qulī Khan, who had

[77] Barthold, *Turkesktan,* (Eng. tr.), p. 313. ⟦For Mahmūd b. Walī's work, see C. A. Storey, *Persian Literature, a Bio-bibliographical Survey,* I (London, 1927), 375-76; Storey-Bregel', II, 1,135-38.⟧

[78] Yate, *Northern Afghanistan,* p. 256.

[79] There is in the citadel a stone from white marble, the throne of Kaykāwūs (A. Burnes, *Travels into Bokhara* [London, 1839], II, 205).

ruled here in the second half of the seventeenth century. Most probably the whole city as depicted in Yate's plan and described in his book belongs to the Uzbek period.[80] The Afghans themselves placed the ruins of the earlier town to the east of the one described, calling them *shahr-i Hinduwān*, and maintained that this Balkh had been destroyed by Chingiz Khan, after which the new town came into being. It is not clear whether this town was contiguous with the citadel described. It is quite possible that the fortress together with the citadel is identical with the citadel of the old town destroyed by Chingiz Khan and rebuilt by the amīr Ḥusayn, and that the *shahristān* of the pre-Mongol period had been on the site of the ruins of *shahr-i Hinduwān*. According to the observations of Burnes, all the ruins visible today above the ground belong to the Islamic period, which is indeed most probably the case;[81] other travelers such as J. P. Ferrier thought they saw in Balkh fragments of bricks with cuneiform script, but this has not been substantiated.[82] Yate ascribes two large kurgans or mounds of the city to the Buddhist period: Takht-i Rustam and Tepe-yi Rustam;[83] judging by their location, it is possible that here were the two edifices of Nawbahār about which Hsüan-tsang wrote in the seventh century. Tepe-yi Rustam was a round building made of unbaked brick, 150 feet in diameter at the base and 50 feet tall;[84] the upper part of the building was faced with fired bricks. The edifice had a flat top; inside were visible four round cells; they were uncovered and open from above because their cupola-shaped roof had collapsed, so that there may be other cells as yet undisturbed. Below, four entrances were dug through. They converged in the center as passageways, but the explorer could not determine whether these passageways had existed from the very beginning or whether they had been dug later,

[80] Yate, *Northern Afghanistan*, p. 257. This is incorrect; not taken into account was the story about the siege of Balkh by the Bukhārans in 1573. Cf. G. Le Strange, *The Lands of the Eastern Caliphate* (Cambridge, 1905), pp. 421 ff., concerning the Nawbahār of Balkh only as a Zoroastrian one; identification of Balkh with Mazār-i Sharīf. Staël-Holstein's observation on Hsüan-tsang, p. 20, is inexact. *Mazār* of Khwāja ʿUkkāsha in Mir ʿAlī Shīr Nawāʾī, *Majālis al-nafāʾis*, ms. Leningrad University, fol. 46a.

[81] Burnes, *Travels*, II, 204.

[82] J. P. Ferrier, *Voyages et aventures en Perse, dans l'Afghanistan, le Beloutshistan et le Turkestan* (Paris, 1870), I, 389.

[83] The local population calls this monument Top-i Rustam; for its excavations see A. Foucher, *La vieille route de l'Inde, Bactres à Taxila*, I, 83-98, 168-69, pls. xix-xx.

[84] The little upper platform is thirty yards in diameter; cf. Yate, *Northern Afghanistan*, p. 259.

possibly by grave robbers; at present they are so filled that it is impossible to pass through them. Takht-i Rustam is a mound of similar size; it is not round, however, but has a trapezoidal shape.[85] There are no traces of bricks; the edifice, it seems, was made of clay. The top is entirely flat and in some places eroded through by rain, but it is not known whether there had been any cells. In the surroundings of the town, there had been other similar mounds in which the explorer thought to recognize the remnants of similar Buddhist structures; the name Takht-i Rustam, according to Yate,[86] is usually applied by local inhabitants to ruins of Buddhist stupas.[87]

We do not know whether there had been any Buddhist or other sanctuary on the place of the present-day principal Islamic sanctuary of the region, Mazār-i Sharīf, situated to the east of Balkh. In the Middle Ages, the village of Khayr had been here.[88] In the first half of the twelfth century, according to the report of the traveler Gharnāṭī, a rumor had spread that the caliph ʿAlī had been born in this place; many affirmed that they had learned about this from the Prophet Muḥammad himself, who had appeared to them in dream. This was discussed in a meeting at the governor's office; one *faqīh* resolutely declared that this was impossible, for ʿAlī had never been in those parts. That night the *faqīh* himself had a vision; in his dream he saw angels who took him to the grave, showed him the undecayed body of the caliph, and heaped on him reproaches and blows because he had suspected the Prophet of lying. The *faqīh* woke up with traces of the blows, hurried to the governor, and told him everything that had happened; the latter came with a large number of people to the designated place, found the undecayed body of the caliph, and ordered that a magnificent mausoleum be erected for him.[89] Despite its fantastic character, the

[85] ⟨⟨See Foucher, *La vieille route*, I, pl. xxi, a.⟩⟩

[86] Yate, *Northern Afghanistan*, p. 321.

[87] ⟨⟨For the history of Balkh and its monuments, see also: R. Hartmann, *EI*¹, art. "Balkh"; R. N. Frye, *EI*², art. "Balkh"; E. Caspani and E. Cagnacci, *Afghanistan, crocevia dell'Asia* (Milan, 1951), pp. 240-42; D. N. Wilber, *Annotated Bibliography of Afghanistan* (New Haven, 1956), pp. 84, 177-78; for photographs of the monuments and a plan of the contemporary city, see: O. von Niedermayer, *Afghanistan* (Leipzig, 1924), pp. 48-64; Foucher, *La vieille route*, I.⟩⟩ ⟦Z. V. Togan, "The Topography of Balkh down to the Middle of the Seventeenth Century," *CAJ* (1970). XIV, 277-88.⟧

[88] Le Strange, *The Lands*, p. 423 (after Khwāndamīr), about the village of Khwāja Khayrān, three leagues from Balkh. From Balkh to Mazār-i Sharīf, according to Ferrier, the distance was two farsakhs (I. Minaev, *Svedeniia*, p. 128; *ibid*., p. 215, according to the itinerary by Faiz Bakhsh, two farsakhs or ten and a half miles).

[89] Barthold, *Turkestan* (Eng. tr.), p. 79.

story told by Gharnāṭī in general faithfully renders what he had heard in Balkh. The same thing is also told in the Persian verses that, according to Yate, are carved on the sarcophagus, even though the present-day structure of the *mazār* is of a later date;[90] it was built in 886/1481 by Sulṭān Ḥusayn [Bāyqarā], a descendant of Tīmūr, the old building having been destroyed by Chingiz Khan. According to the historian Isfizārī, the tomb of ʿAlī was reopened in 885 A.H. (= A.D. 1480).[91] The *mazār* with its blue domes represents the only substantial building in the whole town that grew around the holy place. The governor Nā'ib ʿAlīm Khān, a Shīʿī, in 1866 chose Mazār-i Sharīf as his residence, and since then the town has become the main city of Afghan Turkestān.[92]

In the western part of ancient Bactria, that is, in the area between the Murghāb and Balkh, the character of the country is somewhat different. A certain distance below Balkh, the Āmū Daryā turns northwestward; the mountains, on the other hand, proceed southwestward. In this manner the distance between the river and the cultivated belt (the latter skirting the mountains), widens. The little rivers that flow from the northern slope of the mountains disappear in the sands long before reaching the Āmū Daryā. The waterless, sandy country between the Murghāb and the Āmū Daryā ends on the south with the flat elevation of Kara Bel, 3,500 to 4,000 feet high; from the southern edge of this elevation flow the so-called *shōrs*, little rivers filled with brackish water. These rivulets with little water flow partly into the Kala-Weli, a tributary of the Murghāb, and partly into the river Qayṣār, which after its merger with the Āb-i Maymana and the Shīrīn Tagay is called Āb-i Andkhūy. Even some of the more important streams that belong to the Murghāb system are so impregnated with salt that they are useless not only for drinking but even for irrigation. Nevertheless, the southern part of the steppe wasteland (*chöl*) is habitable, if not by agriculturists at least by nomads. In this respect there is some difference between the steppe around Maymana and that around Andkhūy. Around Maymana there are excellent pastures; below Dawlatābād the pastures change into desert areas covered with moving sands.

The reports of Arab geographers show that in the course of the

[90] Yate, *Northern Afghanistan*, pp. 280-81.

[91] Isfizārī, *Rawḍāt al-jannāt fī awṣāf madīnat Harāt*, ms. Leningrad University, no. 588, fol. 43a.

[92] ⟨⟨See also: Barthold, *EI*[1], art. "Mazār-i Sharīf," *Soch.* III, 478; Masson-Romodin, I, 348; for a photograph of the *mazār*, see Foucher, *La vieille route*, I., pl. ii; Mukhammed Ali, *Afganistan*; G. A. Pugachenkova, *Iskusstvo Afganistana*, pp. 168-69.⟩⟩ ⟦L. Dupree, *Afghanistan*, index.⟧

last millennium the cultivated belt has shrunk very little. Even then there was a desert, partly a sandy one, between Balkh and Marw (Merv). The water of the Balkh Āb reached in the northeast the village of Siyāhgird, five farsakhs from Balkh; there still exists a village of this name, and near it are the ruins of the old town.[93] The canals from the Balkh Āb, however, were conducted in the same direction as now, that is, northwestward. Describing the journey from Balkh to the next important town west of there, Ushbūrqān, Shabūraqān, or Shapūrgān (now Shibargān), the Arabs placed at a distance of seven farsakhs from Balkh the populous, well-watered settlement of Dastjird; water could be brought here only from the Balkh Āb.[94] Beyond it began the steppe; five farsakhs from Dastjird was the village of Sidra; originally, according to Qudāma, there was here only a lotus shrub (*sidra* in Arabic, hence the name of the village), and a post station in the middle of the desert; at the time of the earthquake of 203/818-19 the small spring near the bush became a large source and gave origin to the little river that flowed into the steppe; a copse soon grew around the source and a village appeared.[95] From here it was six farsakhs to Shapūrgān; in this manner the distance from Balkh to Shapūrgān was reckoned to amount to eighteen farsakhs. The modern settlements of Aqcha and Nimlik (the former is still an important town, while the latter is in ruins), approximately correspond to Sidra and Dastjird of the Arabs. There is no mention today of a source that would feed a specific stream; Aqcha is reached by the waters of the Balkh Āb; according to Yate, much water suited for irrigation flows from here into the steppe, but there are not enough people to take advantage of it.[96] In the locality of Unpaykal, northwest of Nimlik, Yate saw the ruins of an old town, comprising a whole row of tall, large houses; evidently each house had once been surrounded by its own orchard and vineyards.[97] These ruins are most probably those mentioned by Ferrier when he says that he saw, one hour before reaching Nimlik, the ruins of an early Bactrian town with

[93] Siyāhgird, according to Yate, *Northern Afghanistan*, p. 247, based on a communication from Peacock, measures ten square kilometers; it used to be a large city, but no one knows when.

[94] Nāṣir-i Khusraw, *Safar-nāma* (Tehran, 1312/1894-1895), lithogr., p. 258, Dastgird; on the way from there to Balkh is the Pul-i Jamūkiyān, *ibid.*, p. 259. Cf. Yāqūt, *Muʿjam al-buldān*, for Dastkird Jumūkiyān bi-Balkh. ⟨⟨Cf. also R. N. Frye, "J̌amūk, Sogdian 'Pearl'?" *JAOS*, LXXI (1951), 143.⟩⟩

[95] Qudāma b. Jaʿfar, *Kitāb al-Kharāj*, ed. and tr. M. J. de Goeje (Leiden, 1889), tr. pp. 161-62.

[96] *Northern Afghanistan*, p. 255.

[97] *Ibid.*, p. 254.

large heaps of fired bricks.[98] If there had indeed been a Bactrian city here, it may have been Eucratidis, built by King Eucratides; Tomaschek locates Eucratidis on the site of Khulm,[99] but Gutschmid cites Ptolemy, according to whom the town was situated on the left bank of the Balkh river below Balkh.[100] The region became depopulated only in the nineteenth century, when it was conquered by the Afghans after a stubborn resistance of the Uzbek population.[101]

Shapūrgān was already part of the area of Gūzgān or Gūzgānān, the Jūzjān of the Arabs. The region comprised the cultivated belt of two rivers that flow out of the mountains and disappear in the sands; today, these rivers do not have names of their own but are called after the towns lying on their courses. The eastern river is usually called Āb-i Shibargān, the western one is formed by the merger of two rivulets: Āb-i Qayṣār (with the Āb-i Maymana tributary) and Shīrīn Tagay; the river resulting from this confluence is called Āb-i Andkhūy. It is unknown in which period Gūzgān began to be considered an independent region; classical geographers do not know such a region, and make Bactria border immediately on Margiana. It was still known in the tenth century that Gūzgān had formerly not been a distinct region but had been associated with that of Balkh.[102] In the ninth century, the name Gūzgān was applied only to the cultivated belt of the Āb-i Shapūrgān and to the mountainous region Gurziwan in the upper reaches of the rivulet Āb-i Maymana.[103] The residence of the Arab governors in the area was Anbār, one day's journey south of Shapūrgān, probably on the site of the modern town Sar-i Pul.[104] The local ruler lived in Gurziwan, in the village of Kundarm, four days' journey from Shapūrgān. The old capital of Gūzgān was Shapūrgān, which is confirmed by one of Ṭabarī's reports.[105] As at the present time, there was a wasteland between the course of the

[98] *Voyages*, I, 387.

[99] *PW*, art. "Baktriane."

[100] *Geschichte Irans*, p. 64.

[101] See Yate, *Northern Afghanistan*, p. 255: "The Balkh river . . . expends immense volumes of spill-water in the desert beyond, all of which might be utilised were there only people to utilise it. But the people have all apparently been killed off."

[102] Maqdisī, p. 298.

[103] Ya'qūbī, *Kitāb al-Buldān*, p. 287. ⟦R. Hartmann, *EI*², art. "Dj̲ūzdj̲ān." The region falls within the modern Afghan provinces of Maymana and Mazār-i Sharīf, see Humlum, *La géographie de l'Afghanistan*, pp. 112-13, 148-49.⟧

[104] ⟨⟨See *Ḥudūd al-ʿālam*, tr. Minorsky, p. 335; Ghirshman, *Les Chionites-hephthalites*, p. 26.⟩⟩

[105] Marquart, *Ērānšahr*, p. 87.

Shapūrgān river and that of the Shīrīn Tagay; this wasteland was called by the Arabs al-Qāʿ, which means a plain or a lowland with stagnant water. The station of al-Qāʿ was probably not far from the place where several smallish rivulets disappear into the sands; the station belonged even in the ninth century to Gūzgān.[106] The main town of the cultivated belt of the Āb-i Qayṣār and the Shīrīn Tagay, Fāryāb, was most probably situated on the site of the modern town of Dawlatābād or somewhat lower, where there is today the village of Khayrābād. Mention is also made of the mountain settlement of Yahūdān or Yahūdiyya, where even in the ninth century—in Yaʿqūbī's time—the ruler of Fāryāb still lived.[107] The settlement was on the site of modern Maymana, although only one day's journey was reckoned between it and Anbār. The name Maymana does not appear in the works of the tenth-century geographers. It is found in those of the thirteenth-century authors [108] in the form Maymand, which had, however, existed earlier; Sulṭān Maḥmūd's (998-1030) vizier [Aḥmad b. Ḥasan] Maymandī was from there.[d] At the end of the tenth century, in Maqdisī's time, Yahūdiyya was considered to be the capital of Gūzgān.[109] The name of the town shows that it had a large Jewish colony.[e]

The tenth-century geographers describe several roads between the towns of Gūzgān and give some information about them, without, however, describing any town in detail. We only learn that in Yahūdiyya there was a Friday mosque with two minarets, but that in Gūzgān it was not customary to erect minarets, and that in Ibn Ḥawqal's time the amīr, the nobles, and the population for a long time would not permit them to be built, on the grounds that it was not good to betray the customs of the ancestors.[110]

The region was still in Maqdisī's time not very thickly popu-

[106] Ibn Khurradādhbih, tr., p. 23; see also Qudāma, tr., p. 161.

[107] Yaʿqūbī, *Kitāb al-Buldān*, p. 287.

[108] Jūzjānī, *Ṭabaqāt-i Nāṣirī*, ed. W. Nassau Lees (Calcutta, 1864), pp. 378, 399-400. ⟨⟨The name Maymana appears in the tenth century in Bīrūnī; see *Ḥudūd al-ʿālam*, tr. Minorsky, p. 335; cf. also R. B. Whitehead, *EI*[1], art. "Maimana"; B. Spuler, *Iran in früh-islamischer Zeit* (Wiesbaden, 1952), p. 216.⟩⟩

[d] It is unlikely that Aḥmad b. Ḥasan Maymandī came from Maymana in Gūzgān, and that the form Maymand ever existed for the town of Maymana is far from certain (see Bosworth, *EI*[2], art, "Maymana"); he was much more likely a native of Maymand in Zābulistān, the region around Ghazna, and Mustawfī's notice of Maymand (*Nuzhat al-qulūb*, ed. Le Strange, p. 147, tr. *idem*, p. 145) clearly refers to this last.

[109] Maqdisī, p. 198.

[e] See on this community, W. J. Fischel, "The Jews of Central Asia (Khorasan) in Mediaeval Hebrew and Islamic Literature," *Historia Judaica*, VII (1945), 29-50.

[110] Ibn Ḥawqal, p. 321.

lated.[111] In the towns situated in the mountains there are mentioned orchards and vineyards; in the case of those situated on the plain, for example Shapūrgān, cultivated fields are said to have predominated, whereas orchards would have been few. As for the northernmost town, Andkhūd or Andkhūy, it is said that "it is a small town in the steppe with seven villages; nomads live there with their flocks of sheep and herds of camels." The distance from Fāryāb to Andkhūy was reckoned to be three days' journey, and from Andkhūy to Karkul, that is, Kerki on the Āmū Daryā, another three days' journey. The ruler of Gūzgān had at one time the title of Gūzgān-Khudāt. In the tenth century, Gūzgān was ruled by the local dynasty of the Farīghūnids (Āl-i Farīghūn), who had the title of amīr; this dynasty was overthrown by Maḥmūd of Ghazna.[112] Subsequently, Shapūrgān and other towns usually shared the fate of Balkh. In the nineteenth century, Shibargān, Sar-i Pul, Maymana, and Andkhūy were capitals of small Uzbek domains. They all consisted of the town proper and of the separate citadel that dominated each town; all suffered greatly during the conquest by the Afghans. Today almost no ancient ruins of town and buildings are left; near Andkhūy one can see extensive ruins of the old town, but even there, according to Yate, no monuments predating the end of the fourteenth century survive. Historians mention more often the citadel of Shapūrgān; according to Sharaf al-Dīn,[113] this citadel is identical with the fortress of Safīd-diz, mentioned in Firdawsi's *Shāh-nāma*. According to Tomaschek, Shapūrgān is identical with the Bactrian city of Surogana, mentioned by the classical geographers.[114] The region of Gūzgān was famous, according to Iṣṭakhrī[115] and Ibn Ḥawqal,[116] for its curried hides, which were exported to other parts of Khurāsān.[117]

[111] Maqdisī, p. 298.

[112] ⟨⟨For the Farīghūnids, see Barthold, *Vvedenie*, pp. 4-7, *Soch*, VIII, 505-509; *Ḥudūd al-ʿālam*, tr. Minorsky, pp. 173-78; Minorsky, "Ibn Farīghūn and the Ḥudūd al-ʿālam," *A Locust's Leg, Studies in Honour of S. H. Taqizadeh* (London, 1962), pp. 189-96; D. M. Dunlop, *EI*², art, "Farīg͟hūnids."⟩⟩

[113] Sharaf al-Dīn Yazdī, *Ẓafar-nāma* (Calcutta, 1885-1888), I, 221.

[114] *PW*, art. "Baktriane."

[115] Iṣṭakhrī, p. 271.

[116] Ibn Ḥawqal, p. 322.

[117] ⟨⟨For Jūzjān, see also: *Ḥudūd al-ʿālam*, tr. Minorsky, pp. 328-37; R. Hartmann, *EI*¹, art. D̲jūzd̲jān"; B. Spuler, *Iran in früh-islamischer Zeit*, index.⟩⟩

CHAPTER II

Marw and the Course of the Murghāb

On the west, Gūzgān was bounded by the cultivated tract of the Murghāb and its affluents, the ancient Margiana. As the largest river in the whole area, the Murghāb flows much farther north than the neighboring streams, but a part of its course crosses a sand desert; elsewhere the cultivated zone astride it is only a narrow belt. For this reason the road between the two largest cities of Arab Khurāsān, Marw and Balkh, left Marw first in a southerly direction along the Murghāb toward the mountains, then proceeded along these mountains northeastward through Fāryāb (that is, Dawlatābād) and Shapūrgān.[1] In the eastern part of the Murghāb basin was the city of Ṭālaqān, which lay at an equal distance (three days' journey) from Marw al-Rūd, situated on the Murghāb, and Fāryāb, that is, Dawlatābād.

The problem of the location of Marw al-Rūd and Ṭālaqān remains unsolved. The question of whether Marw al-Rūd was on the site of modern Marūchak or further south, on the site of Bālā Murghāb, has not been adequately answered to this day.[2] The data that the Arab geographers give in their itineraries seem to speak in favor of Bālā Murghāb. From among the points along this route, the castle of al-Aḥnaf b. Qays (whence a direct road left the Murghāb toward Balkh) could have stood on the site of the small Türkmen settlement of Qaraul-khāna near the confluence of the small river

[1] Nāṣir-i Khusraw (*Safar-nāma*, Tehran lithogr., p. 6) about the journey from Shapūrgān to Marw al-Rūd: "I spent the night in the village of Bādyāb [read Fāryāb? in Schefer's ed., p. 3, Bāryāb] and from there I went by way of Sanglān and Ṭālaqān to Marw al-Rūd." In the same work, p. 257, the return journey. From Sarakhs to Marw al-Rūd: "By way of the Ja'farī ribāṭ and the 'Umrawī [sic] ribāṭ and the Ni'matī ribāṭ, all the three of which are close to each other"; from Marw al-Rūd: "On the nineteenth of the month we arrived in Aryāb by way of Āb-i Garm." ⟨⟨Cf. Barthold. "Merverrud," *Soch.* III, 255 n. 22, and pp. 257-58.⟩⟩ The amīr of Khurāsān, Chaghrī Beg, on the trip from Shapūrgān to his capital Marw: "We went, because of the insecurity of the road[s], toward Sanglān, and from there we came to Balkh by way of Sih-dara." *Ibid.*, p. 258: "Ribāṭ-i Sih-dara, from there to Dastgird."

[2] Article about Marw al-Rūd, *ZVORAO*, XIV ⟨⟨Barthold, "Merverrud"; see also Mir Hussein, "Merve Rud," *Afghanistan*, IX (1954), no. 3, pp. 8-17; no. 4, pp. 19-25.⟩⟩ ⟦Bosworth, *EI*², art. "Marw al-Rūdh."⟧

Qalʿa Walī with the Murghāb;[3] nearby are several mounds with fragments of fired bricks and other traces of buildings.[4] Six miles above Bālā Murghāb was the entrance to the fourteen-mile-long defile,[5] probably the same as the one mentioned by the geographer Qudāma.[6] Near both its northern and southern entrances there are, on top of the cliffs, ancient stone towers guarding the passage; the northern tower is probably identical with the "castle of ʿAmr" of the Arab geographers. Qudāma's statement that the entrance into the defile is at a distance of one farsakh from Marw al-Rūd speaks in favor of Bālā Murghāb and against Marūchak. Insofar as one can judge from Yate's description, there is no defile on the road from Marūchak to Qaraul-khāna;[7] the road proceeds along the right bank of the river by the foothills, and twice cuts through the latter's ridge.[8] Another argument in favor of this identification, less substantial but not without value, is the following: Sharaf al-Dīn Yazdī says that Marw al-Rūd was in his time called Murghāb;[9] Marūchak, as far as is known, never had this name. At the same time, Bālā Murghāb was sometimes called simply Murghāb; this is what the traveler Ferrier still called it in 1845.[10] Qudāma mentions cave dwellings in this area, and there are even today many caves in the cliffs of the Murghāb valley. Some of these on the left bank were examined by Yate, who, however, found nothing of interest there;[11] according to him, there is today nothing in these caves that would allow us to form an idea about the way of life of their

[3] The castle of Aḥnaf, according to Yāqūt (*Muʿjam*, IV, iv, p. 108) was first called Sinuwān; see also III, p. 170, where it is also added: "and that fortress was called Ḥiṣn al-Aḥnaf, it is [the same one called] Sawānjard." In Balādhurī, we read about the *rustāq* (district) of Aḥnaf (p. 406) that it is called (*yudʿā bi-*) Shaqq al-Juradh. The road to Marw al-Rūd; details about military events; Aḥnaf is between the Murghāb and the mountains (*min dākhil al-shiʿb*); the Murghāb is on the right side, the mountains on the left. Balādhurī's idea (p. 406) about the Murghāb: "The Murghāb is a river that flows by Marw al-Rūd, then it disappears under the sands, then it emerges in Marw al-Shāhijān."

[4] Yate, *Northern Afghanistan*, p. 122.

[5] *Ibid.*, p. 219; Darband pass, northern entrance—Band-i Joukar, where the Fīrūzkūhīs place the limit of their *yurt*; near the southern entrance is the bridge to Band-i Kilrekta. ⟨⟨Cf. Barthold, "Merverrud," *Soch.* III, 254.⟩⟩

[6] Qudāma, tr., p. 161.

[7] ⟨⟨Cf. Barthold, "Merverrud," *Soch.* III, 254 n. 15.⟩⟩

[8] Yate, *Northern Afghanistan*, p. 121.

[9] Sharaf al-Dīn Yazdī, I, 311.

[10] *Voyages*, I, 368.

[11] *Northern Afghanistan*, pp. 222-23.

inhabitants.[12] Examined in greater detail were the caves of another locality on the Murghāb, namely, near Panjdih within the Russian border; these caves were described by the English captain F. de Laessoë, who also provided a plan.[13] They are dug out of a sandstone mountain in two stories; the lower level consists of a corridor with a row of cells on each side, approximately identical in size, with a well in each; on the upper floor there was three more cells. No inscriptions were found anywhere; the caves of the lower floor were found entirely empty, but they were so well preserved as to give the impression that they had been vacated just recently.

After leaving the defile, the road was said to proceed upstream along the Murghāb and then again northward along one of the side valleys, across the ridge of Tīrband-i Turkistān and along the valleys of the rivers Qara Jangal and Qalʿa Walī. Ṭālaqān was situated, according to Iṣṭakhrī,[14] in a mountainous place, and according to Yaʿqūbī (who, incidentally, had very vague notions about these regions), between two large mountains;[15] it could have lain either near the fortress of Takht-i Khātūn or on the site of the old fortress of Kaurmakh at the southern edge of the Qalʿa Walī valley. Kaurmakh was until the middle of the nineteenth century the main fortress of the latest inhabitants of the country, the Jamshīds. If the citadel of Ṭālaqān stood here, the town itself could have occupied the area down to the Qalʿa Walī river; the mounds mentioned by Yate in his description of this locality could have been part of it.[16] The citadel of Ṭālaqān is mentioned under the name of Nuṣrat Kūh in connection with Chingiz Khan's campaigns; it defended itself for half a year against the Mongol army.[17] In the ninth century, Ṭālaqān was so large that it had two Friday mosques; it was famous for its woolen fabrics.[18]

The mountainous region on the upper reaches of the Murghāb was called Gharch, Gharj, Gharchistān, or Gharshistān, and its inhabitants were called Gharcha. This ethnonym is still current as

[12] In A. D. Kalmykov's opinion (letter of 3 December 1905), the caves are clearly unsuitable for habitation (they are not located along the exterior ravine but burrow into the depth), but they could serve as a burial ground, although there are no traces of graves. The entrance was not camouflaged.

[13] "Caves and ruins at Penjdeh," *PRGS*, n.s. VII (1885), 584-88.

[14] Iṣṭakhrī, p. 270.

[15] *Kitāb al-Buldān*, p. 287.

[16] *Northern Afghanistan*, p. 211.

[17] ⟨⟨The siege of Nuṣrat Kūh lasted, according to Ibn al-Athīr, ten months, and according to Rashīd al-Dīn, seven. Cf. Barthold, *Turkestan*, p. 439.⟩⟩

[18] Yaʿqūbī, *Kitāb al-Buldān*, p. 287.

Ghalcha, and it is used in Central Asia to designate the Aryan population of the mountainous region along the upper reaches of the Āmū Daryā. This term, in Tomaschek's opinion, goes back to the ancient Bactrian word *ghar*, "mountain";[19] that the word is the same in both cases is, moreover, evident from the fact that the term Gharjistān was also applied to the mountainous region of the upper Zarafshān; the twelfth-century author Samʿānī says about one village that it was situated in the "Gharjistān of Samarqand."[20] The region under discussion here, Murghāb Gharjistān, had its own rulers whose title was *shār*; Iṣṭakhrī[21] and Ibn Ḥawqal[22] name two principal towns of the region, of which one, Pīshīn [Bāshīn] (Afshīn in Jūzjānī) lay on the eastern, right bank of the Murghāb, at a distance of one day's journey above Diza (the village of Diza was situated at the southern end of the above-mentioned defile);[23] the other, Shūrmīn, was in the mountains, one day's journey southward from the former. Islam had already spread into Gharjistān by the tenth century, but the local princes retained their rule; at the end of the tenth century, even Marw al-Rūd was within their domains.[24] This local dynasty was liquidated in the eleventh century by Maḥmūd of Ghazna.[a]

The character of the country along the Murghāb is now quite different from what it was in the time of the Arab geographers. Yate draws attention to the fact that the Arab geographers speak of the orchards of Marw al-Rūd,[25] whereas today there are in neither Marūchak nor Bālā Murghāb either trees or even bushes.[26] The nomadic inhabitants of the area, the Aryan Jamshīds and the

[19] ⟨⟨For the term *galcha*, see also Barthold, "Tadzhiki," *Soch.* II/1, 458. The word *ghar-* ("mountain," Avestan *garay-*, *gairi-*), is represented in eastern Iranian languages; however, in the monuments of the pre-Islamic period the ethnonym **gharchak* or **gharchik* is not attested (in Soghdian *ghrtsyk* = "mountain-," "mountaineer").⟩⟩

[20] Barthold, *Turkestan*, p. 131. Cf. Also Marquart, "Beiträge," p. 666.

[21] Iṣṭakhrī, p. 271-72.

[22] Ibn Ḥawqal, p. 323.

[23] ⟨⟨For the two halves of the village of Diza (Dizak)—the upper one above Marw al-Rūd, and the lower one—see Barthold, "Merverrud," *Soch.* III, 254; Barthold, *Oroshenie*, *Soch.* III, 144.⟩⟩

[24] Maqdisī, p. 314 ⟦See on the region, R. N. Frye, *EI*², art. "Gh̲ard̲jistān."⟧

[a] Muḥammad Nāẓim, *The Life and Times of Sulṭān Maḥmūd of Ghazna* (Cambridge, 1931), pp. 60-62.

[25] *Northern Afghanistan*, p. 224.

[26] According to Kalmykov's letter of 3 December 1905, the Türkmens today do have orchards from Takhta-bāzār to Russian Marūchak (two versts from Afghan Marūchak).

Turkish Türkmens, pay equally little attention to fruit growing, an occupation that demands even greater sacrifices than does agriculture from people who are not inclined to a sedentary way of life in the first place.[27]

There has never been an uninterrupted zone of cultivation along the Murghāb; this is by reason of high sandstone cliffs that sometimes, especially along the right bank, go all the way to the river and break up its valley into separate segments. The Marūchak valley ends three English miles north of the present-day fortress at a place where the bluffs reach the river on both sides.[28] The next oasis on the Murghāb, Panjdih, literally "five villages" (a name distorted by the Türkmens as Pendi), represents, according to Yate's description, a long, narrow valley extending over a distance of twenty-five miles with an average width of two miles.[29] The ruins of a large town, according to de Lassoë, are visible to the south of the village of Old Panjdih.[30] There are more ruins on the right bank, opposite Old Panjdih and further downstream. Panjdih is called by this name for the first time, so far as is known, by Yāqūt at the beginning of the thirteenth century.[31] By Tīmūr's time, the Türkmens had already changed this Persian name to Pendi.[32] At the present time, the number of cultivated fields in the valley of Panjdih is extremely small; Yates observes that the valley cannot feed its population,

[27] ⟨⟨For the Türkmens' irrigation of the Murghāb basin in the nineteenth century, see *Materialy po zemlevodopol'zovaniiu*, pp. 63-185. For the origin of the Jamshīds, see below, p. 48 and note 4. For the ethnogenesis of the Türkmens, see Barthold, "Ocherk istorii turkmenskogo naroda"; A. Ia. Iakubovskii, "Voprosy etnogeneza turkmen, VIII-X vv.," *SE* (1947), no. 3, pp. 48-54; *Ist. Turkmenskoi SSR*, I.⟩⟩

[28] The distances, according to Yate: Tāsh-kurgan—Karaul-khane, 10 miles; Karaul-khane—Marūchak, 12 miles; Khauz-i Khān—Rabāṭ-i Kāshān, 35 miles; Khauz-i Khān—Kala-i Maur, 15 miles; Old Penje—Sarï Yazï, 35 miles; Ak-tepe—Kurbān-i Niyāz, 13 miles; Bend-i Nādir—Pul-i Khishtī, approx. 10 miles; Marūchak—Takhta-bāzār, approx. 12 miles. ⟨⟨Cf. Barthold, *Oroshenie*, *Soch.* III, 144-45, 151. For reports by the Arab geographers about the routes in the Murghāb basin, see Barthold, "Merverrud," *Soch.* III, 253 ff.⟩⟩

[29] *Northern Afghanistan*, p. 184.

[30] "Caves and Ruins of Penjdeh," *Proceedings of the Royal Geographical Society*, n.s. VII (1885), 583-91.

[31] V. A. Zhukovskii, *Razvaliny starogo Merva*, p. 40. Panjdih already in Nāṣir-i Khusraw, eleventh century (*Safar-nāma* [Tehran lithogr.], p. 4; Schefer's ed., p. 2: Panjdīh-i Marw al-Rūd.) Ḥamd Allāh Mustawfī Qazwīnī ascribes the foundation of Panjdih to Malikshāh.

[32] Sharaf al-Dīn Yazdī, I, 353. Irrigation works under Tīmūr; for works carried out under Nādir Shāh, see in the article about the manuscript of Muḥammad Kāẓim (Barthold, "O nekotorykh vostochnykh rukopisiakh, *Soch.* VIII, 347-48).

and until the fixing of the border in 1885, grain was brought here from Maymana.[33] The main settlement of the area today is Takhta Bāzār, a Russian border point whither the Afghan amīr used to allow his subjects to go for the purpose of trade. The railway does not reach this place, but goes only to the brick bridge (Pul-i Khishtī in Persian, Ṭāsh Köprü in Turkish) on the Kūshk not far from the confluence of this stream with the Murghāb,[34] and then proceeds along the valley of the Kūshk to the Afghan border.

The cultivated zone of Panjdih is separated from that of Marw by a sand desert, a situation that we find to have existed even in the ninth and tenth centuries. The northernmost limit of the cultivated zone of Panjdih today is considered to be the site of Sarï Yazï, now a railway station. Clayey promontories and hills of hard sandstone continue for about seventy versts further, down to the post station of Charwakh. The southernmost point connected to Marw was in the Middle Ages considered to be the village of Qarīnayn, some twenty-five farsakhs from Marw; its proper name was Barkdiz, and it received the Arabic nickname of Qarīnayn ("Two Friends") because it used to be attributed now to Marw, now to Marw al-Rūd. The village lay on a high bluff above the river; there were no cultivated fields here, and the inhabitants, who were fire-worshipers, earned their living by hiring out their donkeys to travelers. V. A. Zhukovskii, probably correctly, identifies Qarīnayn with the present site of Imām Bābā, some thirty versts below Sarï Yazï, where there is on a high bluff an old caravanserai, and at its foot an old Muslim cemetery.[35] Besides Qarīnayn, the few other sites that in the tenth century were strung along the Murghāb further downstream consisted only of post stations and caravanserais;[36] even the second stage on the road from Marw to Marw al-Rūd, namely, the tract of six farsakhs between the village of Faz (situated at a distance of seven farsakhs from Marw) and that of Mahdīābād was said to pass through the desert.[37] At present, Zhukovskii writes, "there is here the most excellent postal road, which is crossed by old deep canals and a mass of irrigation ditches, and which passes along fields planted with jugara (sorghum) and melons and is studded

[33] *Northern Afghanistan*, p. 189.

[34] ⟨⟨For this bridge see also Barthold, *Oroshenie, Soch.* III, 151; *idem*, "O nekotorykh vostochnykh rukopisiakh," p. 929.⟩⟩

[35] *Razvaliny starogo Merva*, p. 181.

[36] ⟨⟨For the villages between Marw and Marw al-Rūd, see K. A. Adykov, "Doroga."⟩⟩

[37] Qudāma, text, p. 209; tr., p. 160.

with whole forests of tamarisks."[38] The old irrigation ditches pertain to a later period than that of the Arab geographers, perhaps to the period of Marw's prosperity under the Saljūqs in the twelfth century or to the time of its restoration under the Tīmūrids in the fifteenth.[39] The latter is more likely: the Harāt historian Isfizārī wrote in 1492 that under the reign of Sulṭān Ḥusayn (who ascended the throne in 1469), thanks to newly dug canals, the zone under cultivation both between Bālā Murghāb and Marw and between Marw and Sarakhs was considerably expanded. He further claims that in both areas formerly barren lands became fully irrigated and cultivated, so that continuous belts of cultivation were formed between the above-mentioned towns. This, however, is hardly plausible.[40]

Marw and its oasis is so far the only region of Central Asia about which we have a detailed historical-geographical study, namely, the excellent work of Zhukovskii, *The Ruins of Old Marw*.[41]

The city of Marw lay throughout the Middle Ages in the eastern part of the oasis; its existence was closely linked to that of a dam which is today called Sulṭān Band, and which was recently restored. The dam is first mentioned in the tenth century; it was several times destroyed, sometimes by the waters of the Murghāb, sometimes by conquerors who wanted to force the city to surrender by depriving it of water.[42] Halfway between the dam and the city was the village of Zarq,[43] where the large canal branched out into smaller ones; here stood the watermill where Yazdigird III, the last Sāsānid, was killed. Zhukovskii locates this village at the site of the ruins of Türkmen Kala. The city of Marw itself, as Zhukovskii has proved, gradually moved westward. The earliest part was at the site of Giaur

[38] *Razvaliny starogo Merva*, p. 175.

[39] ⟨⟨For irrigation works done under the Saljuqs in some areas of the Murghāb basin (especially in the Pendi oasis), see Barthold, *Oroshenie, Soch.* III, 149 ff.⟩⟩

[40] Zhukovskii, *Razvaliny starogo Merva*, p. 71. For a continuous cultivated belt between Marw and Sarakhs, see Barthold, *Oroshenie*, p. 66; *ibid.* for the Khīwan narrative about Kucha Kumi (*Soch.* III, 152).

[41] ⟨⟨See also Barthold, "K istorii Merva"; *idem*, "Po povodu"; for the works of Soviet archaeologists investigating Marw, see M. Masson, "Novye dannye"; *idem*, "Kratkaia khronika"; G. A. Pugachenkova, *Puti razvitiia arkhitektury Iuzhnogo Turkmenistana pory rabovladeniia i feodalizma* (Moscow, 1958), *Trudy IUTAKÈ*, VI, 191 (plan of eleventh- to twelfth-century Marw); *Trudy IUTAKÈ*, XI (1962); XII (1963); XIII (1966); Koshelenko, *Kul'tura Parfii*, pp. 76-97.⟩⟩

[42] Zhukovskii, *Razvaliny starogo Merva*, pp. 174-75.

[43] Or Rāziq, see Barthold, *Oroshenie, Soch.* III, 141 n. 24.

Kala.[44] As Zhukovskii has further shown, Giaur Kala is to be identified with the *shahristān,* the inner city of tenth-century Marw. Together with the suburbs, the city occupied an area of some forty square versts. In the tenth century, when Khurāsān and Māwarānnahr were united under the rule of one dynasty, Marw lost its military importance, and its citadel had already been ruined.[45] The *shahristān* had four gates; Zhukovskii places them in the western and eastern walls, in conformity with the location of the gates in later townships. However, in other large cities of Central Asia (Balkh, Harāt, Samarqand) where the *shahristān* had four gates, the latter were situated at the four cardinal points, and there is hardly any reason for assuming that a different situation existed in Marw; for it was precisely here that four roads intersected, namely, those to Sarakhs, Khwārazm, Bukhārā, and Marw al-Rūd.[46]

There also seem to have been ruins to the north and northeast; they were called "Old Marw" and were covered with sand; even in the fifteenth century, the author Ḥāfiẓ-i Abrū relates, there would sometimes appear, when strong winds scattered the sand, traces of walls and other structures.[47]

West of the site of Giaur Kala there was another, Sulṭān Kala; in the very center of the inner square are the ruins of a large dome-shaped building, the mausoleum of Sulṭān Sanjar.[48] The site of Sulṭān Kala corresponds to Marw of the Saljuq period, which had a wall built by Sulṭān Malikshāh. The tall building is the mausoleum of Sulṭān Sanjar, who died in 1157; the mausoleum was built by this monarch in his lifetime, and even at the end of the thirteenth century, according to the historian Rashīd al-Dīn, it was considered to be the tallest Islamic building in the world.[49]

Marw was destroyed by the Mongols in 1221; Zhukovskii pro-

[44] Zhukovskii, *Razvaliny starogo Merva,* pp. 111 ff.

[45] ⟨⟨For the Marw citadel, already destroyed, it would seem, in the second half of the eighth century (Bulgakov, "Iz arabskikh istochnikov o Merve," pp. 219-20), see Usmanova, "Èrk-kala"; Koshelenko, *Kul'tura Parfii,* p. 77.⟩⟩

[46] There was no gate on the southern side: see Barthold, "K istorii Merva," *Soch.* IV, 178; for a different opinion, see Pugachenkova, *Puti razvitiia,* p. 191.

[47] In Zhukovskii, *Razvaliny starogo Merva,* pp. 64, 66; in the excerpt from Ḥāfiẓ-i Abrū it is mentioned that the dam called "Old Marw" was built *bi-dih-i ʿAndaq*; cf. Zhukovskii's conclusion (*ibid.,* pp. 35, 67) about the identity of ʿAndaq with the Andaq of Samʿānī and Yāqūt, that is, a village two or three farsakhs from Marw, in the sands (cf. *ibid.,* p. 47, after Samʿānī).

[48] *Ibid.,* pp. 119 ff.

[49] M. C. D'Ohsson, *Histoire des Mongols, depuis Tchinguiz-Khan jusqu'à Timour bey ou Tamerlan* (The Hague and Amsterdam, 1834-1835), IV, 273.

poses the hypothesis[50] that the Mongol camp was placed on the present site of Shaim Kala (to the southeast of Giaur Kala).[51] Marw was rebuilt in 1409 by Shāhrukh, Tīmūr's son, in a new location; the remains of this town appear to be two sites connected with each other, Bayram ʿAlī and ʿAbdullāh Khānī, but considerably smaller than the former sites.[52]

Zhukovskii also gathered information about the villages of the Marw oasis. From the result of his research it is evident that in the Middle Ages, just as now, the oasis occupied a very modest area in all directions from the city. We have already discussed the southern limit of the oasis. On the northeast, there was a road from Marw to Bukhārā, on which the village of Kushmayhan, now Kishman, was reached after five farsakhs; the sands began here, and for the rest of this road all the way to the banks of the Āmū Daryā only postal stations are mentioned. To the left of this road, at a distance of one farsakh from Kushmayhan and five farsakhs from Marw, was the village of Hurmuzfarrah, whose name was later shortened to Musfara; here passed the road to Khwārazm, also across sands that began immediately after this village. The road to Sarakhs went southwestward; several points are mentioned along it, but even the second, namely, the fortress of Dandānqān, ten farsakhs from Marw, is described as standing in the middle of the desert; the fortress itself occupied only an area of five hundred paces, and beside it was the halting place for caravans.[53]

The isolated position of Marw and the proximity of the desert subjected its trade to constant danger; only in rare periods of strong government was it possible to shield the oasis from the raids of the nomads. This has been used to explain the decline of the city, which was originally situated on the main route from western to eastern Asia. As early as in the third century B.C., Antiochus Soter (280-261 B.C.) founded here the city of Antiochia, and surrounded the whole oasis with a wall 1,500 stadia, or forty miles, long;[54] Zhu-

[50] *Razvaliny starogo Merva*, p. 173.

[51] Cf. Barthold, "K istorii Merva," *Soch.* IV, 189 and n. 108.

[52] The side of ʿAbdullāh-khānī: 300 fathoms; the surface, 37½ desiatinas; the sides of Bayram ʿAlī, 375 and 250 fathoms, its surface, 39¹⁄₁₀ desiatinas.

[53] Zhukovskii, *Razvaliny starogo Merva*, pp. 21-22. ⟦Dandānqān's great claim to fame lies in the fact that it was the site in 1040 of the historic battle between Sultan Masʿūd b. Maḥmūd of Ghazna's army and the Oghuz invaders of Khurāsān led by the Saljuq family, the defeat of the former leading to the total loss of the Ghaznawid lands in the west; see Bosworth, *EI*² Suppl., art. "Dandānḳān."⟧

[54] ⟨⟨For the remains of this wall, see S. A. Viazigin, "Stena Antiokha Sotera."⟩⟩ ⟦R. N. Frye, "The Sasanian System of Walls for Defense," *Studies in Memory of Gaston Wiet*, ed. Miriam Rosen-Ayalon (Jerusalem, 1977), p. 14.⟧

kovskii argues on this basis that the oasis at that time covered approximately the same area as now.[55] The incursions of nomads must have caused a decline in Marw's commercial importance.[56] Isidore of Charax, who wrote around the beginning of our era, does not mention a road through Marw to the Āmū Daryā; the trade route described by him reached the Murghāb (probably near the later Marw al-Rūd), whence it turned southward toward present-day Harāt. On the place of Marw al-Rūd, in Zhukovskii's opinion, was the city of Alexandria in Margiana, founded by Alexander the Great. There are no records about Marw in the Sāsānid period except for the brief remark of a seventh-century Syriac author quoted by Zhukovskii.[57] According to this report, the oasis was at that time surrounded by a wall twelve farsakhs in circuit. The Arab governors of Khurāsān usually resided in Marw; as Zhukovskii correctly remarks, "it was the natural base from which the Arabs spread their rule into the depths of Turkestān."[58]

A certain decline of the city is noticeable following the time when the Ṭāhirids moved the capital of Khurāsān to Nīshāpūr, which then remained the chief city of that province down to the Mongol invasions, despite the fact that Sulṭān Sanjar lived in Marw in the twelfth century;[59] even then, however, the main trade route passed through Marw. According to the description by the ninth- and tenth-century Arab geographers beginning with Ibn Khurradādhbih, this road, departing from Baghdad, went through Hamadān and Ray to Nīshāpūr and from there through Sarakhs to Marw. There it bifurcated: one branch proceeded northeastward to Bukhārā and Samarqand, the other southeastward to Marw al-Rūd and Balkh. Only the Sāmānids succeeded in establishing security and order in the country. Up to the time of their rule in the ninth

[55] Zhukovskii, *Razvaliny starogo Merva*, pp. 4-5.

[56] Cf. Gutschmid, *Geschichte Irans*, p. 29, for the destruction of Antiochia in Margiana by the barbarians (after Pliny).

[57] *Razvaliny starogo Merva*, p. 8. Marw is mentioned only in the Sāsānid inscriptions of the third century, in Manichaean texts and on Sāsānid coins. In the Middle Persian work *The Cities of Ērān-shahr*, the only thing mentioned in regard to Marw is that it was founded by Alexander; the foundation of Mawr al-Rūd is ascribed in this text to Bahrām Gūr; see J. Markwart, *A Catalogue of the Provincial Capitals of Ērānshahr*, ed. G. Messina (Rome, 1931), pp. 11, 44, 45. A. Yu. Yakubovskii-Bosworth, *EI*[2], art. "Marw al-Shāhidjān."

[58] *Razvaliny starogo Merva*, p. 10.

[59] For the rebuilding of the walls of Sulṭān-kale in the period between the end of eleventh century and the Mongol invasion of 1221, see Barthold, "K istorii Merva," *Soch.* IV, 187.

century, according to the geographer Yaʿqūbī, each station on the road from Sarakhs to Marw through the desert had a fortification, in which the inhabitants could defend themselves against the Turks, who often attacked one or another of these stations.[60]

In 1221, Marw was destroyed by the Mongols, and never recovered from this calamity. In 1250 the Mongol governor Arghun erected some structures in the villages of Razīqābād to the south of the city.[61] The village of Mahan, three farsakhs from Marw, became the chief point of the oasis; in the fourteenth century, under Tīmūr, a separate Türkmen governor lived there.[62] Linked with the decline of Marw was the rise of Harāt, also destroyed by the Mongols but already rebuilt, as we shall see below, under Chingiz Khan's successor Ögedey. Marw was restored only in 1409, but this new Marw was much smaller than the pre-Mongol city.[63] Harāt remained under the Tīmūrids the main city of Khurāsān and the capital of the most powerful members of the dynasty. After the foundation of the new Persian state by the Ṣafawids, Marw and its oasis were often subjected to attacks both by the Bukhāran and Khīwan Uzbeks and by the Türkmen vassals of the Khīwans, who gradually occupied the whole region along the Murghāb.[64] As a result of this situation, trade between Persia and Māwarānnahr took a detour via Harāt, which thus became the most important trading link in Central Asia. The rulers of Harāt, beginning with the medieval Kurt dynasty and ending with the nineteenth-century Afghan rulers, endeavored to bring under their control the entire area up to the Murghāb, including the cultivated zone along this river—sometimes not without success. In the nineteenth century, circumstances did not always favor the Afghans; in the 1830s, dur-

[60] Zhukovskii, *Razvaliny starogo Merva*, p. 14. For these stations on the trade route from Sarakhs to Marw, see Adykov, "Glavnye stantsii."

[61] Barthold, *Turkestan*, part I, *Teksty*, p. 117 ⟨⟨Juwaynī's test⟩⟩.

[62] Zhukovskii, *Razvaliny starogo Merva*, pp. 43, 53.

[63] ⟨⟨For Tīmūrid Marw, see O. V. Obel'chenko, "Gorodishcha Starogo Merva Abdulla-khan-kala i Baĭram-Ali-khan-kala v svete rabot IUTAKE 1950g.," *Trudy IUTAKE*, XII (Ashkhabad, 1963), 83-168.⟩⟩

[64] Campaign of the Bukhārans in 1785; passing of Marw to the Khīwans in 1822; foundation of New Marw in 1824 near Mahan; siege of Bayram-ʿAlī by the Khīwans in 1847; restoration of the dam of Sulṭān-Band; complete absence of inhabitants in the valley of the Kūshk at the time of Abbott's journey, 1839-1840; falling into desolation of the area between Panjdih and Yolotan. The number of the Türkmens in the Marw oasis, according to Abbott, was 60,000; they were paying a tax to the Khan of Khīwa, up to 30,000 *tillas*. See J. Abbott, *Narrative of a Journey from Herat to Khiva, Moscow and St. Petersburg, during the late Russian Invasion of Khiva* (London, 1884), I, 18-19, 29, 31, 53 ff.; Barthold, *Oroshenie*, *Soch.* III, 54-156.

ing the siege of Harāt by the Persians, the Khīwans seized the valley of the Murghāb up to Panjdih and the valley of the Kūshk up to Kala-i Maur. After the 1850s, the quarrel over the ownership of the Murghāb valley continued only among the various Türkmen tribes; the tribe of the Saryks, pushed out of Marw by the Tekes, occupied Panjdih and Marūchak. In 1860, the Persian government organized an expedition against Marw, without success. More successful was the movement of the Russians from the north and of the Afghans from the south; in 1884 there occurred the simultaneous occupation of Marw by the Russians and of Bālā Murghāb, Marūchak, and Panjdih by the Afghans.[65] This caused a border dispute that almost led to war between Russia and Britain; the clash ended with the Afghans giving up Panjdih upon the insistence of the Russian government.[66]

[65] Yate, *Northern Afghanistan*, p. 182: The whole Marūchak valley on the right bank and two-thirds of the oasis on the left bank belong to the Afghans.

[66] A. A. Semenov's article "Ocherki iz istorii prisoedineniia vol'noi Turkmenii (1881-1885 gg.). Po arkhivnym dannym," *Turkestanskie Vedomosti* (1909), pp. 83-168; review by A. Samoilovich, "Novoe o turkmenakh." Marw taken for the first time on 3 March 1884; O'Donovan in Marw in 1881; reconciliation of Persia and Bukhārā; Alikhanov and Sokolov (Marw and the caravans in February 1882); the Afghans, their occupation of Marw at the beginning of October 1881; Khīwan governors Yūsuf Bay (died October 1882) and ʿAbd al-Raḥmān Bay, the latter recalled in 1883; English agents, the mysterious Siyāpūsh and his *murīds*, the deportation of him and of Qājār-Khān to European Russia, death in 1885. ⟨⟨For these events, see also Barthold, *Ist. kul'turnoy zhizni Turkestana, Soch.* II/1, 415; *Rossiia i Turkmeniia v XIX veke*, pp. 248 ff.; *Ist. Turkmenskoi SSR*, I/2, 127 ff.; Masson-Romodin, *Istoriia Afganistana*,II, 283-88.⟩⟩ ⟦On this so-called "Panjdih Incident" of 1885, see W. K. Fraser-Tytler, *Afghanistan, a Study of Political Developments in Central and Southern Asia* (London, 1967), pp. 161-67.⟧

CHAPTER III

Harāt and the Course of the Harī Rūd

THE Arab geographers do not give a detailed description of the roads connecting the valley of the Murghāb with that of the next substantial river, the Harī Rūd, where Harāt is located. The distance from Harāt northeastward to Marw al-Rūd was reckoned to be six days' journey, that from Harāt northwestward to Sarakhs, five days' journey. The country between Harāt and Marw al-Rūd was called Ganj Rustāq, and that between Harāt and Sarakhs, Bādghīs; this latter term later acquired a wider meaning and came to designate the whole northwestern part of present-day Afghanistan (even in the fifteenth century, Ḥāfiẓ-i Abrū applies the name Bādghīs to the whole area between the Harī Rūd and the Murghāb).[1] In both Ganj Rustāq and Bādghīs several towns are mentioned that did not have great importance. The rivulets Kūshk and Kāshān flow into the Murghāb from the southwest; they are not remarkable for any great volume of water, and in their lower course they are sometimes completely dry in summer. Even at the time of the Arab geographers, there was in these rivulets too little water for irrigation; in both Ganj Rustāq and Bādghīs fields were irrigated with either rain water or well water. Irrigation with rain water (the so-called dry farming) is frequently practiced in mountain areas, where rains fall more often than in the plains.

Northwestern Afghanistan was the object of detailed explorations by members of the British Boundary Commission in 1885-1886. The main road from Harāt to Marw in the Middle Ages probably ran along the valley of the Kūshk and not of the Kāshān; this is indicated by numerous ruins along the banks of the Kūshk, as well as by an ancient bridge on the site of Chihil Dukhtarān, often mentioned in the history of Tīmūr and the Tīmūrids.[2] Some twelve English miles north of this site is the Russian border post of

[1] ⟨⟨See also Barthold, *EI*[1], art. "Bādghīs."⟩⟩ ⟦Barthold and F. R. Allchin, *EI*[2], art. "Bādghīs."⟧

[2] Yate, *Northern Afghanistan*, p. 222; cf. V. I. Masal'skii, *Turkestanskii krai*, p. 641. Chil-Dukhtar is now a border post on the right bank of the river near a ruin of the same name; it is the southernmost point of the [Russian] empire (35°38′ 17″ N). See *ibid.* for the settlements of Alekseevskoe and Poltavskoe.

Kūshka. On the Kūshk, near the present-day settlement of Qalʿa-i Mor, was the town of Baghshūr, through which passed, in addition to the road from Harāt to Marw al-Rūd, the road from the Murghāb at the castle of Akhnafa (now Karaul Khāne) westward to Bādghīs. The ruins of Baghshūr occupy a large area; in the center, upon an artificial mound of considerable height, the ruins of an old fortress built of brick are visible.[3] Another road to Harāt is mentioned—that from the headwaters of the Murghāb, from the towns of Gharjistān, and passing through the settlement of Karūkh, which still exists (northeast of Harāt). The mountains that form the watershed between the Harī Rūd and the Murghāb systems were known in antiquity by the name of Paropamisus. This name is often used by present-day geographers as well. There is no native term for this mountain system as a whole, but each individual chain has a specific name; thus the westernmost branch, which delimits the valley of Harāt from the north, is called Kaytu or Kūh-i Bābā.[a] The main chain reaches the height of about 10,000 feet, and gradually rises toward the east; the passes are quite steep, but the British still managed to bring in their heavy baggage without any major difficulty. From the northwest, the road to Harāt is entirely open. The northern slopes of the mountains are at present occupied by nomadic and seminomadic peoples: the Jamshīds, a people of Iranian origin, as we have seen; and the Hazāras, Iranized Mongols, who came here in the thirteenth century.[4] The main settlement of the Jamshīds is Kūshk; that of the Hazāras, Qalʿa-i Naw on the Kāshān; in the nineteenth century, the latter was still the residence of an independent Hazāra ruler.[5] Fields under cultivation, both

[3] ⟨⟨For Baghshūr and the fortress, see also Barthold, *Oroshenie*, in *Soch.* III, 137, 150; Le Strange, *The Lands*, pp. 413, 415; *Ḥudūd al-ʿālam*, tr. Minorsky, p. 327.⟩⟩

[a] Although the westernmost section of the Paropamisus Mountains is indeed marked on modern maps as the "Band-i Bābā" and as similar terms, that of Kūh-i Bābā is usually now reserved for the eastern extension of the Paropamisus running toward Kabul, the massif of east-central Afghanistan; see Humlum, *La géographie de l'Afghanistan*, pp. 28 ff., and Bosworth, *EI*², art. "Kūh-i Bābā."

[4] For the border between the Hazāra and the Jamshīds, see Yate, *Northern Afghanistan*, p. 12: "the Tagou-i-Jawal at the head of the Kushk river." The Jamshīds are also in Bālā-Murghāb, *ibid.*, p. 122; the Türkmens in Karaul-khāne; in the past, the Jamshīds lived also to the north of there (*ibid.*, p. 188); for their departure from Bālā-Murghāb, see *ibid.*, p. 217. ⟨⟨For the Jamshīds, see *Narody Perednei Azii*, pp. 124-33; for the Hazāra, see below.⟩⟩

[5] Qalʿa-i Naw, its location on the map and in reality. The fortress of Neretü and its location. ⟨⟨For this fortress see Barthold, *Ulugbek*, *Soch.* II/2, 151 ff.; ⟦*Ulugh-Beg*, tr. V. and T. Minorsky, in *Four Studies on the History of Central Asia*, II (Leiden, 1958), 149 ff.;⟧ for the reading Nayratu in the Bombay lithograph of Khwāndamīr's *Ḥabīb*

irrigated and dry, today occupy a much smaller area than in the past; numerous ruins show that the area used to be much more settled and cultivated. Bādghīs, with its excellent pastures, always used to attract nomads, and this is why a settled civilization could not develop here.[6] War broke out in 1270 between the Mongols of Central Asia and those of Persia because of Bādghīs; Ferrier singles out the pastures around Qalʿa-i Naw as the best in all Asia.[7]

Alexander the Great was considered by the Muslims to be the founder of Harāt, as of Marw. In the case of Harāt, the legend is supported by the accounts of Greek historians about the foundation of the city of Alexandria in the region of Aria, Ἀλεξάνδρεια ἡ ἐν Ἀρείοις; this city is mentioned both by Ptolemy (under the name Aria metropolis) and by Isidore of Charax, as separate from the local capital, Artakoana.[8] The location of the latter has therefore been a subject of argument among scholars; in Tomaschek's opinion, Artakoana was situated on the site of the citadel of Harāt, which later, from the time of the Kurt dynasty (thirteenth-fourteenth centuries), was called Ikhtiyār al-Dīn. Owing to the extraor-

---

al-siyar, see Boldyrev, *Zainaddin Vasifi*, p. 315.⟩⟩ ⟦Bosworth, *EI*² Suppl., arts. "Hazāradjāt" and "Hazāras."⟧

6 See also Khanikoff (C. Ritter, *Iran* [St. Petersburg, 1874], p. 468, after Ḥājjī Khalīfa) for pistachio woods in Bādghīs, where the fortress of Nertuka is located. Cf. letter from A. D. Kalmykov (2 November 1905) about extensive pistachio copses (wild pistachios) protected by our Forest Authority, in the southern part of the Pendin prefecture.

7 *Voyages*, I, 364.

8 Thus also Strabo, ed. H. L. Jones, V, 278 (= book XI, ch. 10): three cities, Ἀρτακάηνα καὶ Ἀλεξάνδρεια καὶ Ἀχαΐα, ἐπώνυμοι τῶν κτισάντων.⟨⟨The Middle Persian work *The Towns of Ērānshahr* also attributes the founding of Harāt to Alexander the Great; see Markwart, *A Catalogue*, pp. 11, 46-47 (the same place gives a list of the cited ancient sources). This tradition is also reflected in the Arabic authors (Ṭabarī, I, 702; Qudāma, text, p. 265, tr., p. 207; Ḥamza Iṣfahānī, *Ta'rīkh sinī mulūk al-arḍ*, ed. J.M.E. Gottwaldt [St. Petersburg and Leipzig, 1844-1848], text, p. 40, tr., p. 29; Thaʿālibī, *Ghurar al-siyar*, ed. and tr. H. Zotenberg [Paris, 1900], p. 415), but it probably goes back to a Middle Persian version of the Alexander romance that has not come down to us. Harāt as the name of a region is mentioned already in Achaemenid inscriptions as well as in the tenth Yasht of the Avesta (in the combination *maurum hārōyum*, literally "to Harāt Marw," which may point to the inclusion of Margiana in the framework of some kind of pre-Achaemenid political formation with its center in the area of Harāt; cf. I. Gershevitch, *The Avestan Hymn to Mithra* [Cambridge, 1959], pp. 81, 176). Harāt is mentioned, in the form *ḥryw* (Harēv or Harē, cf. Harī in early New Persian texts, for example in the *Ḥudūd al-ʿālam*, fols. 6b, 10a, etc.), in the inscription of Shāpūr I at Naqsh-i Rustam (middle of the third century A.D.); in the fifth and sixth centuries, Harāt was an important military base of the Sāsānids in their struggle with the Hephthalites.⟩⟩

dinary fertility of the Harī Rūd valley, Harāt was already in Sāmānid times one of the chief cities of Khurāsān, although it remained aside from the main trade routes; we saw that the main route from Persia to Turkestān passed from Nīshāpūr via Sarakhs and Marw, where a road branched off to Balkh, whither Indian goods were brought. Harāt, however, carried on trade with Sīstān and the southern Persian regions all the way to Fārs. The length and width of the city equaled one farsakh;[9] like other large cities, it consisted of a *shahristān* (the city proper), a *rabaḍ* (the suburb), and a *quhandiz* (the citadel). The city had four gates at the four points of the compass. Of these, the eastern one, the gate of Kūshk, still has the same name. From the northern gate the road led to Balkh; from the western one, to Nīshāpūr; and from the southern one, to Sīstān. Only the northern gate was made of iron, whereas the rest were wooden. The palace of the ruler was situated outside the city to the west of it, at a distance of approximately one-third of a farsakh[10] at a place called Khurāsānābād. Almost the whole city was also surrounded by an outer wall at a distance of thirty paces from the inner one.[11] All these walls were destroyed as a result of the inhabitants' rebellions; the same is also said about other large cities, such as Samarqand. Iṣṭakhrī and Ibn Ḥawqal specify in the case of Harāt, as in that of other large cities, the location of the ruler's palace (see above), of the Friday mosque (in the center of the city), of the jail (to the west of the Friday mosque), and of the bazaars (near each gate and around the Friday mosque).[12] No other Khurāsānian city had as many people who spent all their time at the mosque as had Harāt.[13] The buildings, as everywhere, were made of clay; stones for paving were quarried in the mountains half a farsakh north of the city. The mountains were already at that time stripped of forests, and brushwood from the steppe extending south of the Harī Rūd was used for firewood. On the top of the mountain was a temple of the fire worshipers, and between the

[9] In Iṣṭakhrī, p. 264, *half a farsakh*; the same in Ibn Ḥawqal, p. 316.

[10] ⟨⟨"One-third"—addition by Barthold in the margin.⟩⟩ ⟦Cf. Le Strange, *The Lands*, p. 408.⟧

[11] Three rows of walls.

[12] Iṣṭakhrī, pp. 264-65; Ibn Ḥawqal, pp. 316-17.

[13] Iṣṭakhrī, p. 265, about the fact that in other towns of these regions (*bi-hādhih al-amākin*) ⟨⟨this refers to Khurāsān, Māwarānnahr, Sīstān, and Jibāl⟩⟩ the inhabitants go to the mosque only at the time of the Friday prayer, whereas in Harāt—*ʿalā rasm al-Shām wa 'l-thughūr* "in the manner of the people of Syria and the frontier regions." Mention of *ḥalaq al-fuqahā'* "circles of legal scholars." Besides Harāt ⟨⟨there is reference also⟩⟩ to people in the mosques of Balkh and Zaranj.

mountain and the city was a Christian church. The city was famous for its manufacture of cloth; in the Mongol period, a kind of tissue woven with gold thread with patterns and figures was especially valued. From Harāt were exported, in large quantities, raisins, pistachios, honey, and other sweets. Even today there are many fruit trees on the southern slopes of the mountains that delimit the valley of the Harī Rūd from the north.

The history of Harāt in pre-Mongol times offers little that is noteworthy; the city shared, as a rule, the fate of the rest of Khurāsān and was never the residence of independent and powerful rulers. As a result of its geographical situation, Harāt was conquered before any other Khurāsānian city by the rulers of the mountainous region of Ghūr, who became powerful in the twelfth century; the Harī Rūd as well as the rivers that flow southwestward have their sources in this mountainous region. To the east of Harāt, a few more settlements are mentioned, among them Marābād (Marava on the modern maps) and Awfa (Obeh on present-day maps). Two days' journey from Awfa was also the settlement of Chisht,[14] after which one entered the region of Ghūr; Ghūr bordered on the possessions of the Abū Dāwūdids, with Gūzgān, Gharjistān, and the Harāt region to Farāwa or Farāh. The geographers of the tenth century point out Ghūr as the only region surrounded on all sides by Islamic territories and yet inhabited by infidels. The simple fact of these mountaineers' long resistance to Muslim conquerors indicates the inaccessibility of the region. According to Ferrier, this whole area can be viewed as one huge fortress raised in the central and highest part of the extensive Asian highland.[15] From whichever side one approaches, one must cross high and steep mountains; these cut through the region in several directions, especially from the east. According to Iṣṭakhrī, at the time of the Sāmānids, the only inhabitants of Ghūr who professed Islam were those who lived in immediate vicinity of Islamic territories, and even their conversion was only superficial.[16] The Persian author of the *Ḥudūd al-*

[14] ⟨⟨For the monuments of Chisht (another name: Khwāja-i Chisht), see G. Wiet, "Les coupoles de Tshisht," in Maricq and Wiet, *Le minaret de Djam*, pp. 64-70; G. A. Pugachenkova, *Iskusstvo Afganistana* (Moscow, 1963), pp. 98-99; Masson-Romodin, I, 266 and the bibliography there.⟩⟩

[15] *Voyages*, II, 15.

[16] Iṣṭakhrī, 272. ⟨⟨For a summary of sources about Ghūr in the ninth and tenth centuries, see A. A. Naimi, "Un regard sur Ghor. Préambule: la géographie, l'histoire et les sites historiques," *Afghanistan*, IV (1949), 1-23; C. E. Bosworth, "The Early Islamic History of Ghūr," *CAJ*, VI (1961), 116-33; Masson-Romodin, I, 255-57.⟩⟩

ʿālam asserts that the ruler of Ghūr, whose title was Ghūr Shāh, submitted to the Farīghūnids of Gūzgān, after which a majority of the mountaineers adopted Islam.[17] The first to penetrate the interior of the region was the Ghaznawid sulṭān Masʿūd, in 1020, during the rule of his father Maḥmūd, when Masʿūd was governor of Harāt. The historian Bayhaqī gives a detailed description of this campaign, which resulted in the conquest of several settlements and fortifications of Ghūr and the submission of one of the rulers, whose subjects were considered the most warlike of all the Ghūr people.[18] The residence of this ruler had previously been the capital of Ghūr, and he who possessed this part of the country controlled the entire region. The fortifications served the inhabitants of Ghūr primarily for the protection of women, children, and possessions in time of military campaigns. The language of the people of Ghūr differed so much from that of the inhabitants of the plain that Masʿūd had to communicate with them through an interpreter.[19]

In the eleventh century, the people of Ghūr became Muslims and nominally submitted to the Ghaznawid government, but remained under the rule of the local dynasty of Sūrī. One of the representatives of this dynasty, who was still reigning in Ghūr in the settlement of Āhangarān in Maḥmūd's time, was taken prisoner and ended his life by suicide. (The settlement of Āhangarān itself may perhaps correspond to the place of the same name that still exists on the upper reaches of the Harī Rūd.) In the twelfth century, powerful rulers arose who were descended from this dynasty; they acquired first Ghazna, then Harāt with a part of Khurāsān, all of present-day Afghanistan, and a part of India. The capital of Ghūr was at that time the fortress of Fīrūzkūh, also situated on the upper reaches of the Harī Rūd, apparently not far from Āhangarān.[20] The location of this city, which was at the end of the twelfth and beginning of the thirteenth centuries one of the capitals of a mighty kingdom, and which was embellished by a series of magnificent buildings, cannot be identified with certainty, because the upper

[17] *Ḥudūd al-ʿālam*, fol. 21b ⟦tr. Minorsky, p. 106⟧.

[18] *Taʾrīkh-i Masʿūdī*, ed. W. H. Morley (Calcutta, 1861-1862), pp. 128-34 ⟦ed. Qāsim Ghanī and ʿAlī Akbar Fayyāḍ (Tehran, 1324/1945), pp. 114-20⟧.

[19] ⟨⟨For the dialects of Ghūr in the tenth and eleventh centuries, see also *Ḥudūd al-ʿālam*, tr. Minorsky, p. 344; Wiet, in Maricq and Wiet, *Le minaret de Djam*, p. 46.⟩⟩

[20] Cf. Jūzjānī, tr. Raverty, II, 1,047. ⟦For the history of the Ghūrid dynasty, see Wiet in Maricq and Wiet, *Le minaret de Djam*, "Commentaire historique," pp. 32-54; Bosworth, *EI*², art. Ghūrids"; *idem*, in *Cambridge History of Iran*. V. *The Saljuq and Mongol Periods*, ed. J. A. Boyle (Cambridge, 1968), pp. 157-66.⟧

reaches of the Harī-Rūd are still little explored. When Ferrier was there in 1845, the local prince pointed out for him the ancient town of Shaharak, not far from Dawlat Yār, as the former capital of Ghūr;[21] he also pointed out the town of Qarabāgh, surrounded by ruins, in which people found coins that pertained, according to the British officer who saw them, to Alexander the Great.[22] The dynasty remembered by the name of Ghūrid was extinguished just before the Mongol invasion. The western part of its domains was conquered by the Khwārazmshāh Muḥammad; the mountain fortifications of Ghūr and Gharjistān, however, put up a stiff resistance to the Mongol armies.

Harāt, like other Khurāsānian cities, was taken in 1221 by Chingiz Khan's son Toluy; as the inhabitants surrendered voluntarily before the assault, the city was spared, and Toluy limited his action to the extermination of the garrison, 12,000 strong. In the same year, however, the temporary successes of the Khwārazmshāh Jalāl al-Dīn spurred the inhabitants to rise against the Mongols and caused a new siege of Harāt; the city was taken in 1222 after a six-months' siege and suffered complete destruction. The Mongol armies did not maintain themselves in Khurāsān in Chingiz Khan's lifetime, and the Mongols had to reconquer the region under his successor Ögedey; Khurāsān was thus exposed to new destruction and accordingly recovered much more slowly than Māwarānnahr. Harāt was rebuilt sooner than other large cities of Khurāsān; according to some reports, the Khan Ögedey liked the cloths made by Harāt craftsmen so much that he allowed the craftsmen to return home and establish workshops there.[23] Under the khan Möngke

[21] *Voyages*, I, 444-45.

[22] Holdich, *The Indian Borderland, 1880-1900*, p. 146: "The ancient Afghan capital of Ghor was unearthed." Cf. M. L. Dames, *EI*[1], art. "Fīrūzkōh" (reference to Holdich, *The Gates of India* ⟨⟨R. N. Frye, *EI*[2], art. "Fīrūzkūh"; the ruins of Taywāra in the basin of the upper Farāh Rūd; mention of a convenient link with Harāt, Farāh, and the valley of the Harī Rūd.⟩⟩ ⟦Although the site of the recently discovered minaret of Jam in the upper Harī Rūd valley was confidently identified by Maricq (Maricq and Wiet, *Le minaret de Djam*, p. 55) as that of the Ghūrid capital Fīrūzkūh, an opinion followed by Frye in his *EI*[2] article cited above, doubts remain as to the correctness of this identification. Note the cogent arguments of L. S. Leshnik, "Ghor, Firuzkoh, the Minar-i Jam." *CAJ*, XII (1968), 36-49, suggesting a more probable site in central Ghūr (Jam being on its northern fringe) at Taywāra on the upper Rūd-i Ghōr (not in the valley of the Farāh Rūd); on the other hand, G. Vercellin, "The Identification of Firuzkuh: a Conclusive Proof," *EW*, n.s. XXVI (1976), 337-40, has maintained the correctness of Maricq's original view.⟧

[23] ⟨⟨For Harāt and the Harāt oasis after the Mongol conquest, as well as for the beginning of the city's reconstruction in 1236, see Ṣayfī al-Harawī, *Ta'rīkh-i Harāt*

(1251-1259), Shams al-Dīn Muḥammad Kurt, a man from Ghūr, already in possession of the fortress of Khaysār, was granted Harāt;[24] Khaysār is mentioned by the tenth-century geographers as being on the road from Harāt to Ghūr, two days' journey from the former.[25] Shams al-Dīn laid foundations of the Kurt dynasty, and this was how a dynasty of Ghūrī origin became established in Harāt once more.[26]

From that time onward begins the florescence of Harāt as the chief city of Khurāsān. Through it, as a result of the destruction of Marw and Balkh, now led the trade route from western Asia toward the northeast to Turkestan and China, and toward the southeast to India.[27] The city retained this commercial importance down to the most recent times, until the construction of the Transcaspian railway; thanks to this advantageous commercial position, Harāt always recovered quickly from invasions by nomads and other external enemies. Here, to use Ferrier's expression, converged all the roads leading to the main parts of Asia.[28]

The Kurt dynasty ruled Harāt throughout the time of the Mongol rule in Persia in the thirteenth and fourteenth centuries. Fakhr al-Dīn Kurt (1285-1307)[29] built the present-day citadel of Harāt, which is located in the northern part of the city and which was at that time, as noted above, called Ikhtiyār al-Dīn. Also built under the Kurts was the inaccessible fortress of Amān Kūh, or Eshkilche, some four farsakhs to the southwest of the city. The strongest ruler of this dynasty was Muʿizz al-Dīn Ḥusayn (1331-1370), in whose

---

(Calcutta, 1944), pp. 87-128; Petrushevskii, "Trud Seyfi"; Masson-Romodin, I, 298-99.⟫

[24] ⟪Shams al-Dīn had extended his rule to Harāt by 1244 or 1245; see Masson-Romodin, I, 297; Frye, *EI*², art. "Harāt."⟫

[25] Iṣṭakhrī, p. 285. ⟪For the location of Khaysār, see ⟦Muʿīn al-Dīn⟧ Isfizārī ⟦*Rawḍāt al-jannāt fī awṣāf madīnat Harāt*⟧, tr. A. C. Barbier de Meynard, *JA*, 5th series, XVII (1861), 455 ⟦ed. Sayyid Muḥammad Kāẓim Imām (Tehran, 1338-9/1959-60), I, 358-59⟧; Masson-Romodin, I, 295.⟫

[26] ⟪For various versions of Kurt genealogy, see Masson-Romodin, I, 295 n. 52; for the reading of the dynasty's name (Kurt or Kart), see *ibid.*, I, 294 n. 46, and Barthold, II/2, 55 n. 135.⟫ ⟦B. Spuler, *EI*², art. "Kart."⟧

[27] ⟪For the growth of Harāt's importance under the Kurts, see Masson-Romodin, I, 318-19, and the bibliography cited there; for the attempts of the Mongols to halt the economic rise of Harāt at the end of the thirteenth and the beginning of the fourteenth century, see Petrushevskii, "Trud Seyfi," pp. 141-43, 161.⟫

[28] *Voyages*, I, 315-16.

[29] ⟪Fakhr al-Dīn ruled from 1294-1295 succeeding on the throne his father Rukn al-Dīn (who was Shams al-Dīn the Younger, 1278 to 1294-5), son of Shams al-Dīn Muḥammad; see Masson-Romodin, I, 302.⟫

time the fall of the Persian Mongols took place. Muʿizz al-Dīn Ḥusayn brought under his control all the regions up to the Murghāb, whence he undertook raids still further east; thus in 1368 he plundered Shapūrgān.[30] Until 1353 he recognized nominally the suzerainty of the last representative of the Il-Khanid dynasty, Tugay Tīmūr; after the latter's death, he made himself a fully independent ruler and remained such until his death, although as early as 1354 he had been defeated by the amīr Kazagan, governor of the Chaghatay state.[31] Under his son Ghiyāth al-Dīn Pīr-ʿAlī, in 1381, there took place the conquest of Harāt by Tīmūr. The historian ʿAbd al-Razzāq Samarqandī, whose source was the Khurāsānian historian Ḥāfiẓ-i Abrū, gives us fairly detailed information about the personality of the last king of Harāt. He was noted for his gentle character and did not harm his subjects; during the defense of the city he showed personal valor, but he had been too devoted to pleasure to prepare himself in time for the siege.[32] He had not taken care to gather an army that could repel the attack, but expressed the conviction that "everybody would fight for women and children." In the meantime, Tīmūr promised at the very start of the siege the inviolability of life and possessions to everybody who would remain in his house and refrain from taking part in armed resistance. Under such conditions, nobody paid attention to Ghiyāth al-Dīn's orders; he was advised to execute several people as an example to others, but preferred to surrender the city to Tīmūr. The latter razed the inner and outer walls and imposed a large fine on the inhabitants; a still larger sum was taken after an unsuccessful uprising in 1383. Ghiyāth al-Dīn was at first allowed to stay on as governor of Harāt, but in 1382 he was taken to Samarqand and in the following year he was killed.[33]

[30] ⟨⟨For the limits of Muʿizz al-Dīn's domains, see Petrushevskii, "Trud Seyfi," pp. 143-44; Masson-Romodin, I, 316.⟩⟩

[31] ⟨⟨In V. A. Romodin's opinion (Masson-Romodin, I, 316), Muʿizz al-Dīn became not only a *de facto* but also a formally independent sovereign after the death of Abū Saʿīd (1335).⟩⟩

[32] ʿAbd al-Razzāq, *Maṭlaʿ al-saʿdayn,* ms. fol. 74b. ⟨⟨For a description of the siege of Harāt, see also Niẓām al-Dīn Shāmī, *Ẓafar-nāma,* ed. F. Tauer (Prague, 1937-1956), I, 82-84.⟩⟩ ⟦For ʿAbd al-Razzāq Samarqandī, see Storey, *Persian Literature* I, 293-98, 1276-77; Storey-Bregel', II, 820-28; Barthold-Moḥammad Shafi, *EI*², s.v. The *Maṭlaʿ al-saʿdayn* has now been edited by Shafi (Lahore, 1360-8/1941-9). For Ḥāfiẓ-i Abrū, see Storey, I, 86-89, 1235-36; Storey-Bregel', I, 341-49; F. Tauer, *EI*², s.v.⟧

[33] For the destruction of the last representative of the Kurt dynasty by Tīmūr's

The city quickly recovered from this destruction, and remained the capital of Khurāsān under Tīmūr and the Tīmūrids. The governor of the region was for several years Tīmūr's son Mīrānshāh, followed from 1397 onward by his second son Shāhrukh, who stayed in Harāt even after Tīmūr's death, when he became the sovereign of the whole empire. In 1415 Shāhrukh rebuilt the fortifications of Harāt destroyed by Tīmūr. Among other powerful Tīmūrids who resided in Harāt, Abū Saʿīd lived there in 1458-1469[34] and Sulṭān Ḥusayn [Bāyqarā] from 1469 to 1506.[35] The period of the Tīmūrids was the most brilliant in the history of Harāt.[36] The names of Shāhrukh and Sulṭān Ḥusayn are to this day alive in the memory of the population; according to Ferrier, these names are known to everyone, even in the most miserable hovel, and they are never pronounced with other than respect.[37] To this period also belong some surviving buildings. In the city itself, only one stands out: the Friday mosque, built as early as 1201 by the Ghūrid sulṭān Ghiyāth al-Dīn, and later restored under the Kurts.[38] It is located in the northeastern part of the city. More beautiful are the buildings around Harāt. The best of these was to the northwest of the city and had the name of Muṣallā, that is, "place of prayer"; this term was applied to places in the outskirts of large towns where Muslims would go in order to celebrate the two important festivals, namely, that of breaking the fast after Ramaḍān, and that of the sacrifices, the *ʿīd al-qurbān*, on 10 Dhū 'l-Ḥijja. The Muṣallā of Harāt consisted of three structures: the madrasa, of which there remained in Yate's time only two arches and four minarets; the domelike structure with tombs of several Tīmūrids; and the large mosque. According to [Muʿīn al-Dīn] Isfizārī,[39] both the mosque and the madrasa were built in the reign

---

son Mīrānshāh, see Barthold, *Ulugbek, Soch.* II/2, 55 ⟦*Ulugh-Beg*, tr. Minorsky, p. 33⟧.

[34] ⟨⟨For a detailed exposition of the events, see Barthold, *Ulugbek, Soch.* II/2, 170-71.⟩⟩ ⟦*Ulugh-Beg*, tr. Minorsky, pp. 172-73.⟧

[35] For Harāt in the time of Sulṭān Ḥusayn [Bāyqarā], see *Bābur-nāma*, ed. A. S. Beveridge (London, 1905), p. 188.

[36] According to Schiltberger, *Puteshestviia* (see below, Ch. VII n. 25), p. 45, there were in Harāt 300,000 houses. ⟨⟨Cf. Ḥamd Allāh Mustawfī, *Nuzhat al-qulūb*, ed. Le Strange (London, 1915), p. 152, tr. *idem* (London, 1919), p. 151: 444,000 houses.⟩⟩

[37] Ferrier, *Voyages*, I, 338.

[38] Isfizārī, University ms., fols. 10a, 131b ⟦ed. Kāzim Imām, I, 30 ff., 254.⟧ ⟨⟨For traces of architectural decoration of the Friday mosque pertaining to the pre-Mongol period, see Masson-Romodin, I, 266.⟩⟩

[39] Isfizārī, University ms., fols. 10a, 170b ⟦ed. Kāzim Imām, I, 30 ff., 271-72⟧.

of Shāhrukh by the queen Gawhar-shād Begum, whose tomb was also in the Muṣallā; on it is indicated the date of her death (861/1457).[40] The mosque was considered to be the second Friday mosque of Harāt. Ferrier and Yate were enraptured by the proportions and elegance of the dome and arches and variety of ornamentation. Today these structures no longer exist, because in 1885 the Afghan amīr ʿAbd al-Raḥmān had them torn down on the insistence of British engineers, who were then expecting a siege of Harāt by the Russians.[41]

In the environs of Harāt, the artificial mound called Tall-i Bangiyān ("Mound of the Users of Opium") to the north of the city is also remarkable. Here, Yate had been told, the orgies of those addicted to this vice took place.[42] Ferrier heard a legend that he himself found hard to believe: Nādir Shāh was supposed to have erected this mound in order to shell the citadel of Harāt.[43] It is more likely that this is the citadel of pre-Mongol Harāt.[44]

East of there and some two English miles to the northeast of the city is the place Gazur-gāh (corruption of Kārzār-gāh, "place of the battle"; according to Isfizārī, a battle took place there in 206 A.H.).[45] This was one of the residences of former rulers of Harāt, together with the mausoleum of the eleventh-century shaykh ʿAbd Allāh

[40] In Wāṣifī (fol. 59a), mention is made of the madrasa of the pious late sovereign Mīrzā Shāhrukh, which is situated below the citadel of Harāt (cf. Boldyrev, *Ocherki*, p. 339). In Wāṣifī, fol. 61b, it is said that the great sovereign, ʿAlīshīr, had completed the work of restoring the Friday mosque of Harāt. There are two *ta'rīkhs* ⟨⟨composed by the Sayyid Ikhtiyār al-Dīn Ḥasan⟩⟩, one in Arabic and one in Persian; the former is "on the northern [?] side of the maqṣūra aywān," and the latter "on the façade framing the aywān." ⟨⟨Both these *ta'rīkhs* give the date 904 A.H., the date of the completion of the restoration works on the Harāt Friday mosque; the same date appears in Khwāndamīr, see Boldyrev, "Memuary Vosifi," pp. 238-39; *idem, Zaynaddin Vasifi*, pp. 74, 323-24.⟩⟩ Wāṣifī, *Badā'iʿ al-waqā'iʿ*, fol. 216a, mentions the "caravanserai of Mīrak Ṣarrāf which is [located] in the Iraq gate." On the way from here to the "king's gate" is the "place of amusement which is the abode of pleasure of Khurāsān and the home of revelry of the city of Harāt. Nowhere in the inhabited part of the world is a drinking-house like it mentioned by any traveler."

[41] Holdich, *The Indian Borderland*, pp. 142-43.

[42] *Northern Afghanistan*, p. 33.

[43] *Voyages*, I, 342.

[44] Isfizārī, University ms., fol. 21a ⟦ed. Kāẓim Imām, I, 77.⟧

[45] *Ibid.* ⟦ed. Kāẓim Imām, I, 382, placing this battle during the governorship of Hārūn b. Ḥusayn, which he says lasted for thirty-seven months after the brief governorship (six months during the year 200/815-6) of Muḥammad b. Saddād. *Ibid.*, II, 50-51, however, the battle—between the Khārijī rebel Ḥamza b. Ādharak and the ʿAbbāsid governor ʿAbd al-Raḥmān b. ʿAbd Allāh b. ʿAmmār—indeed took place in 206/821-2.⟧

Anṣārī, "the holy man of Harāt"; the mausoleum was erected in the fifteenth century by the Tīmūrids, and next to it stands a magnificent monument made from white marble. Here are also buried some other personalities, among them the renowned Afghan amīr Dūst Muḥammad, who died in 1863. For the construction of monuments and tombstones, white marble quarried near the settlement of Obeh and black marble from the deposit of Shāh Maqṣūd in the mountains north of Qandahār, were used.[b]

In Ferrier's opinion, all of these structures had once been part of the urban area, whereas the modern city corresponds to what in Harāt's brilliant epoch was the citadel. There is, however, no ground for making such an assumption. Contemporary historians, especially Isfizārī, give us fairly detailed information on what kind of city Harāt was in the Tīmūrid period. From Isfizārī's testimony, we see that the layout of the city was then the same as it is today.[46] The city was surrounded by a wall[47] with five gates, of which two were on the northern side. The names of the gates were the same as today, except for that of the southern gate, which had the same name as in the tenth century, that is, Fīrūzābād;[48] now it is called the Qandahār Gate. Isfizārī ordered his students to measure the length of the walls. It turned out that their circumference was 7,300 paces; from the northern gate to the southern one, the length was 1,900 paces, and an equal number from the eastern to the western one.[49] These data fully correspond to the dimensions of the modern city, whose circumference, according to John Login (who lived here a long time), equals one farsakh.[50]

After the Tīmūrids,[51] Harāt was incorporated into the Ṣafawid

[b] For the Gāzurgāh shrine complex, see Lisa Golombek, *The Timurid Shrine at Gazur Gah* (Toronto, 1969).

[46] Isfizārī, University ms., fol. 21a ⟦ed. Kāzim Imām, I, 19ff.⟧.

[47] Cf. also Faṣīḥ, fols. 428b-429a, under the year 844: "Construction of the moat, rampart, and battlements of the fortress of the city of Harāt began on the sixteenth of Safar [844]" (17 June 1440).

[48] Cf. Yāqūt, *Muʿjam*, III, 928: "and Fīrūzābādh is also a place outside Harāt; there is in it a Ṣūfī *khānaqāh*."

[49] Samarqand, according to Bābur, was 10,600 paces in length; Marw, according to Ḥamd Allāh Mustawfī, was 12,300 paces long.

[50] Ferrier, *Voyages*, I, 233. There is a map in von Niedermeyer, *Afghanistan*; the length of the eastern side was 1,476 meters, and of the southern side, 1,206 meters.

[51] ⟨⟨For Harāt under the Tīmūrids, see also Barthold, *Ulugbek* ⟦tr. Minorsky, *Ulugh-Beg*⟧; Barthold, *Mir-Ali-Shir* ⟦tr. Minorsky, *Mīr ʿAlī Shīr*⟧; Belenitskii, "Istoricheskaia topografiia Gerata"; M. Masson, "K istoricheskoi topografii Gerata"; Masson-Romodin, I, 332-48 and bibliography; L. Bouvat, "Essai sur la civilisation timouride," *JA*,

state, but was several times conquered by the Uzbeks; at the end of the sixteenth century, Shāh ʿAbbās restored Persian rule here and endeavored to revive the city's importance. In the eighteenth and nineteenth centuries, Harāt was a bone of contention between the Afghan rulers and Persian shāhs, and the number of its inhabitants, if one may believe the travelers' accounts, was subject to great fluctuations. According to Ferrier, there were in the city prior to the siege by the Persians 70,000 inhabitants; after the siege, only 6,000 to 7,000 remained.[52] The energetic ruler of Harāt, Yār Muḥammad Khān (1842-1853), whose personality made a strong impression on Ferrier and British travelers, endeavored to attract the inhabitants back, and by means of a general amnesty encouraged the return of those who during earlier wars had gone over to the Persian or British side; in 1845, when Ferrier visited Harāt, there were there already between 20,000 and 22,000 inhabitants. Grodekov, who visited Harāt in 1878, estimated the number of inhabitants to be up to 50,000.[53] The panic spread by the Russian movements in 1885 again caused a depopulation of the city; Yate estimated that hardly 10,000 inhabitants of either sex remained there.[54] In 1893 Yate visited Harāt for the second time; then, he says, there were up to 3,000 families.[55] The city is surrounded on all sides by a high earthen rampart, on top of which there is a wall;[56] it is traversed by two streets, one from east to west and one from north to south, and these streets are paved with square wooden

CCVIII (1926), 193-299; Wilber, *Annotated Bibliography*, nos. 378, 953, 978, 998. ⟦1). Brandenburg, *Herat, eine Timuridische Haupstadt* (Graz, 1977)⟧⟩⟩

[52] *Voyages*, I, 326.

[53] Kostenko, *Turkestanskii krai*, II, 174. The taking of Harāt by the Persians in 1852 and 1855, by the Afghans in 1863. ⟨⟨For these events see Bushev, *Gerat i angloiranskaya voyna*.⟩⟩

[54] *Northern Afghanistan*, p. 29. According to Yate, the city had become depopulated earlier—there were, according to the census made several years before, only 1,700 families; "now there are 2,000 families, hardly more than 10,000 inhabitants" (the date of this passage in Yate's diary: 30 August 1885). According to the *Imperial Gazetteer of India*, V, 78, there are in Harāt 10,000 to 14,000 inhabitants, in Qandahār about 31,000. In Marw there are up to 16,000 (Masal'skii, *Turkestanskii krai*, p. 638). ⟦The estimated population of Harāt in 1969 was 86,000, according to Dupree, *Afghanistan*, p. 161.⟧

[55] *Khurasan and Sistan* (Edinburgh and London, 1900), p. 18.

[56] The height of the rampart is fifty feet, that of the wall on top of it, twenty-five feet. Grodekov ("Poezdka") mentions a stone wall some four fathoms high, provided with towers. See also Ḥāfiẓ-i Tanïsh, *ʿAbdallāh-nāma*, fol. 489b: "The fortress of Ikhtiyār al-Dīn, which is [also] known as Bālā-Furghāy."

beams. At the intersection of the streets there was a dome—the *chārsū (chahār-sū)*; this center and the sections of the streets that are adjacent to it are paved with fired bricks. The ruler's palace (Chahār Bāgh), located near the Friday mosque, is nothing remarkable. Altogether, almost all the buildings of the city are built of clay; there are no stone buildings at all, and very few brick ones.[57]

Below Harāt in the valley of the Harī Rūd there are a few more settlements;[58] each of these, according to latest travelers, includes in addition to inhabited dwellings a considerable number of empty clay buildings, so that such a settlement at first sight appeared much more populous than it really was. This decline was caused here, as in all of Bādghīs, by the raids of the Türkmens. In the Middle Ages, there was on the Harī Rūd at a distance of one march from Harāt on the road to Nīshāpūr the town of Būshang, home of the Ṭāhirid dynasty; some other settlements were also attached to Būshang.[59] Here it was still possible to use the water of the Harī Rūd, which then as now had so little water further downstream

[57] Yate, *Northern Afghanistan*, p. 29. See G. Forster, *A Journey from Bengal to England through the Northern Part of India, Kashmir, Afghanistan and Persia and into Russia by the Caspian-sea* (London, 1798), II, 120, about Harāt in the second half of the eighteenth century: "Herat is a smaller city than Kandahar, but maintains a respectable trade"; for the nineteenth century see Holdich, *The Indian Borderland*, p. 171: "The city is a poor one, and its bazaar quite third-rate, as compare either Kandahar or Kabul," ⟨⟨For Harāt in the nineteenth century see also G. B. Malleson, *Herat, the Granary and Garden of Central Asia* (London, 1880); for a description of Harāt's monuments, see Afghān Khālidī, *Āthār-i Harāt* (Harāt, 1309-10/1930-1); see also Wilber, *Annotated bibliography*, nos. 343, 362, 1067; R. N. Frye, *EI*², art. "Harāt."⟩⟩ ⟦For the surviving array of mosques, madrasas, and other public buildings of Harāt, see Z. V. Togan, *Islâm Ansiklopedisi*, art. "Herat"; Terry Allen, *A Catalogue of the Toponyms and Monuments of Timurid Herat*, Studies in Islamic Architecture 1, Aga Khan Program for Islamic Architecture (Cambridge, Mass., 1981).⟧

[58] The valley of Harāt, after Ibn Rusta, *al-Aʿlāq al-nafīsa* (Leiden, 1892), p. 173: 400 villages, among these also 47 *dastkaras*, in each 10 to 20 souls, 324 mills; cf. Barthold, *Soch.* IV, 296 n. 13. A large number of villages in Haraiva, according to the *Vendidad*: see Geiger, *Ostīrānische Kultur im Alterthum*, p. 72. ⟨⟨The subject of argument is the interpretation of the word *viš.harāzana*, which appears in the first *fargard* of the *Vendidad* (#8) as attribute to *harōiva-* "Harāt." Bartholomae and a number of other scholars translate *viš.harāzana-* as "⟨⟨with⟩⟩ abandoned houses," whereas A. Christensen as well as Geiger prefer the translation "with villages scattered ⟨⟨around⟩⟩"; see Christensen, *Le premier chapitre du Vendidad et l'histoire primitive des tribus iraniennes* (Copenhagen, 1943), pp. 18-20.⟩⟩

[59] According to Yāqūt, *Muʿjam*, I, 758, Būshanj was some ten farsakhs from Harāt; Yāqūt saw it from a distance on his journey from Nīshāpūr to Harāt. ⟨⟨For a list of sources on Būshanj, see Barthold, *EI*¹, art. "Bū<u>sh</u>and<u>j</u>"; Barthold-Spuler, *EI*², art. "Bū<u>sh</u>and<u>j</u>."⟩⟩

that it could not even be used for irrigation. In 1885, members of the British Boundary Commission crossed the Harī Rūd below Harāt at a distance of not more than forty versts from the city. The river fanned out here into several branches, none of which was at that time of the year (November) more than two feet deep.[60] The valley gradually becomes narrower; near the bridge of Tīrpul, some twenty-five versts from Harāt, the width is not so much as one English mile. The bridge had an elegant and solid structure, and needed only small repairs. After Tīrpul, the valley broadens again without reaching the settlement of Kuhsān, which is situated at a distance of one English mile from the right bank of the river.[61] In 1885, Kuhsān was the last inhabited point along the western border of Afghanistan.[62] The fortress was in ruins; as early as 1845, Ferrier found only four hundred inhabited houses in Kuhsān, whereas the ruins of the ancient town occupied a much wider area.[63] The border between Afghanistan and Persia follows the Harī Rūd to the site of Zulfikār, which in 1885 came close to causing a breakdown of negotiations between Russia and Britain and the opening of hostilities. The significance of this place rests in the fact that here a passage opens in the chain of rocky bluffs on the right bank of the river; the rocks extend northward without interruption for about forty more versts up to the bridge of Pul-i Khātūn. Yate admits that the occupation of Zulfikār was indispensable to the Russians for the sake of rounding out their borders and in order that they might possess a border point that would meet their strategic needs and that would provide a direct link between the lines of attack along the Harī Rūd and the Kūshk river.[64] For the same reason, the Afghans and the British could not leave this point to the Russians, who in this case had to back down; as a result, access

[60] Holdich, "Afghan Boundary Commission: Geographical Notes," p. 277.

[61] Holdich, *The Indian Borderland*, p. 171: "In fact, the actual wealth of the Hari Rud valley is all centered between Obeh and Kuhsān. There is not much more than a hundred miles of it in length." According to Strabo, book XI, ch. 10, the length of Aria was 2,000 stadia (350 versts), the width of the valley, 300 stadia (less than 50 versts). The Arabs considered the distance from Obeh to Harāt to be five days' journey (Iṣṭakhrī), and three days' journey from Harāt to Kūrisār (Ibn Rusta). The size of the town was one-sixth that of Harāt.

[62] Yate, *Northern Afghanistan*, p. 51. Toman-Aga some twelve miles downstream below Kuhsān (*ibid.*).

[63] *Voyages*, I, 271.

[64] Yate, *Northern Afghanistan*, p. 76.

from the east to a part of the Harī Rūd valley south of Pul-i Khātūn was closed to them.

Pul-i Khātūn represents the same kind of structure as Tīrpul; the resemblance is so great that the British considered the two bridges to be the work of the same architect.[65] The Harī Rūd serves here as the border between Russia and Persia up to the town of Sarakhs; Old Sarakhs, to the right of the Harī Rūd, is on the Russian side, New Sarakhs on the Persian. As early as the tenth century, in Iṣṭakhrī's time, the waters of the Harī Rūd did not reach Sarakhs in the dry season;[66] today, according to Lessar, who was here in 1882, the river bed is usually dry.[67] Under such circumstances, even in the tenth century the inhabitants could water their fields only with rain water or well water.[68] There were, on the whole, few cultivated fields; pastures predominated in the environs of the town, and the main wealth of the inhabitants was in camels. Because of its location on the main road from Nīshāpūr to Marw, the town had great commercial importance, and it was one-half the size of Marw. Since the construction of the Transcaspian railway, however, the importance of Sarakhs is exclusively strategic. Russian Sarakhs includes only one hundred houses, the Persian only a fortress, built in 1850, with a small garrison.[69]

Below Sarakhs, the Harī Rūd (or, as it is called on its lower course,

[65] The Pul-i Khātūn, according to Masal'skii (*Turkestanskii Krai*, p. 635) was rebuilt in 1899 by our military engineering authority. On the Persian side of the river there are ruins of a fortress made of hewn stone. See also Logofet, *Na granitsakh Srednei Azii*, I, 226.

[66] Iṣṭakhrī, p. 272.

[67] Curzon, *Persia and the Persian Question*, I, 195.

[68] According to Ibn Rusta, p. 173, the canal that irrigated Sarakhs ran two farsakhs from the town. According to Geier, *Putevoditel' po Turkestanu*, p. 82, today the principal canal Salïr begins at the mountains Kïzïm-Kay; some ten versts above Sarakhs the trunk course feeds two secondary branches, the Khan-Yab and the Davlet-Magomet-bay. Two versts further down, the trunk course divides into three canals, after the number of three generations of the Türkmen clan of Salïr; one of these canals irrigates the town of Sarakhs. For the absence of water in Sarakhs in mid-May of the extremely dry year 1040, see Barthold, *Oroshenie*, in *Soch.* III, 135 n. 10.

[69] According to Yate (*Khurasan and Sistan*, p. 34), there were in Russian Sarakhs up to 2,000 Salors and a small German colony; five-sixths of the water served Russian Sarakhs, and one-sixth Persian Sarakhs. According to the 1897 census, there were 1,748 souls in Sarakhs: 1,492 men and 256 women (Geier); according to Masal'skii, up to 2,500 inhabitants. The German settlement of Krestovyi was some eleven versts from Sarakhs on the canal Khan-Yab (*Turkestanskii krai*, pp. 332, 635).

the Tejen) soon disappears in the sands; the river bed crosses the Central Asian railway near the station of Tejen [Tedzhen] some 118 versts from Marw.[70] It is difficult to say whether the river ever had more water; the area was seldom visited by travelers, so that the most fantastic ideas existed about the river. As late as 1845, Ferrier[71] was able to believe a local legend according to which the Harī Rūd had merged, eighty years before his visit—that is, in the eighteenth century—with the Murghāb.[72]

[70] Tedzhen, according to Geier, had 382 souls; according to Masal'skii, 550.

[71] *Voyages*, I, 270.

[72] Cf. also Bagrov's book *Materialy* and the review by Barthold in *ZVORAO*, XXI, 149, *Soch.* III, 293. Comparison with information in Ibn Rusta, p. 173: "and this river flows to a place called al-Ajma, [it is] between Sarakhs and Abīward; there is an abundance of tamarisk there as well as cultivated fields; the government levies the tithe from it." ⟨⟨For irrigation of the region of Sarakhs, see also Barthold, *Oroshenie*, in *Soch.* III, 134-35; Adykov, "Glavnye stantsii," p. 220; for the monuments see Mahdī Bāmdād, *Āthār-i ta'rīkhī-yi Kilāt wa Sarakhs* (Tehran, 1333/1954).⟩⟩

CHAPTER IV

Sīstān, the Southern Part of Afghanistan and Balūchistān

WE have seen that Harāt, even at a time when it lay off the northern trade route, was the center of commerce with Sīstān and the southern regions of Persia. A fire worshiper built a bridge across the Harī Rūd which, according to Maqdisī, had no equal in all of Khurāsān.[1] In Tīmūrid times, Isfizārī mentions the bridge by its present name, Pul-i Mālān; in English books, it appears as Pul-i-Malun, whereas Ferrier calls it Peul-Malane.[2] In the nineteenth century, the bridge was restored by Yār Muḥammad. Ferrier states that such a bridge would have been a wholly commonplace phenomenon in Europe, but in Afghanistan it caused universal admiration; it was built from fired bricks and was divided into twenty-six arches;[3] there was also a dike made of sand to protect the bridge from floods.

In the tenth century, orchards extended to the south of Harāt for one farsakh;[4] three days' march from that city was the district of Isfizār, which belonged to the province of Harāt.[5] It was under excellent cultivation, with four minor towns; the name of one of these, Adraskan, has maintained itself to this day in the name of Adraskand, a village two marches from Harāt; the same name is applied to the upper course of the Harūd, a stream that irrigates

[1] Maqdisī, p. 330.

[2] Ferrier, *Voyages*, II, 29. According to Holdich (*The Indian Borderland*, p. 174), the bridge was three English miles from Harāt.

[3] Cf. Wāṣifī, fol. 86a: "The bridge of Mālān, which is one farsakh from the city of Harāt: it is that crossing which comprises twenty-eight arches, and for ages the Architect of the Firmament has considered one of its arches as a model for the River of the Milky Way, and He builds one side with the New Moon, but fails to complete the other side. And these arches, time and again, become so flooded that the waters, finding no way to pass, destroy one side of an arch and [then] pass." In Khanikoff, *Mémoire*, p. 126: 23 arches.

[4] According to Iṣṭakhrī, p. 266, there were orchards along the road to Sīstān over a distance of one march.

[5] In Yāqūt, *Muʿjam*, I, 248, the vocalization is Asfizār/Asfuzār; the same in Iṣṭakhrī, p. 267.

the district and flows southwestward into Lake Hāmūn. The whole district, which covers an area of three marches, was under cultivation, and there were no barren stretches whatsoever. The town of Isfizār was one march south of Adraskand; its name also appears in the abbreviated variants Sabzawār or Sabzār.[6] In 1383, even more terrible destruction than that suffered by Harāt befell it, because the inhabitants rose against Tīmur and killed his governor. When the city was taken, Tīmūr ordered a tower of 2,000 living persons to be erected; they were bound, laid one upon another and covered with soil and pieces of bricks.[7] In contrast to Harāt, Isfizār did not recover under Tīmūr's successors because of continuous uprisings and the resulting military repressions. The above-mentioned historian Muʿīn al-Dīn Isfizārī, describing his native region, speaks of nothing but ruins of towns and of large fortresses. In the nineteenth century the region suffered, according to Ferrier, from wars between the rulers of Harāt and Qandahār; only ruins and dried-up canals bore testimony to past prosperity, which may have occurred during the rule of Shāh ʿAbbās, that is, the end of the sixteenth and beginning of the seventeenth century.[8] To Shāh ʿAbbās, who took Harāt from the Uzbeks and installed his own rule there, is attributed the construction of a series of caravanserais to the south of the city on the way to Qandahār. Among the ruins described by Ferrier is the large fortress of Saba, built on a mountain at a half hour's distance from Isfizār; local inhabitants attributed its construction to Alexander the Great.[9] The same ruins are described by Isfizārī, who calls this fortress Muẓaffar Kūh.[10] His description, which mentions a Friday mosque, suggests that the fortress was still inhabited in Islamic times. In Isfizārī's time its builder was said to be a certain Alp-Ghāzī.

Along this entire road, one must cross mountain chains that present no obstacles to travel. The road led to the province of Sīstān or Sijistān. In the Middle Ages Sīstān occupied a much larger area than the present province; it was later divided up, according to the

[6] The altitude of Harāt is 2,600 feet, of Sabzawār 3,550, of Farāh 2,500; from Harāt to Qandahār the distance is 360 miles, from Farāh to Girishk 150, from Girishk to Qandahār 70. ⟨⟨For the district of Isfizār (the Sabzawār of Harāt) see also Le Strange, *The Lands*, p. 412; *Ḥudūd al-ʿālam*, tr. Minorsky, pp. 199, 327.⟩⟩ ⟦Sabzawār-i Harāt is the modern Shindand; see Humlum, *La géographie de l'Afghanistan*, p. 145.⟧

[7] Sharaf al-Dīn Yazdī, I, 360.

[8] *Voyages*, II, 37.

[9] *Ibid.*, p. 363.

[10] Isfizārī, *Rawḍāt al-jannāt*, ms., fol. 19b ff.

agreement of 1872, between Persia and Afghanistan. The tenth-century geographers make Sīstān border directly on the province of Harāt, but there are some contradictions as to the delimitation of their respective boundaries; Iṣṭakhrī in one place attributes the settlement of Dara (two marches south of Isfizār) to Harāt province,[11] but in another he attributes to Sīstān not only Dara but also Kustān, a village one march to the north.[12] At any rate, the town of Farāh which lay one march south of Dara, and which has conserved its name to this day, was attributed to Sīstān; according to Ferrier, the inhabitants of Farāh now refuse to include their town in Sīstān. In Tīmūr's time, there was in Farāh a local ruler who voluntarily submitted to the conqueror in 1383. Farāh is situated on the left, southern bank of the Farāh Rūd; in the tenth century it straddled the river. Ferrier considers as most ancient the ruins south of the Farāh Rūd, half an hour from the modern town, in a gorge flanked on three sides by mountains. This town, according to him, had been built long before Alexander the Great's campaign, but he gives no proof to support his opinion.[13] The city of Fra is mentioned by Isidore of Charax (first century B.C.), but without any closer indication of its location. The modern town is constructed after the same pattern as Harāt, but is much smaller; it too is surrounded by a high wall.[14]

Present-day Sīstān is divided into three parts that, according to Curzon, alternately turn into a lake, a marsh, or dry, hard land, depending on the time of year and the quantity of water.[15] The rivers Harūd Rūd, Farāh Rūd, Khwash Rūd, and Hilmand form two lakes or marshes: Hāmūn-i Farāh (into which flow the former

[11] Iṣṭakhrī, p. 282.

[12] *Ibid.*, p. 249.

[13] *Voyages*, II, 278.

[14] Today the ancient city is completely abandoned, and only military encampments appear there; Yate, *Khurasan and Sistan*, pp. 15-16. The old fortress, Qal'a-yi Dukhtar, is some three miles to the south of the city. On the other bank of the river, opposite the fortress, are the ruins of the old city. For the almost complete desertion of Farāh by its inhabitants, see also *The Imperial Gazetteer of India*, V, 75 ("almost deserted, the governor and his escort being the principal inhabitants"), although one of the six provinces of Afghanistan is named after Farāh (*ibid.*, p. 79: Kābul, Qandahār, Harāt, Farāh, Badakhshān, Afghan Turkestan). M. L. Dames's *EI*[1] art. "Farāh": in the *Vendidad*, Fradātha (lit. "progress") corresponds to the Farāh Rūd. ⟨⟨Cf. Chr. Bartholomae, *Altiranisches Wörterbuch* (Strassburg, 1904), p. 982, s. vv. *fradaθa-, fradaθā-*⟩⟩; the Greek translation was Προφθασία, in Pliny ὁ Φράδος, in Isidore of Charax Φρά. According to Dames, the city is in decay, but nonetheless it conserves some importance as the chief center of a fertile province and an intersection of caravan routes to Sīstān and the Hilmand.

[15] *Persia*, I, 226.

two) and Hāmūn-i Sawarān (into which flow the latter two). The area between these lakes is called Nayzār, and is covered with thick overgrowths of reeds; at the time of high water, the lakes unite and flood Nayzār. In the case of a still higher crest, the whole plain of Hāmūn, which extends further south, is inundated; on rare occasions water covers not only the entire Hāmūn but also a third depression, that of Zarah. This last had not taken place, as the members of the British Boundary Commission heard in 1885, within the memory of the living inhabitants; in fact, one can much more frequently see the beds of all the rivers dry than all the basins flooded. Such a degree of dependence on the fluctuating quantity of rainfall caused frequent changes in the region: the lakes sometimes filled with water, sometimes grew shallower or even disappeared altogether. The rivers changed courses; sometimes, as also happens in other parts of Central Asia, the main course of the river would follow a man-made canal, which would then quickly assume the physiognomy of a natural course. The silt brought by the rivers made the region exceptionally fertile, but frequent floods forced the inhabitants to abandon their towns and villages and build new ones. In Curzon's opinion, nowhere else could one find in so restricted an area so many ruins of towns and villages. The tenth-century geographers spoke only of one lake, Zarah (the *Aria palus* of classical authors), which occupied an area thirty farsakhs long and some four to eight farsakhs (one march) wide.[16] All the four above-mentioned rivers flowed into this lake. The size of the lake was even then subject to periodical fluctuations.

The most fertile part of the province at present appears to lie between Hāmūn and the left bank of the Hilmand, where its principal towns, Sihkūheh [17] and Nuṣratābād (or Nāṣirābād) are located. In the Middle Ages, Zaranj, the chief city of Sīstān, lay on the right side of the Hilmand;[18] the name of Drangiana and of its people,

[16] Iṣṭakhrī, p. 243.

[17] Sihkūheh is the southernmost inhabited point, if one does not count the settlement of Warmal (seven miles further on, see Yate, *Khurasan and Sistan*, p. 91). Cf. also the itinerary in Ibn Khurradādhbih, text, pp. 49-50: from Fahraj through the desert for seventy farsakhs; from Fahraj to Zaranj, seventy-two farsakhs (road from Bam to Narmashīr). Coincidence with the route of Arab conquerors (following Balādhurī, p. 393).

[18] Description of Zaranj in Iṣṭakhrī, pp. 239-40: five gates, two on the western side; the most densely inhabited were the quarters by the southern gate; the citadel was in the northeastern corner; the canals entered the city by the western and southern gates; half a farsakh from the western gate of the *shahristān* to the western gate of the *rabaḍ*. ⟨⟨Cf. Le Strange, *The Lands*, pp. 335-37.⟩⟩

the Σαράγγαι was preserved in the name of this city.[19] The ruins of Zaranj are situated between the town of Nād ʿAlī and the settlement Zāhidān Jahānābād.[20] The name Sīstān, as is known, derives from the work Sakistān, land of the Saka, Isidore of Charax's Σακαστηνή. Isidore identifies Sakastene not with Drangiana but with Paratakene, Παρατακηνή (between Drangiana and Arachosia or White India). This shows that the Saka had earlier occupied the southern part of present Sīstān.[21] In order to distinguish the native population of Sīstān from the Balūchīs and other later elements, the term Sīstānī is used today, whereas in the Middle Ages the term *Sagazī* was also encountered. According to Rawlinson, the Sīstānīs are "Persians of the purest Aryan type," and together with the Jamshīds of Harāt can even be considered to be the only representatives of the early Aryan race in Persia;[22] they have preserved, better than others, the tongue and physical type of the Achaemenid period.[23]

[19] ⟨⟨Greek Σαράγγαι, Ζαράγγαι reflects the eastern Iranian name of the region (and people) of Zranka-, attested in Achaemenid inscriptions; Greek Δραγγιακνή, Δραγγήνη goes back to the Old Persian form.⟩⟩

[20] Tomaschek, *Zur historischen Topographie von Persien*, II, *SBWAW*, CVIII, no. 2 (1885), 207; Yate, *Khurasan and Sistan*, p. 113. The situation of Zaranj near the contemporary fortress of Nād-ʿAlī, built by ʿAlī Khān Sanjarānī. Description in Tate, *Seistan*, pt. 3, pp. 199 ff. A plan of Binā-yi Kaj is inserted. According to this plan, the outer city measured diagonally three and one-third English miles, the inner city a little over one mile. The distance between the respective western gates was one and a half miles. Image of a "London of the East": 86 miles from Qalʿa-yi Fatḥ to Lām-Juwayn), see A.H.S. Landor, *Across Coveted Lands, or a Journey from Flushing (Holland) to Calcutta, Overland* (London, 1902), II, 194. Zāhidān: ruins of the city from Tīmūr's and the Tīmūrids' time. ⟨⟨A different location for the ancient capital of Drangiana-Sīstān was recently proposed by Italian archaeologists; see U. Scerrato, "Excavations at Dahan-i Ghulaman (Seistan-Iran). First Preliminary Report," *EW*, n.s. XVI (1966), 9-30.⟩⟩

[21] Cf. Huart, *La Perse antique*, p. 48, for Cyrus: "Il soumit les Saces, déjà installés dans la Sacastène, le Sistan actuel"; p. 130 for the second century B.C., the Yüeh-chih and the fall of the Graeco-Bactrian kingdom: "C'est à la même époque que l'on voit les Saces (Saka) s'installer dans le Nord de la Drangiane et donner au pays le nom de Sakastana (Sîstan actuel)." ⟨⟨For the settlement of the Saka on the territory of Drangiana and the neighboring districts, see Herzfeld, "Sakastan, geschichtliche Untersuchungen zu den Ausgrabungen am Kūh i Khwādja," *AMI*, IV (1932), 1-116; Debevoise, *A Political History of Parthia*, pp. 60 ff.; Masson-Romodin, I, 134 ff.; P. Daffinà, *L'immigrazione dei Sakā nella Drangiana* (Rome, 1967). For pre-Islamic monuments in the territory of Sīstān, see Vanden Berghe, *Archéologie de l'Iran ancien*, pp. 15-17, 145; Koshelenko, *Kul'tura Parfii*, pp. 98-106; Ṣamadī, *Sīstān az naẓar-i bāstān-shināsī* (Tehran, 1334/1956); G. Gullini, *Architettura iranica degli Achemenidi ai Sasanidi. Il palazzo di Kuh-i Khagia, Seistan* (Turin, 1964).⟩⟩

[22] Curzon, *Persia*, I, 232.

[23] ⟨⟨The idioms of Sīstānī or Seistani appear to be dialectical forms of New Persian

The region is distinguished for its fertility and warm climate, despite strong winds that are mentioned as early as Iṣṭakhrī's time and were used in his time to turn windmills.[24] According to Holdich, a member of the British Boundary Commission, the northwest wind blows in Sīstān with such force that, in comparison, the northwest wind in England could be called a light breeze.[25] The wind raises sand, whose proximity caused constant danger to cultivated land; in Iṣṭakhrī's time the inhabitants had recourse to wooden barriers as defense against spreading sand.[26] Also noteworthy was a peculiarity of the houses in Sīstān mentioned by Iṣṭakhrī: in their construction people did not use wooden frames, as in other towns of Central Asia, but built them directly from clay in the form of archlike vaults; wood could not be used because it was gnawed by worms and quickly rotted.[27] According to Ferrier, houses in Sīstān are today built with reed and tamarisk branches covered by a thick layer of clay;[28] in other words, they do not differ from the usual type of construction in Central Asia.[29]

The Hilmand, the principal river of the region, was already at that time not distinguished for the volume of its water, although Ferrier calls it a real river, the only one in the whole stretch between

---

(see Griunberg, "Seistanskii dialekt"; J. W. Weryho, "Sistani-Persian Folklore," *IIJ*, VI (1962), 276-307. By the term *Sagzī*, mentioned in medieval sources (especially in Persian-Persian dictionaries) was meant, it would seem, only a Persian dialect (cf. R. Gauthiot, *Essai de grammaire sogdienne. I. Phonétique* (Paris, 1914-1923), pp. VII-VIII.)⟫

24 Iṣṭakhrī, p. 242.

25 "Afghan Boundary Commission," p. 162. ⟦These winds include the famous seasonal "wind of 120 days," *bād-i ṣad u bīst rūz*, beginning each July and described with feeling by other travelers in the region such as Yate and Tate.⟧

26 Iṣṭakhrī, p. 242.

27 *Ibid.*, p. 241.

28 *Voyages*, II, 317.

29 The tamarisk is being gradually exterminated (Yate, *Khurasan and Sistan*, p. 112). The primitive character of the buildings is still true today. For the situation of the population, see *ibid.*, pp. 83-84: "The cultivators and people of Sistan generally were in a wretched state of poverty. . . . There were no landowners in Sistan. All the land and water belonged to the Government, who took a third share of the produce." The peasants have no oxen, but rent them from the nomads of Nayzar. Absence of land ownership; capricious rotation of the tenants by the administrator, also rotation of the *katkhudā*, who previously used to be hereditary. Eye diseases; absence of fever. See the article of Miller, "Proshloe i nastoiashchee Seistana." ⟦See now for an exhaustive archaeological, geographical, and demographic survey of Sīstān, K. Fischer, D. Morgenstern, and V. Thewalt, *Nimruz*; also Humlum, *La géographie de l'Afghanistan*, pp. 251 ff., and Dupree, *Afghanistan*, pp. 26-31, who notes that the tamarisk is in fact abundant in the section of the Hilmand flood plain not used for agriculture.⟧

the Tigris and Indus; Ferrier is convinced that if the Hilmand belonged to Europeans, steamers would sail on it.[30] In Iṣṭakhrī's time, ships could sail between Bust (present Qalʿa-yi Bist) and Zaranj, which was accessible to the Sanarūd canal only at high water.[31] One march above Zaranj there was a dam connected by canals with the Hilmand. This may be the same dam that is mentioned in the Middle Ages under the name of Band-i Rustam and that is attributed to the legendary hero who came, as is well known, from Sīstān; this tradition would point to a pre-Islamic origin of the dam. It was destroyed in 1383 by Tīmūr and once more by Shāhrukh; at present, there is on the site of Kūhak a dam made from tamarisk branches, pales, and clay, built in order to divert water into a canal dug to Sihkūheh.

In the first centuries of Islam, Sīstān was a refuge of the Khārijīs, who launched their uprisings and incursions into the neighboring Khurāsānian towns from there.[32] Besides regular troops, volunteers called *muṭawwiʿa*, "warriors for the faith," participated in the fight against the Khārijīs; they were a class that in reality consisted of people who could not find a proper occupation or were incapable of earning their living by work. From this class arose the dynasty of the Ṣaffārids; Yaʿqūb, the founder of this line, distinguished himself through his abilities in one such detachment, became its leader, and defeated the Khārijīs or drew them to his side. He went on to eliminate the local ruling power and became the sole master of Sīstān. Yaʿqūb then gradually conquered the remaining regions of present-day Afghanistan, the southern parts of Persia, and Khurāsān. Between 873 and 900, Yaʿqūb and after him his brother ʿAmr were the most powerful rulers in the eastern part of the Islamic world, but, as is evident from Iṣṭakhrī's report about the buildings erected in Zaranj by the two of them, they did not neglect their homeland.[33] The Ṣaffārids may also be responsible for those

[30] *Voyages*, II, 339.

[31] Iṣṭakhrī, p. 243.

[32] ⟨⟨For the history of Sīstān from the ninth until the thirteenth century, the fundamental sources are now the *Taʾrīkh-i Sīstān* and the *Iḥyāʾ al-mulūk* (the latter was known to Barthold).⟩⟩ ⟦The *Taʾrīkh-i Sīstān* was edited by Malik al-Shuʿarāʾ Bahār (Tehran, 1314/1935). English tr. Milton Gold (Rome, 1976), and the *Iḥyāʾ al-mulūk* edited by Manūchihr Sutūda (Tehran, 1344/1966); cf. Storey, I, 364-65; Storey-Bregel', II, 1078-81. The early Islamic history of Sīstān, including the activities of the Khārijīs there, is examined by Bosworth in his *Sīstān under the Arabs, from the Islamic Conquest to the Rise of the Ṣaffārids (30-250/651-864)* (Rome, 1968).⟧

[33] Iṣṭakhrī, p. 241. ⟨⟨For the Ṣaffārids, see also Barthold, "Zur Geschichte der Ṣaffāriden," *Orientalistische Studien . . . zu Th. Nöldeke gewidmet* (Giessen, 1906), I,

bridges and other constructions that are mentioned by the tenth-century geographers. There was a pontoon bridge on the Hilmand not far from Bust, modern Qalʿa-yi Bist.[34] A bridge over the Hilmand is also mentioned on the northern road from Zaranj toward the towns of Juwayn (which has retained its name to this day) and Farāh;[35] finally, there was a brick bridge across the Khwash Rūd[36] on the way from Zaranj to Bust.[37] Among the ruins, those of Pīshāwārān immediately north of Nayzār are especially extensive. Noteworthy also is the fortress of Ṭāq, situated one march south of Zaranj and still mentioned by the nineteenth-century traveler Conolly. The tenth-century geographers mention Ṭāq as only a minor town, but by the eleventh century it was a large fortress that Maḥmūd of Ghazna took in 1003 only with great effort. The fortress was surrounded by seven rows of walls and a deep ditch passable only by means of a drawbridge.[38]

The might of the Ṣaffārid dynasty, which had originated in Sīstān, did not last long, but it left a deep impression on the memory of the local inhabitants; all the subsequent rulers up to modern times have claimed descent from Yaʿqūb, ʿAmr, or their brothers, and have used their names in order to draw the population to their side. The province remained under the rule of such successors throughout the Middle Ages almost to the present, except for brief interruptions; the dynasty of the Ṣaffārids, which survived in the persons of its real or fictitious descendants, thus lasted through both the Mongol conquest and the epoch of Tīmūr. The Mongols devastated Sīstān in 1222 and definitively conquered it in 1229, but they preserved the local dynasty; Tīmūr acted likewise in 1383. Like Isfizār, Sīstān, as a result of frequent rebellions of local rulers relying on the support of a population devoted to them, failed to recover under Tīmūr's successors. From the sixteenth century onward, the local rulers were vassals of the Safawids, then of Nādir

171-91, and *Soch.* VII 337-53.⟫ ⟦Bosworth, "The Ṭāhirids and Ṣaffārids," in *Cambridge History of Iran.* IV, 90-135.⟧

[34] Maqdisī, p. 304.

[35] Iṣṭakhrī, p. 248.

[36] Today, Takht-i Pul, aside from Yate, *Khurasan and Sistan*, pp. 118 ff., Barthold, "Zur Geschichte der Ṣaffāriden," p. 183 n. 4 (*Soch.* VII, 347 n. 68); see Tate, *Sistan*, pp. 205 ff., and illustration there.

[37] Iṣṭakhrī, p. 249. Three farsakhs from Zaranj to Karkūy, four farsakhs from there to Bashtar, a bridge on this road; from Bashtar, one day's march to Juwayn (Iṣṭakhrī, p. 248).

[38] ʿUtbī, *al-Taʾrīkh al-Yamīnī*, ms. INA C 342 (510), fol. 72. ⟦Nāẓim, *Sulṭān Maḥmūd*, pp. 68-69.⟧

Shāh, and in the second half of the eighteenth century of Afghanistan; in the nineteenth century, Sīstān was a bone of contention between the rulers of Harāt and Qandahār.[39] In 1846, when Ferrier visited it, the Khwash Rūd was considered to be the boundary between the two. After the unification of Afghanistan by Dūst Muḥammad, who died in 1863, wars were waged for Sīstān between Persia and Afghanistan; the delimitation of boundaries was carried out in 1872 by a British commission presided over by General Goldsmith, with the better area, all the way to the Hilmand, being allotted to the Persians.

The main road from Harāt to India leads from Farāh through the regions of Bakwā and Zamīndāwar; the latter was already important in the tenth century because it bordered on the possessions of the inhabitants of Ghūr and other independent peoples, among whom are mentioned the Khalaj Turks. The reading of this ethnonym is based on etymologies cited by Rashīd al-Dīn and certain Turkish authors;[40] in India, where this people produced one of the dynasties, this ethnonym is pronounced *Khilj*. The Khalaj later adopted the Afghan language and fused with the Afghans, among whom they are today the largest group.[41] In Zamīndāwar, guard posts were maintained against incursions of the inhabitants of Ghūr; it was from here that Maḥmūd of Ghazna undertook his campaigns against Ghūr.[42] The inhabitants of Zamīndāwar are well known to this day for their warlike spirit and fanaticism.

In the tenth century, the main trade route passed further to the south, through Bust, which was one of the depositories for wares

[39] Conquest of Qāyin; Mīr ʿĀlam Khān (died in 1891), from the Arab tribe of the Khuzayma (amīrs of Qāyin at the close of the seventeenth century). His elder son in Sīstān, the second son in Qāyin (Yate, *Khurasan and Sistan*, p. 66).

[40] V. V. Radlov, *K voprosu ob uigurakh*, pp. 26, 35, 51.

[41] In Marquart's opinion (*Ērānšahr*, pp. 251-53), one should read Khūlaj. Information from Minorsky about Khalajistān, to the west of Tehran and to the north of Sāwa; the majority of the Khalaj speak a Persian dialect, but some speak Turkish (Türkmen). ⟨⟨For the Khalaj, see also Barthold, *EI*[1], art. "Khaladj" (*Soch.* VII, 511).⟩⟩ ⟦Bosworth, and G. Doerfer, *EI*[2], art. "Khaladj"; F. Köprülü, *İA*, art, "Halaç"; T. W. Haigh, *EI*[1], art. "Khaldjī"; *Hudūd al-ʿālam*, tr. Minorsky, pp. 347-48; Minorsky. "The Language of the Khalaj," *BSOS*, X (1940-1942), 417-37; Z. V. Togan, "Die Bedeutung der türkischen Ortsnamen in Ostiran für die vorislamische Geschichte der Türken," *Proceedings of the Eighth International Congress of Onomastic Studies* (The Hague and Paris, 1966), pp. 542-43; G. Doerfer and S. Tezcan, *Wörterbuch des Chaladsch* (Budapest, 1980), and bibliography on pp. 71-75.⟧

[42] Bayhaqī, ed. Morley, p. 123. For Zamīndāwar, see J. Marquart and J. J. de Groot, "Das Reich Zābul und der Gott Zūn vom 6.-9. Jahrhundert," *Festschrift E. Sachau* (Berlin, 1915), p. 285; *Ḥudūd al-ʿālam*, tr. Minorsky, p. 345.

on the way to India. We have fewer data about the middle course of the Hilmand between Bust and Zaranj. In 1885, several members of the British Boundary Commission traveled along the river from Khwāja ʿAlī to the Hāmūn; according to them, the whole area between Landī and Qalʿa-yi Fatḥ is covered with ruins of fortresses, villages, and remants of ancient irrigation canals.[43] The fortress of Qalʿa-yi Fatḥ is considered, according to tradition, to have been the capital of the dynasty of the Kiyānids, celebrated in the *Shāh-nāma*. Only one village, Rūdbār, is mentioned by its present appellation in the accounts of the Arab conquest.[44] The region is known by the name of the Garmsīr ("warm country"). According to Curzon, no other part of Afghanistan suffered so much from human passions as the Garmsīr. Curzon quotes another explorer, Bellew, who enthusiastically describes the fertility of its soil and abundance of its water, and states that if strong and just rule were established in the Garmsīr, the region would recover its former prosperity, and the whole course of the river all the way to Sīstān would be lined with one uninterrupted orchard.[45]

The Arghandāb flows into the Hilmand near Bust. The region along this river and its tributaries, ancient Arachosia, always had considerable commercial and strategic importance; the road from Western Asia to India branches out from there in two directions: the northeastern road to the northern part of the Panjāb, and the southeastern road to Multān and the delta of the Indus. In the tenth century, the region was called al-Rukhkhaj (sometimes al-Rukhkhadh), obviously identical with that ancient name which the Greeks transmitted as Arachosia.[46] The strategic position of the

[43] Holdich, "The Afghan Boundary Commission," p. 161.

[44] Balādhurī, p. 434.

[45] H. W. Bellew, *Record on the March of the Mission to Seistan* (Calcutta, 1873). ⟦For the sandy desert region to the south and east of the Garmsīr region of the middle Hilmand, the Rīgistān, virtually uninhabited except by nomads, see Balsan, *Au Registan inexploré*. This Garmsīr region has been developed agriculturally in recent decades with the help of American aid to the Afghan government, and a Hilmand Valley Authority was formed in 1952; see Humlum, *La géographie de l'Afghanistan*, pp. 236 ff., and Dupree, *Afghanistan*, pp. 482-84, 499-507.⟧

[46] In Marquart's opinion, *Ērānšahr nach der Geographie des Ps. Moses Xorenacʿi*, *AGWG*, n.s. III/2 (Berlin, 1901). 37, Harachwat. Χοροχοάδ of Isidore of Charax. Cf. A. Forbiger, *Handbuch der alten Geographie aus den Quellen bearbeitet* (Hamburg, 1875-1877), II, 537, for the river 'Αραχωτόί, according to Isidore of Charax. Le Strange, *The Lands*, p. 345, following Maqdisī, p. 304 line 18, the river Kh.r.d.ruy (variant Kh.r.d.w.r.y). ⟨⟨The Old Persian name was Harahuvatī-, Avestan Harxᵛaitī-; for the etymology and relationship with al-Rukhkhaj, see Eilers, "Demawend," pp. 275, 279.⟩⟩

fortress of Girishk, occupying a passage across the Hilmand on the road from Qandahār to Harāt and that of Qandahār itself, suggest that the towns of the region have existed since time immemorial, although their names appear much later. On the site of Girishk there was in the tenth century the town of Fīrūzqand, the first stage on the way from Bust to Zamīndāwar and Ghazna.[47] In the works of the principal tenth-century geographers, the name Qandahār is not applied to the Afghan city; these authors mean by Qandahār the region Gandhara on the Indus along the lower course of the Kabul river; only a few authors such as Balādhurī, Yaʿqūbī, and Masʿūdī mention the city of Qandahār by its present name.[48] The tenth-century geographers cite Panjwāy and Tiginābād as the principal towns of al-Rukhkhaj. Tiginābād is situated one march from Panjwāy on the road to Ghazna. It had a certain significance in the history of the Ghaznawids as a strong fortress and, in W. Anderson's opinion, it corresponded to the location of Qandahār.[49] Up to the eighteenth century, Qandahār lay halfway between the present city and the banks of the Arghandāb, among high and steep cliffs, on three terraces that rose one above the other. Nādir Shāh attempted to move the city some distance to the west, but Nādirābād, which he thus founded, was soon destroyed as well; the new city was built by the founder of the Afghan state, Aḥmad Shāh, and its plan did not differ from that of Harāt.[50] Situated in the middle of a plain

[47] Iṣṭakhrī, pp. 248, 250; cf. Marquart, *Ērānšahr*, pp. 255, 280. ⟨⟨In the same source it appears also as Fīrūzqand, see Le Strange, *The Lands*, p. 344; *Ḥudūd al-ʿālam*, tr. Minorsky, p. 345.⟩⟩

[48] Marquart, *Ērānšahr*, pp. 270-72. Qandahār; Alexandropolis; Panjwāy; Tigīnābād; foundation of the city in a plain under Nādir Shāh. ⟨⟨For the history of Qandahār and its monuments, see also M. L. Dames, *EI*[1], art. "Ḳandahār"; K. Fischer, "Kandahar in Arachosien," *Zeitschrift der Martin-Luther-Universität zu Halle-Wittenberg*, VII (1958), 1151-64; G. Fussman, "Notes sur la topographie de l'ancienne Kandahar," *Arts Asiatiques*, XIII (1966), 33-58, and the bibliography there. For Tigīnābād and Panjwāy under the Ghaznawids, see Gardīzī, *Zayn al-akhbār*, ed. Muhammad Nāẓim (Berlin, 1928), p. 14; for the data in Bīrūnī, see *Ḥudūd al-ʿālam*, tr. Minorsky, p. 332. ⟦Fischer, "Zur Lage von Kandahar an Landverbindungen zwischen Iran and Indien," *Bonner Jahrbücher des Rheinischen Landmuseum in Bonn*, CLXVII (1967), 129-232; Bosworth, *EI*[2], art. "Ḳandahār."⟧

[49] "Ibn Houkul's Account of Seestan," *JASB*, XXI (1852), 374. ⟦This identification seems probable; see the works of Fischer and Bosworth cited in the previous note.⟧

[50] The city was often called Aḥmad-Shāhī by ʿAbd al-Karīm Bukhārī also on coins (M. L. Dames, *EI*[1], art. "Afghānistān"). Aḥmad Shāh's father was Zamān Khān, the place of his burial was Rawḍa-yi Bāgh (to the south of Harāt: ʿAbd al-Karīm Bukhārī, *Histoire de l'Asie Centrale (Afghanistan, Boukhara, Khiva, Khoqand): depuis les dernières années du règne de Nadir Chah (1153), jusqu'en 1233 de l'Hegire (1740-1818)*, Persian text (Bulaq, 1290/1873-4), p. 39. ⟨⟨For Aḥmad Shāh and his successors, see Gankovskii, "Nezavisimoe Afganskoe gosudarstvo," as well as his *Imperiia Durrani*.⟩⟩

and surrounded by higher places, this city cannot compare with ancient Qandahār in terms of strategic importance.

In the tenth century, a road led from Panjwāy northeastward toward Ghazna, and another southeastward into the northeastern part of present Balūchistān. The direct trade route from Sīstān to Balūchistān passed through the Garmsīr; this road, which, judging by the ruins preserved in the Garmsīr, must have existed for some time, and which the British are now successfully trying to restore, is not mentioned in the tenth-century sources. The geographers of that time know only the road from Bust to Panjwāy and from there to the region of Bālis, with the towns of Isfanjāy and Sīvī, now Sībī.[51] The northeastern part of Balūchistān was at that time called Ṭūrān; its principal city was Quṣdār, which still exists and has the same name. At present, Quṣdār is the capital of the minor Balūchī khanate of Jalawān, vassal of the main center of the entire region, Kalāt. In the tenth century, Quṣdār seems to have had the importance that Kalāt has today. The ruler of Quṣdār did not recognize any authority except that of the caliph; in the eleventh century, Sulṭān Maḥmūd had to wage war strenuously against Quṣdār. The importance of Quṣdār was probably due to the fact that here the road to India was joined by a road from western Persia that passed through the southern part of Kirmān and the town of Jalk; the latter still exists on the border between Persia and Balūchistān. Annual income from commercial taxes raised in Quṣdār reached one million dirhams.[52] Within the confines of Ṭūrān was also the town of Qandābīl on the road from Bālis to Quṣdār; today called Gandawa, it is the center of the most fertile region of Balūchistān, a country otherwise notorious for its stony and sandy soil; the khanate of Kūch Gandawa is an exception and, according to British observers, if it were well cultivated, it could feed all of Balūchistān. To Qandābīl used to come for the sake of commerce members of the nomadic pagan people al-Badaha; this appellation is clearly to be understood as that of the Brahui (perhaps it should be read al-Baraha).[53] In the seventeenth century the Brahui took the rule over from the Balūchīs, and are now the dominant group in Balūchistān, although the Balūchīs share with them their exemption from taxes, which are collected only among the sedentary immi-

[51] Iṣṭakhrī, pp. 244, 252. ⟨⟨For Bālis, see also Markwart, *Wehrot und Arang*, p. 124; *Ḥudūd al-ʿālam*, tr. Minorsky, p. 346.⟩⟩

[52] Maqdisī, p. 485. ⟦Minorsky, *EI*¹, art. "Ṭūrān"; Bosworth, *EI*², arts. "Kilāt," "Ḳuṣdār"; Nāẓim, *Sulṭān Maḥmūd*, p. 74.⟧

[53] Iṣṭakhrī, p. 176.

grants from Afghanistan to India.[54] In the tenth century, the Brahuis' principal occupation was camel breeding; they sent stud camels even to Khurāsān and Fārs.

There are several bays on the coast of Balūchistān, which to a certain extent function as harbors; at the time of the Arab geographers, these bays did not have any commercial importance, however, and all trade was channeled to the port of Daybul located to the west of Indus estuary (today it is called Lar-i Bandar).

The southeastern part of Afghanistan, the nucleus from which the modern Afghan state sprang, had much greater historical importance than Baluchistan.[55] A road led from Panjwāy to Ghazna and Kābul; both were depots for Indian goods. The political situation of the region in pre-Islamic times is not quite clear; the same geographers who in one instance count Ghazna among the regions dependent on Sīstān attribute it in another instance to a region belonging to the ruler of Bāmiyān.[56] At any rate, there were in-

[54] The Brahui belonged to the Dravidian race. Cf. F. Hultzsch, "The Brahui Language. Part I. Introduction and Grammar," *ZDMG*, LXV (1911), 149, for the language of the Brahui, "whose total disappearance is only a matter of time." ⟨⟨For the present-day situation of the Brahuis, see Gankovskii, *Narody Pakistana*, p. 235; M. G. Pikulin, *Bragui* (Moscow, 1967); for the language of the Brahui, see now M. B. Emeneau, *Brahui and Dravidian Comparative Grammar* (Berkeley and Los Angeles, 1962).⟩⟩

[55] Cf. Geiger, "Die Sprache der Balutschen," *GIPh*, I, 232, for the two main dialects of the Balūchīs, the northeastern and southwestern (Makrānī). ⟨⟨For the latest works on the Balūchī language and dialectology, see V. A. Frolova, *Beludzhskii iazyk*; Gankovskii, *Narody Pakistana*.⟩⟩ Abodes of the Balūchīs in the tenth century, according to Iṣṭakhrī, p. 164, in the southwestern part of Kirmān, to the west of Bashākird. In Ibn Khurradādhbih, however, Muqāṭaʿat al-Balūṣ on the way from al-Fahraj through Makrān to Fannazbūr. The distances: Muqāṭaʿat al-Balūṣ to al-Fahraj, 102 farsakhs; further on to Fannazbūr, 28 farsakhs; further to Quṣdār, 50 farsakhs. Fahraj is on the edge of the desert, four farsakhs from Narmāshīr. The Balūchīs occupy today the southeastern part of Iran, but occur in the north up to the central part of Khurāsān and in the west to 58° east of Greenwich. ⟨⟨For the contemporary distribution of the Balūchīs, see M. G. Pikulin, *Beludzhi* (Moscow, 1959); Oranskii, *Vvedenie*, pp. 323-26; Gankovskii, *Narody Pakistana*.⟩⟩ From among the populations of Balūchistān, the Afghans were the most devoted to their language, the Brahuis the least (*Census of India, 1911*. IV. *Baluchistan*, 128). See *The Imperial Gazetteer of India*, V, 30, for the sect of the Zikrīs or Dāʿīs in Makrān; they believe in a Mahdī from Jawnpūr, and they have a Kaʿba on the Kūh-i Murād near Turbat, where they carry out the rituals of pilgrimage. ⟦J. H. Elfenbein, *The Baluch Language, a Dialectology with Texts* (London, 1966); B. M. Spooner, "Notes on the Baluchī Spoken in Persian Baluchistan," *Iran, JBIPS*, V (1967), 51-71; Bosworth, *EI*² Suppl., "Dhikrīs".⟧

[56] Cf. Iṣṭakhrī, pp, 239, 280.

dividual local rulers both in Kābul and Ghazna, and the ruler of Kābul bore the title of Kābul Shāh.

The Arab conquerors never managed to occupy the region beyond the Hindū Kush, and had to content themselves with receiving tribute from the Kābul Shāh and other rulers;[57] the region was firmly incorporated into the Islamic domains only in the ninth century by the founder of the Ṣaffārid dynasty, Yaʿqūb; in this connection, mention is made of an individual Muslim ruler in Gardīz,[58] one march from Ghazna on the way to India.[59] After the fall of the Ṣaffārids, there were again local rulers in Ghazna and Kābul.[60] In the tenth century, the Sāmānid general Alptigīn, having quarreled with his sovereign, crossed the Hindū Kush, conquered Ghazna, and prepared the ground for the Ghaznawid dynasty. As is well known, during the rule of Maḥmūd (998-1030), Ghazna was the capital of a large empire and one of the centers of learning and the arts; ruins of this city lie some 25 versts north of modern Ghazna.[61] The city's prosperity was disturbed by a whole series of calamities; the first and hardest blow was struck in 1148 by the Ghūrids, led by ʿAlāʾ al-Dīn Ḥusayn, who received as a result of his destruction of Ghazna the title Jahān Sūz.[62] In 1221, Chingiz Khan subjected the inhabitants of Ghazna to general slaughter, except for the artisans who were carried off as prisoners.[63] Finally, in 1326 the city was destroyed by the Mongols of Persia, who had routed the army of the Chaghatay khan Tarmashīrīn; at that point the tomb of Maḥmūd was disturbed, those living in its vicinity were carried off as prisoners, and Qurʾān manuscripts and other books

[57] ⟨⟨The data that are in the *Akhbār Makka* "Chronicles of the City of Mecca" by Abu 'l-Walīd Muḥammad al-Azraqī point to an occupation of the regions of Kābul and Qandahār as early as 812-813, see A. I. Mikhaĭlova, "Novye epigraficheskie dannye dlia istorii Sredneĭ Azii IX v.," *Epigrafika Vostoka*, V (1951), 10-20. Masson-Romodin, I, 22.⟩⟩ ⟦Bosworth, *EI*², art. "Kābul."⟧

[58] Gardīzī, Cambridge ms., fol. 84b ⟦ed. Nāẓim (Berlin, 1928), p. 11; Bosworth, "Notes on the Pre-Ghaznavid History of Eastern Afghanistan," *IQ*, IX (1965), 17 ff.⟧

[59] Maqdisī, p. 349.

[60] Cf. the situation under Nādir Shāh: Qandahār was Afghan, Ghazna and Kābul Indian; the border was present-day Mukūr, in Muḥammad Mahdī Khān Astarābādī's *Taʾrīkh-i Nādirī* (Tabrīz, 1265/1849), p. 115, events of 1738: "The spring of Makhūr which is on the border of the kingdoms of Iran and India."

[61] According to M. L. Dames, *EI*¹, art. "Ghazna," about four kilometers; according to the *Imperial Gazetteer of India*, V, 63, it was three miles.

[62] Ghazna was considered as being in the hands of the Ghūrids from 1161 onward.

[63] Barthold, *Turkestan*, p. 445, *Soch.* I, 512.

were burned or torn apart.[64] Present-day Ghazna, although it counts some 10,000 inhabitants in all, retains a certain commercial importance thanks to its position on the caravan route to India.[65] The streams on which Ghazna and Gardīz used to be situated flow into the lake of the Āb-i Istāda, the last landlocked basin on the way to the Indus system.

The mountainous region between the Indus and the basins of the Hilmand and the Āb-i Istāda is known as the Sulaymān mountains; the chains of this system along the frontier are called by the British the Eastern and Western Sulaymān ranges. These mountains were in prehistoric times already inhabited by Afghans, a people of Iranian stock. The Afghans for their part call themselves Pukhtūn or Pushtūn, pl. Pukhtāna or Pushtāna,[66] the Paktioi of Herodotus.[67] The origin of the name Afghan is unknown; it is first used by the eleventh-century historian ʿUtbī, in connection with the campaign of Maḥmūd of Ghazna against the Afghans.[68] In their almost inaccessible mountainous homeland, the Afghans long resisted both the domination of Islamic rulers and the cultural influence of Islam; even at the end of the fourteenth century, during Tīmūr's campaigns, the majority of Afghans were pagans.[69]

[64] *Dhayl-i Jāmiʿ al-tawārīkh*, ms. *INA* D 66, fol. 508.

[65] The article of Dames, *EI*[1], "Ghazna." Description of the tomb of Maḥmūd in G. T. Vigne, *Ghazni and Afghanistan* (London, 1840) (he was there in 1836); cf. in Khanikoff (K. C. Ritter, *Iran* [St. Petersburg, 1874]), pp. 573 ff. A plan of the surroundings of Ghazna, *ibid.*, p. 579. ⟨⟨For the history and mounuments of Ghazna, see also C. E. Bosworth, *EI*[2], art. "Ghazna," and its bibliography; Wilber, *Annotated Bibliography*, nos. 973, 1,010, 1013, 1,036, 1,048, 1,051, 1,052; Bosworth, *The Ghaznavids*; Masson-Romodin, I; G. A. Pugachenkova, *Iskusstvo Afghanistana* (Moscow, 1963), pp. 163-65.⟩⟩

[66] The principal dialects: northern (*kh* = Pakhtō—Kābul, Peshawar, Swat) and southern (*sh* = Pashtō). ⟨⟨For the dialects of the Afghan language and the territory of their distribution, see now G. Morgenstierne, *An Etymological Vocabulary of Pashto* (Oslo, 1927); *idem*, "The Wanetsi Dialect of Pashto," *NTS*, IV (1930), 156-75; *idem*, "Archaisms and Innovations in Pashto Morphology," *NTS*, XII (1942), 88-114; Oranskii, *Vvedenie*, pp. 304-306; Dvoriankov, *Iazyk pushtu*.⟩⟩

[67] According to M. L. Dames (*EI*[1], art. "Afghanistan"), the forms with *sh* are earlier than those with *kh*, for this reason Dames rejects the theory of identity of the Pashtuns and Paktis. ⟨⟨See now also Morgenstierne, *EI*[2], art. "Afghān"; Masson-Romodin, I, 67-69.⟩⟩ ⟦Caroe, *The Pathans.*⟧

[68] For earlier data about the Afghans, see in the Tumanskii ms. of the *Ḥudūd al-ʿālam*, fol. 16a. ⟨⟨See Barthold, *Vvedenie*, p. 21, and *Ḥudūd al-ʿālam*, tr. Minorsky, pp. 252, 349 n. 2. For possible mention of the Afghans in Indian and Chinese sources of the sixth and seventh centuries, see G. Morgenstierne, *EI*[2], "Afghān"; Masson-Romodin, I, 211-12.⟩⟩

[69] Cf. Masson-Romodin, I, 305-13.

The conquest of the lower reaches of the Indus, all the way to Multān, was carried out by the Arabs from the south, while the mountainous region between Kābul and Ghazna on one side and the banks of the Indus on the other remained unsubjugated. The extent to which the raids of the Afghans complicated the commercial relations between these regions is indicated by the fact that, according to Maqdisī,[70] the journey from Ghazna to Multān sometimes took three months.[71] Maḥmūd was the first to invade India from the west, and he firmly occupied Panjāb; nonetheless, the Afghans retained their independence under the Ghaznawids and the following dynasty, that of the Ghūrids. After Ghazna's destruction by the Mongols, the Afghans could make incursions into the neighboring civilized areas unhindered. The fourteenth-century traveler Ibn Baṭṭūṭa already mentions the Afghans in Kābul; besides spreading into the basin of the Kābul river, they also gradually started to settle in that of the Hilmand. In the same century the term "Afghanistan" begins to appear as the name of the country of the Afghans. As they settled over the countryside, the Afghans were to fuse with other ethnic groups, the latter then adopting the language of the majority. One such group consisted of the above-mentioned Khalaj Turks.[72] Qandahār, Kābul, and Ghazna came within the framework of the empire of Tīmūr and his successors. Bābur undertook his Indian campaign, which led to the founding of the empire of the Great Mughals, from Kābul. In the sixteenth century, Qandahār came within the framework of the Persian state of the Ṣafawids, but occasionally it was under the rule of the Great Mughals. In the beginning of the eighteenth century, the decline of both states was seized upon by the Afghans, who rose as rapidly as the mountaineers of Ghūr had done in the twelfth century. In 1709, the leader of the Khalaj, Mīr Ways, made himself master of Qandahār; in 1722 his son Maḥmūd even conquered Persia and made himself ruler of Persia. By 1729, however, Maḥmūd's nephew Ashraf was driven out of Persia by Nādir Shāh, whose successes halted for some time the rise of the Afghans. Nādir Shāh again subjugated Afghanistan and devasted India. He appointed as lead-

[70] *Ibid.* and Maqdisī, p. 486, for the road from Manṣūra through Quṣdār to Ghazna.

[71] Description of the road between India and Ghazna in Bīrūnī, *India*, tr. E. C. Sachau (London, 1888), I, 206: Wayhind, capital of Gandhara; Purshawar, 14 farsakhs; Dunpūr, 15 farsakhs; Kābul, 12 farsakhs; Ghazna, 17 farsakhs. The road through Gardīz (in Maqdisī, p. 349; see above, p. 77) also lends to Wayhind. ⟨⟨For this road, see also *Ḥudūd al-ʿālam*, tr. Minorsky, pp. 251-54.⟩⟩

[72] Aristov, "Anglo-Indiiskii 'Kavkaz,' " p. 25.

ers of his Afghan armies the elders of the other Afghan group, the Abdālīs, in order to undermine the power of the Khalaj.[a] After Nādir Shah's death in 1747, Aḥmad, leader of the Abdālīs, cut his ties with the Persians, seized Qandahār, and laid the foundations of an independent state. Aḥmad Shāh died in Qandahār in 1733;[73] his tomb is the most magnificent construction in that city to this day. Aḥmad's successor Tīmūr Shāh (1773-1793) transferred the government to Kābul, which has since remained the capital city of Afghanistan.[74] The borders of the state were subject to frequent modifications; for some time, they encompassed also Kashmīr, a part of Panjāb, and Sind.[75] The rule of the Afghans in India did not last, however; not even the original homeland of the Afghans comes within borders of modern Afghanistan, although the majority of Afghans live there even today. In the opinion of the Russian scholar N. A. Aristov,[76] the Afghans number some four and a half to five million in all, of whom only some two million live in the territory of the amīr.[77] The inhabitants of the Sulaymān moun-

[a] See L. Lockhart, *Nadir Shah, a Critical Study Based Mainly upon Contemporary Sources* (London, 1938); *idem, EI*², art. "Abdālī."

[73] According to the *Mujmil al-ta'rīkh-i ba'd-Nādiriyya,* ed. O. Mann (Leiden, 1891-1896), p. 148, the death of Aḥmad Shāh was at the end of Jumādā II, 1185 (beginning of October 1771). In M. L. Dames, "Afg͟hānistān," the year 1773 (1187 A.H.); the same in *idem, EI*¹, art. "Aḥmed Shāh Durrānī," where there is a misprint: 1184. In ʿAbd al-Karīm Bukhārī, p. 9, the year is 1185. See Dames, "Afg͟hanistān," for the Durrānī control over the other Afghan tribes to the present day. Mention of the Bārakzay clan in the historical part of Dames's article "Afg͟hānistān," at p. 170, and not in his description of the tribes (*ibid.*, pp. 149 ff.), cf. J. S. Cotton, *EI*¹, art. "Bārakzai." The appellation Durrānī was adopted by Aḥmad Shāh instead of ʿAbdalī. The clan of Sadōzay.

[74] See *Mujmil al-ta'rīkh-i baʿd-Nādiriyya,* p. 155: episode from the times of trouble at the beginning of the reign of Tīmūr Shāh.

[75] Cf. Muḥammad Jaʿfar al-Ḥusaynī Khūrmūjī, the author of the *Ta'rīkh-i Shīrāz,* compiled in 1276/1859-60: "Afghanistan, which in reality is an ancient part and dependency of the noble state of Iran. . . . For almost one hundred years each of the regions of this country has been under the sway of the Afghan khans. The government of England, with the preservation of India and her own national interests in mind, is endeavoring to establish this country [that is, Afghanistan] as a separate state, and to achieve the goal of her wishes within the limits of [her] power; [while] the noble state of Iran will of course also, so far as possible, be mindful of realizing its own right[s]. And we will see what the wishes of the Master of the World are in this regard." The author gives information about himself in the description of the village of M.nq.l. ⟨⟨For Muḥammad Jaʿfar K͟hūrmūjī, the author of the works *Ta'rīkh-i Shīrāz* (also known as *Āthār-i Jaʿfarī*) and *Ḥaqā'iq al-akhbār-i Nāṣirī,* see Storey, *Persian Literature,* I, 343-44, 352.⟩⟩

[76] "Anglo-Indiiskii 'Kavkaz'," p. 50.

[77] Different statistics in MacGregor, *Narrative of a Journey*: there are about 3,500,000

tains are subjected to nominal "control" by Britain; in reality, the subjugation of these mountaineers, for which the British aim, will cost the latter, in Aristov's opinion, even more dearly than subjugation of the Caucasus cost the Russians.[b]

The mountainous region that forms the central part of Afghanistan is inhabited primarily by peoples of non-Afghan origin. We have seen how in the Middle Ages the powerful dynasty of the Ghūrids, which had originated in Ghūr, played an important part in historical events. From among the inhabitants of Ghūr may have originated several nomadic peoples who, despite their Aryan origin and Iranian language, are known by the generic Turkish term Aymaq (properly *oymaq*, "clan" or "tribe").[78] These nomads differ sharply in both customs and dialect from the sedentary inhabitants of cultivated areas, the so-called Pārswāns (properly *pārsī zabān*, "Persian speaking"). The Aymaqs are divided into a whole series of separate groups, whose names—Jamshīdīs, Taymanīs, and so on—are absent in medieval literary sources; so little research has been done on the history of Afghanistan that it is impossible to say when these groups first made their appearance. Along both slopes of the Tīrband-i Turkistān range and in the valley of the Harī Rūd

---

Afghans in all; from among these, 1,080,931 are within the British confines and 2,359,000 in Afghanistān. In Dames's *EI*[1] art. "Afghanistān" there are no figures. ⟨⟨For contemporary data about the distribution and size of the Afghan population in Afghanistan and Pakistan, see *Narody Perednei Azii*, p. 56; *Sovremennyi Afganistan; Afghānistān* (Kābul, 1334/1955 onward); *Statistical Digest of Pakistan*, 1950; J. W. Spain, *The Pathan Borderland* (The Hague, 1963).⟩⟩ ⟦Dupree, *Afghanistan*, p. 59, estimates (in 1973) the Pushtuns at about 6,500,000 in Afghanistan and roughly the same number across the border in Pakistan.⟧

[b] There is irony in the fact that it is now, eighty years later, not the British but the Russians who, as an occupying force in Afghanistan, are finding its subjugation a "second Caucasus."

[78] Chahār-Aymaq: Jamshīds, Hazāras, Fīrūzkūhīs, and Taymanīs. The Taymanīs certainly already in Tīmūr's time. For the Moghols in Afghanistan, see Ramstedt, "Otchet," (they live between Qandahār, Harāt, and Kābul); also *idem*, "Mogholica, Beiträge zur Kenntnis der Moghol-Sprache in Afghanistan," *JSFOu*, XXIII (1905), I-IV, 1-60, and my remark in *Etnograficheskoe obozrenie* (1910), nos. 1-2; ⟨⟨Barthold, "K voprosu o kaitakakh," about the Moghols of Afghanistan, p. 44 and nn. 3-4; Barthold, "Popravka"; see now *Narody Perednei Azii*, pp. 107-33, 555; Schurmann, *The Mongols of Afghanistan*; K. Ferdinand, "Ethnographical Notes on Chahâr Aimâq, Hazâra and Moghôl," *AO*, XXVIII (1964), 175-203; E. Bacon, "An Inquiry into the History of the Hazara Mongols of Afghanistan," *Southwestern Journal of Anthropology*, VII (1951), 230-47; G. Jarring, *On the Distribution of Turk Tribes in Afghanistan* (Lund, 1939); for the languages see Efimov, *Iazyk afganskikh khazara*; Ligeti, "Recherches sur les dialectes mongols et turcs de l'Afghanistan," *AOHung.*, IV (1954), 93-117, and the bibliography in these works.⟩⟩

live the Fīrūzkūhī, a people whose name, they say, stems not from that of the medieval capital of Ghūr but from the name of the stronghold Fīrūzkūh in Persia on the fringes of Māzandarān; the latter was taken by Tīmūr in 1404, and the entire garrison was transferred to Harāt.

Iranian in speech but Mongol by origin seem to be the so-called Hazāras, now the most numerous and powerful ethnic group in this region. They live to the north as well as to the south of the principal ranges. Their name is derived from the Persian word *hazāra* ("thousand"), used in the Arabic plural *hazārajāt.*[c] This term was applied by the Persians to one of the chief divisions of the Mongol army, and it then seems to have been adopted by the Mongols themselves. Subjugation of this mountainous region and conquest of the strong fortresses of Ghūr required great effort on the part of the Mongols. After the completion of the conquest, Mongol detachments were left in the country; these then gradually adopted the language of the vanquished. They were subsequently, it would seem, joined by other Mongol detachments, which also settled here and called themselves by the names of their leaders; outstanding among these were the Niküderīs, who arrived here in the thirteenth century and at first were a detachment led by the Chaghatay prince Niküder. Niküder served Hülegü, the conqueror of Persia, but then betrayed him.[d] In Bābur's time (that is, the sixteenth century), part of the Hazāra and Niküderīs, who lived in the mountains west of Kābul, spoke Mongolian.[79] In the area between Harāt and Qandahār there seems to be even today a tribe that has retained its Mongolian language. In 1838 Lieutenant R. Leech published in the *Journal of Asiatic Society of Bengal* a dictionary of the language of this tribe;[80] H. C. von der Gabelentz then proved that this dialect belongs to the Mongolian languages in both lexical content and grammatical structure.[81] On the upper reaches of the Murghāb lives a tribe whose members call themselves Mongols but speak Persian; its neighbors know the leaders of this tribe, according to Ferrier, as Saharāhīs (from Arabic *ṣaḥārā*, pl. of

[c] See on the region and the people, the references given in Chapter III n. 5 above.

[d] See on these military groups, J. Aubin, "L'ethnogénèse des Qaraunas," *Turcica*, I (1969), 65-94.

[79] *Bābur-nāma*, ed. Il'minskii (Kazan, 1857), p. 161.

[80] ⟨⟨Leech, "A Vocabulary of the Language of the Moghal Aimaks," *JASB*, VII (1838), 785-87.⟩⟩

[81] ⟨⟨Von der Gabelentz, "Ueber die Sprache der Hazâras und Aimaks," *ZDMG*, XX (1866), 326-35.⟩⟩

ṣaḥrā', "steppe," "desert").[82] Tīmūr and his successors had to undertake expeditions against the Hazāras. In the middle of the nineteenth century, when Ferrier traveled in the area, the Hazāras were virtually independent and obeyed only their own leaders or sardārs, although the Afghan rulers, especially Yār Muḥammad of Harāt, did try to subjugate them.

A totally special case is that of the mountain dwellers of the Hindū Kush, who still to this day have not fully submitted to the influence of Islam. We have seen that in the tenth century the main routes through the Hindū Kush led to the valley of the Panjshīr, one of the tributaries of the Kābul river.[83] There is, furthermore, mention of a road from Badakhshān to "Tibet," that is, to the upper reaches of the Indus inhabited by Tibetans; today this includes the regions of Gilgit, Kanjut, and Ladakh, subjugated by the British. Along these routes the influence of Islam gradually spread; the extensive mountain region between the two routes, however, remained outside the sphere of this influence. Even the present Muslim region of Chitrāl (Chitrār), whose rulers bore the Iranian title of Mihtar, and which was in 1895 conquered by the British, became wholly Islamic in relatively recent times. Bābur, who wrote at the beginning of the sixteenth century, still attributes Katūr, that is, Chitrāl, to Kāfiristān. The form Chitrār appears in the work of the seventeenth-century author Maḥmūd b. Walī; the ruler of "Chitrār," Shāh Bābur, declared himself subject of the khan of Bukhārā, Imām Qulī.[84] In Chitrāl, just as in medieval Ghūr, each village represented a minor fortress in its own right; rulers of villages were at the same time military commanders and, as the Mihtar's vassals, they joined his campaigns with a specified number of men. The importance of Chitrāl resided in the fact that here two roads branch out southward from the road that leads from Badakhshān to Gilgit and Kashmīr: one through Dīr and the Malakand pass to Peshāwar, the other through Kunār along the banks of a river of the same name (Chitrāl itself is situated along the banks of this river on its upper reaches, where it is better known as the Chitrāl river), to

[82] *Voyages*, I, 431.

[83] The Hindu Kush is here the limit of the Iranian dialects; one exception is the dialect of Yidga (Geiger, "Kleinere Dialekte und Dialektgruppen," *GIPh*, I, 291); Munjān and the valley in Injigān, to the south of the Dōrāh pass. ⟨⟨For the Munjān language and the Yidga dialect, see now I. I. Zarubin, "K kharakteristike mundzhanskogo iazyka," *Iran*, I (19 Leningrad, 1927), pp. 111-99; G. Morgenstierne, "The Name Munǰān and some Other Names of Places and Peoples in the Hindu Kush," *BSOS*, VI (1931), 439-44; *idem*, *Indo-Iranian Frontier Languages*. II. *Iranian Pamir Languages* (Oslo, 1938).⟩⟩

[84] *Baḥr al-asrār*, fol. 276b.

Jalālābād and Kābul. All these roads present enormous difficulties and in winter they are considered impassable. Still more arduous is access to the area between the Panjshīr and the Kunār, Kāfiristān proper, which was conquered only in the most recent years by the amīr ʿAbd al-Raḥmān. In addition to the name Kāfirs, the inhabitants are also called Siyāhpūsh (after their black clothes); for their own part they call themselves, according to some reports, Bolors—a term that appears already in Chinese historical sources of the first century A.D.[85] Both in Chinese sources up to the eighteenth century and in those of the Muslims—for example in the work of Muḥammad Ḥaydar, who wrote in the middle of the sixteenth century[86]—the term "Bolor" and "Boloristān" are applied to the whole region from the Kābul valley northeastward to Kashmīr, Yarkand, and Kashgar.[87] Today the term "Bolor" seems to be seldom used even by the Bolors themselves, who, when they want to distinguish their people from the Muslims, use, according to J. Biddulph, the term "Kapira"—obviously a corruption of the Arabic *kāfir*.[88] The country of the Siyāhpūsh represents the most inaccessible part of the slopes of the Hindū Kush; to use Muḥammad Ḥaydar's words, "the whole area is covered with mountains, valleys, and gorges; with some exaggeration one could say that in all of Boloristān there is no single plain, were it but one farsakh wide." According to Dr. Robertson, who spent ten months in Kāfiristān,

> the valleys there, carved out by rapid and overflowing streams, in many places represent impassable defiles. One rarely encounters a stretch of an even road that would extend for some one or two hundred fathoms; the road consists mostly of stony paths, winding along cliffs, precipices, and narrow ledges.

[85] The Siyāhpūsh form a part of the Kāfirs, the others are the Waiguli ⟨⟨Waigeli⟩⟩ and Presunguli ⟨⟨Presun, Prasun⟩⟩. The Kati are a part of the Siyāhpūsh. The Presun are called Wiron by the Muslims; they are clearly a very ancient group who have conserved their old religious beliefs in their greatest purity and their respect for the *pshurs* or priests, shamans. ⟨⟨For the Kāfirs, see now Vavilov-Bukinich, *Zemledel'cheskii Afghanistan; Narody Perednei Azii*, pp. 133-48, 555; Masson-Romodin, I, 301-304; P. Snoy, *Die Kafiren, Formen der Wirtschaft und geistigen Kultur* (Giessen, 1962); Sch. Jones, *The Political Organization of the Kam Kafirs* (Copenhagen, 1967), and also the literature given in *idem, An Annotated Bibliography of Nuristan (Kafiristan) and the Kalash Kafirs of Chitral* (Copenhagen, 1966).⟩⟩ ⟦C. S. Coon, *Caravan, the Story of the Middle East* (New York, 1951), pp. 65-73; Humlum, *La géographie de l'Afghanistan*, pp. 107-10; Bosworth, *EI*², art. "Kāfiristān."⟧

[86] Muḥammad Ḥaydar, *Ta'rīkh-i Rashīdī*, tr. and comm. N. Elias and E. D. Ross (London, 1895), pp. 384-86. ⟨⟨Cf. Barthold, "Kāfiristān v XVI v."⟩⟩

[87] The Dards and the country of Dardistān.

[88] *Tribes of the Hindoo Koosh* (Calcutta, 1880), p. 128.

> Sometimes there are bridges that span the rivers, but these are at best dug-out thick tree trunks, whose edges are often studded with long staffs tipped by beautifully carved heads of animals. More often the bridges consist of one or two beams thrown over the streams, or it is simply a fallen tree that serves this purpose. For a good part of the year there is no communication between the valleys whatsoever.[89]

In this kind of country there can naturally be no question either of national or of political unity among its inhabitants. The language of the Siyāhpūsh, about which some data are given by Biddulph, is considered to belong to the Indian branch of Aryan languages, but dialects of the various clans differ so sharply that their speakers are sometimes totally unable to understand one another.[90] There were among the clans of the Siyāhpūsh in Muḥammad Ḥaydar's time as well as at the end of the nineteenth century unending fratricidal wars, in comparison with which the clashes between them and the Muslims appear insignificant. Detachments of Muslim conquerors, consisting primarily of cavalry, could not achieve a lasting success in this region; Tīmūr, Bābur, and Muḥammad Ḥaydar could carry out only plundering raids in the land of the Kāfirs. Tīmūr mounted an expedition against the Siyāhpūsh in 1398 while on his way to India, in response to complaints by the citizens of the trading city of Andarāb about the incursions of the Kāfirs. The conqueror penetrated their country from the north, through the Khawak pass, where he restored an old dismantled fortress.[91] After Tīmūr, as far as is known, neither armies nor travelers entered Kāfiristān from this direction. The Kāfirs, according to Sharaf al-Dīn, spoke a peculiar language that resembled neither Persian nor Turkish nor Indian, and they mostly wore no clothes at all; their elders bore the title *ʿadā* or *ʿadāshū*;[92]today Kāfir elders call themselves *jashtams* or *jastams*.[93]

[89] ⟨⟨Sir G. S. Robertson, "Kafiristan," *GJ*, IV (1894), 193-218; cf. also *idem*, *The Kafirs of the Hindu Kush* (London, 1896), and *idem*, Russ. tr., *Kafiry Gindukusha.*⟩⟩ ⟦Robertson's classic work has recently been reprinted (Karachi, 1974) with a valuable introduction by L. Dupree. Marco Polo refers to the region of the Pamirs to the east of Badakhshān as Bolor; see *The Book of Ser Marco Polo* (1871 ed.), I, 163, 168-69.⟧

[90] ⟨⟨For the Kafir languages, see Edel'man, *Dardskie iazyki*, and the bibliography there.⟩⟩

[91] Descent from the pass: lowering people on lines, including Tīmūr himself. Fortress, river, mountain, inscription.

[92] Sharaf al-Dīn Yazdī, II, 22.

[93] ⟨⟨For survivals of the patriarchal-kinship organization and the institution of

Aside from this raid from the northwest, other incursions into Kāfiristān were undertaken from the north via Badakhshān, from the south via the Kābul river valley, and from the east via Chitrāl.[e] Access to the region seems to have been somewhat easier from the east, and Kāfiristān had especially close economic ties with Chitrāl; some tribes were even politically dependent on the ruler of Chitrāl.[94] Muslim traders could enter the country only in the company of a Kāfir, but then they enjoyed security; Kāfirs returning from Chitrāl were sometimes accompanied by curious persons who wished to see the country and take advantage of the celebrated hospitality of savages. Europeans began to penetrate Kāfiristān only very recently. In 1885, Lockhart entered it with his mission via Chitrāl, as did in 1889 the above-mentioned Robertson.[95] Only the Afghan amīr ʿAbd al-Raḥmān succeeded in conquering Kāfiristān. The first campaign took place in the winter of 1895-1896 under the command of General Ghulām Ḥaydar; the Kāfirs, still armed mostly with bows and arrows (rifles of coarse workmanship had only recently begun to be introduced there) could not stand up against Afghan artillery. The armies were followed by mullas in order to propagate Islam. Finally, ʿAbd al-Raḥmān had recourse to a measure used by all conquerors: Kāfir families were forced to move to inner regions of Afghanistan, and their place was taken by Afghan mountaineers. In this manner the region, flanked on three sides by Afghan possessions and on the east bordering the valley of Chitrāl, a province subjugated by Britain, will soon become definitively incorporated into the framework of Afghanistan.[96]

---

elders among the Kafirs, see A. Herrlich, "Beitrag zur Rassen- und Stammeskunde der Hindukusch-Kafiren," in *Deutsche im Hindukusch* (Berlin, 1937), pp. 168-246; *Narody Perednei Azii*, pp. 139-42.⟫

[e] One abortive expedition from the Kābul river valley into the region of Laghmān or Lamghān was made in the late sixteenth century by the Mughal prince of Kābul, Muḥammad Ḥakīm; see G. Scarcia, *Ṣifat-nāma-yi Darvīš Ḫān-i Ġāzī. Cronaca di una crociata musulmana contro i Kafiri di Laġmān nell'anno 1582* (Rome, 1965).

[94] The people of Hunza (district of Kanjut) and its special language; opinion of N. Ia. Marr about the Japhetids. ⟪For the Kanjut (Burish-Vershin) language, see I. I. Zarubin, "Vershikskoe narechie"; D.L.R. Lorimer, *The Burushaski Language* (Oslo, 1935). For attempts to connect the Kanjut language with the "Japhetic" languages, see Zarubin, "N. Ia. Marr i kandzhutskii (burishsko-vershinskii) iazyk," *Iazyk i Myshlenie*, VIII (1937), 165-70; Klimov-Edel'man, *Iazyk burushaski.*⟫ ⟦D. N. MacKenzie, *EI*[2] Suppl., "Burushaski."⟧

[95] Robertson was there for a long time ⟦actually, thirteen months⟧, 1890-1891. See his book *The Kafirs of the Hindu Kush*.

[96] After its subjugation by ʿAbd al-Raḥmān, Kāfiristān was renamed Nūristān, see Niedermayer, *Afghanistan*, p. 30.

CHAPTER V

Khurāsān

We have no information as to how and when the Aryans moved from the eastern to the western part of Iran. The Medes (Amada, later Madai) are mentioned for the first time in 835 B.C. in an inscription of the Assyrian king Shalmaneser II; it is not clear whether these Medes were Aryans from the outset, or whether Aryan conquerors had adopted the name of earlier occupants of the country.[1] Aryan proper names appear only with the inscriptions of Sargon (721-705 B.C.).[2] Furthermore, we do not know whether the Aryan migration occurred only along the northern route, that of the Medes, or whether it also followed the southern route from Sīstān to Kirmān and from there to Fārs. The latter seems more likely, considering the fact that the Persians who asserted themselves in Fārs included, according to Herodotus (I.125), the Gedrosians (Δηρουσιαῖοι in the text) and Germanians or Kirmanians (Γερμάνιοι), which meant that the entire southern part of modern Persia was occupied by one branch of Iranians who called themselves Persians, Pārsa. Since the Medes appeared in history before the Persians, it is very likely that the migration along the northern route occurred earlier.

The movement of the Aryans through the northern part of Persia probably followed the age-old route between western and eastern Asia, in other words, along the southern slope of the mountains that constitute the northern limit of the Iranian plateau. Certain itineraries suggest that in antiquity a part of this route passed further to the north; thus, according to Isidore of Charax, the road from the region of Κομισηνή (called Qūmis by the Arabs) with the towns of Dāmghān and Simnān proceeded northward to Hyrcania, that is, to the banks of the Gurgān, a river that flows into the Caspian sea. From there it continued into the country of the Parthians, whose earliest capital—Ἄστακα or Ἄρσακα on the site of the Arabic Khabūshān or modern Qūchān, and Νισαία, the Arabic Nasā,

[1] ⟨⟨Cf. now I. D'iakonov, *Istoriia Midii.*⟩⟩

[2] ⟨⟨For a discussion of this subject and an up-to-date bibliography, see Grantovskii, "Iranskie imena"; *idem, Iranoiazychnye plemena Perednei Azii.*⟩⟩

now ruins near ʿAshqābād, were located to the north of the later, principal route. The movement of the Aryans may thus have skirted the banks of the Gurgān; the name Hyrcania (from Wrkāna, "land of wolves"), is purely Indo-European. The migration then proceeded along the southern slope of the mountains, since the southern shore of the Caspian was occupied right down to the time of the Persian rule by populations of non-Aryan stock. Besides the route through Hyrcania, the present-day main route is mentioned, as well: already Arrian (III, 23, 1) writes that Hyrcania was to the left of the road from Media to Parthia.

Herodotus, as is known, includes the Parthians, Choresmians, Soghdians, and Arians (Areioi) in one satrapy; in all the cuneiform inscriptions, however, Parthia is listed separately from Choresmia, Soghdia, and Areia. The satrap of Parthia, at the beginning of Darius's reign, was his father Gushtasp, who in 518 B.C. had to quell an uprising of the Parthians and Hyrcanians.[3] In Achaemenid times the region did not have much importance; according to Strabo, the Persian kings, during their tours of the country, strove to pass through Parthia as quickly as possible, because the region was too poor to sustain their large retinues. As a result of this poverty and the necessity of defending themselves against incursions by nomads, the Parthians remained faithful to the simple, soldierlike way of life of the eastern Iranians, and after the fall of the Achaemenids proved to be the solid element that succeeded in rebuilding a strong Iranian state and repelling even Roman expansion.

A natural border between Turkestān and the southern part of the Caspian basin is constituted by the mountains of the Greater and Lesser Balkhān, Küren-Dagh, Köpet-Dagh, and those of Khurāsān, which form today the border between Russia and Persia. According to Curzon, nothing can match the gloomy spectacle of these sterile heights of gray limestone, watered only by few springs and deprived of any vegetation except sparse juniper. In antiquity and the Middle Ages, the oases along the northern slope of these mountains were inhabited by Iranians; their location left them exposed to especially frequent incursions by Turkish nomads, so that

[3] Ménant, *Les Achéménides et les inscriptions de la Perse*, p. 114. ⟨⟨In harmony with the chronology of events in the first years of Darius I's reign as it is accepted by most present-day scholars, the quelling of the uprising of the Parthians and Hyrcanians, mentioned in the Behistun inscription, is dated to the period from 8 March to 12 July 521 B.C. See Dandamaev, *Iran*, p. 272; cf. also Kent, *Old Persian, Grammar, Texts, Lexicon*, p. 161; Hallock, "The 'One Year' of Darius I," *JNES*, XIX (1960), 36-39.⟩⟩

in the end they came under the latter's domination. From that time onward the area received the Turkish name Atek, or more exactly Etek (Ītāk, "edge, hem, foot of a mountain").[4]

Among the towns of this region, those most often mentioned in the Middle Ages were Nasā and Abīward.[5] The former is located not far from modern ʿAshqābād, whereas the latter still exists as a modest settlement 110 versts from ʿAshqābād. In the district of Nasā was the *ribāṭ* of Farāwa (Afrāwa), some four days' journey from Nasā; it was built in the ninth century by the Ṭāhirid ʿAbd Allāh, and consisted of three interconnected fortifications (the modern Kïzïl Arvat).[6] From there a direct road led across the steppe to the town of Gurgānj (near modern Kunya-Urgench, in the northern part of the khanate of Khīwa). Mentioned in the district of Abīward is the town of Mihna or Mayhana. A settlement of the same name still exists to the south of the railroad on the border between Russia and Persia; it is noteworthy as the birthplace as well as the place of last repose of the well-known Ṣūfī Abū Saʿīd Mayhanī (eleventh century). From Abīward, a direct road led to Marw. As has already been pointed out, Etek was on account of its geographical position subjected to inroads by Central Asian nomads; moreover, the region was always the object of ambitions for conquest by the nearest Central Asian rulers, namely, the sovereigns of Khwārazm. Already in Herodotus (III, 117) there is a report,

[4] Akhal and Etek. For Akhal, see Mu'nis, *Firdaws al-iqbāl*, Asiatic Museum ms. S 571 (590 oa), fol. 88a: " 'Akhal' in Türkmen means areas of drainage and water. The region, which is a dependency of Nasā and Bāwurd, consists mostly of flooded places and rice paddies, and this is probably why they call it 'Akhal.' " According to Masal'skii, *Turkestanskii krai*, pp. 633-44, the Etek oasis begins at the station of Giaurs and intermittently extends to the station of Dushak; the center of the oasis and the residence of the Etek district officer is at the station of Kaakhka.

[5] Zhukovskii's investigations (see his report in *Otchety [Imp.] Arkheologichestoĭ Komissii* [St. Petersburg, 1896], pp. 104-105): Anau, two sites Nasā, Pīshtak (Old Abīward) and Mayhana (Meana, fifty to fifty-five versts from Dushak); the tomb of Abū Saʿīd; a plan to publish a description of the monuments and a corpus of the historical-geographical data. See also Semenov, *Musul'manskii mistik*, p. 15 (Nasā, some eighteen versts from ʿAshqābād and twelve versts from the station of Bezmein) and p. 13 (about Abīward: some five versts from Kaakhka, where "mosques with magnificent tiles" have been preserved). For the two sites of Nasā, the southwestern one and the southeastern one, see Barthold, *Oroshenie*, p. 39. ⟨⟨*Soch.* III, 128; for the sites of Nasā and the history of their study, see now M. Masson, "Gorodishcha Nisy"; also cf. Barthold, *EI*[1], art. "Āk͟hāl Tekke" (*Soch.* II, 242-43); *idem, EI*[1], art, "Atek" (*Soch.* III, 337); Semenov, "Razvaliny Abiverda"; Minorsky, *EI*[1] Suppl., art. "Bāward."⟩⟩

[6] ⟨⟨For this *ribāṭ*, see Barthold, *Oroshenie*, in *Soch.* III, 129-30.⟩⟩

so far not satisfactorily explained, about a valley surrounded by five mountains with mountain passes; a river called Ἄκης that flowed through this valley had originally belonged to the Choresmians, and was located between the possessions of the Choresmians, Hyrcanians, Parthians, Sarangians, and Tamanians. This report shows that even in remote times, prior to the formation of the Achaemenid empire, the rule of the Choresmians extended to the mountainous regions to the south of the steppe.[7]

In the tenth century, the Sāmānid Nūḥ b. Manṣūr presented the ruler of the northern part of Khwārazm, Ma'mūn, with Nasā, and the ruler of the southern part, the Khwārazmshāh Abū ʿAbd Allāh, with Abīward; the latter did not actually receive this gift because of resistance by the Khurasanian governor Abū ʿAlī Simjūrī.[8] After the unification of Khwārazm at the end of the tenth century under the rule of Ma'mūn, who assumed the title of Khwārazmshāh, Nasā and Farāwa belonged to the Khwārazmians down to the conquest of Khwārazm by the Ghaznawid Maḥmūd in 1017. When in 1035 the Türkmens led by the Saljuqs invaded Khurāsān, Sultan Masʿūd was forced to deliver Nasā and Farāwa to them.[9] In the twelfth century, when a new dynasty of Khwārazmshāhs grew in strength, Nasā passed under their rule before other towns of Khurāsān.[10] Also mentioned in this period is the town of Shahristān on the road from Khwārazm to Nasā; it was located at a distance of one farsakh from the latter, on the edge of the sands; Yāqūt, who was here in 1220[11] states that as a result of its location there were no orchards in the environs of the town, and that the cultivated fields were far away.[12]

After the Mongol invasion, Khwārazm did not have an independent dynasty of its own—except for a brief interlude in the fourteenth century—until the area's conquest by the Uzbeks at the beginning of the sixteenth century. In the sixteenth and seven-

[7] The commander-in-chief of the Parthians and Khwārazmians in the army of Xerxes (Herodotus, VII, 66); Artabaz, Persian notable (Herodotus, VIII, 126; IX, 41); an army 40,000 men strong (Herodotus, IX, 66).

[8] Barthold, *Turkestan*, p. 261. ⟦Bosworth, *EI*², arts. "Khʷārazm" and "Khʷārazm-Shāhs."⟧

[9] Bayhaqī, ed. Morley, p. 611 ⟦ed. Ghanī and Fayyāḍ, p. 585⟧.

[10] Barthold, *Turkestan* (Eng. tr.), p. 335.

[11] *Muʿjam*, III, 343.

[12] Darun (Durun) near the station Baharden, sixty versts from Bam and fifty-two versts from Gök-Tepe. Shahristan-Islam and the ruins. In Masal'skii (*Turkestanskii krai*, p. 628) there is mention of Shahr-Islam; to the north of the station, Baharden on the fringe of the sands.

teenth centuries, the towns of Etek were usually under the rule of the Khwārazmian Uzbeks. According to Abu 'l-Ghāzī, Etek was at this time called *tagh boyï* ("side of the mountain, mountainside") in opposition to *su boyï* ("side, banks of the river"), as the banks of the Āmū Daryā were called, that is, Khwārazm proper. At the same time, the khans of Khīwa were always trying to bring the Türkmen tribes under their control. As early as the sixteenth century, these tribes held the entire eastern shore of the Caspian sea all the way to the Gurgān, and then gradually, as the might of the shāhs of Persia and the khans of Khīwa was declining, they spread their rule eastward all the way to Marw. Shāh ʿAbbās the Great (1587-1628) for all practical purposes renounced Etek, although he and his successors nominally considered the Uzbek rulers of Etek as their vassals. In order to safeguard the country from the inroads of the Türkmens and Uzbeks, ʿAbbās decided to resettle here warlike Kurds from the west. He established five Kurdish districts all along the border from Astarābādh to Chinārān. Three of these still exist: Bujnūrd, Qūchān, and Deregez; in Deregez there is today not a Kurdish but an Uzbek dynasty.[13] The strongest of the three rulers, that of Qūchān, bears the Turkish title of *il-khanï* (that is, "khan of the tribe").[14] In the Middle Ages, Qūchān was usually called Khabūshān, although the form Khūjān is already found in Maqdisī.[15] In the tenth century it was the chief town of the district of Ustuwā, which corresponds to the 'Ασταβηνή or 'Ασταυηνή of Isidore of Charax; as early as the twelfth century, at the time of the rise in importance of the Khwārazmshāhs, it was one of the chief points on the road to the central part of Khurāsān.[16] Aside

[13] Yate, *Khurasan and Sistan*, p. 165. According to Sykes, *A History of Persia*, II, photograph accompanying p. 126, there is in Deregez the mausoleum called *Ḥaḍrat-i Sulṭān* which was, however, built in the twelfth century by Mu'ayyid (1162-1174).

[14] The title *il-khanï* is also that of the governor of Bujnurd; see *Safar-nāma-yi Nāṣir al-Dīn Shāh Qājār ba-Khurāsān (Safar-i duwwum)* (Tehran, 1306/1889), p. 100.

[15] Maqdisī, p. 319. Khūjān in Bayhaqī, ed. Morley, p. 761, ⟦ed. Ghanī and Fayyāḍ, p. 604⟧. Cf. Rashīd al-Dīn, *Jāmiʿal-tawārīkh*, ed. and tr. E. Quatremère, I, 183: "They arrived in Khabūshān which the Mongols call Qūjān."

[16] ⟨⟨Cf. Ustuwā and Khūjān in *Ḥudūd al-ʿālam*, fols. 11a, 19b. In Juwaynī, *Ta'rikh-i Jahān-gushāy*, ed M. M. Qazwīnī (Leiden and London, 1912-1937), II, 13; Khabūshān-i Ustuwā. For Qūchān, see also Minorsky, *Iranica, Twenty Articles*, pp. 169-70; Barthold, *EI*¹, art. "Ḳučan" (*Soch.* III, 473-74).⟩⟩ ⟦Bosworth, *EI*², art. "Ḳūčān." On the historical corridor for east-west communication across northern and western Khurāsān, see Aubin, "Réseau pastoral et réseau caravanier. Les grand' routes du Khorassan à l'époque mongole," *Le monde iranien et l'Islam*, I (1971), pp. 105-30, and also B. Spooner, "Arghiyān. The Area of Jājarm in Western Khurāsān," *Iran, JBIPS*, III (1965), 97-107; and Bosworth, *EI*², Suppl., art. "Dj̲ādj̲arm."⟧

from its location, the town owed its importance to the outstanding fertility of its environs; according to Curzon,[17] there is no single more fertile and better watered place in the northern part of Persia.[18] The resettlement of the Kurds did not stop the Türkmen incursions; the adversaries proved to be of equal strength; neither side was able to obtain a decisive victory, and the Kurds could only retaliate for Türkmen raids by devastating the fields of the Etek.[19] The Kurdish ruler of Qūchān participated in Nādir Shāh's march on Samarqand and Bukhārā and, so J. B. Fraser tells us, carried off from Samarqand the Qur'ān that lay on Tīmūr's tomb and that had been copied by his grandson Bāysonghor.[20] The manuscript was torn apart into separate leaves by the Kurds, then partly reassembled by the ruler's son and placed on the tomb of the imām interred in Qūchān. Fraser saw some of the leaves; according to his description, this magnificent specimen of the art of calligraphy was kept very carelessly. It apparently fell victim to the most recent earthquake (1895).[21] On a hill near Qūchān, which is even today called Nādir-tepe, the killing of Nādir Shāh took place in 1747.[22] The town suffered a great deal during the quelling of the *il-khanī*'s uprising by ʿAbbās Mīrzā in 1833, as well as from the earthquakes of 1851 and 1872; after these calamities Qūchān, according to Curzon, had scarcely 12,000 inhabitants.[23] The earthquake of 1895 definitively ruined the town; new Qūchān was built about twelve versts to the east of the old one.[24]

[17] *Persia*, I, 111.

[18] A description of the Qūchān valley is given in the *Safar-nāma . . . ba-Khurāsān*, p. 114. Cf. Yate, *Khurasan and Sistan*, p. 297. From Qūchān, it is nine farsakhs to Muḥammadābād, the chief city of Daragaz (*Safar-nāma . . . ba-Khurāsān*, p. 120).

[19] The Kurds Zaʿfarānlū in Qūchān, Shādillū ones in Bujnūrd; see *Safar-nāma . . . ba-Khurāsān*, pp. 96, 120, and Yate, *Khurasan and Sistan*, p. 179. Also Kaywānlū in Rādkān and ʿImārlū near Nīshāpūr (*Ta'rīkh-i baʿd-Nādiriyya*, p. 43).

[20] *Narrative of a Journey into Khorasan, in the Years 1821 and 1822* (London, 1825), 574.

[21] Tomb of the *imām* Shāhzāda Ibrāhīm, the son of ʿAlī Riḍā, in Qūchān (*Safar-nāma . . . ba-Khurāsān*, p. 119). For the Qur'ān see *ibid.*, p. 124: "We ordered that two pages from it be brought to Tehran and, after their restoration, be placed in the State Museum; they are very large pages, but torn to pieces; each page is a sheet of 'khanbaligh' paper." A Qur'ān manuscript by Bāysonghor is also in Mashhad (*ibid.*, p. 153).

[22] The hill called Nādir-tepe is to the southeast of Qūchān. The settlement there has three names: Nādir-tepe, Fatḥābād (a *chaman* by this name was there) and Qalʿa-yi Kalb-Āqāsī (this *nawkar*, Alhiyār Khān Āṣaf al-Dawla, was the founder of the settlement).

[23] *Persia*, I, 109.

[24] The ruins of old Qūchān are three farsakhs to the west of the modern (recent)

Another border point bound up with Nādir Shāh's name was the important fortress of Kalāt. Nature itself created this inaccessible mountain fortress: the platform, some 2,500 feet above sea level, is about twenty English miles long and five to seven miles wide, and is surrounded on all sides by a natural wall consisting of bare steep rocks between seven hundred and one thousand feet above the valley. This wall is cut through only by two narrow passages that can easily be fortified; there are, however, mountain paths by means of which one can penetrate the fortress. The main gate, through which flows the stream that irrigates the valley, is called Darband-i Arghun Shāh, after the name of the person who recorded his construction in the inscription on the polished surface of one of the rocks. Curzon and others identified this Arghun Shāh with Arghun, the Mongol khan of Persia (1284-1291 A.D.). It is indeed said about Arghun that he sought refuge in Kalāt when, even before his succession to the throne, he was defeated by his uncle Aḥmad; the fortress was at that time in ruins and Arghun surrendered at the approach of Aḥmad's army without resistance.[25] It is not certain whether it is possible to tell from the text of the inscription if the builder of the fortress was indeed the khan Arghun; attempts to make a copy of the inscription have so far met with little success.[26] It would be more natural to assume that the person in question was the local ruler Arghun Shāh, father of ʿAlī Beg, with whom Tīmūr had fought.

In 1382, Kalāt was besieged by Tīmūr; several gates are mentioned in connection with this event, the *darband-i Arghun Shāh* among them.[27] ʿAlī Beg expressed submission, but then he betrayed Tīmūr, who built, as a counterweight to Kalāt, the fortress of Qahqaha between Abīward and Kalāt, clearly on the site of the present-day railway station Kaakhka.[28] The person who took full advantage of the natural features of Kalāt was Nādir Shāh, and the fortress received its present name of Kalāt-i Nādirī at that time. According to Curzon, Nādir Shāh wanted to build here an inaccessible stronghold and a safe depository for the treasures that he had brought from India. There is a description of Kalāt by a con-

one, on the road from Shīrwān, near the settlement of Najafābād (see *Safar-nāma . . . ba-Khurāsān*, p. 115). Tīmūr and the Tīmūrids traveled from Central Asia to Gurgān and Astarābād sometimes by way of Abīward, Nasā, and Darūn, sometimes by way of Qūchān. A Buddhist temple in Qūchān in Ghazan Khan's time.

[25] D'Ohsson, *Histoire des Mongols*, III, 594-95.

[26] Yate, *Khurasan and Sistan*, p. 156.

[27] Sharaf al-Din Yazdī, I, 337.

[28] *Ibid.*, p. 343.

temporary of Nādir Shāh, the Greek traveler Basil Vatatses.[29] According to him, Nādir Shāh wished to construct a city that had no equal, where the inhabitants could find everything, without any need of importing goods; the booty from the Indian campaign covered the expenses of the construction.[30] The rocks were hewn from inside and from outside, and whenever an attack could be expected guard towers were erected. After Nādir Shāh's time and until 1885, Kalāt was the capital of a minor khanate, nominally a vassal of Persia, into which were also incorporated, until the Russo-Persian border delimitation of 1881, Abīward and a few other points in Etek.

Curzon describes the northwestern, mountainous part of Khurāsān in the following manner:

> A series of lofty mountain ridges, with an axis inclined from north-west to south-east, run parallel to each other at varying distances, the intervening hollows being in the more northern parts deep gorges admitting little more than a torrent bed at their bottom, while further south they widen into valleys watered by mountain streams and dotted with villages, and eventually into broad, rich plains, such as that of Kuchan to the north and Nishapur to the south of the Binalud Kuh mountains. Transverse ravines cut these ridges, often at right angles, and provide a way of communication from valley to valley. These gorges are frequently of almost inconceivable abruptness and grandeur. Each one presents a score of positions of absolute impregnability; and I do not suppose that a more savage mountain scenery, in zones below the snow line, exists anywhere in the world. The base of these defiles seldom admits more than a torrent bed blocked with enormous boulders, and the walls are frequently vertical to a height of from 500 to 1,000 feet. The higher mountains rarely display even the scantiest vegetation, being sterile, stony, and forbidding to a degree, though the loftiest peaks are majestic with splintered outline, and occasionally some astonishing natural phenomenon is encountered, like the southern wall of Kelat. Cultivation is almost

[29] E. Legrand, "Voyages de Basile Vatace en Europe et en Asie," *Nouveaux mélanges orientaux*, II, 209-14.

[30] For Nādir Shāh, see, besides Vatatses, also the *Ta'rīkh-i baʿd-Nādiriyya*, pp. 22 ff. Inscription of Shaybānī on the way from Kalāt to Mashhad (Yate, *Khurasan and Sistan*, p. 153). ⟦J. K. Tod, "Kalat-i Nadiri," *GJ*, LXII (1923), 366-70; L. Lockhart, *Nadir Shah*, p. 254; R. M. Savory, *EI*², art. "Kilāt-i Nādirī."⟧

> wholly confined to the valley bottoms, and is there dependent upon precarious streams and watercourses dug therefrom to the arable plots. Each village is like an oasis in a brown desert; and the squalid mud huts, with their fringe of green poplars and orchards, present an appearance almost as refreshing to the wayfarer as the snuggest of English homesteads.[31]

In the environs of Nīshāpūr, however, fields under cultivation are found even on mountain slopes, from which flow the streams that irrigate the valley; these fields occur, according to Ferrier, even on the highest elevations.[32] The fields on mountain slopes are separately terraced. Due to the abundance of water, there are in this valley more settlements than elsewhere; here too, as in other parts of Persia, the vegetation is not continuous, but the arable plots are separated from each other by only minor intervals. The small river that flows past Nīshāpūr is called Shūrīrūd, after the bitter and salty taste of its water.[33]

Nīshāpūr was so often subjected to earthquakes[a] and devastating invasions, and in its present state differs so much, both in terms of its area and of its population, from the medieval capital of Khurāsān, that the study and clarification of the latter's topography present major difficulties. The only certain thing about ancient, pre-Islamic Nīshāpūr is that it was called Abarshahr (Abrashahr of the Arab geographers);[34] and that it received its present name from

[31] *Persia*, I, 142.

[32] *Voyages*, I, 199.

[33] For the soil of the Nīshāpūr valley, see *Safar-nāma . . . ba-Khurāsān*, p. 171: "The whole area of Nīshāpūr is well tilled and consists of a soft soil; there is no other place better suited for agriculture and fruit-growing than this one; if all of the region of Nīshāpūr were passed through a sieve, not a single stone would appear."

[a] See for these, C. Melville, "Earthquakes in the History of Nishapur," *Iran, JBIPS*, XVIII (1980), pp. 103-20.

[34] Interpretation of the word Abarshahr. A different interpretation is in A.V.W. Jackson, *From Constantinople to the Home of Omar Khayyam. Travels in Transcaucasia and Northern Persia for Historic and Literary Research* (New York, 1911), p. 247: *abr shahr*, "cloud city." ⟨⟨For this term, see also Markwart, *A Catalogue*, p. 52; E. Honigmann and A. Maricq, "Recherches sur les Res Gestae Divi Saporis," in *Mémoires de l'Académie Royale de Belgique*, Cl. des Lettres et des Sciences Morales et Politiques, XLVII/4 (Brussels, 1953), 106-107, 175 n. 1; J. Walker, *EI*[2], art. "Abarshahr"; Henning, "Mitteliranisch," *HOr*, 1/4, *Iranistik*, 1. *Linguistik* (Leiden-Cologne, 1958), p. 95; Frye, *Heritage*, pp. 172, 265.⟩⟩ For the pre-Islamic dynasty in Nīshāpūr see Marquart, *Ērānšahr*, pp. 74-75 ⟨⟨see also Markwart, *A Catalogue*, p. 52; Henning, "Mitteliranisch," p. 95; R. N. Frye, *The Histories of Nishapur* (The Hague, 1965), p.

one of the Sāsānid kings, Shāpūr I (third century A.D.) or Shāpūr II (fourth century).[35] This last fact disproves the often-expressed opinion about the identity of Nīshāpūr with the Parthian city of Νισαία. Both in Sāsānid times and under the first Arab governors, the capital of Khurāsān was Marw; Nīshāpūr acquired the role of a capital only with the dynasty of the Ṭāhirids in the ninth century.

The fame of Nīshāpūr is closely linked with that of ʿAbd Allāh b. Ṭāhir (830-844), first ruler of Khurāsān. In my dissertation *Turkestan down to the Mongol Invasion,* I strove to portray this remarkable administrator, who, according to the historian Yaʿqūbī, governed Khurāsān as no one had done before.[36] He was concerned with the interests of the peasants as people who produce nourishment for the rest of the population; he ordered that a set of rules be compiled on the utilization of water for irrigation;[b] and he was far ahead of his time in his views on the significance of knowledge, which, in his opinion, should be made accessible to all those desirous of it; desire for knowledge alone should distinguish between those worthy of it and those unworthy.

The Sīstānī dynasty of the Ṣaffārids, which overthrew the Ṭāhirids in 873, also transferred its capital to Nīshāpūr. In 900 the Ṣāffarid ʿAmr b. Layth was defeated by the Sāmānid Ismāʿīl b. Aḥmad, after which Khurāsān was incorporated into the Sāmānid state. The capital of the Sāmānids, as is well known, was Bukhārā; the lands to the south of the Āmū Daryā were under the rule of a separate governor who bore the title of *Sipāhsālār* and lived in Nīshāpūr.[37]

Nīshāpūr of the Sāmānid period is described in detail by the tenth-century Arab geographers. The city was situated on a plain, but immediately adjacent to the mountains;[38] according to Ibn Rusta,

---

8.⟫ For the significant role of Khurāsān in the renaissance of Persian literature, and the opposite contemporary reputation of the Khurāsānians, see T. Nöldeke, "Das iranische Nationalepos," *GIPh,* II, 144 n. 3.

[35] Ṭabarī, tr. Nöldeke, *Geschichte der Perser und Araber zur Zeit der Sasaniden* (Leiden, 1879), p. 59.

[36] *Turkestan,* p. 213. ⟦See also Bosworth, "The Ṭāhirids and Ṣaffārids," in *Cambridge History of Iran,* IV, 97-101; and for ʿAbd Allāh b. Ṭāhir as a Maecenas and patron of literature and music, see *idem,* "The Ṭāhirids and Arabic Culture," *JSS,* XIV (1969), 58-67.⟧

[b] This *Kitāb al-Qunī* was still used in Khurāsān during Ghaznawid times two centuries later, according to Gardīzī (Barthold, *Turkestan* [Eng. tr.], p. 213).

[37] *Ibid.,* p. 229.

[38] The mountain panorama according to the *Safar-nāma . . . ba-Khurāsān,* p. 167: "They are mountains that are beautiful to look at, and colored in a variety of hues such as yellow, red, blue, and violet." *Ibid.,* p. 168, mentions a great number of settlements on the road from Qadamgāh; the settlement of Ar.d.qish (Dawlatshāh,

there was a high mountain bordering the city on the west.[39] Nīshāpūr was one farsakh long and one wide; it consisted, like other large cities of Central Asia, of a *quhandiz*, that is, citadel, a *shahristān* or the city proper, and a *rabaḍ* or suburb. The citadel was not part of the *shahristān* but was contiguous with it, separated from it by only a ditch. In the tenth century, the life of the city, doubtless as a result of the development of trade and industry, moved wholly to the *rabaḍ*, mainly, it would seem, to its southern part. Describing the bazaars, Iṣṭakhrī remarks among other things that on the north they extend to the "head of the bridge,"[40] and in an earlier passage he mentions, among the gates of the *shahristān*, that "of the head of the bridge."[41] As in other large cities, there were four such gates. The number of the gates of the *rabaḍ* was considerable: according to Maqdisī, over fifty.[42] The center of the bazaar was the so-called "large quadrangular open place" (*al-murabbaʿa al-kabīra*), whence rows of shops and hostels spread in all four directions: eastward to the Friday mosque, northward to the *shahristān*, westward past the "little quadrangular open place" (*al-murabbaʿa al-ṣaghīra*), and southward to the "graves of the descendants of Ḥusayn." In the western part, not far from the "little quadrangular open place," was the palace built by ʿAmr b. Layth on the "square of the descendants of Ḥusayn" (*maydān al-Ḥusayniyyīn*), and alongside it, the jail. The Friday mosque was apparently on a site called *al-muʿaskar*, "military camp."[43] This building is described in detail by Maqdisī.[44] It consisted of six parts; the main building, in which was the pulpit (*minbar*) of the imām, was built in part as early as the eighth century by Abū Muslim, well known for the role he played in the establishment of the ʿAbbāsids, and in part at the end of the ninth century by ʿAmr b. Layth.[45] The building erected by Abū Muslim

Tadhkirat al-shuʿarā, ed. E. G. Browne [London and Leiden, 1901] p. 280: Ar. dūgh-sh); the Turks, resettled by Nādir Shāh, have conserved their Turkish language.

[39] Ibn Rusta, p. 171.

[40] Iṣṭakhrī, p. 255.

[41] *Ibid.*, p. 254.

[42] Maqdisī, p. 316.

[43] One farskh from the Friday mosque to the palace and jail (*ibid.*).

[44] *Ibid.*

[45] For the beginnings of Ṣūfism in Nīshāpūr and Khurāsān, see Hujwīrī, *Kashf al-maḥjūb*, tr. R. A. Nicholson (Leiden and London, 1911), p. 134. Abū ʿUthmān Saʿīd b. Ismāʿīl al-Ḥīrī, a contemporary of Junayd, who died in 297/910. ⟨⟨For the Khurasanian school of Ṣūfī shaykhs, see E. E. Bertel's, "Proiskhozhdenie sufizma"; *idem*, "Baba Kukhi," and the bibliography there; for Junayd, see now Abdel-Kader Ali Hassan, *The Life, Personality and Writings of al-Junayd. A Study of a Third/Ninth Century Mystic, with an Edition and Translation of His Writings* (London, 1962).⟩⟩

was supported by wooden columns, whereas that by ʿAmr rested on round brick pillars; on its sides there were three porticoes and in the center a "gilded structure" (probably a cupola) with eleven doors and with columns made from multicolor marble. To the Friday mosque there also belonged, most probably, the minaret that is mentioned by Yaʿqūbī as built by ʿAbd Allāh b. Ṭāhir.[46]

The canals that brought water to Nīshāpūr were mostly dug underground. The number of steps that led to them sometimes reached one hundred; beyond the city the water came to the surface and was used for irrigation. Nīshāpūr was famous for its silk and cotton fabrics that were exported, according to Iṣṭakhrī, even beyond the confines of the Islamic world.[47] According to Maqdisī, the city was a warehouse for products both of Fārs, Kirmān, and Sind, that is, of the southern regions, and of Ray, Gurgān, and Khwārazm.[48] According to Ibn Hawqal, the shops and inns of Nīshāpur were crowded with representatives of the most varied crafts and trades.[49] In the nearby mountains, copper, iron, silver, turquoise, and other minerals were mined; the turquoise mines, located some thirty-six English miles (about fifty versts) to the northwest of Nīshāpūr on the road to Qūchān, have retained their importance to this day, and appear to be the only turquoise mines in the world that are worked profitably.[c]

Nīshāpūr remained the capital of Khurāsān under the Ghaznawids and Saljuqs as well,[50] despite the preference for Marw shown by some members of the latter dynasty. In 1153 the city was subjected to a devastating raid by the nomadic Ghuzz, who had risen against Sulṭān Sanjar; these Ghuzz plundered the city and razed

[46] *Kitāb al-Buldān*, p. 278.

[47] Iṣṭakhrī, p. 255.

[48] Maqdisī, 315.

[49] Ibn Ḥawqal, p. 311.

[c] For the contemporary turquoise cutting industry in Khurāsān, see Hans E. Wulff, *The Traditional Crafts of Persia* (Cambridge, Mass., 1966), pp. 38-40. Abū Dulaf, *Travels in Iran*, tr. pp. 59-60, #60, mentions only the copper mines of the Nīshāpūr region.

[50] Cf. Nāṣir-i Khusraw, *Safar-nāma* (Tehran lithogr.), p. 171 (who was in Nīshāpūr in spring 1046): Toghrïl Beg (although Khurāsān was under Chaghrï Beg) "ordered a *madrasa* to be built near the saddlers' market; it was [then] used as an *imārat* [=welfare hospice]." ⟦For Nīshāpūr in the Ghaznawid and Saljuq periods, see Bosworth, *The Ghaznavids*, pp. 145-202; specifically on the ulema and bourgeosie there, R. Bulliet, *The Patricians of Nishapur: a Study in Medieval Islamic Social History* (Cambridge, Mass., 1972); more generally, *idem*, "Medieval Nishapur: a Topographic and Demographic Reconstruction," *Studia Iranica*, V (1976), 67-89, and Lockhart, *Persian Cities* (London, 1960), pp. 80-86.⟧

it. The poet Khāqānī says, with some exaggeration, that when the inhabitants returned after the enemy had departed, they could not locate their own dwellings. The new town sprang up to the west of the old one in a place called Shādyākh (sometimes spelled Shaykān);[51] the quarter of Shādyākh had existed, however, even earlier, and was founded by ʿAbd Allāh b. Ṭāhir.[52] There was a high hill here, on which the citadel was built. Thanks to its fortunate location, the town speedily recovered in the same century, and the buildings occupied the entire area from the hill to the old city. According to Yāqūt, Nīshāpūr became again "the most flourishing of God's cities" (*aʿmar bilād Allāh*), as well as the richest and most populous one; he correctly attributes the rapid recovery of Nīshāpūr to its location: it was, so to speak, "the entrance hall of the entire Orient" (*dihlīz al-mashriq*), and caravans could not bypass it.[53]

Much more far-reaching in consequence was the calamity of 1221. Half a year earlier, a son-in-law of Chingiz Khan was killed by an arrow under the walls of Nīshāpūr; as a result, when Chingiz Khan's son Toluy besieged the city, all the prayers of the inhabitants for pardon were rejected outright. The city was taken by storm, and the population was massacred, except for four hundred craftsmen who were led away as prisoners; the buildings were razed and the site ploughed. A detachment of four hundred men was left there in order to exterminate those remnants of the population who might have hidden among the ruins.[54] Chingiz Khan's troops did not manage to maintain themselves in Khurāsān, however, and his successors had to reconquer the country; futile resistance only hampered its recovery. Consequently, the towns of Khurāsān remained ruined much longer than those of Māwarānnahr.

After the conquest, Khurāsān was initially a personal fief of the whole Mongol dynasty, as their common patrimony; the governor was appointed by the Great Khan, but there were by his side the representatives of the other principal members of the House of Chingiz Khan. In the middle of the thirteenth century, the newly established Il-Khanid Mongol state in Persia annexed Khurāsān, but, according to Ḥamd Allāh Mustawfī Qazwīnī, the province had

[51] Ibn Ḥawqal, p. 312 note a.

[52] Yaʿqūbī, *Kitāb al-Buldān*, p. 278.

[53] Yāqūt, *Muʿjam*, IV, 858. ⟦On the various displacements of Nīshāpūr and Shādyākh during these times, see C. Melville, "Earthquakes in the History of Nīshāpūr," *Iran, JBIPS*, XVIII (1980), 103-20.⟧

[54] Barthold, *Turkestan* (Eng. tr.), pp. 446-47. ⟦Boyle, in *Cambridge History of Iran*, V, 314-15.⟧

a separate administrative and financial system; revenues from it were not incorporated into the general revenues of the Il-Khanid dynasty.[55] The river Āmū Daryā was considered to be the border between the latter's domains and those of the Chaghatayids in Māwarānnahr; this border, however, was frequently violated, especially by the Chaghatayid princes. When Khurāsān was part of the Il-Khanid possessions, it was usually governed by one of the members of the dynasty, generally the khan's son or the heir presumptive. The Mongol rulers usually preferred Ṭūs and the valley of the Kashaf Rūd (a tributary of the Harī Rūd), situated to the north of the Binālūd Kūh chain, to Nīshāpūr. After the fall of the Mongol rule in Persia, Nīshāpūr was incorporated in the 1340s into the domains of the Sarbadārs, who had become established in Sabzawār; in 1381 the last sovereign of this dynasty submitted to Tīmūr, so that Nīshāpūr escaped that conqueror's ferocity. The brilliance of Harāt under the Tīmūrids and the religious significance of Mashhad under the Ṣafawids were bound to overshadow Nīshāpūr, which nevertheless remained an important city down to the middle of the eighteenth century, when it was destroyed by the Afghan Aḥmad Shāh. According to tradition, not a single habitable dwelling remained in the city after this devastation.[56] Aḥmad Shāh gave the city to the Turkish prince ʿAbbās Qulī Khān, who took measures to restore it;[57] at the end of the same century, Nīshāpūr passed under the rule of the present Persian dynasty of the Qājārs. Efforts both by ʿAbbās Qulī Khān and others to restore the city's former importance failed. In 1821, according to Fraser,[58] the length of its walls amounted to 4,000 paces in circumference;[59] if this area had been inhabited, the number of the inhabitants would have amounted to 30,000 to 40,000, but the greater part of it still lay in ruins. The Persians counted 2,000 inhabited houses in the city, but Fraser's estimate was that the number of inhabitants did not exceed

[55] *Nuzhat al-qulūb*, ms. of the Asiatic Museum, 603 bbc, fol. 183b (in the Leningrad University ms. 171, fol. 190 b, a part of the sentence is omitted) ⟦ed. Le Strange, p. 147, tr. *idem*, pp. 146-47⟧.

[56] When the town was taken, the inhabitants were forced to gather in the Friday mosque, leaving all their possessions; everything was plundered, burned, and flooded.

[57] ʿAbbās Qulī Khān became governor of Nīshāpūr as early as at the time of the first, unsuccessful siege by Aḥmad Shāh.

[58] *Khorasan*, p. 404.

[59] Five thousand paces in circumference, according to Ḥamd Allāh Qazwīnī Mustawfī. ⟦In *Nuzhat al-qulūb*, ed. Le Strange, p. 148, tr. *idem*, p. 147, actually fifteen thousand paces.⟧

5,000.[60] Textiles were made there exclusively for local consumption; the only article of export was turquoise. Nīshāpūr made a roughly similar impression on Ferrier in 1845; he estimated that the number of the inhabitants did not rise above 8,000 souls.[61] The earthen walls were in poor condition, there was no water in the moat, the citadel lay in ruins; the bazaars and the Friday mosque were surprisingly small. At the time of Curzon's journey in 1889, the totally useless walls were being repaired, with no detectable purpose. Curzon considers it possible that by this time the number of inhabitants had risen to 10,000.[62]

We lack a detailed study and description of the antiquities of Nīshāpūr; Fraser, and more recently Yate, have offered some information on this topic.[63] History records, and the present state of the ruins show, that Nīshāpūr, like Marw and Balkh, gradually moved from east to west. Immediately contiguous with the modern town are the ruins, made partly from clay, partly from brick; according to tradition, this is where the citadel of the ancient city used to stand. Fraser does not say whether there is an elevation here; according to Yate's description, these ruins no longer exist and remnants of the ancient city begin at a distance of one English mile to the southeast of the modern one. The citadel is on a high hill in the southwestern corner of these ruins; the Persians told Fraser that this was where the citadel of the most ancient Nīshāpūr, built in Sāsānid times, had stood, which is hardly likely. At the southeastern corner of the citadel is the tomb of the famous Ṣūfī Farīd al-Dīn ʿAṭṭār, who was killed at the conquest of the city by the Mongols; the memorial monument, from black marble with a Persian inscription, is surrounded by a brick wall. This tomb is the only medieval monument in Nīshāpūr that can be dated; it was built at the end of the fifteenth century under Sulṭān Ḥusayn Bāyqarā

[60] Fraser, *Khorasan*, p. 405.

[61] Ferrier, *Voyages*, I, 201.

[62] *Persia*, I, 261. ⟦According to the *Farhang-i Jughrāfiyā-yi Īrān-zamīn* (repr. Tehran, 2535 *shāhānshāhī*/1335 A.S.H./1966), ed.Razmārā, IX, 431, the population in ca. 1950 was 24, 270; in 1976, it was 59,101 (*Le monde iranien et l'Islam*, IV [1976-1977], 242).⟧

[63] Fraser, *Khorasan*, pp. 397-401; Yate, *Khurasan and Sistan*, pp. 401-12. ⟨⟨See also Honigmann, *EI*[1], art. "Nīshāpūr"; *Survey of Persian Art*, II, V; Vanden Berghe, *Archéologie de l'Iran ancien*, pp. 15, 144 (and the bibliography there for the pre-Islamic monuments of Khurāsān).⟩⟩ ⟦For reports of the excavations conducted under American auspices in the nineteen thirties and nineteen forties, see C. K. Wilkinson, *et al.* in *Bulletin of the Metropolitan Museum of Art* (1934, 1936-1938, 1942), and Wilkinson's book, *Nishapur, Pottery of the Early Islamic Period* (New York, 1975).⟧

by the vizier Mīr ʿAlī Shīr Nawāʾī, who was a famous poet in Persian and especially in the Turkish language, and a patron of the arts.[64] Nearby is also the tomb of one of the ʿAlids built by Shāh Ṭahmāsp in the sixteenth century; according to tradition, the person buried here is the *imāmzāda* Muḥammad Maḥrūq, brother of ʿAlī al-Riḍā b. Mūsā al-Riḍā, the principal saint of Persia, whose mausoleum is in Mashhad. Tombs of relatives of this imām are of course hardly authentic, shown as they are in almost every Persian town of any importance. By the side of this sanctuary is the tomb of the astronomer and freethinking poet ʿUmar al-Khayyām, in the midst of a neglected and weed-infested park.[65]

The high mountain chain of the Binālūd Kūh separates the plain of Nīshāpūr from the valley of the Kashaf Rūd and the modern capital of Khurāsān, Mashhad, situated some twenty-five versts to the southeast of ancient Ṭūs. When describing the road between Nīshāpūr and Ṭūs, the Arab geographers must have had in mind, judging by the distance, one of the roads across the mountain ridge followed by most modern travelers;[66] the present-day postal track makes a detour, avoiding the principal ridge and cutting across relatively low slopes. The name Ṭūs was applied in the tenth century to the whole district, with the towns of Nūqān and Ṭābarān and the village of Sanābād, where in 809 were interred the caliph Hārūn al-Rashīd and the ʿAlid imām ʿAlī b. Mūsā al-Riḍā;[67] the

[64] Isfizārī, University ms., fol. 70a.

[65] According to the *Maṭlaʿ al-shams*, the ruins were 9,000 *dhirāʿs* in circumference; on the northeast was the *kurgan* of Alp-Arslān; the citadel was at the southwestern end. By the southeastern corner of the citadel was the tomb of ʿAṭṭār; half a mile to the east of there was the tomb of Imāmzāda Muḥammad-i Maḥrūq. The *kurgan* of Alp-Arslān was three miles to the east of the modern city, near the settlement of Turbābād (Yate, *Khurasan and Sistan* pp. 410-12); the so-called old Shādyākh; legend about the marriage of Malikshāh with Ögedey Khan's daughter. Diagrams in Jackson's *From Constantinople to the Home of Omar Khayyam*, at pp. 152, 158. Sykes' opinion ("A Sixth Journey in Persia," *GJ*, XXXVII (1911), 1-19, 149-65), regarding the interval between the modern city and the ruins of the old one. Shādyākh, according to Sykes, lies at the southwestern end of the ruins (the citadel). ⟦In 1934, the Iranian government restored the tomb and garden of ʿUmar Khayyām, together with the nearby one of Farīd al-Dīn ʿAṭṭār and the tomb of Firdawsī at Ṭūs; see Lockhart, *Famous Cities of Iran* (London, 1939), pp. 44-45.⟧

[66] Cf. Abū Dulaf in Yāqūt, *Muʿjam*, III, 560, for the *qaṣr* between Ṭūs and Nīshāpūr.

[67] Qadamgāh is the place of Imām ʿAlī Riḍā's visit and miracle. All the inhabitants are *sayyids*; cf. Jackson, *From Constantinople to the Home of Omar Khayyam*, p. 261; Yate, *Khurasan and Sistan*, p. 415. Cf. also *Safar-nāma . . . ba-Khurāsān*, p. 143, for the settlement of T.r.q.ba to the northwest of Mashhad, in a parallel position with the settlement of Gulistān; the latter, according to Yate, *Khurasan and Sistan*, p. 348,

caliph Ma'mūn, to please the Shīʿīs, had at first declared the imām al-Riḍā his successor to the throne, but then, as they claimed, had had him poisoned. There is no detailed description of medieval Ṭūs; at the time of the Arab geographers it was still rather modest in size, because of the flourishing state of Nīshāpūr. Like Nīshāpūr, Ṭūs was destroyed by Toluy, Chingiz Khan's son, and was rebuilt under Chingiz Khan's successor Ögedey; subsequently it was several times the residence of the Mongol governors. After the fall of the Mongols of Persia, Ṭūs, together with Qūchān, Kalāt, Abīward, Nasā, and the Marw oasis, came within the framework of a small state formed by the amīr Arghun Shāh, chieftain of the Jūn Gharbānī tribe; Arghun Shāh was succeeded by his sons Muḥammad Beg and ʿAlī Beg.[68] ʿAlī Beg had to submit to Tīmūr in 1382, was transferred to Farghāna, and in the following year killed. In 1389, after an unsuccessful uprising, Ṭūs was devastated: 10,000 people were killed. Following the custom, towers of the heads of those slain were erected by the gate of the town.[69] The fortress of Ṭūs was rebuilt immediately after Tīmūr's death in 1405. In the following period, Ṭūs was usually mentioned together with Mashhad, but the latter, because of its religious importance, gradually eclipsed its neighbor and became the chief city of Khurāsān. The gradual migration of the inhabitants of Ṭūs to Mashhad is discussed by an Indian traveler who was a contemporary of Nādir Shāh. His testimony is cited by the Persian minister Ṣanīʿ al-Dawla (who later had the title Iʿtimād al-Salṭana) in his work *Maṭlaʿ al-shams*; we find in his book the most detailed description of the ruins of Ṭūs in their present state.[70] There are no dated monuments among the

---

is a "curious structure with high walls, . . . the houses being built two and three storeys high."

[68] Ḥāfiẓ-i Abrū, ms. GPB, fol. 276a. Expression of the Tīmūrid age concerning the Khurāsān of ʿAlī Beg and that of ʿAlī Mu'ayyad.

[69] Sharaf al-Dīn Yazdī, I, 469.

[70] A ground plan of the ruins of Ṭūs is in Jackson, *From Constantinople to the Home of Omar Khayyam*, at p. 294. The diagonal length, from southwest to northeast, was 2,300 yards = 6,900 feet = 985 5/7 fathoms. The hill *Kharābī-yi Ṭūs*, [water from] the spring Chashma-yi Kīlās was conducted to Mashhad under the Ṣafawids, according to the *Safar-nāma . . . ba-Khurāsān*, whereas Yate dates this differently. The weir of the source was built as a *ṣila* or gift of Sultan Maḥmūd for the *Shāh-nāma*, cf. the story in Niẓāmī ʿArūḍī, *Chahār maqāla*, ed. M. M. Qazwīnī (Leiden and London, 1910), p. 51, about the *ribāṭ-i chāha* at the beginning of the road from Ṭūs to Nīshāpūr and Marw. ⟨⟨For the history of Ṭūs and its monuments, see also Minorsky, *EI*[1], art. "Ṭūs" and the bibliography there; Muḥammad Mahdī al-ʿAlawī, *Ta'rīkh Ṭūs wa 'l-Mashhad al-Riḍawī* (Baghdad, 1346/1927).⟩⟩ ⟦Abū Dulaf Misʿar b. Muhalhil, *Travels in Iran (circa A.D. 950)*, ed. and tr. Minorsky (Cairo, 1955), tr. pp.

ruins. Ṣanīʿ al-Dawla describes the walls of the city, which were over one farsakh in circumference; the citadel, located in the northeastern part; and a large building, probably a mosque, within the precincts of the city. The length, width, and height of the walls, towers, and other ruins are given in each case. Within the citadel there was yet another minor fortress on an artificial mound, and a drawing of the mosque is also included in the book; this building is known to the Persians as the *naqqāra-khāna*.[71] Fraser, describing Ṭūs, mentions a smallish minaret (not far from the mosque) and a cupola above Firdawsī's grave, the latter outside the city's precincts,[72] not far from the southeastern gate; tradition ascribes the building of this cupola to the sixteenth-century Bukhāran khan ʿUbayd Allāh. The cupola no longer existed in 1858, at the time of Khanikoff's journey, and the place where the poet's grave had been was sown with wheat.[73] Zhukovskii visited the site in 1890 and found only a disturbed mound, which consisted of complete as well as broken bricks and of fragments of tiles, doubtless the remains of the collapsed and now settled structure, perhaps the same one seen by Fraser.[74] The mound stood inside a quadrangle formed by a new earthern wall. According to the peasants, the ground of the mound had been disturbed by the former governor of Khurāsān Āṣaf al-Dawla, who paved the newly formed platform with bricks, erected the earthen wall, and planned to build a tower, but died before he could finish the project.[75] Near Firdawsī's grave were at one time the tombs of the famous imāms Aḥmad and Muḥammad Ghazālī, the latter of whom was the author of the renowned work

58-59, #59, mentions briefly the monuments of Ṭūs, but concentrates his attention on a fortress between Ṭūs and Nīshāpūr allegedly constructed by one of the ancient Tubbaʿ kings of South Arabia.]

[71] According to Jackson, *From Constantinople to the Home of Omar Khayyam*, p. 289, the edifice was a *mazār*, a *qaṣr*, or a *gunbadh*; he rejects the opinion that this was the grave of Firdawsī; it resembles the mausoleum of Sulṭān Sanjar; illustration at p. 290. Jackson's opinion (*ibid.*, p. 288) regarding Ḥumayd b. Qaḥṭaba, with a reference to Yāqūt. Cf. *Muʿjam*, III, 560, quoting Abū Dulaf on Ḥumayd b. Qaḥṭaba; Qaḥṭaba [b. Shabīb] fell in the battle near the Euphrates in 749 (Ṭabarī, III, 14).

[72] Thus Nöldeke, "Das iranische Nationalepos," p. 157; according to Jackson, *From Constantinople to the Home of Omar Khayyam*, p. 284, it was within the gates; according to Zhukovskii, "Mogila Firdousi," p. 311, the grave was within the city.

[73] Khanikoff, *Mémoire sur l'ethnographie de la Perse* (Paris, 1866), p. 110.

[74] An illustration of the site of Firdawsī's mausoleum, besides being in Zhukovskii's article "Mogila Firdousi," is in Jackson, *From Constantinople to the Home of Omar Khayyam*, at p. 293.

[75] Āṣaf al-Dawla, according to Zhukovskii, "Mogila Firdousi," was appointed governor of Khurāsān in 1884.

Iḥyā' ʿulūm al-dīn.[76] The grave of Muḥammad Ghazālī is still mentioned in the account of the fourteenth-century traveler Ibn Baṭṭūṭa, but since then it has disappeared without a trace.[77]

Ṭūs was located on the northern side of the Kashaf Rūd. Not far from the southeastern gate of the city, on the road to Mashhad, there was an eight-arch bridge over the small river; today it is in a semiruined state. This bridge is described by both Fraser and Ṣanīʿ al-Dawla; the latter author even indicates the dimensions of each arch. In a better, though by no means perfect, state is the bridge located somewhat further downstream on the road from Kalāt to Mashhad (some five miles from the latter city). This bridge, which consists of eleven arches, has the epithet of "imperial" (Pul-i shāh); its impressive size, according to Curzon, is in no way matched by the width of the river bed (not more than twenty-five feet).[78]

The city of Mashhad, as we have seen, originated around the tomb of Imām ʿAlī b. Mūsā al-Riḍā, who was buried in the village of Sanābād some four farsakhs from Ṭūs, by the side of the grave of the caliph Hārūn al-Rashīd. Even in Ibn Ḥawqal's time (tenth century), the village was already surrounded by a strong wall and the tomb was considered a sanctuary.[79] In the same century, Maqdisī uses the term *al-mashhad* for it.[80] In Mustawfī's time (fourteenth century), Mashhad was already a city; another contemporary traveler, Ibn Baṭṭūṭa, describes the cupola-shaped structure built over the tomb, embellished with silk cover and golden lamps.[81] Opposite the tomb of Imām al-Riḍā, under the same dome, was the tomb of the caliph Hārūn al-Rashīd, also with lamps burning above it; Shīʿī pilgrims, having bowed before the imām's tomb, would then kick that of the ʿAbbāsid caliph. The number of pilgrims must have risen dramatically in the sixteenth century, when the Ṣafawid dynasty declared Shīʿism to be the official religion in Persia. When the other Shīʿī sanctuaries, namely, the tomb of ʿAlī in Najaf and that of Ḥusayn in Karbalā, were in the seventeenth century definitively incorporated into the Ottoman empire, the grave of the

[76] Zhukovskii (after Mustawfī) places it in the eastern part of the city. According to Yāqūt, *Muʿjam*, III, 561, the tomb of the imām Ghazālī is "outside al-Ṭabarān."

[77] Ibn Baṭṭūṭa, III, 77.

[78] For the bridge across the Kashaf Rūd, see also Jackson, *From Constantinople to the Home of Omar Khayyam*, p. 285 (illustration at p. 284); the length was 100 yards, the width 18 feet, and the width of the pathway 14 feet.

[79] Ibn Ḥawqal, p. 313.

[80] P. 352; *ibid.*, p. 333 regarding the mosque built by Fā'iq, "the best in Khurāsān."

[81] *Riḥla*, III, 78-79.

imām al-Riḍā became the principal Shīʿī sanctuary of Persia, and was annually visited by some 100,000 pilgrims. Places of pilgrimage always functioned as centers of trade as well; the bazaars of Mashhad, according to travelers, offer a vivid panorama of the greatest variety of oriental peoples.[82] Several times the city was subjected, because of the wealth of its sanctuary and of its bazaars, to plundering raids by the Uzbeks.

Modern Mashhad is surrounded by a mud wall with guard towers; the circumference of this wall is variously estimated, from four and one half to six English miles; an exact determination is made difficult by the irregularity of the ground plan.[83] Mashhad differs from Harāt and other cities in that it is not crossed by two streets perpendicular to each other, but instead is cut through by a principal avenue running diagonally from northwest to southeast; in its middle are the edifices that surround the imām's grave. This main street is known by the term *khiyābān*, that is "avenue, boulevard." The term *khiyābān* does not appear in the works of the tenth-century geographers, but it did exist in Tīmūr's and the Tīmūrid's time; Isfizārī, who wrote at the end of the fifteenth century, mentions the *khiyābān* of Harāt in a fourteenth-century context.[84] The *khiyābān* of Mashhad, according to Curzon, enjoyed among the Persians a widespread, although hardly justified, fame: the trees planted along its sides were grossly neglected; a canal, or more exactly a filthy ditch, whose water was used equally for drinking, washing of clothes, and as a dumping place for carcasses of animals, was dug in the middle. Altogether, the water in Mashhad was totally unfit for drinking; Curzon writes that he left his razor in the water for one night and that the next morning it was black as a rifle barrel. There are many cemeteries in Mashhad, even within the city, as a result of the Shīʿīs' wish to be buried as close to their imām as possible; the corpses are brought from hundreds of versts

[82] The population of Mashhad, according to Jackson, *From Constantinople to the Home of Omar Khayyam*, p. 265, was up to 60,000 people. ⟦The population figure for Mashhad in ca. 1950 was 206,900 (*Farhang*, IX, 399); in 1976, it was 670,180, Mashhad thus being the third largest city of Iran, after Tehran and Iṣfahān and before Tabrīz and Shīrāz (*Le monde iranien et l'Islam*, IV [1976-1977], 242).⟧

[83] Cf. L. F. Bogdanov, *Persiia*, p. 31, the circumference of the wall is up to 15 kilometers. ⟨⟨For the history of Mashhad and its monuments, see also M. Streck, *EI*[1], art. "Meshhed" (with bibliography); Mahdī al-ʿAlawī, *Ta'rīkh; Survey of Persian Art*, II, V; Maḥmūd ʿIlmī, "Ta'rīkhcha-yi Mashhad wa āthār-i abniya-yi ta'rīkhī-yi ān," *Majalla-yi Bāstānshināsī*, no. 3-4 (1338/1959), pp. 63-79.⟩⟩ ⟦Lockhart, *Persian Cities*, pp. 32-41.⟧

[84] University ms., fol. 139b.

away. Nevertheless, the health of the population here is better than in other Persian towns. This may be due to the advantageous position of the city, for it lies to the north of the mountain ridge that protects it from hot desert winds.

The sanctuary, situated in the center of Mashhad, is to this day closed to infidels; European travelers have entered it only in rare cases, exposing themselves to great danger.[85] The whole complex is surrounded by a rampart. The main street still continues for a short distance beyond the entrance arch (for about forty-five fathoms); here is the center of the bazaar. The pilgrim who has crossed the rampart is on sacred soil and enjoys the right of asylum (*bast*). Beyond the bazaar, a second, principal arch leads to the main courtyard of the mosque, the so-called "old courtyard" (*ṣaḥn-i kuhna*), which is sixty-five fathoms long and thirty fathoms wide. Similar to courtyards of other mosques and madrasas, it is encompassed on all four sides by rows of niches on two levels; the lower level was still in Frazer's time rented as shop space to merchants. The intervals between the niches and the space above them are inlaid with decorated tiles. In the center of each side was a portal in the form of a high rectangular arch or *īwān* with Kūfic inscriptions on it. In the center of the courtyard was an octagonal fountain for ablution with a gilt roof. Projecting above the western gate is the lattice overhang for muezzins, which takes the place of a minaret in Shīʿī Islam. The southern portal leads to the main sanctuary, and, in contrast with the others, its upper half is gold-encrusted. The work of gilding is due to Nādir Shāh, who used for this purpose the gold that he had seized on his Indian campaign; the construction of the fountain is also attributed to him. The main courtyard includes two minarets; the one on the side of the mausoleum was built in the sixteenth century and restored in the nineteenth (after 1834); the other one, at the opposite entrance, was built by Nādir Shāh. The upper parts of both minarets are encrusted with gilt copper plates that blaze from a distance like fire; both are equipped, following the style of Persian mosques, with a lattice gallery. The whole surface of the courtyard is inlaid with tombstone slabs over the graves of rich people buried there.

At the entrance to the mausoleum, there is a large room with a marble floor covered with expensive rugs. Embellished tiles with

[85] A description of the sanctuary is in Sykes, *A History of Persia*, II, 235-36. Inscription about the restoration of the tomb by Sanjar in 512/1118. A second inscription is dated 612/1215. ⟨⟨For these inscriptions, see Sykes, "Historical Notes on Khurasan," *JRAS* (1910), pp. 1140-44.⟩⟩

Arabic inscriptions cover the walls. The whole edifice is topped by a gilded cupola, which the pilgrims can see from far away, although its height is, according to Curzon, only eleven fathoms in all. Under the main cupola are, besides the imām's grave, those of the caliph Hārūn al-Rashīd and of ʿAbbās Mīrzā, Fatḥ ʿAlī Shāh's son, who died in 1834.

To the south of the mausoleum there is a magnificent mosque built in 1418 by Shāhrukh's wife Gawhar Shād (the same person who built the above-mentioned mosque of Harāt); this mosque was restored in the seventeenth century.[86] Its courtyard (*ṣaḥn-i Gawhar Shād*) is similar to that of the mausoleum. The Gawhar Shād mosque has only one cupola, and one high arch with a minaret on each side. The cupola is higher and wider than that of the mausoleum; it is embellished with tiles ornamented in blue, green, and orange, but in some places these ornaments have already been destroyed by time. Fraser states that the mosque of Gawhar Shād was the most magnificent edifice he saw in Persia.[87] The third, "new courtyard" (*ṣaḥn-i naw*), is on the eastern side of the mosque and was built by Fatḥ ʿAlī Shāh in the nineteenth century. The plan of all the courtyards and edifices is found in Ṣāniʿ al-Dawla's work and was subsequently used by Yate.[88] Mentioned, moreover, are several madrasas and the library described in 1858 by Khanikoff.[89]

The plain on which Mashhad is located was still in Ferrier's time (thus in 1845), quite bare and barren, a result of incursions by the

[86] The inscription about the construction of the Gawhar-Shād mosque was composed by Bāysonghor in 821/1418 (Sykes, *A History of Persia*, II, 237); the Mahdī, it is said, appears from the *minbar* of this mosque (*ibid.*, I, 45). The architect of the Gawhar-Shād mosque was Qawām al-Dīn Miʿmār Shīrāzī, who died in 842/1439 (according to ʿAbd al-Razzāq); his art is also mentioned by Dawlatshāh, ed. Browne, p. 340.

[87] *Khorasan*, p. 447.

[88] *Khurasan and Sistan*, p. 322. Ground plans of the edifice are in *Maṭlaʿ al-shams*, III, between pp. 144 and 145. The Gawhar-Shād mosque is discussed on pp. 138 ff.; see *ibid.* for inscriptions that tell about the restoration works and about the books that had been donated; among these is one that mentions Shāh ʿAbbās II and the date 1052/1642.

[89] *Mémoire*, pp. 100-102. Wāṣifī, fol. 224a, mentions in Mashhad the madrasa-yi Amīr Walī Bīk. *Ibid.*, fol. 226a: "The baths of Mashhad are the best baths of the inhabited world." The library is a *waqf* by ʿAbbās, who donated to it his Arabic books; cf. Iskandar Munshī, *Taʾrīkh-i ʿĀlam-ārā-yi ʿAbbāsī*, ms., fol. 202b; tr. R. M. Savory (Boulder, Col., 1978), pp. 954-55. A list of the books is also in Ṣanīʿ al-Dawla Muḥammad Ḥasan Khān, *Maṭlaʿ al-shams-i Nāṣirī* (Tehran, 1301-3/1884-6), II, 469 ff.

Uzbeks, Afghans, and Türkmens.[90] This observation might be questioned, however, for Fraser saw in 1822 along the road from Mashhad to Ṭūs many cultivated fields.[91] Now, with the danger of Türkmen raids removed as a result of the occupation of Etek by the Russians, the valley of the Kashaf Rūd is of course under better cultivation. Noteworthy in this same valley above Ṭūs on the road to Qūchān is also the settlement of Rādkān or Raykān, mentioned by the tenth-century geographers;[92] half a farsakh to the southeast of Rādkān there is an old brick tower known as *mīl-i Rādkān* with a conical top. There is a detailed description of this tower, with an illustration, in Ṣāniʿ al-Dawla's book.[93] Inside, the tower has the shape of an octagon. On the outside it consists of thirty-six round [half]-columns; between the columns and the conical top are traces of a Kūfic inscription. In Ṣāniʿ al-Dawla's opinion, this tower may have been the tomb of one of the medieval sultans or important personages, and could be dated to the time of the Būyids, that is, to the tenth and eleventh centuries. Other opinions have been expressed: the traveler O'Donovan believes that this edifice could have been neither a dwelling nor a tomb;[94] nevertheless, Ṣanīʿ al-Dawla's opinion is most probably correct on the count of both its purpose and its dating.[95] This is evident from the close resemblance of its outer appearance to the decagonal tower on the southern bank of the river Gurgān; the latter tower, as we know from its inscription and from historical sources, was beyond any doubt the tomb of the local ruler Qābūs b. Wushmgīr, built during his own lifetime in 397/1006-7 (see below for a description of the ruins of Jurjān)[96]

[90] *Voyages*, I, 223.

[91] *Khorasan*, p. 517.

[92] Iṣṭakhrī, p. 257.

[93] *Maṭlaʿ al-shams-i Nāṣirī*, I, 172 ff. (illustration at p. 173). For a ground plan of the structure and its details see also Jackson, *From Constantinople to the Home of Omar Khayyan*, p. 273.

[94] Curzon, *Persia*, I, 120. ⟨⟨E. O'Donovan, *The Merv Oasis. Travels and Adventures East of the Caspian during the Years 1879-80-81* (London, 1882), pp. 22-24.⟩⟩

[95] Cf. Jackson, *From Constantinople to the Home of Omar Khayyam*, p. 273; Diez, *Churasanische Baudenkmäler*, pp. 43 ff.; M. Van Berchem ⟨⟨"Die Inschriften der Grabtürme," in Diez, *Churasanische Baudenkmäler*, pp. 107 ff.; cf. also Barthold, "Bashnia Kabusa," *Soch.* IV, 266; E. Schroeder, "The Seljuq Period," *Survey of Persian Art*, II, 1,022.⟩⟩

[96] On the tower of Rādkān, near Astarābād, see B. Dorn, "Über die Einfälle der alten Russen in Tabaristan nebst Zugaben über andere von ihnen auf dem Kaspischen Meere und in den anliegenden Ländern ausgeführten Unternehmungen," *Mémoires de l'Académie Impériale des Sciences de St.-Petersbourg*, 7th sér., XXIII/1 (1875);

The Arab geographers describe the roads that connect Nīshāpūr with Harāt, Sarakhs, the shores of the Caspian sea, and western Persia; and across the desert with the southern regions. The road that was always the most important one went from Khurāsān to western Persia; it passed through the district of Bayhaq and its town of Sabzawār and Khusrūjird.[97] Sabzawār still exists and is surrounded by a mud-brick wall; ruins of the citadel are on a hill in the northern part of the town.[98]

Sabzawār was noted in history as one of the centers of Shīʿī fanaticism, and enjoyed this reputation as early as Saljuq times. The Shīʿī dynasty of the Sarbadārids originated there in the fourteenth century; its last representative voluntarily submitted to Tīmūr in 1381.[d] The modern town was built at the beginning of the nineteenth century by the rebellious khan ʿAlī Yār. Fraser erroneously assumed that at some period in the past, down to the beginning of the thirteenth century, Sabzawār and Khusrūjird were one and the same city.[99] Arab geographical sources show that even in the tenth century there was a distance of one farsakh between them,[100] which fully corresponds to the interval between modern Sabzawār and the still standing minaret of Khusrūjird, one of the interesting surviving medieval edifices. As is evident from its Kūfic inscription, it was built under the Saljuqs in 505/1111-2. A drawing of the minaret can be found in Curzon's book.[101]

Diez, *Churasanische Baudenkmäler*, pp. 36 ff.; Van Berchem ⟨⟨"Die Inschriften der Grabtürme," pp. 87 ff.; Barthold, "Bashnia Kabusa," *Soch.* IV, 266 n. 28. For the inscriptions on this monument, see also Herzfeld, "Postsasanidische Inschriften. I. Mīl i Rādkān," *AMI*, IV (1932), 140-46; Henning, "Mitteliranisch," p. 51 n. 1.⟩⟩ ⟦On Qābūs, see Bosworth, *EI*², art. "Ḳābūs b. Wus͟hmagīr b. Ziyār."⟧

[97] For Bayhaq, see Tabarī, II, 1772, line 14, as "the furthest region in Khurāsān and the one closest to Qūmis." For Bayhaq as a Shīʿī center, see also Yaʿqūbī, *Ta'rīkh* (Leiden, 1883), II, 397 ff. ⟨⟨See also Ibn Funduq, *Ta'rīkh-i Bayhaq*, ed. Aḥmad Bahmanyār, Tehran, 1317/1938.⟩⟩ ⟦Aubin, "L'aristocratie urbaine dans l'Iran seldjukide: l'exemple de Sabzavâr," *Mélanges offerts à René Crozet* (Poitiers, 1966), pp. 323-32.⟧

[98] In Sabzawār, there are now some 10,000 to 15,000 inhabitants (Jackson, *From Constantinople to the Home of Omar Khayyam*, p. 22).

[d] J. M. Smith, *The History of the Sarbadār Dynasty, 1336-1481 A.D., and Its Sources* (The Hague, 1970); Aubin, "La fin de l'état sarbadār du Khorassan," *JA*, CCLXII (1974), 95-118.

[99] *Khorasan*, p. 380.

[100] Thus in Maqdisī, p. 318; according to Iṣṭakhrī, p. 284, it is about two farsakhs. In Ibn Rusta, p. 171, Khusrūjird appears as *qaṣabat Bayhaq* and Sabzawār as *qarya nabīla*. Cf. Samʿānī, *Kitāb al-Ansāb*, facs. ed. D. S. Margoliouth, fol. 198b: "Khusrūjird: it is a village in the district of Bayhaq; it used to be its district center, then Sabzawār became the center." Similarly, Yāqūt, *Muʿjam*, II, 441.

[101] *Persia*, I, 270. Similarly in Jackson, *From Constantinople to the Home of Omar*

Further on along this road are mentioned the settlements of Mihr, Mazīnān, and Bahmanābād, all of which still exist. From Bahmanābād, six more farsakhs were reckoned to Asadābād, the westernmost Khurāsānian city. The western border of Khurāsān thus passed near the present settlement of ʿAbbāsābād,[102] founded at the beginning of the seventeenth century by Shāh ʿAbbās the Great for Georgian immigrants, who have long since adopted Islam and the Persian language, although their dialect is said to show traces of their ancestors' tongue. Contiguous with Mazīnān on the east are the extensive ruins of Masnadābād, a town built at the beginning of the nineteenth century by the above-mentioned rebellious khan ʿAlī Yār and demolished after the quelling of his uprising.[103]

The part of Khurāsān that has been described in this chapter has always had prime importance in the history of this region; in the tenth century, even the districts lying on the other side of the mountains that delimit the Nīshāpūr plain on the south, such as the district of Pūsht with its main town of Turshīz, were considered to pertain to Nīshāpūr. The latter's name is now applied to the whole district; the town itself is mentioned either by this name or by the name of Sulṭānābād.[104] As early as the tenth century, this district was noted for its unusual fertility; as a result of its warm climate, fruits ripened there earlier than in other parts of Khurāsān.[105]

Khayyam, p. 218; the height is about 120 feet. For the tower (*minār*), see also *Maṭlaʿ al-shams-i Nāṣirī*, III, 222 ff.

[102] The border of Khurāsān is also different in the *Taʾrīkh-i baʿd-Nādiriyya*, p. 131: "Ṭabas, which is on the border of Khurasan and Iraq." ⟦See Minorsky, *EI*², art. "ʿAbbāsābād."⟧

[103] Cf. Jackson, *From Constantinople to the Home of Omar Khayyam*, p. 226, where there is a reference to Fraser, *Khorasan*, p. 381; Yate, *Khurasan and Sistan*, p. 397.

[104] Turbat-i Ḥaydar to the east of Sulṭānābād.

[105] Maqdisī, p. 318.

CHAPTER VI

Qūmis and Gurgān

One part of the principal road between the present-day settlements of ʿAbbāsābād [on the east] and Lāsgird [on the west] was included by the Arab geographers in the region of Qūmis, which appears, as Κωμισηνή, as early as the work of Isidore of Charax. In the tenth century, Qūmis came within the framework of the possessions of the Buwayhids who, however, paid part of the revenues from this region, as well as from the neighboring Ray—200,000 dinars in all—to the Sāmānids. Clearly, this political boundary was purely artificial and therefore underwent frequent modifications. At the time of the Arab conquest, the eastern portion of Qūmis was part of Khurāsān; Yaʿqūbī still refers to Dāmghān as the first town in Khurāsān.[1]

In the eastern part of Qūmis, between ʿAbbāsābād and Shāhrūd, there seems never to have been any important settlements. Here the last spurs of the Khurāsān mountains descend into the plain; the road passes by the foothills and occasionally through them. These gradually diminishing ridges offered a suitable corridor for Türkmen raids, which ceased only with the conquest of Etek by the Russians. Until that time, it was considered unsafe to cross this stretch without an armed escort; twice a month small military detachments would depart, one eastward from Shāhrūd, one westward from Māzinān; the two would meet in the village of Miyāndasht and exchange their roles; there is in Miyāndasht an old caravanserai built by Shāh ʿAbbās the Great and a new one constructed in a fortresslike fashion from fired brick.

There is a fertile stretch along the river Shāhrūd, which flows from the snowy mountains of Shāh Kūh, a branch of the Alburz chain that separates the Caspian coastland from the Iranian pla-

[1] Yaʿqūbī, *Kitāb al-Buldān*, p. 276. ⟨⟨For the history and monuments of Dāmghān, see now Iqbāl Yaghmāʾī, *Jughrāfiyā-yi taʾrīkhī-yi Dāmghān* (Tehran, 1336/1957); D. N. Wilber, *EI*², art. "Dāmg͟hān."⟩⟩ ⟦For the province of Qūmis, see Bosworth, *EI*², art. "Ḳūmis," and for the region in general (now in the modern administrative district [*farmāndārī-yi kull*] of Simnān) and the town of Dāmghān, see Chahryâr Adle, "Contribution à la géographie historique du Damghan," *Le monde iranien et l'Islam*, I (1971), 69-104.⟧

teau, and that reaches here a height of 13,000 feet. The town of Shāhrūd itself was never of any great significance in the past, and is not mentioned by the tenth-century geographers, who place the post station at Badhash;[2] a settlement by the name of Badasht, three and a half English miles to the east of Shāhrūd, is mentioned by Fraser.[3] The town of Bisṭām, situated somewhat above Shāhrūd in the same fertile river valley, has had greater historical importance. It is believed to have been founded in the sixth century by Bisṭām, governor of Khurāsān, Qūmis, Gurgān, and Ṭabaristān, who in the time of troubles tried to seize the throne.[4] In the ninth century, one of the first Ṣūfī shaykhs, Bāyazīd (more correctly Abū Yazīd Bisṭāmī) lived here;[5] at the time of the Arab geographers, Bisṭām was a modest but prosperous town.[6] Its celebrity is assured to this day by the tomb of the shaykh Abū Yazīd, whom the inhabitants of Bisṭām drove out of their town twelve times; it is related that each time the shaykh would make the following remark: "Blessed is the town in which lives the heretic Bāyazīd!" Ṣanīʿ al-Dawla bitterly remarks that "now they all are worshipers of the shaykh's tomb; although communication with his noble person had been beyond their faculties [in his lifetime], the most intimate kinship unites them with his grave which consists of stone and clay" (". . . *wa aknūn hama muʿtaqid-i qabr u turbat-i ū-yand wa īn az ān-ast ki īshān-rā bā shakhṣ-i sharīf-i ū mujālasatī nabūd ammā bā qabr-i ū ki sang u kulūkh-ast munāsabat-i tamām dārand*").[7]

The existing edifice of the shaykh's mausoleum, like other old buildings of Bisṭām, goes back to the fourteenth century. A detailed description of the mausoleum, together with a drawing of it, is in Ṣanīʿ al-Dawla's book.[8] Inside the building, at a passage from one part to another, is an Arabic inscription indicating the date of the

[2] Ibn Rusta, p. 170; Maqdisī, p. 371.

[3] *Khorasan*, p. 345.

[4] Marquart, *Ērānšahr*, p. 71. ⟨⟨For Bisṭām and its monuments see also M. Streck, *EI*[1], art. "Bisṭām"; Herzfeld, "Khorasan. Denkmalsgeographische Studien zur Kulturgeschichte des Islam in Iran," *Isl.*, XI (1921), 168-69; Iqbāl Yaghmā'ī, *Bisṭām wa Bāyazīd-i Bisṭāmī* (Tehran, 1317/1938).⟩⟩

[5] Biography of Bāyazīd in Farīd al-Dīn ʿAttār, *Tadhkirat al-awliyā'*, ed. R. A. Nicholson (London and Leiden, 1905-1907), I, 194 ff.; cf. Hujwīrī, *Kashf al-maḥjūb*, tr. Nicholson, pp. 106 ff. ⟨⟨For Bāyazīd Bisṭāmī, see also Nicholson, *EI*[1] Suppl., art. "al-Bisṭāmī"; Bertel's, "Proiskhozhdenie sufizma," pp. 32-34, and his "Nūr-al-ʿulūm"; ʿAbd al-Raḥmān Badawī, *Shaṭaḥāt al-Ṣūfiyya (Abū Yazīd Bisṭāmī)* (Cairo, 1944).⟩⟩

[6] Iṣṭakhrī, p. 211; Maqdisī, p. 356.

[7] *Maṭlaʿ al-shams-i Nāṣirī*, I, 78-79. ⟨⟨See also Barthold, *Islam, Soch.* VI, 116.⟩⟩

[8] *Maṭlaʿ al-shams-i Nāṣirī*, I, 69.

construction, 702/1302.[9] The mausoleum is in the southwestern corner of a courtyard that is flanked by a few other buildings; among these is the tomb of one of the ʿAlids, Muḥammad b. Jaʿfar, built in the sixteenth century, and a mosque that is believed to antedate Bāyazīd's mausoleum. This mosque is flanked by a minaret distinctive in that it moves when people stand on its top. Fraser explains this by the fact that the tower is built with very thin bricks and leans slightly sideways: this, in his opinion, does not adversely affect the solidity of its structure.[10] Near the mausoleum is also an edifice in which a dried mummy is kept; Fraser was told that it is the body of the founder of the town, Bisṭām Mīrzā. A passage leads from this courtyard into a madrasa, in it there is a beautiful arch with an inscription indicating the date of the construction: 713/1313.[11] From among the older monuments of Bisṭām, the Friday mosque (716/1316-17) is also noteworthy.

Despite its shrines, Bisṭām eventually had to fall behind Shāhrūd, which is situated on the main route from western to eastern Persia, at a point where this route is joined by almost all the roads from the north. Shāhrūd is separated from Astarābād and the southeastern shore of the Caspian sea by mountains that are crossed by high but not particularly difficult passes; a road goes from Shāhrūd to the northern part of Khurāsān through Bisṭām, Jājarm, and the valley of Isfarāyin, where in the Middle Ages there used to be a town of the same name.[12] This Isfarāyin was destroyed by Tīmūr in 1381 and once more by the Afghans in 1731, so that today only ruins are left; they are called Shahr-i Bilqīs or Shahr-i Sabā', and have been described by Yate.[13] This road was also joined in Isfarāyin by another that led from Nīshāpūr to the banks of the Gurgān and the city of Gurgān, capital of ancient Hyrcania; Gurgān was also linked by a road with Bisṭām. Finally, a road went from Bisṭām through Jājarm toward the northern border of Khurāsān, and to

[9] The inscription is quoted by Ṣanīʿ al-Dawla; see also his description of the edifice and its dimensions.

[10] *Khorasan*, p. 337.

[11] The inscription with a date; there is also the name of the shaykh, Muḥammad b. Faḍl Allāh b. Bāyazīd, who built this edifice, and the name of the craftsman, Muḥammad b. al-Ḥasan al-Jaṣṣāṣ (the word al-Jaṣṣāṣ means "the artisan who prepares gypsum, plaster"). Cf. the opinion of Ṣanīʿ al-Dawla, *Maṭlaʿ al-shams-i Nāṣirī*, I, 74.

[12] Cf. Juwaynī, for Isfarāyin to the north of Sabzawār.

[13] *Khurasan and Sistan*, pp. 378-80. ⟦For the district (now a *shahristān* of the province of Khurāsān, with its chief town at Miyānābād) and medieval town of Isfarāyin, see Bosworth, *EI*², s.v.⟧

the banks of the Atrek and into the Kurdish khanates of Bujnurd, Qūchān and Daragaz; these khanates are still called Kurdistān in Fraser's book.[14] Thus if one can surmise that the migration of the Aryans into Persia proceeded through Etek and the basin of the Gurgān river, it was in the area around Bisṭām and Shāhrūd that this movement would have joined the modern high road. Curzon correctly observes that an army that has seized Astarābād, Bisṭām, and Shāhrūd has *ipso facto* cut Khurāsān off from western Persia.[15]

In antiquity, Hyrcania also encompassed the eastern portion of modern Māzandarān; by the time of the Arab geographers, however, the border between Ṭabaristān, as Māzandarān was then called, and Jurjān or Gurgān passed not far to the west of Astarābād. In terms of climatic conditions, the area between the Alburz, Gurgān, and the Caspian coast differs fundamentally from Khurāsān; here, as in other Caspian regions of Persia, precipitation is very high, so that the region has luscious vegetation.[16] Fraser, who reached the banks of the Gurgān coming from Bujnurd on the east, relates in glowing terms the impression that the change made on him.[17] The earthen walls and flat earthen roofs of Khurāsānī dwellings, whose color fully corresponds to that of the soil, were replaced by constructions that were built chiefly of wooden pales held together with clay, and which had wooden floors; household utensils were also made from wood. On the other hand, the humidity that condenses in the forests makes the climate of this region quite harmful to the health. Furthermore, the country is totally open to inroads by nomads from the north, against whom fortifications were built as early as Sāsānid times.

The Arabs conquered Gurgān much later than Khurāsān (in fact, only in 717 A.D.). Until the conquest of Gurgān, travel through Qūmis was considered unsafe, and even the governors of Khurāsān appointed by the caliph usually preferred to take the southern route through Fārs and Kirmān; only Qutayba b. Muslim, in 705,

[14] *Khorasan*, p. 249.

[15] *Persia*, I, 189.

[16] Between Gurgān and the mountains there is a lovely plain with magnificent forests; the climate is much healthier than in Māzandarān, and the soil is better. Only the area to the south of the river is irrigated; that to the north cannot be irrigated because the river flows in a deep gorge (letter from A. D. Kalmykov). ⟪For the pre-Islamic monuments of Gurgān, see Vanden Berghe, *Archéologie de l'Iran ancien*, pp. 7-14, 142-44; for the history of the region, see Ḥamza b. Yūsuf al-Sahmī, *Ta'rīkh-i Jurjān*, ed. Niẓām al-Dīn, Hyderabad, Dcn., 1950.⟫ ⟦R. Hartmann-Boyle, *EI*², art. "Gurgān."⟧

[17] Fraser, *Khorasan*, p. 610.

realized the journey through Ray and Qūmis.[18] In the time of the Arab geographers, Gurgān was the capital of the local dynasty of the Ziyārids, whose founder, Mardāwīj b. Ziyār (928-935) conquered a part of Persia and was beginning to dream of a restoration of the throne of the Sāsānids when he was killed by his slaves.[19] His successors had to submit to the mightier dynasties of the Būyids, the Ghaznawids and ultimately the Saljuqs; in the second half of the eleventh century, the dynasty was annihilated by the notorious sect of the Ismāʿīlīs or Assassins.[a] The city of Gurgān thus no longer had any political importance after Mardāwīj, but it remained, judging from descriptions by the Arab geographers, the largest city of the Caspian regions. Iṣṭakhrī speaks with enthusiasm of the fertility in this country, where the growing of crops of warm as well as cold climates converged, where it snowed in winter but where nonetheless palms could grow.[20] Gurgān, together with Ṭabaristān, was also renowned for its silk.

The city of Gurgān, Jurjān in Arabic, straddled the river of the same name; the river divided it into two parts,[21] Shahristān and Bakrābād,[22] which were linked by a bridge. Shahristān was on the right bank, Bakrābād on the left.[23] As early as the tenth century, the city went into a decline caused by chronic wars between the Sāmānids and the Būyids, a struggle in which the Ziyārids kept submitting to whichever side was winning. To the epoch of the Ziyārids also pertains the tomb of Qābūs b. Wushmgīr, built in 397/1006-7;[24] the edifice has been described by Fraser,[25] Yates,[26] and, in greater detail, by I. T. Poslavskii.[27] Still clearly visible today is a

[18] Ṭabarī, II, 1,322.

[19] Ibn al-Athīr, *al-Kāmil fi 'l-ta'rīkh*, ed. C. J. Tornberg (Leiden, 1851-1876), VIII, 226. ⟦W. Madelung, "Minor Dynasties of Northern Iran," in *Cambridge History of Iran*, IV, pp. 212-13; H. Busse, "Iran under the Būyids," *ibid.*, pp. 254-57.⟧

[a] See Bosworth, "On the Chronology of the Ziyārids in Gurgān and Ṭabaristān," *Isl.*, XL (1964), 25-34.

[20] Iṣṭakhrī, p. 213.

[21] In Ibn Ḥawqal, p. 213, the eastern and western sides. The city of Gurgān did not yet exist at the time of the Arab conquest: Ṭabarī, II, 1,324, line 13. Cf. the cities of antiquity and the Middle Ages in Forbiger, *Handbuch*, II, 571.

[22] Maḥalla-yi Bakrābād in the romance about Abū Muslim Ṭarṭūsī, ms. Asiatic Museum 280ae, fol. 121a, the passage about Shāh Ṭāliba-yi Bakrābādī.

[23] Ibn Ḥawqal, p. 273. According to Maqdisī, p. 358, the *Shahristān* had had nine gates. ⟦Abū Dulaf, *Travels in Iran*, p. 58, #57.⟧

[24] In Sykes, *A History of Persia*, II, 93, erroneously 375 = 997.

[25] *Khorasan*, pp. 612-14.

[26] *Khurasan and Sistan*, pp. 240-48.

[27] ⟨⟨Poslavskii, "Iz poezdki," pp. 184-90, see also Barthold, "Bashnia Kabusa"; A. Godard, "Gurgān and the Gunbād-i Qābūs," *Survey of Persian Art*, II, 967-74,

Kūfic inscription that is quoted by Samʿānī, who visited this monument in the twelfth century.[28] The harbor of Abaskūn served as the port of Gurgān; it was probably situated at the estuary of the Gurgān river on the site of the present-day settlement of Gümüshtepe.[b] Alongside Abaskūn, Astarābād is also mentioned, not as the trading center that it is today, but as a manufacturing town; the inhabitants were renowned for their mastery in silk weaving. Today only woolen rugs were woven in Astarābād,[29] but more widely known are other kinds of industry that did not exist there in the Middle Ages, in particular, soap boiling and the manufacture of gunpowder.

To the north of Abaskūn, on the eastern shore of the Caspian sea, there was only one inhabited place, Dihistān, six days' journey from Abaskūn. Here was the border between Muslim domains and those of the nomads, the Ghuzz Turks. For this reason there was a *ribāṭ* here; in this case the term was used in its original sense of a military post at a frontier. The foundation of Dihistān was attributed to the Parthians; European scholars usually connect the word Dihistān with the name of the Δάαι or Dahae, a nation that, according to the classical geographers, lived to the east of the Caspian sea. According to Ṭabarī, there was at a distance of five farsakhs from Dihistān an island,[30] or, more exactly, a peninsula (as in the work of the anonymous tenth-century Persian geographer)[31] on which a certain Turkish prince lived. Iṣṭakhrī[32] and Ibn Ḥawqal[33] knew Dihistān only as a minor settlement on the seacoast[34] inhab-

---

and the bibliographies to these works.⟩⟩ ⟦A.D.H. Bivar, *EI*², art. "Gunbadh-i Ḳābūs."⟧

[28] Barthold, *Turkestan*, pt. 1, p. 63. Kufic script; see B. Moritz, *EI*¹, art. "Arabia. d. Arabic Writing": in Persia there are no monuments with this script. The inscription of the Chifteh minaret in Erzurum is apocryphal (351/962-3), and the earliest monuments in Kūfic are the tomb of Yūsuf b. Quṣayyir (557/1162) and the mausoleum of Mu'min Khātūn (582/1106-7) in Nakhchevān. ⟨⟨Cf. also Barthold, "Bashnia Kabusa," *Soch.* IV, 263 and n. 12.⟩⟩

[b] For Abaskūn, see Minorsky, *EI*², s.v.

[29] Rugs are no longer made in Astarābād; in mountain villages woolen kilims are made from a thick but smooth fabric. In the city itself there are two ancient citadels, with a dirt-filled underground passage between them. ⟨⟨For Astarābād, see also Streck, *EI*¹, s.v.; H. L. Rabino, *Mázandarán and Astarábád*; R. N. Frye, *EI*², s.v.; and bibliographies there.⟩⟩

[30] Ṭabarī, II, 1323.

[31] *Ḥudūd al-ʿālam*, fol. 5b ⟦tr. Minorsky, p. 60⟧.

[32] Iṣṭakhrī, p. 219.

[33] Ibn Ḥawqal, p. 277.

[34] This is an error, arising from a confusion of the *ribāṭ* of Dihistān with the place called Dihistānān-Sūr (this error also in Le Strange, *The Lands*, p. 379). See also

ited by fishermen; on the other hand, in Maqdisī's description, tenth-century Dihistān was a district consisting of a whole series of settlements, twenty-four in number.[35] The center of this district or *rustāq* was the town of Ākhur, situated on the right-hand side of a road that went toward the *ribāṭ* at the frontier; the minaret of Ākhur was visible from far away. The *ribāṭ* used to be surrounded by a wall, but even by Maqdisī's time it had been demolished on the order of the government, and the former frontier outpost became a peaceful, flourishing settlement. Many bazaars and mosques were to be found there; from among the latter, Maqdisī singles out the old mosque with wooden columns and another with a minaret; this mosque was, in contrast to the rest, not of the Ḥanafī but of the Shāfiʿī school. Until the question of how much the eastern shoreline of the Caspian sea has changed in the course of the last millennium is answered, we shall not be able to pinpoint the whereabouts of this frontier outpost of Muslim territory. Historical sources about this area are exceedingly scant; we do not know when Dihistān ceased to exist and when the last vestiges of Persian culture and urban civilization disappeared from here. There are traces along the Atrek[36] of an extensive irrigation system, but contemporary explorers such as Poslavskii admit the possibility of artificial irrigation here only under the condition that some time in the past there used to be in the Atrek, Sumbar, and Chandyr rivers incomparably more water than today, and that the water did not have the bitter-salty taste it has now.[37] A change in the course of the Atrek is also assumed on the basis of the site of a city whose ruins are known by the name of Mashhad-i Miṣrīyān, that is, "place of the martyrdom of the Egyptians" (on maps it often appears as Mastorian).[38] These ruins were described at the beginning of the 1830s by the traveler A. Conolly,[39] and in greater detail, together

---

Barthold, *Oroshenie*, p. 33, *Soch.* III, 122. In the romance about Abū Muslim Ṭarṭūsī, ms. Asiatic Museum 280 ae, fol. 229a, the names are Dihistan and Bāz.r.

[35] Maqdisī, pp. 358-59. ⟨⟨Cf. Barthold, *Oroshenie, Soch.* III, 122.⟩⟩ ⟦For Dihistān, see *Ḥudūd al-ʿālam*, tr. p. 133, comm. pp. 385-86; B. Spuler, *EI*², s.v.⟧

[36] Atrek, cf. Maḥmūd Kāshgharī, *Dīwān lughāt al-Turk*, ed. Kilisli Muʿallim Rifʿat (Istanbul, 1333-5/1915-7), I, 93: a Ghuzz word that means *al-ashqar min al-rijāl* (of men, "ruddy, handsome, blond, or red-haired").

[37] ⟨⟨Artificial irrigation seems to have appeared in Dihistān as early as the middle of the second millennium B.C., but around the middle of the first millennium B.C. it fell into decay; see V. Masson, "Arkheologicheskie raboty," p. 67 (map); *idem*, *Margiana*, p. 97.⟩⟩

[38] Mashhad-i Miṣrīyān in Muḥammad Mahdī Khān Astarābādī, *Ta'rīkh-i Nādirī*, p. 67, concerning the events of 1732. ⟦Minorsky, *EI*¹, art. "Meshhed-i Miṣriyān."⟧

[39] *Journey to the North of India, Overland from England, through Russia, Persia and Afghanistan* (London, 1838), pp. 76-77.

with a plan, by A. M. Konshin.[40] The city occupied an area of 120 desiatinas [that is, 324 acres], and was surrounded by a pentagonal wall built from fired brick, with bastions on its southern side. In the center were two tall minarets pertaining to a stuccoed mosque, which is well preserved; at the city's two extremities were visible traces of tall, arched gates with blue tiles of the kind that occur today in Persian royal palaces. By the eastern gate stood another large white mosque, which is also well preserved. Local tradition attributes the destruction of the city to the Kalmucks, who appeared in these parts at the end of the sixteenth and beginning of the seventeenth century. A canal from the Atrek, fifty versts long, was led to the city. These ruins are so far from the present-day coast that it is hard to guess whether they are in any way related to Dihistān of the tenth century, which consisted, as we have seen, of a group of settlements, of which at least the principal one lay immediately on the coast.[41] The extant ruins of the city pertain, as can be seen from their description, to a relatively recent date.[42] Historical sources do not discuss, as far as we know, the question of when the city of Dihistān ceased to exist or whether it was destroyed by the Kalmucks.[43]

In the tenth century, there were no large towns in Qūmis, although the cotton and fur textiles manufactured there enjoyed wide distribution. The largest city of the region was Dāmghān, but even it is referred to by Maqdisī as a minor town.[44] Between Dāmghān and another town, Simnān, there were in the Middle Ages, just as today, two roads: Ibn Rusta describes the direct route through Akhuwān as the post road (it is still in active use today);[45] Iṣṭakhrī as well as the other tenth-century geographers describe a circuitous route through the settlement of Frat.[46] There are medieval minarets in Dāmghān and Simnān (two in Dāmghān[47] and one in

[40] Konshin, *Raz"iasnenie*, pp. 152-53. ⟨⟨For the ruins of Mashhad-i Miṣrīyān, see also Barthold, *Oroshenie*, *Soch.* III, 122 ff.⟩⟩

[41] ⟨⟨Cf. *ibid.*, p. 127 n. 34.⟩⟩

[42] There is a mosque with an inscription of the Khwārazmshāh Muḥammad (1200-1220), see Semenov, "Nadpisi na portale."

[43] ⟨⟨Cf. Barthold, *Oroshenie*, *Soch.* III, 124-26.⟩⟩

[44] Maqdisī, p. 355. ⟦Abū Dulaf, *Travels in Iran*, tr. p. 57. #55; Lockhart, *Persian Cities*, pp. 87-93. In about 1950 Dāmghān's population was approximately 10,000 (*Farhang*, III, 116).⟧

[45] Ibn Rusta, pp. 169-70.

[46] Iṣṭakhrī, pp. 215-16. ⟦For Simnān, see Abū Dulaf, *Travels in Iran*, tr. pp. 56-57, #54, comm. p. 104.⟧

[47] Pictures of both in the *Safar-nāma . . . ba-Khurāsān*, pp. 203-204, one near the Masjid-i Chihil Sutūn (construction of Muʿāwinī?), the other near the Masjid-i Jāmiʿ;

Simnān[48]), which architecturally resemble the minaret of Khusrūjird. The area is also noteworthy because the capital of Parthia, which is known to us only under its Greek name Ἑκατόμπυλος, Hekatompylos, that is, "The City of a Hundred Gates," used to be here. The exact location of this city remains a matter of debate; Tomaschek follows the opinion of one of his predecessors, Schindler, according to whom Hekatompylos lay in the center of a triangle formed by Dāmghān and the settlements of Frat and Gūsha.[49]

---

see also in Jackson, *From Constantinople to the Home of Omar Khayyam*, pp. 147, 167 ff., 172. ⟦The minarets mentioned here are presumably those of the Tārī(k)-Khāna mosque (basically eighth-century, minaret from the eleventh century). See A. Godard, "Les anciennes mosquées de l'Iran," *AI*, I (1936), 187 ff.; Sylvia Matheson, *Persia; an Archaeological Guide* (London, 1972), pp. 193-94.⟧

[48] The Masjid-i Shāh in Simnān is a construction of Fatḥ ʿAlī Shāh (*Safar-nāma . . . ba-Khurāsān*, p. 213); the *ark u ʿimārat* were built in the same reign by the shāh's son Ḥājjī Bahāʾ al-Dawla, *ibid.*, p. 212); description of the bazaar (p. 213) and of the surroundings (p. 210). For Qūmis, see *ibid.*, p. 207. On the road from Dāmghān to Mīrābād (three farsakhs), approximately halfway, one sees (through the *dūrbīn* ⟦telescope⟧) the fortress of Girdkūh, see *ibid.*, pp. 204, 206-207. The fortress is also visible from the road from Mīrābād to Gūsh. In 658/1260 Girdkūh was not yet taken (see Juzjānī, tr. Raverty, II, 1,208-11). For Girdkūh, see also Rashīd al-Dīn, ed. Quatremère, pp. 212, 278 (according to Quatremère, p. 212, twenty years after 1256, this fortress was still in the hands of the Ismāʿīlīs). Cf. also Yāqūt, *Muʿjam*, II, 539 (Yāqūt on the way to Khurāsān in 613/1216-7: "He who stands in Dāmghān sees it in the middle of the mountains"). One day's journey from Dāmghān to Girdkūh. According to Ḥamd Allāh Mustawfī Qazwīnī, it is three farsakhs, cf. Le Strange, *The Lands*, p. 365. For the road from Simnān to Dāmghān, see Jackson, *From Constantinople to the Home of Omar Khayyam*, p. 153. The caravanserai of Shāh ʿAbbās the Great and the stone *ribāṭ* of Anūshirwān (pp. 156 ff.), a square of 45 yards' length on each side. ⟨⟨See also Kramers, *EI*¹, art. "Semnān."⟩⟩ ⟦The medieval minaret mentioned here is presumably that of the Masjid-i Jāmiʿ (eleventh century). See Matheson, *Persia*, pp. 190-91; Ch. Adle, "Le minaret du Masjed-e Jâmeʿ de Semnân," *Studia iranica*, IV (1975), 177-86.⟧

[49] Tomaschek, *Zur historischen Topographie*, I, 223. ⟨⟨The best synopsis of the classical sources regarding this city is still the article by A. D. Mordtmann, "Hekatompylos. Ein Beitrag zur vergleichenden Geographie Persiens," *SB Bayr. AW*, I (1869), 497-536.⟩⟩ ⟦The site of Hekatompylos has been identified with virtual certainty by J. Hansman as lying at the modern spot called Shahr-i Qūmis to the southwest of Dāmghān near Gūsha/Qūsha on the Simnān road. See his "The Problem of Qūmis," *JRAS* (1968), pp. 111-39; *idem* and D. Stronach, "Excavations at Shahr-i Qūmis, 1967," *JRAS* (1970), pp. 29-62; *eidem*, "Excavations at Shahr-i Qūmis, Iran," *National Geographical Society Research Reports, 1970 Projects* (Washington, D.C., 1979); Matheson, *Persia*, pp. 191-92; Georgina Herrmann, *The Iranian Revival* (Oxford, 1977), pp. 36-38. A full account of the extensive work undertaken by the British Institute of Persian Studies at Shahr-i Qūmis has not yet appeared.⟧

CHAPTER VII

Ray and Hamadān

THE western limit of Qūmis was considered to be the station Ra's al-Kalb, in the low mountain spurs to the west of Lāsgird; this place was separated from the fertile district of Khuwār[1] (the Χόαρα of Ptolemy and Χοαρηνή of Isidore of Charax)[2] by a salt desert in which the village of Dih-i Namak or Diz-i Namak, the Qaṣr al-Milḥ of the Arabs, is located. The chief settlement of the district of Khuwār now bears the Turkish name Qïshlaq ("winter quarters").[3] Travelers describe the guard towers and walls that until recently served as protection from incursions by the Turkomans; one can see from Ibn Rusta's account that such towers[4] were there as early as the beginning of the tenth century.[5] The district of Khuwār is separated from Ray by a mountain passage; this passage, now wider, now narrower, winds its way in helicoid fashion through the mountain chain; it is, in most scholars' opinion, identical with the "Caspian Gates" of the ancients, through which Alexander the Great passed in his pursuit of Bessus. Ibn Rusta counts three farsakhs from the western end of this passage to the village Afrīdūn, and from there nine more to the city of Ray.[6]

[1] Khuwār, according to Yāqūt, *Muʿjam*, II, 479, was a large town ("one of the districts of al-Rayy"), but when he passed through it at the beginning of 1217 it was in decay. Khuwār is a town at the western limit of Qūmis; see Le Strange, *The Lands*, pp. 367 ff., as well as Ibn Ḥawqal, pp. 269-70, and Maqdisī, p. 258.

[2] Choarene as a part of Parthia, see Forbiger, *Handbuch*, II, 549.

[3] For Qïshlaq and its environs, see *Safar-nāma . . . ba-Khurāsān*, pp. 218-19, 222-23; from Qïshlaq, one-and-a-half farsakhs to the "entrance of Khuwār," and a further two farsakhs to Aywān Kayf (it is mentioned also by Ḥamd Allāh Mustawfī Qazwīnī, *Nuzhat al-qulūb*), from there six (or seven to eight) farsakhs to Khātūnābād. Concerning Aywān Kayf, see also Jackson, *From Constantinople to the Home of Omar Khayyam*, pp. 123 ff. (ruins of Qalʿa-yi Mādar and Qalʿa-yi Qīz).

[4] *Ḥiṣn mithl al-manāra.*

[5] Ibn Rusta, p. 169.

[6] These nine farsakhs through the Sawād al-Ray (the place is irrigated, the canals comprising *hashtādh rūdhān*), then one more hour, then steppes. To Ray by the Sawād al-Ray, seven farsakhs from Q.sṭāna, description of villages on both the right and left sides (Ibn Rusta, pp. 168-70). Khushkrūdh before Ray. According to *idem*, p. 169, from Afrīdūn to Khuwār, eight farsakhs, of which the last five through a ravine.

Ray, ancient Raga, was one of the earliest cities of Iran; Raga, a city in Media, is already mentioned in Darius's inscriptions of the sixth century B.C. Because of its antiquity, it had the nickname Shaykh al-Bilād or, like Balkh, Umm al-Bilād.[7] Subsequently, the Seleucids founded next to the mountain passage itself the town of Charax, the medieval Arazi,[8] where the Parthian king Phraates I in the first half of the second century A.D. resettled the people of Mardoi.[9] Ray was conquered by the Arabs in the seventh century, and sometimes served as residence of governors who were in charge of the entire eastern half of Iran, including Khurāsān. One such governor was the future caliph Mahdī (father of Hārūn al-Rashīd), stationed here as governor during the caliphate of his father Manṣūr. He developed the city and named it after himself, al-Muḥammadiyya; this name is often found on the coins struck by Mahdī while he was heir presumptive.[a] At the time of the tenth-century geographers, Ray was a considerable town, although it remained behind Nīshāpūr in terms of size and wealth.[10] Like other large towns, Ray consisted of a *quhandiz*, a *shahristān*, and a *rabaḍ*; the Friday mosque, built by Mahdī, stood, as in Samarqand and Bukhārā, between the citadel and the *shahristān*.[11] Ibn Rusta says that

[7] Cf. Dīnawarī, *al-Akhbār al-ṭiwāl*, ed. W. Guirgass and I. J. Kratschkowski (Leiden, 1888-1912), p. 40, regarding the construction of Ray under the Sāsānid Fīrūz in the fifth century. See also Ṭabarī, tr. Nöldeke, p. 123. For Ragae, see Strabo, #524.

[8] In Ibn al-Faqīh, p. 269, Azārī, twelve farsakhs from Ray, on the road to Khuwār. The citadel of Ray, al-Z.y.n.b.dī (Ibn al-Faqīh, p. 269, see Marquart, *Ērānšahr*, p. 124); Qalʿat al-Farrukhān. Friday mosque at the foot of the cliff. For the fortress of Zaybandī (or Zaynabdī) see Yāqūt, *Muʿjam*, II, 895; IV, 431 (where it is al-Zabīdiyya), also Balādhurī, p. 219. Cf. Le Strange, *The Lands*, p. 215; Jackson, *From Constantinople to the Home of Omar Khayyam*, p. 131 (*ibid.* for the clash between the Afghans and Nādir Shāh, after Mahdī Khān, *Taʾrīkh-i Nādirī*, p. 36); Jackson, *Persia Past and Present*, p. 432 (Rei-bandi). ⟨⟨See also Barthold, *ZVORAO*, XVII, 104; *Soch.* III, 279.⟩⟩

[9] Tomaschek, *Zur historischen Topographie*, I, 221.

[a] The new mint name of al-Muḥammadiyya, instead of al-Ray, first appears in 148/765 and continues to be used until 407/1016-7, that is, until just before the Ghaznawid conquest of the town from the Buwayhids in 420/1029; see G. C. Miles, *The Numismatic History of Ray* (New York, 1938), pp. 31 ff. Al-Muḥammadiyya was properly the town below the citadel.

[10] Maqdisī, p. 391.

[11] According to Iṣṭakhrī, p. 208, in the *shahristān*; in Maqdisī, p. 391, "on the side of the city enclosed within the citadel"; in Ibn Rusta, p. 168, the fortress was in front of the mosque. The outer and inner city, in addition the *rabaḍ*, bazaars in it; cf. Ibn al-Faqīh, p. 269. Story in Ṭabarī, I, 2,655 about the destruction of old Ray and construction of a new one. The taxes of Ray, according to Ibn al-Faqīh, p. 270, were twelve million dirhams up to Maḥmūd, ten million after him. Under the Mongols, seven hundred tūmāns = seven million dinars or forty-two million dirhams.

the citadel was on a steep hill and that from the top of this hill a view opened up over the entire city.[12] The length and breadth of Ray equaled, according to some reports, one farsakh;[13] according to others, one and one-half farsakhs.[14] Both the citadel and the *shahristān* were in the tenth century abandoned by the inhabitants, whose life, as in other commercial and manufacturing towns, completely shifted to the *rabaḍ*, where there were many bazaars. The chief market was called Rūda, after the name of the small river that flowed through it. Besides the water of two small rivers, the inhabitants used well water. The district was famous for its fertility and warm climate because it was protected from northerly winds; at the same time, however, the climate of Ray, like the present climate of Tehran, was considered very harmful to health, especially in summer. One could see the volcano of Damāwand, 5,900 meters high, from any part of the city and even from a considerable distance further south. The tenth-century sources do not report it as active, but smoke was seen rising from its top at all times.[15] As is known, Damāwand is reputed in Persian mythology to be the place where the evil Ḍaḥḥāk, defeated by Farīdūn, was imprisoned.[b]

Ray suffered in the eleventh century from incursions of the Ghuzz, but it recovered under the Saljuqs; the founder of this dynasty's might, Ṭoghrïl Beg, was buried here.[16] The fatal blow was struck in the Mongol invasion of 1220. According to Yāqūt, however, Ray had already become almost depopulated before that date as a result of factional strife between the Ḥanafīs and Shāfiʿīs.[17] Much earlier,

[12] Ibn Rusta, p. 169. ⟦Abū Dulaf, *Travels in Iran*, tr. p. 51, #48, cf. comm. p. 100, mentions the castle built by the supporter of the former Ṭāhirid governors, Rāfiʿ b. Harthama, in the late ninth century, but in ruins at the time of his visit two or three generations later, and also the nearby mountain of Ṭabarak, with its pre-Islamic buildings and fire temples, much mentioned in subsequent Būyid, Ghaznawid, and Saljuq times (see below, note 24).⟧

[13] Maqdisī, p. 391.

[14] Iṣṭakhrī, p. 207.

[15] *Ibid.*, p. 210. ⟦Abū Dulaf, *Travels in Iran*, tr. pp. 51-53, #51, climbed Damāwand in order to check popular reports that a rebellious demon had been imprisoned in the mountain by Sulaymān b. Dāwūd, and found vapor rising from a sulphurous spring.⟧

[b] See M. Streck, *EI*[2], s.v.

[16] Ray was considered a capital also under Alp Arslān, al-Bundārī, *Zubdat al-nuṣra*, ed. M. T. Houtsma, in *Recueil de textes relatifs à l'historie des Seldjoucides*, II (Leiden, 1889), 36, 41; and Malikshāh (*ibid.*, p. 55). Enthronement of his son in Iṣfahān (*ibid.*, p. 82) where Malikshāh, too, often stayed (pp. 55, 71); *ibid.*, p. 85, remnants of *al-dawla al-Khātūniyya*. For the treasures in the fortress of Iṣfahān, see *ibid.*, p. 156.

[17] *Muʿjam*, II, 893-94. Yāqūt, *ibid.*, about employment of blue tiles in Ray. In the

Maqdisī mentions in the tenth century the rivalry of these two groups and states that at the Friday mosque the function of imām was discharged one day by a Ḥanafī, the next day by a Shāfiʿī.[18] In the thirteenth century, the dissensions assumed the character of armed struggle; Yāqūt's narrative indicates that one legal school predominated among the city dwellers, the other among the villagers: this would suggest that the rivalry had economic rather than religious causes.[19]

After the Mongol calamity, Ray did not recover its former importance. One of the nine districts or *tūmāns* into which Persian ʿIrāq,[20] that is, ancient Media, was divided under the Mongols was Ray, together with its local towns and villages,[21] but the chief city of this *tūmān* was not Ray but Warāmīn, which now also lies in ruins. As a village, Warāmīn is already mentioned by the tenth-century geographers.[22] The district was administered under the Mongols by special hereditary governors.[23] Ray was partly restored under the reign of the il-khan Ghazan (1295-1304); also built (or rather restored) was the fortress called Ṭabarak in the northern part of the city at the foot of the mountain, which had already existed in the twelfth century.[24] The inhabitants of the district were

---

tenth century, the buildings were from clay and wood; in Yāqūt's time, the greater part of the city was ruined, but the city walls were untouched.

18 Maqdisī, p. 391.

19 According to Mīrkhwānd (D'Ohsson, *Histoire des Mongols*, I, 249), the Shāfiʿīs invited the Mongols against the Ḥanafīs. Participation of the Shīʿīs; in the midst of the *ahl-i rustāq*, the majority were Shīʿīs; a small number of Ḥanafīs, but no Shāfiʿīs at all. Cf. Ibn Ḥawqal, pp. 270, 289; Yāqūt, *Muʿjam*, II, 572, 833, 893-94; Le Strange, *The Lands*, p. 216. ⟦For this general phenomenon of factional strife, *ʿaṣabiyya*, in the towns of Iran, see Cl. Cahen, *Mouvements populaires et autonomisme urbain dans l'Asie musulmane du Moyen Age* (Leiden, 1959), originally in *Arabica*, V-VI [1958-1959]; and for Khurāsān in particular, Bosworth, *The Ghaznavids*, pp. 163-71.⟧

20 For the origin of the name, see Le Strange, *The Lands*, pp. 185 ff. In Yāqūt, *Muʿjam*, II, 15, s.v. "al-Jibāl." In the election law of 1902, ʿIrāq was a district of Sulṭānābād, as it is also on the map in Jackson, *Zoroaster*. ⟦For the town and district (*shahristān*) of Sulṭānābād, see Minorsky, *EI*¹, s.v.; the present name for these is now Arāk (< ʿIrāq), see *Farhang*, II, 6. The town's prosperity increased considerably after 1938 when the Persian Gulf-Tehran railway, which passed through it, was completed. In 1976, the population of the town of Arāk was 114,507 (*Le monde iranien et l'Islam*, IV [1976-1977], 242.)⟧

21 Mustawfī, *Nuzhat al-qulūb*, extract in Schefer's ed. of Niẓām al-Mulk's *Siyāsat-nāma* (Paris, 1897), pp. 166-72 ⟦ed. Le Strange, pp. 52-55, tr. *idem*, pp. 58-60⟧.

22 Iṣṭakhrī, p. 209.

23 Warāmīn as a small town, according to Yāqūt, *Muʿjam*, IV, 918, some thirty miles from Ray on the road to Iṣfahān. Iṣṭakhrī concerning the dimensions of the settlements.

24 Ibn al-Athīr, ed. Tornberg, IX, 268. In Ẓahīr al-Dīn Marʿashī, *Taʾrīkh-i Ṭa-*

at that time mostly Shīʿīs, and only a few villages remained aligned behind the Ḥanafīs. After the collapse of the Il-Khanids, Ray, as in the tenth century, shared the lot of the Caspian provinces and became part of the possessions of the amīr Walī, who had established his control over Astarābād and Māzandarān. In 1384 Walī was beaten near Astarābād by Tīmūr, whose armies in that same year took Ray without resistance. The city was thus spared calamity under Tīmūr. Ray is mentioned several times in connection with Tīmūr's campaigns, but the district rather than the town is meant in this context. Clavijo, who passed through it in 1404, found only ruins on the place of the former Ray.[25] The preference that the population had acquired for Warāmīn can be partly explained by the supply of water in the latter, which benefited from the most substantial watercourse in the district, the Jāj Rūd. Besides Warāmīn, however, Tehran, the present capital of Iran, to which the residents of Ray and Warāmīn must have moved, was already an important city by the fifteenth century.

The ruins of Ray have been described more than once, by R. Ker Porter in the 1820s among others.[26] The plan of the ruins that he made will never lose its relevance, because the remnants of the buildings and walls are no longer as evident today as they were in his time;[27] the inhabitants of Tehran have used and sometimes still use the bricks of the ancient buildings as materials for the construction of their own dwellings. The most notable feature among these ruins is, of course, the citadel, which stands on a steep cliff; Ferrier states that the local inhabitants call this cliff al-Burj, "the

---

baristān va Rūyān va Māzandarān, ed. B. Dorn (St. Petersburg, 1850), p. 15, *qalʿa-yi Ṭabarak*, a stronghold on the *tapa-yi buzurg* built by Manūchihr, the earliest of all the fortresses; *ṭabar* = "mountain" in Ṭabaristānī. Also in Yāqūt, *Muʿjam*, III, 507 ff. *Ibid.* for the destruction of the fortress by Sultan Ṭoghrïl in 588/1192. His relationship with Qïzïl-Arslān (killed in 1191); death of Ṭoghrïl in 1194; his capital was Hamadān.

[25] *Travels*, ed. I. I. Sreznevskii, p. 187 ⟦tr. Le Strange, *Embassy to Tamerlane 1403-1404* (London, 1928), p. 167⟧. Schiltberger, *Puteshestviia*, p. 47, remarks that the inhabitants of Ray "differ from other heathens" in their Shīʿī beliefs. ⟦The narrative of the Bavarian soldier Hans Schiltberger's *Reisebuch* (he spent over thirty years in Tīmūrīd Iran) was published by V. Langmantel (Tübingen, 1885); F. Brui's Russian version, used by Barthold, had appeared earlier (Odessa, 1866). Cf. A Gabriel, *Die Erforschung Persiens, die Entwicklung der abendländischen Kenntnis der Geographie Persiens* (Vienna, 1952), pp. 42-48, on these two Spanish and German sources.⟧

[26] *Travels in Georgia, Persia, Armenia, Ancient Babylonia, etc. during the years 1817, 1818, 1819, and 1820* (London, 1821-1822), I, 358-64.

[27] A plan, after Ker Porter, is in Jackson, *Persia Past and Present*, p. 435. The area is about 4,000 or 3,500 yards, approximately three and one-third or three versts.

tower."[28] At the foot of the hill is yet another citadel, obviously the stronghold Ṭabarak built under Ghazan Khan. The entire ground plan of the ruins has the shape of a triangle whose top is constituted by the cliff with the citadel on it. Among other noteworthy buildings are two towers with Kūfic inscriptions; one of these towers is called, like the one in Ṭūs, the Naqqāra-Khāna. According to Curzon, it was subjected to a restoration just before his visit, that is, at the close of the 1880s; this restoration disfigured it beyond recognition. There are, however, representations of the tower in its original form, for example in L. Dubeux's book *La Perse*.[29] There used to be in Ray a bas-relief from Sāsānid times with a portrait of the king on horseback and a lance in his hand; in the nineteenth century, at the close of Fatḥ ʿAlī Shāh's reign, this bas-relief was effaced and there was substituted a representation of the latter monarch piercing a lion with a lance.[30]

There are also several beautiful medieval constructions among the ruins of Warāmīn.[31] Especially remarkable is the fourteenth-century mosque whose building is attributed to the il-khan Abū Saʿīd (1316-1335). A picture and a description of it are to be found in J. Dieulafoy's book.[32]

Tehran, which has replaced these cities, is so new that a detailed description of it is not appropriate to a discussion of historical geography. In its original form, the city differed little from other Persian towns; it had a quadrangular shape, with a gate in the middle of each side and two more gates as well as a citadel in the northern section, where there is still today the palace of the shāh.[33]

[28] *Voyages*, I, 107.

[29] *La Perse* (Paris, 1841), fig. 37.

[30] Curzon, *Persia*, I, 352. Bas-relief in Jackson, *Persia Past and Present*, p. 439.

[31] For Warāmīn, see also Iskandar Munshī, *Ta'rīkh-i ʿĀlam-ārā-yi ʿAbbāsī* (Tehran, 1313-4/1895-7), I, 256 (under 997 A.H.): "The fortress of Warāmīn near Ray: it is in the center of the country of Iraq and has excellent caravanserais." ⟨⟨For the history and monuments of Ray and Warāmīn, see also A.V.W. Jackson, "Historical sketch of Ragha," *Spiegel Memorial Volume* (Bombay, 1908), pp. 237-45; Herzfeld, "Zarathustra. V. Awestische Topographie," *AMI*, II (1930), 95-98; Minorsky, *EI*¹, arts. "Raiy" and "Warāmīn"; *Survey of Persian Art*, II, V; Mīr Ḥusayn Yakrangiyān, *Jughrafiyā-yi ta'rīkhī* (Tehran, 1332/1953).⟩⟩ ⟦Abū Dulaf, *Travels in Iran*, tr. pp. 51-53. ##47-50, comm. pp. 99-101.⟧

[32] ⟨⟨*La Perse, la Chaldée et la Susiane* (Paris, 1887).⟩⟩

[33] For the village of Tehran, see Yāqūt, *Muʿjam*, III, 564. Tehran in J. Chardin (1674), "petite ville du pays Comisène" (*Voyages en Perse, et autres lieux de l'Orient*, ed. L. Langlès [Paris, 1811], VIII, 174). ⟨⟨The earliest certain mention of Tehran is in the *Fārs-nāma* of Ibn al-Balkhī, ed. Le Strange and Nicholson (London, 1921), p. 134, see Minorsky, *EI*¹, art. "Tehran"; for the history and monuments of Tehran,

Modern Tehran is a creation of the late Nāṣir al-Dīn Shāh, who in 1870-1872 expanded and rebuilt the city after the manner in which Paris was rebuilt under Napoleon III. Tehran now has the shape of an octagon,[34] and is more than fifteen versts in circumference, with twelve gates;[35] the fortifications are built on the pattern of those in Paris from before the Franco-Prussian War, but are not equipped with cannon, and in general are totally useless for defense of the city. Some of the gates represent monumental constructions; inside, avenues have been conducted through the city, squares have been laid out, and several beautiful buildings have been added. Curzon states that however much remains to be done for the welfare of the city, Nāṣir al-Dīn has by and large successfully solved the problem of reconstructing Tehran on a European model without adversely affecting its special Oriental charm.[36]

Like other large cities of Iran, Tehran has it religious sanctuary: the mausoleum of Shāh ʿAbd al-ʿAẓīm, one of ʿAlī's descendants, who fled to Ray from the caliph Mutawakkil and died here in 861; an Imāmzāda ʿAbd al-ʿAẓīm is mentioned among the personages buried in Ray by Ḥamd Allāh Mustawfī Qazwīnī, although not as the most prominent one.[37] Connected with Ray is the name of yet another ʿAlid, Ḥamza, son of the imām Mūsā and brother of ʿAlī al-Riḍā; in Mustawfī's time, a cave in the vicinity of Tehran was

aside from the works listed in the bibliography that accompanies Minorsky's article, see also Yakrangiyān, *Jughrāfiyā-yi ta'rīkhī*; ʿAbd al-ʿAzīz, *Ta'rīkh-i Tihrān* (Tehran, 1325/1946); S. Abdalian, *La région de Tehran* (Tehran, 1948).⟩⟩

[34] In E. G. Browne, *A Year amongst the Persians* (London, 1893), p. 86, "roughly speaking circular in shape."

[35] Listed in Browne (*ibid.*); twelve gates also in Jackson, *Persia Past and Present*, p. 420; the city is over ten miles in circuit. According to the election law of 1906, Tehran elected 32 deputies to the Majlis from among 128; according to the law of 1909, 15 out of 120 (all Azerbaijan, according to the 1906 law, elected 12; according to the 1909 law, 19). The text of the 1909 law is in M. Ardatov, *Poslednee politicheskoe dvizhenie v Persii*, fasc. 2, pp. 82 ff. (the ruling about the elections in fasc. 1, pp. 60 ff.; for the number of deputies, article 6). ⟨⟨A different set of data, especially 60 deputies from Tehran according to the law of 9 September 1906 (20 Rajab 1324), are in the book *Majmūʿa-yi maṣūbāt-i adwār-i awwal va duwwum*, pp. 43-48. See also M. Ivanov, *Iranskaia revoliutsiia*, pp. 88-95.⟩⟩

[36] *Persia*, I, 306-307. ⟦Lockhart, *Persian Cities*, pp. 1-9. From a large literature on the urbanization of Tehran and attendant problems, see H. Bahrambeygui, *Tehran, an Urban Analysis* (Tehran, 1977). The population of Tehran in 1976 was 4,496,159, according to a census conducted in November of that year by the Markaz-i Āmār-i Īrān; cf. *Le monde iranien et l'Islam*, IV [1976-1977], pp. 237-43.⟧

[37] *Nuzhat al-qulūb*, extract in Schefer's edition of Niẓām al-Mulk, p. 176 ⟦ed. Le Strange, p. 173, tr. *idem*, p. 168⟧.

shown where this saint, hiding from his pursuers, disappeared.[38] The modern structure above the tomb of ʿAbd al-ʿAẓīm mentioned earlier[39] was built, as is shown by an inscription on the frontal, by Nāṣir al-Dīn Shāh, and is considered a sanctuary, *bast*, from which the infidels are barred and where a Muslim enjoys the right of asylum; the right is outwardly symbolized by a string stretched in front of the building. The mausoleum lies nine versts from Tehran, with which it is linked by a railway, so far the only one in Iran.

In the course of their westward migration, the Aryans entered in Ray a country into which the Assyrian armies occasionally penetrated and which thus could come under a certain influence from Mesopotamian civilization. The Assyrians under King Esarhaddon (681-668 B.C.) reached Alburz and Damāwand, but these campaigns had the character of incursions and did not prevent the Medes from creating a strong kingdom at a time that coincided with the reign of the following Assyrian king, Ashshurbanipal (668-626 B.C.). They seized the opportunity for this at a moment when the Assyrians were busy elsewhere, especially in Khūzistān.[40] This unification of small clan units into one political organism was achieved by the Medes in the area where Hamadān is located, that is, next to the mountain chains that separate Iran from Mesopotamia. Here was the "land of Dayaukku," the center of activity of that real or mythical founder of the Median empire.

According to Tomaschek's findings, the ancient road from Hamadān to Ray (that is, from Ekbatana to Raga), coincided with the present road and passed through Zarand;[41] the Arab geographers write about a roundabout way, via the town of Sāwa. The shortest route from Hamadān to Ray is reckoned to measure 49 farsakhs (302½ versts). Although this road crosses some mountains, no single pass presents serious obstacles to pack transport except for the 50 versts-long section between Kushkan and Mazdakan, which is sometimes blocked by snowdrifts, even to wheeled transport.[42] The roundabout way, according to the Arab geographers, was 61 farsakhs long. Noteworthy on this road was the village of Mashkūya, some 8 farsakhs from Sāwa and 15 farsakhs from Ray. Ibn Rusta mentions the existence, in this village, of an interesting palace of pre-Islamic date, with figures carved from wood and a gilt roof; the palace had a park with a spring from which a stream issued

[38] *Ibid.*, p. 174.
[39] Curzon, *Persia*, I, 346.
[40] ⟨⟨See now I. D'iakonov, *Istoriia Midii.*⟩⟩
[41] *Zur historischen Topographie*, I, 154.
[42] Tumanskii, *Ot Kaspiiskogo moria*, p. 29.

and watered the neighboring fields.[43] Between Mashkūya and the next station, the road to Ray came to a river now called Āb-i Shūr; the road crossed it on a bridge made of brick, with arches; from this bridge one could see Mount Damāwand.

The "roundabout road" thus must have originated not because of some real obstacles on the main road but as a result of the importance of the city of Sāwa; the district of Zarand, which lies on the main road, is subordinate to it even now. Here one of the roads to southern Persia branches off. The district of Sāwa comes within the confines of the region of Qum, to which it is ascribed as early as the tenth-century author Ibn al-Faqīh.[44] In the political sense, Sāwa was subordinate to Ray rather than to Hamadān; the customs-house of the ruler of Ray was located, according to Ibn Rusta,[45] somewhat further west of where the roads to Sāwa and to Zarand bifurcated, a little distance east of the village of Pūsta, which already existed at that time.[46] Sāwa was said to have been built in the Islamic period; it does not seem to have had great importance before the Il-Khanids, although narratives about the Mongol conquest mention the burning of a rich library.[47] Here too, as in Ray, a struggle was going on between the townspeople, Shāfiʿī Sunnīs, and the peasants of the countryside, who were Shīʿīs. The village of Āwa, a short distance to the south of the city,[48] was the center of Shīʿism in this struggle.[49] Sāwa was rebuilt by a local ruler in the fourteenth century, apparently on a larger scale than before. It remained Sunnī, although in it there was one of the Shīʿī sanctuaries, the tomb of Imām al-Riḍā's brother Isḥāq. Moreover, in the neighborhood of Sāwa was shown, then as now, the grave of the prophet Samuel.[50]

The broad and fertile valley in which, according to Herodotus,

[43] Ibn Rusta, p. 168. The township mentioned in Yāqūt, *Muʿjam*, IV, 543. Mashkūya as a geographical appellation and as a personal name; Ibn Miskawayh. ⟨⟨Cf. Barthold, *Turkestan*, p. 32 n. 1, *Soch.* I, 78, n. 3.⟩⟩

[44] Ibn al-Faqīh, p. 265; tr. p. 318.

[45] Ibn Rusta, p. 168.

[46] Būsta somewhat to the west of Mazdakān. Cf. Balādhurī, p. 318, for Dastabā.

[47] Yāqūt, *Muʿjam*, III, 24. According to Yāqūt, this was the largest in the world. Cf. Le Strange, *The Lands*, p. 211 (also according to Mustawfī, *Nuzhat al-qulūb*).

[48] There were two settlements called Āwa; the second was on the road from Hamadān to Ray (it is marked on the map).

[49] According to Yāqūt, two farsakhs (Āwa); between Zanjān and Hamadān, Uwa. The *nisba* Āwaqī, *Muʿjam* , I, 408; Āwa on the road from Karaj to Ray (Maqdisī, p. 401).

[50] Mustawfī, *Nuzhat al-qulūb*, extract in Schefer's edition of Niẓām al-Mulk, p. 180 ⟦ed. Le Strange, p. 63, tr. *idem*, p. 68⟧.

Deioces (Dayaukku) founded his capital, is surrounded by seven rows of walls formed by two spurs of the mountain Alwand or Arwand, the Orontes of the Greeks, and it is watered by the stream Murad Bek Chay and a number of wells. Thanks to an abundant water supply, Hamadān and its environs always had many orchards with fruit trees and grapes. There were also fields under cultivation, but the grain was of poor quality,[51] probably because of the cold climate: the valley has an elevation of 6,000 feet above sea level. The present name, Hamadān, is a modified form of the Old Persian Hagmatana, Greek ʼΑγβάτανα.

Ekbatana remained a royal residence even after the fall of the Median kingdom, under the Achaemenids; the Persian kings spent their summers here, because of the high altitude of the valley and the resulting cool climate. Several columns and the statue of a lion preserved in the city are dated to the Achaemenid period. Ibn al-Faqīh mentions the latter, and quotes an Arab poet who celebrates this lion in his verse; the statue, which stood at that time by the gate of the city,[52] made such an impression of antiquity on this poet that the latter addresses the lion with the question of whether he was prior to time or whether time was prior to him: *a qablaka kāna al-dahru am kunta qablahu?*[53]

As under the Median kings, so under the Achaemenids the citadel of Ekbatana was considered the strongest in the kingdom and the safest depository for royal treasures; Alexander the Great placed here the booty of his campaigns. The city played the same role under the Parthians: according to Polybius (second century B.C.), there was at the foot of the citadel a palace, richly inlaid with golden and silver plates, and alongside was a temple with gilt columns. Isidore of Charax locates in Ekbatana the treasury (θησαυροφυλάκιον) and temple of Anahita, the Iranian goddess of fertility. The site of the citadel of Ekbatana is usually identified with the present hill of Muṣallā, the final spur of Alwand, to the southeast of the city, on which are remnants of the ancient structure. In the Middle Ages, however, as we know from Yāqūt's account, the as-

[51] *Ibid.*, p. 189.

[52] Perhaps under the gate—"by the gate of the town" (Ibn al-Faqīh, p. 240), at any rate on the side of Alwand, "opposite Arwand." Cf. *EI*² art. "Hamadhān," reference to Masʿūdī, *Murūj*, IX, 21, for the destruction of the *bāb al-asad* in 319/911 by the army of Mardāwīj b. Ziyār, in which the statue was toppled over; see the photograph in Jackson, *Persia Past and Present*, p. 160. Inscriptions of Darius and Xerxes; the gorge of ʿAbbāsābād three kilometers from the city, inscriptions five kilometers from the entrance to the gorge. In Ibn al-Faqīh, p. 243; tr. p. 294 at Tabanābar.

[53] Ibn al-Faqīh, p. 241.

sociation was made with the ruins of an ancient castle in the village of Sinjābād, two farsakhs from the Islamic city.[54] According to tradition, the kings took their treasures away because of the evil and treacherous disposition of the inhabitants; this latter feature, as well as the city's bad climate, was also a subject of complaints voiced by the Arab geographers.[55] In the Sāsānid period, Hamadān does not seem to have had great importance, and it was not one of the royal residences. Ibn al-Faqīh points out that the constructions of the Sāsānids were distributed all along the space between their capital al-Madā'in and the mountain pass that separates the cities of Asadābād and Hamadān on the road from Baghdad to Khurāsān, but that no such buildings existed anywhere beyond this pass, even in Hamadān.[56]

The Arabs took Hamadān half a year after the murder of the caliph 'Umar, in the spring of 645. There were so few monuments from earlier times in the city that Ibn Ḥawqal could characterize it as "new, built in Islamic times."[57] The length and width of the city equaled one farsakh; a tradition claimed that in the past it had been much more spacious and occupied the enormous area of four farsakhs in diameter.[58] The Arab geographers describing Hamadān do not mention the citadel, and only speak of the *shahristān* with four iron gates; this *shahristān* occupied the center of the town and had by then already become quite dilapidated.[59] The bazaars and the Friday mosque were in the *rabaḍ* that surrounded the *shahristān*.

In terms of its population and wealth, Hamadān remained behind Ray. During the tenth and eleventh centuries, the city was the capital of a few rulers, especially under the Buwayhids, but in general it did not play any outstanding political or military role; on the other hand, it has kept to this day its importance as a large commercial center, despite periods of temporary decline. As the most important city of southwestern Iran, Hamadān functioned as

[54] *Muʿjam*, IV, 981. ⟦Abū Dulaf, *Travels in Iran*, tr. pp. 47-49, #41, clearly refers, however, to the mound of ancient Ekbatana when he speaks of "the ancient town" (*al-madīna al-ʿatīqa*) on its mound.⟧

[55] Maqdisī, p. 392.

[56] Ibn al-Faqīh, p. 229; tr. p. 277.

[57] Ibn Ḥawqal, p. 260.

[58] Ibn al-Faqīh, p. 218; tr. p. 265.

[59] Maqdisī, p. 392. His statement that "the city in the middle of the district which the *rabaḍ* surrounds is ruined." Ibn al-Faqīh, p. 219: Alexander the Great "built in its center a massive castle overlooking [it], it had three sides, and he called it Sārūq." Yāqūt, *Muʿjam*, IV 982 ff., about the buildings of Persian kings; *ibid.*, p. 981, Sanjābād two farsakhs from Hamadān.

a transshipment center in the trade of these regions with the west; here were brought the goods to be sent to Tabriz and from there to Trebizond and the Black Sea; here were brought also, after the development of Anglo-Indian trade via Basra and Baghdad, goods destined for the southeastern provinces of Iran. According to Tumanskii, "the large and lively Hamadān bazaar is stocked full with Anglo-Indian goods."[60] From Hamadān the caravans, loaded with these goods, head also for Tehran and on another road for Rasht across the town of Āwa. According to Curzon, at the time of his visit (1889), there were no more than 20,000 inhabitants in Hamadān,[61] but Tumanskii, who visited it just five years later, estimated the population already at some 40,000 to 50,000; according to him, the city had grown quickly in the course of the previous twenty years as a result of British trade through Baghdad.[62] There are also in Hamadān a fair number of Jews (according to Curzon, 1,500 to 2,000), both local and from Baghdad; the latter, according to Tumanskii, are the dominant element in the commerce of Hamadān. The attitude of the local population toward the Jews, according to Curzon, is exceedingly hostile, although the Muslims venerate the Jewish sanctuaries in the city, the presumed tombs of Esther and Mordecai.[63] The cupola crowning the building has, according to Curzon, the character of an undoubtedly new structure; the bodies are kept in wooden coffins covered with Hebrew letters. Ker Porter heard that the present mausoleum had been built after Tīmūr's time and was restored in the seventeenth century.[64] Near it was the tomb of the famous eleventh-century philosopher Avicenna (that is, Abū ʿAlī Ibn Sīnā).[65]

[60] *Ot Kaspiiskogo moria*, p. 30.

[61] *Persia*, I, 566.

[62] According to Jackson, *Persia Past and Present*, p. 148, in 1903 about 25,000. Article of A. F. Shtal', "Khamadan": area of the city, nine square versts, 50,000 to 60,000 inhabitants. For Hamadan, see also Le Strange, *The Lands*, pp. 194 ff. ⟦H. L. Rabino, "Hamadan," *RMM*, XLIII (1921), 221-27; Lockhart, *Persian Cities*, pp. 94-100. The population of the town in ca. 1950 was 120,000 (*Farhang*, V, 482); in 1976, it was 155,846 (*Le monde iranien et l'Islam*, IV [1976-1977], 242).⟧

[63] Doubtful, but the same appears in Jackson, *Persia Past and Present*, pp. 168-69.

[64] *Travels*, II, 108.

[65] For the history and monuments of Hamadān, see also the bibliography in Vanden Berghe, *Archéologie de l'Iran ancien*, pp. 108-10; *Survey of Persian Art*, II, V; Frye, *EI*², art. "Hamadhān"; *Rāhnamā-yi shahr-i Hamadān* (Tehran, 1331/1952). ⟦Matheson, *Persia, an Archaeological Guide*, pp. 109-12.⟧

CHAPTER VIII

Qūhistān, Kirmān, and Makrān

THE settlement of the southern part of Iran by the Aryans took place, most probably, independently of the movement of the Medes described above. The Iranians of the southern regions are subsumed by Herodotus (I, 125), in distinction from the Medes, under the common name Πέρσαι, Persai; among the Persai are also reckoned the Δηρουσιαῖοι and Γερμάνιοι, from whom the southeastern regions Gedrosia (now Makrān) and Kirmān received their names. This movement also probably proceeded from east to west. These Aryans became separated from the northern branch of the Iranians, perhaps in Khurāsān. They occupied Sīstān, where the tribe mentioned by Herodotus under the name Σαράγγαι remained; subsequently the more frequent names for this people were Ζαράγγοι (Arrianes), Zarangae (Pliny), Δράγγαι (Arrianes, Strabo), Drangae (Pliny), and the name of the region became Δραγγιανη, Drangiana. As we have seen, this name was preserved in the Middle Ages in the name of the capital of Sīstān, Zaranj. H. Kiepert likewise assumes a separate movement of the Aryans southward across Sīstān.[1]

Moving on from Sīstān, the Aryans must have first of all crossed the desert on the way into the northeastern part of the present province of Kirmān toward the mountain spurs that belonged, in their geological formation and northwest-southeastward orientation, to the Zagros system; this system forms the western border of Iran and cuts, by means of individual mountain chains, through the plateau itself. In historical times, the important road led from Sīstān to Bam. The cultivated belt is separated here from Sīstān by an extensive steppe area, but one less extensive than the vast desert stretching northward. A low row of hills, extending toward the town of Khabīṣ, divides this desert into two parts, the Dasht-i Kawīr and the Dasht-i Lūṭ; the Arab geographers subsumed both these parts under one name, the Wilderness of Khurāsān (*Mafāzat Khu-*

[1] *Lehrbuch der alten Geographie* (Berlin, 1878), p. 67, no. 2. Uncertainty of the movement itself.

rāsān).[2] The etymology of the word *kawīr* is not yet fully understood; Tomaschek sees in it the Old Iranian word *gawer* (*kawir*), from *gaw* (cf. Latin *cavitas*).[3] It is more likely, however, that the word stems from the Arabic root *q-f-r: qafr* pl. *qifār* or *qufūr*, meaning "a desert without water or vegetation." The characteristic outer marks of *kawīrs* are a completely flat surface, black clayey soil, green pools of water, and great quantity of salt, sometimes lying in the form of separate white spots, sometimes covering vaster areas in the form of a thin white crust that crunches under one's feet and from a distance resembles ice. In rainy weather, the *kawīr* acquires the appearance of a dirty marsh or even of a large lake. The "Wilderness of Khurāsān" impressed even the Arabs as a desert of extreme sterility, even when compared with those of Arabia and northern Africa with which they were so familiar. Iṣṭakhrī says that in the latter countries all the deserts, except for limited areas, include good pasture lands, and are therefore divided up among various nomadic tribes, whereas the desert of Khurāsān has almost no inhabitants at all; one sees only the road and the post stations along it.[4] The words of the same geographer, however, suggest that nomads nevertheless passed through even these parts, for caravans were exposed not only to natural dangers of the desert but also to the raids of brigands,[5] whose temerity was enhanced by the fact that the areas bordering the desert were under the rule of different

[2] Ṭabarī, II, 1637, about the building of the *aywānāt* in the *mafāza* under Asad b. ʿAbd Allāh al-Qaṣrī, governor of Khurāsān. ⟦On the central deserts, see Gabriel, *Durch Persiens Wüsten*; *idem*, "The Southern Lut and Iranian Baluchistan," *GJ*, XCII (1938), 193-210; W. B. Fisher, in *Cambridge History of Iran*, I, 90-101. As Gabriel points out elsewhere (*Die Erforschung Persiens*, pp. 301-302 n. 49), the names "Dasht-i Kawīr" and "Dasht-i Lūṭ" are not used by the local people, and the first expression is something of a tautology.⟧

[3] Tomaschek, *Zur historischen Topographie*, II, 582.

[4] Iṣṭakhrī, pp. 227-28.

[5] For the raids of the Kūfichān, see also Nāṣir-i Khusraw, *Safar-nāma* (Tehran lithogr.), p. 250. For their pacification by Qāwurd and for the latter's constructions, see Muḥammad b. Ibrāhīm, *Ta'rīkh-i Saljūqiyān-i Kirmān*, ed. M. T. Houtsma (Leiden, 1886), pp. 5 ff. ⟦ed. Muḥammad Ibrāhīm Bāstānī-Pārīzī (Tehran, 1343/1964), pp. 4 ff.⟧; cf. Sykes, *Ten Thousand Miles in Persia*, pp. 416 ff.; for the towers, p. 418. See the description of the road through the desert between Nāyin and Ṭabas in Nāṣir-i Khusraw, *Safar-nāma*, pp. 250-51 (from Iṣfahān to Ṭabas, 110 farsakhs; from Nāyin to Garma, 43 farsakhs; from there onward the desert; along this desert road, every two farsakhs *gunbadak-hā* [small domed structures] were erected (*sic*); moving sands; Ribāṭ-i Zubayda (called Ribāṭ-i Maranī); Ṭabas, *ibid.*, p. 252). From there forty farsakhs to the north was Nīshāpūr, and the same distance to the south, Khabīṣ; to the east was a *kūhī muḥkam* [fortified mountain?]. The ruler was Gīlakī b. Muḥammad (see pp. 252-53 for their customs).

governments; brigands could escape pursuit by one government by fleeing to the possessions of another. The raids seem to have been carried out by the Balūchīs and Kūfichīs (al-Qufṣ, see below). According to Maqdisī, the Buwayhid ʿAḍud al-Dawla (949-983) defeated these peoples and took from them eighty youths as hostages; these stayed in permanent captivity in Shīrāz and were released only in exchange for an equal number of others. After these measures, the brigands did not touch those caravans that had an escort from the sulṭān or authority of Fārs, that is, ʿAḍud al-Dawla; only the possessions and caravans of the Sāmānids remained the target of the brigands' raids.[6]

Several roads connect Kirmān with Qūhistān, the mountainous region in the southern part of Khurāsān; mentioned especially often is the road through Rāwar and the oasis of Nayband to Khūr, and that through Khabīṣ to Khusb. Qūhistān did not have a great significance in the history of Iran. As early as the tenth century the villages were separated from each other by extensive areas where only nomads could live; there were no rivers there, but only wells and underground canals.[7] Palm trees grew in the southern part of Qūhistān, but the rest of the province was counted among the "cold regions." Tomaschek remarks that Qūhistān gives an idea of what Iran may look like many thousands of years hence, as a result of dessication and weathering of the soils.[8] Qāyin[9] and Tūn[10] were

[6] Maqdisī, p. 489. ⟦This passage is translated in Bosworth, "The Kūfichīs or Qufṣ in Persian History," *Iran, JBIPS*, XIV (1976), 14-15.⟧

[7] Iṣṭakhrī, pp. 274-75.

[8] *Zur historischen Topographie*, II, 572. See J. H. Kramers, *EI*[2], art. "Ḳūhistān"; Fisher, in *Cambridge History of Iran*, I, 73-76.

[9] Yate, *Khurasan and Sistan*, pp. 53-64, regarding Qāyin: only a few houses inside the city wall; the bazaar, mosque, madrasa, and the greater part of the town are all outside. The mosque was built in 1368 (inscription). Its trade: two-thirds of the goods go to Bandar ʿAbbās, one-third to Mashhad and Sabzawār. The ruins of a fortress to the south of the town, and of another (Qal ʿa-yi Dukhtar) to the east. Only 4,000 inhabitants in Qāyin (Sykes, *Ten Thousand Miles*, p. 407). Today, the chief city is Birjand (up to 25,000 inhabitants), see Yate, *Khurasan and Sistan*, p. 69; but the title "ruler (*ḥukumrān*) of Qāyin" as before "amīr of Qāyin" (*ibid.*). "Qāʾin territory" to the south all the way to Bandān (*ibid.*, p. 74), that is, to the border of Sīstān. The term Qāʾināt.

[10] The road from Ṭabas to Tūn according to Nāṣir-i Khusraw, *Safar-nāma* (Tehran lithogr.), p. 253: twelve farsakhs from Ṭabas was Raqqa (a Friday mosque); twenty farsakhs further on, Tūn. Description of Tūn: *ibid.*, pp. 253-54. Eighteen farsakhs further on, Qāyin (*ibid.*, p. 255, description of the town). From Qāyin, eighteen miles to the northeast was Zawzan, and thirty farsakhs to the south, Harāt. Nāṣir-i Khusraw's journey from Qāyin to Sarakhs (*ibid.*, p. 257).

the chief towns, so that the whole region is called Tunocain or Tonocain by Marco Polo.[11] Only Qāyin had commercial importance; Maqdisī calls it "the warehouse of the goods of Khurāsān and the treasure-trove of Kirmān" (*furḍat Khurāsān wa-khizānat Kirmān*).[12] There were, moreover, many mountain castles in this region, so that Qūhistān became in the eleventh century one of the centers of power for the Ismāʿīlīs.[13]

The deserts of Kirmān, Makrān, and Sind were considered less sterile than that of Khurāsān, and they were inhabited by nomadic tribes. The areas near mountains were suited for agriculture and fruit growing, and here the inhabitants soon adopted a sedentary way of life. Herodotus counts the people of Kirmān among the sedentary tribes of Persia. The Arabs divided the cultivated areas according to the kind of crops grown there, into *ṣurūd* (cold areas) and *jurūm* (warm areas), from the Persian words *sard* (cold) and *garm* (hot). In Kirmān, only the northern districts, occupying approximately one-fourth of the whole region, were reckoned as *ṣurūd*, the rest were *jurūm*; and whereas the crops of the former-cold-region could absolutely not be grown in the southern regions, the reverse did occasionally occur.[14] Cultivation of the most characteristic tree of the south, the date palm, stops at present, according to Tumanskii, a fair distance south of the city of Kirmān;[15] several stunted palm trees, however, were unexpectedly seen by him considerably further north, on the road from Yazd to Tehran, in the village of ʿAqda.[16] The cultivated lands in Kirmān lay in separate patches and thus differed from the more continuous areas under cultivation in Fārs.

The towns of Kirmān mentioned by the Arab geographers have partly conserved their former names, as, for example, Bam, Khabīṣ,

[11] Minaev's translation, pp. 45-46, 56-57 ⟦Eng. tr. Yule, I, 79, 119⟧.

[12] Maqdisī, p. 321.

[13] According to Juzjānī's *Ṭabaqāt-i Nāṣirī*, 70 out of the 105 Ismāʿīlī strongholds were in Qūhistān; according to Juwaynī (see Rashīd al-Dīn, ed. Quatremère, p. 174), 110 were in Qūhistān. *Ibid.* for the title *Muḥtashim.* ⟦P.R.E. Wiley, "The Assassins in Quhistan," *JRCAS*, LV (1968), 180-83.⟧

[14] Iṣṭakhrī, p. 159.

[15] "Ot Kaspiiskogo moria," p. 129.

[16] From Beliaev's letter: the mountain plateau with the city of Kirmān is, as it were, a promontory in the low-lying plain of Dasht-i Kawīr, Bāfq, etc. The palm trees in ʿAqda are a direct continuation of those of Bāfq, where they reach normal size and yield abundant fruit. For the considerable size of palms in Bāfq, see also Sykes, *Ten Thousand Miles*, p. 264; see also Beliaev, *Otchet*, no. 1, p. 37, for the climate of Bam and the neighboring but much lower-lying Khabīṣ.

Zarand, and some smaller places like Māhān. The last-named town is noted for the fact that the only monument from the Achaemenid period found in Kirmān was located there: in the mausoleum of Niʿmat Allāh Walī, a saint who lived in the fifteenth century and who founded the Niʿmatallāhī order of dervishes. The find was a small pyramid on a triangular base, with a trilingual inscription (Persian, Assyrian, and the language of Susiana):[17] "I, Darius, great king, king of kings, king of the regions, king of this land, son of Gushtasp, the Achaemenid." We do not know whence this monument had been brought to Māhān.[18] The names of some other cities mentioned by the tenth-century geographers are now applied primarily to their corresponding districts, such as Narmāshīr, Bardasīr, Jīruft, and so on. The Arabs mention Sirjān as the chief city of Kirmān. Its location was probably not identical with that of Saʿīdābād, the present capital of the district of Sirjān, but must have been to the northeast of it, in the present district of Rafsinjān, with its chief town, Bahrāmābād: this probability is based on the fact that the Arab geographers count only two days' march from Sirjān to Zarand.[19]

In Tomaschek's opinion, Sirjān became the capital of the province only in Arab times; prior to that the capital would have been the city of Kirmān, built by Ardashīr, the founder of the Sāsānid dynasty, who named it Weh-Ardashīr, a name transformed by the Arabs into Bardasīr.[20] The city of Bardasīr is described in detail by Maqdisī, and at the close of the tenth century it was the administrative and military center of the region.[21] Sirjān, nevertheless, had already been the capital of the province of Kirmān in pre-Islamic times. The town created by Ardashīr seems to have been just a military camp; only in the second half of the tenth century,

[17] ⟨⟨That is, in Old Persian, Akkadian, and Elamite.⟩⟩

[18] The monument was in St. Petersburg. F. H. Weissbach's article in *IAN* ser. 6, vol. IV (1910) ("Die sogenannte Inschrift von Kerman"). Picture of the Akkadian text also in Jackson, *Persia Past and Present*, pp. 184 ff. ⟨⟨The monument in question is a stone weight with an inscription of Darius I, originally in the Asiatic Museum and now in the Hermitage; for editions of the inscription, see Kent, *Old Persian*, p. 114.⟩⟩

[19] Le Strange, "The Cities of Kirman in the Time of Ḥamd Allāh . . . Mustawfī and Marco Polo," *JRAS* (1901), p. 289. ⟦Aubin, "La question de Sīrǧān au XIIIe siècle," *Studia iranica*, VI (1977), 285-90.⟧

[20] Zur historischen Topographie, I, 176.

[21] Maqdisī, 461. *Qalʿa* inside the town. ⟨⟨See now Mīr Ḥaydar, "Gudhārish az yak muṭālaʿa-yi jughrāfiyāʾī," *Majalla-yi Dānishkada-yi Adabiyyāt va ʿUlūm-i Insānī* (Tabrīz), no. 4 (1346/1967), pp. 466-85.⟩⟩

under the Buwayhids, did it become the capital of the province. It conserved this place under the Saljuqs, who ruled here in the eleventh and twelfth centuries. The most detailed information about the latter dynasty is given by Muḥammad b. Ibrāhīm, who wrote in the seventeenth century, but who used earlier sources that he identified.[22] The Saljuq rulers spent seven months of the year in Bardasīr, and the remaining five further south, in Jīruft. The founder of this branch of the dynasty was Qāwurd, brother of Sulṭān Alp Arslān. Besides Qāwurd, who was especially concerned with the construction of caravanserais and other buildings so as to facilitate travel through the desert, Mughīth al-Dīn Muḥammad I (1141-1156), a bloodthirsty tyrant who, however, protected the religious class and enjoyed its support, is credited with a whole series of buildings. He built a number of madrasas, *ribāṭs*, mosques, and hospitals in Bardasīr and Jīruft; at the Friday mosque of Bardasīr he founded a library containing 5,000 volumes in various branches of learning.[23]

Local traditions and ruins of the old city prove that the city of Bardasīr, or Guwāshīr (a name it still bore in the fourteenth century), stood on the site of the modern city of Kirmān. A plan of the city accompanies Khanikoff's book.[24] From among its buildings, the mosque of Malik is considered the most ancient one; tradition ascribes its foundation to Sulṭān Malikshāh (1072-1092), but according to historical sources, it was built by the local ruler Tūrānshāh (1085-1097) in the *rabaḍ* that was created only at that time.[25] The Friday mosque was built in the fourteenth century under the Muẓaffarids; there is an inscription with the date of the foundation (1 Shawwāl 750/13 December 1349). In the tenth cen-

[22] For Abū Ḥāmid Muḥammad b. Ibrāhīm, see Barthold, *Turkestan, Soch.* I, 76 n. 7. ⟦At this place in his *Turkestan* (Eng. tr., p. 30 n. 7), Barthold cites Abū Ḥāmid Muḥammad b. Ibrāhīm as an authority mentioned by Rashīd al-Dīn and as being in fact identical with Muḥammad b. ʿAlī Rāwandī, author at the beginning of the thirteenth century of the history of the Great Saljuqs, the *Rāḥat al-ṣudūr wa-āyat al-surūr.* This Abū Ḥāmid Muḥammad b. Ibrāhīm/Muḥammad b. ʿAlī Rāwandī is obviously different from the author of the *Ta'rīkh-i Saljūqiyān-i Kirmān,* on whom see Storey, *Persian Literature,* I, 358, and Storey-Bregel', II, 1,059-60. See for a summary German translation of the work, M. T. Houtsma, "Zur Geschichte der Selǵuqen von Kermân," *ZDMG,* XXXIX (1885), 362-402. The history of the Kirmān Saljuqs is touched upon by Bosworth, in *Cambridge History of Iran,* V, 58-59, 87-90, 174-75, but there now exists a monograph on this dynasty by Erdoğan Merçil, *Kirmân Selçuklulan* (Istanbul, 1980).⟧

[23] Muḥammad b. Ibrāhīm, *Ta'rīkh-i Saljūqiyān-i Kirmān,* pp. 32-33.

[24] Khanikoff, *Mémoire.*

[25] Muḥammad b. Ibrāhīm, *Ta'rīkh-i Saljūqiyān-i Kirmān,* pp. 20-21.

tury, according to Maqdisī, an uninterrupted row of orchards stretched from Bardasīr to Māhān;[26] now, according to Khanikoff, this area is a desert almost as desolate as the Dasht-i Lūṭ.[27]

In the tenth century, the towns of Kirmān differed little from those of the rest of Persia and Central Asia. Most were surrounded by a wall with four gates; only the capital, Sirjān, is said to have possessed eight gates.[28] Also noteworthy is Iṣṭakhrī's remark that because of the lack of timber, the dwellings had the form of domelike structures.[29] A similar type of structure exists in Kirmān even today; Tumanskii, who was there in 1894, says about the village of Nigār:[30] "A great number of homesteads have domelike roofs, which suggests a lack of construction timber."[31] After Sirjān, the most important city was Bam, the industrial center of the province; the cotton fabrics manufactured here were exported all over the Islamic world, including Egypt.[32] These fabrics were remarkable for their durability; one set of clothes made from this cloth could be worn for from five to twenty years. The manufacture of Kirmān shawls, famous to this day, became concentrated in Bam. At that time, according to Ibn Ḥawqal, the price of one shawl could be as much as 30 dinars, that is, 150 rubles.[33] At present, besides the Kirmān

[26] Maqdisī, p. 462.

[27] Khanikoff, *Mémoire*, p. 199. A plan of Kirmān is in Sykes, *Ten Thousand Miles*, p. 188. There are 50,000 inhabitants in the city (*ibid.*, p. 195); see also Rittikh, *Otchet o poezdke*, I, 204. The surface extent of the city is, according to Sykes (*Ten Thousand Miles*, p. 193), one mile from west to east and a little more from north to south. Kirmān at the time of the struggle between Luṭf ʿAlī and Āghā Muḥammad: 70,000 men blinded, 20,000 women and children sold in slavery. ⟨⟨For the history and monuments of Bardasīr and Kirmān, see also Aḥmad ʿAlī Khān Wazīr Kirmānī, *Taʾrīkh-i Kirmān (Sālāriyya)*, ed. Bāstānī-Pārīzī (Tehran, 1340/1961); Kramers, *EI*[1], art. "Kirmān; A.K.S. Lambton, *EI*[2], art. "Kirmān."⟩⟩ ⟦Lockhart, *Persian Cities*, pp. 112-19. On the demography and agrarian structure of the region, see P. W. English, *City and Village in Iran: Settlement and Economy in the Kirman Basin* (Madison, Wis., 1966), and thereto, B. Spooner and P. C. Salzman, "Kirman and the Middle East: Paul Ward English's City and Village in Iran . . . ," *Iran, JBIPS*, VII (1969), 107-13. The population of the town of Kirmān in ca. 1950 was 50,000 (*Farhang*, VIII, 317); in 1976, it was 140,309 (*Le monde iranien et l'Islam*, IV [1976-1977], p. 242).⟧

[28] Maqdisī, p. 464.

[29] Iṣṭakhrī, p. 167.

[30] *Ot Kaspiiskogo moria*, p. 126.

[31] There is yet another reason: the nature of the soil. Here the soil is sandy; there the roofs are on beams, although construction timber is just as scarce (from D. D. Beliaev's letter).

[32] Bam and the contemporary fortress, picture in Sykes, *Ten Thousand Miles*, p. 218. See also photographs in Aḥmad ʿAlī Khān, *Taʾrīkh-i Kirmān*, facing p. 1.

[33] Ibn Ḥawqal, 223.

shawls, the Kirmān carpets are especially famous. The tenth-century geographers do not mention them, but this art of weaving already existed in the fourteenth century under Tīmūr; the master craftsmen of Fārs and Kirmān supplied silk rugs for the Friday mosque built by Tīmūr in Samarqand, now known by the name of Bībī Khānïm.[34] In the northern part of Kirmān, in Kūbanān, according to Yāqūt[35] and Marco Polo,[36] was concentrated the production of zinc oxide or tutty; this was exported from Kirmān to other countries as a medicine for eye ailments.

Of course, the Iranians penetrated into the southern part of Kirmān, the so-called "warm lands" (*garmsīr*), later than they did into the northern part; here the autochthonous population has to this day partly retained its distinctiveness from the Iranian conquerors. In the geographical sense, these parts have not yet been fully explored; even the question of where the interior basins end and where that of the Indian Ocean begins has not been adequately answered. The district of Jīruft is watered by the rivulet Khalīl Rūd (some travelers call it the Khalīrī). Tomaschek[37] refutes the assertion of E. A. Floyer,[38] an early nineteenth-century traveler, that this rivulet flows into the sea, and he suggests that it disappears in the sands;[39] yet in 1894, Tumanskii again heard that it flows into the sea.[40]

Jīruft was separated from the northeastern districts of Kirmān by the mountains of Bāriz, now Jibāl Bāriz.[41] The population of

[34] ʿAbd al-Razzāq Samarqandī, *Maṭlaʿ al-saʿdayn*, ms., fol. 18a.

[35] *Muʿjam*, IV, 316.

[36] Minaev's translation, p. 56 ⟦tr. Yule, I, 117-19 ("Cobinan"); cf. Wulff, *The Traditional Crafts of Persia*, p. 12.⟧

[37] *Zur historischen Topographie*, I, 183.

[38] *Unexplored Baluchistan* (London, 1882). ⟦Floyer was actually an official of the Anglo-Indian Telegraph Company stationed at Jāsk on the northern coast of the Gulf of Oman, who did not begin his travels into the interior of Makrān and Balūchistān till the 1870s; among his credits was that of being the first modern European to describe Bashkardia (see Gabriel, *Die Erforschung Persiens*, pp. 225-26.⟧

[39] The marshy lake called Jaz Muryān, some fifty miles long ⟨⟨approximately ninety miles from Bampūr⟩⟩; Sykes, *Ten Thousand Miles*, p. 143. Along the southern side of the lake, northward from the mountains. Bashākird was crossed for the first time by Sykes in 1893 (*ibid.*, pp. 306-308). In summer the lake dries up either completely or for the most part (*ibid.*, p. 143). In P. Schwarz, *Iran im Mittelalter nach den arabischen Geographen* (Leipzig-Zwickau, Stuttgart-Berlin, 1896-1936), III, 217, quotation from Ibn Ḥawqal, p. 220 line 12, about the absence of lakes (*buḥayra*) in Kirmān.

[40] *Ot Kaspiiskogo moria*, p. 124.

[41] Beliaev, *Otchet*, I, 68, about the Jibāl Bāriz as the first serious barrier to winds bringing moisture from the ocean, from here on rains. ⟦Bosworth, *EI*² Suppl., art. "Bāriz, D̲jabal."⟧

these mountains adopted Islam only in ʿAbbāsid times; and only under the Ṣaffārids, at the close of the ninth century, did it actually submit to Muslim rulers.[42] The city of Jīruft, whose ruins lie not far from the village of Karīmābād, was in pre-Mongol times one of the richest towns of the Islamic world. Here the road coming from the Persian Gulf port of Hurmuz (near modern Bandar ʿAbbās) converged with the road coming from India through Jālk, and the goods brought to Jīruft[43] from India were then distributed to other Persian provinces. In the tenth century, the city ceded primacy in terms of size to Sirjān and Bam,[44] but its prosperity seems to have risen under the Saljuq rulers of Kirmān to the point where it was one of the two capitals of the realm, alongside Bardasīr. Foreign merchants lived mostly in the suburb of Qamādīn, which, according to Muḥammad b. Ibrāhīm, was "the treasury of the wealthy and the warehouse of the owners of products of the East and West": *khazīna-i mutamawwilān wa ganj-khāna-i arbāb-i baḍāʾiʿ-i sharq wa gharb*).[45] Jīruft is mentioned under the name of Camadi by Marco Polo, in whose time the city was already completely ruined.[46]

The road from Jīruft to the sea went through the district of Rūdbār, also mentioned by Marco Polo. Between Rūdbār and the seacoast, in the mountains, primarily to the east of the road, lived the Kūfichīs or Qufṣ, in Persian Kūch or Kūfij, a people who spoke a special language of their own; according to Iṣṭakhrī, they claimed Arab origin.[47] There were seven mountain chains in the region, each of which had its own chieftain; altogether, up to 10,000 men were counted among the inhabitants of the mountains. These mountaineers had no horses and undertook their incursions on foot; nevertheless, their raids spread fear all over Kirmān and the adjacent districts of Fārs and Sīstān. In religious terms, they favored

[42] Iṣṭakhrī, p. 164.

[43] *Ibid.*, p. 169; Maqdisī, p. 486.

[44] Iṣṭakhrī, p. 167.

[45] Muḥammad b. Ibrāhīm, *Taʾrīkh-i Saljūqiyān-i Kirmān*, I, 49.

[46] Minaev's translation, p. 49 ⟦tr. Yule, I, 91-92⟧. The same identification in Sykes, *Ten Thousand Miles*, p. 267 ⟨⟨Camadin as a borough of Jīruft⟩⟩, where there is also a reference to the article by A. Houtum-Schindler, "Notes on Marco Polo's Itinerary in Southern Persia," *JRAS* (1881), p. 495: "Camadi is a contraction of Kuhn-i Muhammedi, the canal or watercourse of Muhammed." According to Sykes, the ruins lie near Sarjaz, in the valley of the Khalīl Rūd, on the right bank. The fortress is square, each side measuring 286 yards (*Ten Thousand Miles*, p. 267). For these ruins, see also Beliaev, *Otchet*, I, 85 ff. On Yate's map, Sarjaz is on the same site where Camadi was recorded by Sykes (somewhat to the north of Karīmābād; in Beliaev, the ruins are delimited to the west of the meridian that links Sarjaz and Karīmābād).

[47] Iṣṭakhrī, 164. ⟦Bosworth, "The Kūfichīs or Qufṣ in Persian History."⟧

the cause of Shīʿism and recognized the authority of the Fāṭimid caliphs.[48] The might of the Buwayhids put an end to their depredations, but these were resumed at the beginning of the eleventh century, when Buwayhid power declined. The mountaineers then seized control over all southern Kirmān and the city of Jīruft, and the founder of the Kirmān Seljuqs, Qāwurd, managed only by treachery to take these districts away from them and to subject the Kūfichīs to his rule.[49] Tomaschek identifies the country of the Kūfichīs with the present region of Bashākird, which is divided into six districts; their chieftains obey a sultan who lives in the town of Angurān, and the authority of the Persian government is virtually ignored.[50] Access to the region is extremely difficult, and as pack animals, only asses of local breed are used. The whole population is reckoned not to exceed 2,000 souls; aside from the ruling class of Persian and Balūch origin, there are natives of the Dravidian race, in whom Tomaschek sees the descendants of the Kūfichīs. Despite the proximity of the sea, the region has been little explored, and the natives are on an extremely low level of civilization.[51]

Of the whole coast of Persia, only the littoral of the Persian Gulf has had any importance in history, although adequate bays and anchorages are also found further east. The Strait of Hurmuz, separating the gulf from the ocean, received this name from the famous harbor that, down to the fourteenth century, lay on the mainland, somewhat to the east of the modern port of Bandar ʿAbbās. One day's journey was reckoned between Hurmuz and the village of Sūrū, where fishermen lived and through which passed the road from Fārs to Hurmuz.[52] In the tenth century, Hurmuz was the port of the province of Kirmān, although it did not have a large population.[53] Subsequently, maritime trade with India cen-

[48] Ibn Ḥawqal, p. 221.

[49] Muḥammad b. Ibrāhīm, *Ta'rīkh-i Saljūqiyān-i Kirmān*, pp. 5-8.

[50] *Zur historischen Topographie*, I, 190. ⟦The authority of the central government in Tehran has been imposed in Persian Balūchistān only during recent decades.⟧

[51] Sykes, *Ten Thousand Miles*, pp. 304-309, for Bashākird: 8,000 inhabitants; four districts: Sindark, Jakdan, Anguhran, Marz; the inhabitants each paid forty pounds a year; Durrān Khān of Rūdbār tax farms the district, but he is also accountable for the results of incursions. Cf. Beliaev, *Otchet*, I, 98, Bashāgerd, and pp. 102 ff. (Bashākerd). ⟨⟨See also Spooner, "Kūch u Balūch and Ichthyophagi," *Iran, JBIPS*, II (1964), pp. 53-67; I. Gershevitch, "Travels in Bashkardia," *JRCAS*, XLV (1959), 213-25.⟩⟩ ⟦Bosworth, *EI*² Suppl., art. "Bashkard"; according to the *Farhang*, VIII, 49, the population of the region ca. 1950 was only about 6,700.⟧

[52] Iṣṭakhrī, pp. 167, 170.

[53] *Ibid.*, p. 166.

tered principally on two points, Hurmuz and Kīsh, the latter on an island of the same name (now called Qays) in the Persian Gulf.[54] Because of commercial rivalry, there were always hostilities between the rulers of Kīsh and Hurmuz; each tried to harm his rival and stop his ships, to the great detriment of trade.[55] At the close of the twelfth century, when the Ghuzz led by Malik Dīnār took possession of Kirmān,[56] the ruler of Kīsh begged him to cede Hurmuz to him, promising to pay every year the sum of 100,000 dinars and to send fifty Arabian horses.[57]

The commercial importance of Hurmuz and Kīsh continued under the Mongols. According to Marco Polo, the main articles of export from Hurmuz, Kīsh, and other points to India, in exchange for Indian goods, were horses.[58] Marco Polo also informs us that the ruler of Hurmuz acknowledged himself a vassal of Kirmān, but that he was often remiss in paying the tribute and waged war against his suzerain.[59] He also ruled over the Arab coast and harbor of

[54] In Waṣṣāf, *Ta'rīkh* (Bombay ed.), pp. 170 ff., there is the history of the Banū Qayṣar, who ruled on the island for three hundred years until its conquest by the Atābek Abū Bakr under the ruler Malik Sulṭān. The ancestor was an inhabitant of Sīrāf; for the name of the island (after Qays, the son of Qayṣar), see *ibid.*, p. 174. There is in Waṣṣāf, p. 175, the following reference: "And the imam Saʿd al-Dīn Arshad (the imamate and primacy in Qays is still held by his descendants) compiled a history of the kings of the Banī Qaysar." In Mustawfī, *Nuzhat al-qulūb*, ed. Le Strange, p. 120, the coastal points are mentioned as dependencies of the House of Qays. Shift of commercial importance from Sīrāf to Qays under the Daylamīs (*ibid.*, p. 117). Also Yāqūt, *Muʿjam*, IV, 215 ff., about Qays and its ruler. Cf. also Rashīd al-Dīn, *Mukātabāt*, ed. M. Shafīʿ (Lahore, 1364/1965), p. 197. According to Muḥammad Jaʿfar Ḥusaynī Khūrmūjī, *Āthār-i Jaʿfarī* (Tehran, 1276/1860), "The island of Qays, although it is one of the largest islands of the Persian Gulf, is barren and uninhabited." ⟨⟨For the island of Qays, see also Streck, *EI*[1], art. "Ḳais."⟩⟩ ⟦J. Lassner, *EI*[2], art. "Ḳays."⟧

[55] Barthold, *Turkestan, Soch.* I, 462.

[56] For Dīnār, the history of Afḍal Kirmānī was compiled in 584/1188; it was lithographed in 1876 in Tehran (the *ʿIqd al-ʿulā*). For this work, see also Sykes, *Ten Thousand Miles*, p. 48 n. 3; also mentioned in Rozen, *ZVORAO*, II, 182, and C. Rieu, *Supplement to the Catalogue of the Persian Manuscripts in the British Museum* (London, 1895), pp. 90-91. ⟨⟨Or. 2887; Or. 3584; cf. Storey, *Persian Literature*, I, 357, 1297.⟩⟩ ⟦Storey-Bregel', II, 1,056-57; there are various more recent printed texts of the *ʿIqd al-ʿulā* than the 1293/1876 lithograph, such as that of Muḥammad ʿĀmirī Nā'inī (Tehran, 1311/1932).⟧

[57] Muḥammad b. Ibrāhīm, *Ta'rīkh-i Saljuqiyān-i Kirmān*, pp. 160-61.

[58] Minaev's translation, p. 261 ⟦Eng. tr. Yule, II, 276-77⟧. ⟨⟨See also Rashīd al-Dīn, *Mukātabāt*, pp. 196 ff.⟩⟩ ⟦On this trade in horses, see S. Digby, *War-horse and Elephant in the Delhi Sultanate, a Study of Military Supplies* (Oxford, 1971), pp. 30-31.⟧

[59] Minaev's translation, p. 308 ⟦Eng. tr. Yule, II, 381-82⟧. Data about the island of Baḥrayn in Khūrmūjī, *Āthār-i Jaʿfarī*; in 663/1235-6, the atabek Abū Bakr con-

Qalhāt to the southeast of Masqaṭ, whither he withdrew whenever the ruler of Kirmān sent an army against him; he would then seize the ships sailing into the Persian Gulf.[60] The ruler of Kirmān suffered such a loss of revenue that he was forced to conclude a peace. The rulers of Hurmuz were clearly of Arab origin, for the name of the dynasty's founder was Maḥmūd Qalhātī.[61] The Aryans of Central Asia could not quite overcome their fear of the sea, while the natives of the Arab littoral, ʿUmān, were always daring sea rovers. Only the mightiest rulers of Persia, such as the Buwayhids in the pre-Mongol period (especially ʿAḍud al-Dawla) and the Saljuqs were able to extend their authority over ʿUmān.

At the beginning of the fourteenth century, the plundering carried out by the Mongols in Kirmān forced the ruler of Hurmuz to transfer his seat to the island of Zarūn or Jirūn, now Hurmuz. Here, three farsakhs from Old Hurmuz, there grew up New Hurmuz.[62] The port remained in Arab hands.[63] At the beginning of

---

quered it, and eight years later he added also Qaṭīf and Laḥsā to his domains. Under the Atabeks and Mongols, the island was a dependency of Fārs, under the Salāṭīn-i Turkmāniyya, of the ruler of Hurmuz; under Shāh ʿAbbās I it was again united with Fārs; under the last Ṣafawids it was seized by the Arabs of the coastal zone of Fārs and Lāristān, who had rebelled; under Nādir Shāh it was again united with Fārs; in 1209/1794-5, the rebellious Banū ʿUtba Arabs seized it. ⟨⟨Cf. Sir Arnold T. Wilson, *The Persian Gulf, an Historical Sketch from the Earliest Times to the Beginning of the Twentieth Century* (Oxford, 1930).⟩⟩ Pearls: for pearl fishing, see now Sykes, *Ten Thousand Miles*, p. 241: about one million pounds, of which one-half from Baḥrayn. According to Mustawfī, *Nuzhat al-qulūb*, ed. Le Strange, p. 138, the greatest quantity of pearls is acquired from the island of Khārk. ⟨⟨For Khārk, see also below, as well as Le Strange, *The Lands*, p. 261; Jalāl Āl-i Aḥmad, *Durr-i yatīm, jazīra-yi Khārg* (Tehran, 1339/1960); R. Ghirshman, *Île de Kharg* (Tehran, 1960); for Baḥrayn, see Bodianskii, *Bakhrein*; G. Rentz and W. Mulligan, *EI*², art. "al-Baḥrayn."⟩⟩ ⟦Aubin, "Les princes d'Ormuz du XIIIe au XVe siècle," *JA*, CCXLI (1953), pp. 77-138. For pearl fishing, see Mohammad Mokri, "La pêche des perles dans le Golfe Persique," *JA*, CCXLVIII (1960), 381-97 = *Recherches de Kurdologie. Contribution scientifique aux études iraniennes* (Paris, 1970), pp. 261-77.⟧

[60] For Qalhāt and the ruins of the old town, see J. R. Welsted, *Reisen in Arabien* (Halle, 1842), I, 32 ff. ⟨⟨See also the bibliography in the article by J. Schleifer, *EI*¹, art. "Ḳalhāt."⟩⟩ ⟦J. C. Wilkinson, *EI*², art. "Ḳalhāt."⟧

[61] *The Book of Ser Marco Polo*, ed. and tr. Sir H. Yule and H. Cordier (London, 1903), I, 113.

[62] Cf. Forbiger, *Handbuch*, II, 553-54. Sykes's opinion (*Ten Thousand Miles*, pp. 85, 302) about Mīnāb (site of the ruins of Old Hurmuz). ⟨⟨See also Le Strange, *The Lands*, p. 318; a different opinion in Schwarz, *Iran im Mittelalter*, III, 243 ff. For Hurmuz, see also R. Stube, "Zur Geschichte des Hafens von Hormuz," *Xenia Nicolaitana. Festschrift zur Feier der 400 Jahre des Bestehens der Nikolaischule in Leipzig* (Leipzig, 1912), pp. 177-96; *idem*, *EI*¹, art. "Hormuz"; L. Lockhart, *EI*², art. "Hurmuz."⟩⟩

[63] Cf. Clavijo, ed. Sreznevskii, pp. 178 ff. ⟦tr. Le Strange, pp. 160-61⟧, for the

the sixteenth century, the ruler was forced to submit to the Portuguese, who also seized the island of Qishm; in 1622 they in turn were driven out from both points by Shāh ʿAbbās. After Shāh ʿAbbās, the island lost its importance, and the town of Gombrun, now Bandar ʿAbbās, became the chief commercial port.[64] The climate on both the island and the mainland is extremely inhospitable for Europeans; the debilitating heat is compounded by humidity and dust, although it stays below the level that it reaches on the Arab coast of the gulf.[65] Maritime trade here as well as on the Makrān coast was in Arab hands; the Persians constituted the agricultural population. From the period of the reign of Nādir Shāh down to that of Nāṣir al-Dīn Shāh, Bandar ʿAbbās and some other coastal points were even in the political sense under the sway of the sulṭān of Masqaṭ; in Nāṣir al-Dīn's time, however, the Persian government succeeded in establishing its authority here. At present, the sulṭān or imām of Masqat owns on the northern coast only the harbor and district of Gwādur, within the confines of Balūchistān.[a]

The Aryans obviously occupied the littoral of Makrān only after having occupied Kirmān. The Greek name, Gedrosia, seems to be derived from that branch of the Persians which was called by Herodotus Δηρουσιαῖοι. The present name, Makrān, is not of Aryan origin but stems, most scholars believe, from the name of that people of Dravidian origin which appears in Greek sources as Μάκαι or Μύκαι, and in cuneiform inscriptions as Maka or Masiia.[66] In the work of one Greek geographer, Stephanus Byzantinus, we find the name of the region as Μακαρηνή; Muslim authors use, in addition to the form Makrān, also the form Makurān.[67] Even today,

---

submission of Hurmuz to Tīmūr. Fantastic idea about the journey from China: ten days by sea, ten days up a river to Hurmuz.

[64] In della Valle ⟨⟨instead of Gombrun there is⟩⟩ Combū and Combrū; Pietro della Valle, *The Travels . . . in India*, tr. G. Havers (London, 1892), I, 3, 8.

[65] On the island of Zarūn there is no water; it was brought there by boat from Qishm (Iskandar Munshī, ms., fol. 318b, ed. Tehran, II, 959-60, tr. Savory, II, 1181); *ibid.*, Bandar-i ʿAbbāsī; its former name was Bandar-i Kambrū; the leader of the Persians in the war of 1622; Shāh ʿAbbās was at that moment besieging Qandahār, which he took two or three days after the arrival of the news about the fall of Hurmuz (fol. 320a), *ibid.*, ed. Tehran, II, 979-82, tr. Savory, II, 1200-1204.

[a] The port of Gwādur, long a center for gun-running into Balūchistān and Afghanistan, was sold to Pakistan by Oman in 1958; see J. B. Kelly, *EI*² Suppl., s.v.

[66] Old Persian Maka-, Mačiya-, see Kent, *Old Persian*, p. 201.

[67] Marquart, *Ērānšahr*, p. 31. ⟦The etymology of the name Makrān has been much discussed. Recently, Hansman has suggested that the ancient Maga of Mesopotamian cuneiform texts equals what is now substantially Persian Makrān, and the more distant region of Melukhkha equals Pakistani Makrān; see "A Periplus of Magan

the population differs little, in terms of its civilization, from those *ichthyophagoi* whom Nearchos had seen here. The Arab geographers likewise mention fish as the staple food of the inhabitants. Because of its poverty and unfavorable climatic conditions, the littoral of Makrān had little attraction for mariners, and the history of this region remained virtually untouched by the lively maritime trade that had always existed between the estuary of the Shaṭṭ al-ʿArab and that of the Indus. From the whole littoral between Hurmuz and the port of Daybul, situated somewhat to the west of the Indus estuaries, the Arab geographers mention only one port of call, the island of Tīz off the coast of Makrān.[68] The harbor of Tīz still exists on the coast of the same bay on which the harbor of Chāhbār is situated.[69] The Arabs mention the people called al-Zuṭṭ or al-Jut, probably of Indian origin, who lived in Makrān.[b] The chief cities of Makrān were always in the interior of the country, where agriculture could be practiced, although the whole region, according to Ibn Ḥawqal, suffered from lack of water; as a result, the predominant type of population was nomadic.[70] The number of rivers is rather high, but their beds are dry for the greater part of the year. The capital of Makrān before the Arabs was Panjpūr, identical, as Marquart suggests, with Diz in the district of Panjpūr in Balūchistān not far from the Persian border.[71] Under the Arabs, the town of Kēj, the Kīj or Kīz of the Arab geographers, arose and

and Meluhha," *BSOAS*, XXXVI (1973), 554-87, but the intrusive *r* of Makrān is a difficulty here.]

[68] Description of the coast from Tīz to Daybul in Bīrūnī, *India*, tr. Sachau (London, 1888), I, 208-209 (Tīz was considered to be the beginning of the Indian coast). Cf. N. Zarudnyi's journey in 1900 ("Otchet," pp. 153 ff.); Sykes, *Ten Thousand Miles*, pp. 131, 356, regarding the Kūh-i Tāftan near Ladis (illustration with p. 132). For the old citadel of Tīz, see Zarudnyi, "Otchet," p. 163.

[69] In Chāhbār, according to Zarudnyi, "Otchet," p. 160, about 300 houses, mostly simple huts, and about 30 shops. According to Sykes (*Ten Thousand Miles*, pp. 90, 110), it is a village; Tīz is better situated. [Chāhbahār is now an important base for the Iranian Navy; see *The Persian Gulf States, A General Survey*, ed. A. J. Cottrell et al. (Baltimore, 1980), p. 158. In ca. 1950 it had a population of some 20,000 (*Farhang*, VIII, 108).]

[b] These are the Jhāts, an Indo-European people, originally centered on the Panjab but spreading westwards in early Islamic times as far as the head of the Persian Gulf; see G. Ferrand, *EI*[1], art. "Zoṭṭ," and A. S. Bazmee Ansari, *EI*[2], art. "Djāts."

[70] P. 235.

[71] Panjgūr is one of the best and most fertile regions of Makrān, and its inhabitants, the most civilized (Hughes, *The Country of Balochistan*, p. 157); the city of Panjgūr (Diz?) and its commercial importance (*ibid.*, p. 161); the term Kalāt-i Makrān (*ibid.*, passim).

remained the chief city of the region in the Middle Ages. The writers of the thirteenth to the fifteenth centuries often used the term Kīj wa Makrān in order to designate the whole province, so that Marco Polo calls it Kesmakoran[72] and reckons it as belonging to India.[73] Today Kēj also lies within the confines of Balūchistān.[74] The main city of Makrān and Persian Balūchistān is Bampūr; the governor of this region, who resides there, is a subordinate of the governor of Kirmān.[75]

[72] Marco Polo, Minaev's translation, p. 290 ⟦tr. Yule, II, 334-35⟧.

[73] The region Kīj wa Makrān was still part of India (the empire of the Great Mughals) in the seventeenth century, up to 1621; see Iskandar Munshī, ms. fol. 306b ⟦ed. Tehran, II, 861-62, tr. Savory, II, 1073-74⟧.

[74] Kēj is today not a town but a combination of several fortifications and villages; formerly there were 3,000 houses; trade with Kalāt, Shikārpūr, the ports of Gwādur and Chāhbār; now it has considerably declined (Hughes, *The Country of Balochistan*, p. 158); place where the tax collector from Kalāt stayed; Kēj and the khan of Kalāt.

[75] Bampūr, according to Sykes, *Ten Thousand Miles*, p. 122: there were two hundred huts in all. For Bampūr and Fahraj, see also *ibid.*, index. ⟨⟨For the history of Makrān and its monuments, see also Stein, *An Archaeological Tour in Gedrosia* and *Archaeological Reconnaissances in North-Western India and Southern Iran*; Vanden Berghe, *Archéologie de l'Iran ancien*, pp. 17-18, 145-46; M. L. Dames, *EI*[1], art. "Balōčistān"; Frye, *EI*[2], art. "Balūčistān."⟩⟩ ⟦Bosworth, *EI*[2], art. "Makrān"; for the geography of the region, W. B. Fisher, in *Cambridge History of Iran*, I, 81-90. As indicated by Stein, the Bampūr-Jaz Muryān basin is rich in archaeological sites, the detailed investigation of which has only recently begun; see Beatrice de Cardi, "Excavations at Bampūr, S.E. Iran: a Brief Report," *Iran, JBIPS*, VI (1968), 135-255.⟧

CHAPTER IX

Fārs

AFTER Kirmān, the Aryans must have occupied Fārs, a region that, as the name suggests, became the focal point of the Persian nation. Here the representatives of the southern branch of the Iranians achieved political unity and created a strong state. Later, when the Persian kings transferred their residence to richer regions, Fārs did not lose its significance for them; this is testified even today by the ruins of the buildings erected here by the Achaemenids and Sāsānids. From Fārs originated not only the founders of the Persian state in the sixth century B.C., but also the dynasty that in the third century A.D. restored the might of Persian nationhood and religion and that successfully put an end to the ambitions of the Roman empire at a moment when the Romans, unaware of the Persian national resurgence, considered final victory over a weakened Parthian state only a matter of time (Strabo, VI, 4). Even in the Muslim period, Fārs retained its importance for Persian national feeling; the language of Fārs, *zabān-i Fārsī*, remained the literary idiom of all Persians.[a]

Strabo, as well as the Arab geographers, divides Fārs into three climatic zones: a cold, a temperate, and a hot one.[1] In the intermediate, most fertile zone converged the characteristic vegetation of both the cold and warm lands. The basin of the large salty lake of Bakhtigān was considered part of the cold zone, together with all the districts to the north of it; even Yazd and its district, geographically more closely linked with Kirmān, were considered a part of Fārs.[2] During their movement from Kirmān into Fārs, the

[a] The exact meaning of the linguistic term *pārsī/fārsī* in early Islamic writers like Ibn al-Muqaffaʿ is a more complex question than Barthold thought; it seems to include both the literary and priestly MP language and the current spoken Persian of Fārs; see G. Lazard, "Pahlavi, Pârsi, Dari. Les langues de l'Iran d'après Ibn al-Muqaffaʿ," *Iran and Islam. In Memory of the Late Vladimir Minorsky*, ed. Bosworth (Edinburgh, 1971), pp. 360-91.

[1] Analogically, also Schwarz, *Iran im Mittelalter*, I, 11.

[2] The Arabs knew that Yazd had formerly been attributed to Kirmān (*ibid.*, p. 3, with a reference to Iṣṭakhrī, p. 101 line 1, where, however, the locality in question is al-Rūdān, which, according to other reports, lay considerably further to the south of Yazd, near Shahr-i Bābak; see *ibid.*, pp. 135, 168).

Aryans occupied first the northern part of the latter, penetrating there, along one of the three roads that, according to the description of the Arab geographers, connected Sirjān with Fārs. One of these roads led to the city of Iṣṭakhr, located near the ruins of ancient Persepolis. The valleys of the rivers Kur and its affluent called Parwāb, Pulwār, or Murghāb remained the center of Fārs until the beginning of the dynasty of the Sāsānids. The valley of the Pulwār is divided into two parts, northern and southern, by the gorge in which the village of Sīwand is located; in the northern part are the ruins of Takht-i Mādar-i Sulaymān, in which most scholars see the ruins of Pasargadae, the ancient capital of Persia.[3]

The most noteworthy structure among these ruins is the so-called tomb of Cyrus, which the natives consider to be the "tomb of Solomon's mother," *qabr-i mādar-i Sulaymān*.[4] The traditions about Solomon had obviously been brought there by the Arabs; we know from Iṣṭakhrī that the Persians identified Solomon with their mythical king Jamshīd.[5] Already at that time, people showed "Solomon's mosque" in the vicinity of Iṣṭakhr. The ruins of Persepolis, now

[3] The platform of the citadel of Pasargadae (Takht-i Sulaymān) measured, according to Ménant (*Les Achémenides*, p. 17), 80 x 60 meters; according to Jackson (*Persia Past and Present*, p. 280), 200 x 50 feet; a little further to the south is the Zindān-i Sulaymān, in reality the remnants of a fire temple (*ibid.*, p. 281); still a little further to the south are the remnants of the palace with Cyrus's inscription; to the east of them is Cyrus's bas-relief, to the west, his tomb. A picture of the tomb *ibid.*, pp. 279, 291 (cf. also, with Persepolis on p. 311). For Pasargadae, see also Herzfeld, "Pasargadae. Untersuchungen zur persischen Archaeologie," *Klio. Beiträge zur alten Geschichte*, VIII (1908), 1-68 (dimensions of the city: 1,250 x 750 meters, *ibid.*, p. 29). ⟨⟨For Pasargadae, see now F. Wachtsmuth, "Achaemenid Architecture. The Principal Monuments," *Survey of Persian Art*, I, 309-20; Vanden Berghe, *Archéologie de l'Iran ancien*, pp. 20-23, 147-48; Ghirshman, *Perse. Proto-iraniens, Mèdes, Achéménides*; Ali Sami, *Pasargadae* (Shiraz, 1956); ʿAlī Sāmī, "Pāsārgād," *Gudhārish-hā-yi Bāstān-shināsī*, IV (1338/1959), 1-172; *idem*, "Shahr-i kāwish-hā wa khākbardārī-hā wa taʿmīrāt-i Takht-i Jamshīd," *ibid.*, pp. 195-278; Frye, *Heritage*; D. Stronach, "Excavations at Pasargadae. Preliminary Reports," *Iran, JBIPS*, I-III (1963-1965).⟩⟩ ⟦*Idem, Pasargadae, a Report on the Excavations of the British Institute of Persian Studies* (Oxford, 1978).⟧

[4] Or *masjid-i mādar-i Sulaymān*, and in Ibn al-Balkhī, *Fārs-nāma*; p. 155, it is *gūr-i mādar-i Sulaymān*; today the tomb is arranged as a mosque, with a *miḥrāb*, Arabic inscriptions on the righthand side from the entrance, and copies of the Qur'ān. See Browne, *A Year amongst the Persians*, pp. 241-42.

[5] P. 123. Cf. Nöldeke, "Das iranische Nationalepos," p. 140. ⟦See the important study of A. S. Melikian-Chirvani, "Le royaume de Salomon, les inscriptions persanes de sites achéménides, *Le monde iranien et l'Islam*, I (1971), 1-41, who notes (pp. 1-20) the inscription of the Salghurid Atābeks of Fārs (see below, p. 156, note b) at Pasargadae, with the characteristic formula in their titulature of *wārith-i mulk-i Sulaymān* "heir to Solomon's kingdom."⟧

known as Takht-i Jamshīd, were said to have been built for Solomon by the jinns under his command. As for the "tomb of Solomon's mother," not all scholars have accepted that it is that of Cyrus even to this day. This structure resembles in its inner arrangement the tombs of Lycia and Pamphylia; its outward aspect is believed to betray traces of Egyptian and even Greek architecture. It is hard to say how much the present appearance of the structure corresponds to the original one; according to Arrianes, Alexander the Great found the tomb ruined and ordered Aristobulos to restore it. The manner in which Cyrus was buried differed considerably from that of the burial of other Persian kings, and reveals traces of Egyptian influence; this is explained by the fact that Cyrus was married to an Egyptian princess.[6] The Persian and Greek inscriptions on the tomb, which are mentioned by Arrianes and other authors,[7] have not been preserved. Nearby are visible the remnants of Cyrus's palace, now known as the "palace of the *dīws*"; an inscription in three languages, as is customary, was preserved on one wall: "I, king, Cyrus, the Achaemenid." We have here the earliest Persian cuneiform inscription, if indeed it can be ascribed to Cyrus. There was a bas-relief representing a winged genius in imitation of Assyrian statues; because of the above-mentioned inscription some have interpreted it as representing Cyrus; others, such as Justi,[8] objected, saying that such a representation would have been impossible while Cyrus was alive, and that the inscription simply means that Cyrus is the builder of the structure.[9]

Having passed through the gorge of Sīwand, the Pulwār issues from the valley of Ḥājjīābād into the fertile plain of Marwdasht.[10] According to contemporary travelers,[11] this plain, extending to the

[6] ⟨⟨See now G. Widengren, *Die Religionen Irans* (Stuttgart, 1965), pp. 132-34.⟩⟩

[7] ⟨⟨For the degree of trustworthiness of these reports by Greek authors, see Dandamaev, *Iran*, pp. 36-38.⟩⟩

[8] *Geschichte des orientalischen Völker*, p. 376. The inscription on the bas-relief has now disappeared. Stolze did not see it again (Herzfeld, "Pasargadae," p. 60).

[9] F. H. Weissbach, "Die altpersischen Inschriften," *GIPh*, II, 61, attributes this inscription to Cyrus the Younger, with a reference to his article "Das Grab des Cyrus und die Inschriften von Murghāb," *ZDMG*, XLVIII (1894), 653 ff. ⟨⟨The question of whether the Old Persian inscriptions in Pasargadae belong to Cyrus (II), whose name they mention, remains a matter of debate. See the survey of literature on the subject in Dandamaev, *Iran*, pp. 34-40; cf. also Oranskii,"Neskol'ko zamechanii"; Ghirshman, "À propos de l'écriture cunéiforme vieux-perse," *JNES*, XXIV (1966), 244-50.⟩⟩

[10] Marw al-Shādhān in Ṭabarī, II, 1978 ff.

[11] Tumanskii, *Ot Kaspiiskogo moria*, p. 71.

place where the Pulwār flows into the Kur, could even today be perfectly irrigated and cultivated; at present, however, only a small portion is under cultivation. Here is the city founded under Darius; it is known to us only by its Greek name, Persepolis. Various hypotheses have been advanced as to what it was called by the Persians themselves. The palaces of Darius and his successors were built on an elevated terrace on the advanced protrusion of a mountain of gray marble that descends into the valley from the east and almost reaches the banks of the Pulwār.[12] These magnificent ruins have been depicted and described many times. The palaces of Persepolis differ from the structures of Assyrian kings first of all in their columns. These are attributed to Greek architects, whose participation is also mentioned by ancient authors; some other decorations may be ascribed to them, too, but there these masters used Asian motifs.[13] A certain distance to the north of these ruins[14] there are, carved in a rock of white marble, the tombs of the kings of the Achaemenid dynasty, now known by the name of Naqsh-i Rustam.[15]

The town that in the Middle Ages was called Iṣṭakhr lay on both banks of the Pulwār. In the tenth century, it occupied a rather small

[12] The dimensions of the terrace, according to Ménant, *Les Achémenides*: 463 x 286 meters.

[13] Cf. Justi, "Geschichte Irans," *GIPh*, II, 449, about Greek artists; remarks of Farmakovskii, *Khudozhestvennyi ideal*, pp. 51 ff.; Herodotus, IV, 88, about Mandrocles.

[14] One hour's journey from the village of Iṣṭakhr. There are four tombs; similar tombs are in Persepolis itself in the rock that dominates the valley. The distance from Iṣṭakhr to Persepolis is five kilometers.

[15] ⟨⟨For the pre-Achaemenid and Achaemenid monuments in the district of Persepolis, see now Wachtsmuth, "Achaemenid architecture"; Godard, "Les travaux de Persepolis," *Archaeologia Orientalia in Memoriam Ernst Herzfeld* (New York, 1952), pp. 119-28; Vanden Berghe, *Archéologie de l'Iran ancien*, pp. 24-37, 150-53; M. D'iakonov, *Ocherk*, pp. 13, 32-33, 123 ff., 346, 356, 383; Schmidt, *Persepolis*, 2 vols.; Ghirshman, *Perse*; Frye, *Heritage*, pp. 96-97.⟩⟩ ⟦For the Sāsānid reliefs of Naqsh-i Rustam, depicting Shāpūr I's victory over the Roman Emperor Valerian, see Christensen, *L'Iran sous les Sassanides*, pp. 221 ff.; Herrmann, *The Iranian Revival*, pp. 86, 89, 94, 96-97, 100. For inscriptions carved at Persepolis in the fourteenth century by the local rulers in Fārs, the Injū'ids and Muẓaffarids, expressing, as with the Pasargadae Islamic inscriptions (see above, note 5), continuity of rule with the Solomonic power, see A. S. Melikian-Chirvani, "Le royaume de Salomon, les inscriptions persanes de sites achéménides," *Le monde iranien et l'Islam*, I (1971), 20 ff. Some four centuries previously, the Buwayhid amīr ʿAḍud al-Dawla had visited Persepolis, had gotten a local Zoroastrian priest to interpret for him the Pahlavi inscriptions there, and had caused an Arabic inscription to be carved in commemoration of his visit; see Bosworth, "The Heritage of Rulership in Early Islamic Iran and the Search for Dynastic Connections," *Iran, JBIPS*, XI (1973), 57.⟧

area, about one mile (about two versts) wide, extending primarily on the western side of the river; outside the city walls was the so-called Khurāsān bridge (Qanṭarat Khurāsān), beyond which there were only a few new buildings.[16] The Friday mosque was surrounded by a row of columns. Maqdisī makes the curious remark that on top of each column there was a figure of the head of a cow;[17] the mosque had originally been a temple of fire worshipers.

Iṣṭakhr remained the chief town of Fārs under the Sāsānids. Ardashīr raised his principal structures in the southern part of the province, but he placed the bas-relief representing his victory over Artaban the Parthian, which made him the King of Kings, at Naqsh-i Rustam above the tombs of the Achaemenids.[18]

From this time onward, the towns of the middle and southern zone began to overshadow Iṣṭakhr;[19] in the tenth century there were four towns in Fārs that surpassed Iṣṭakhr in size: Shīrāz, Fasā, Sīrāf, and Arrajān; the former two were considered part of the middle zone, the latter two, of the southern zone.[20] The whole province was divided in Arab times—and probably also in Sāsānid times—into five districts, *kūras*; in Nöldeke's opinion this word goes back, through Syriac, to the Greek word χώρα.[21] Its Persian counterpart was most probably the term *shahr*, Old Persian *khshatra*;[22] only in New Persian did the word *shahr* acquire the meaning "town, city." These five districts were Iṣṭakhr, Ardashīr-Khurra, Dārābjird,

[16] Iṣṭakhrī, p. 123. For the word *qanṭara*, see Le Strange, *The Lands*, p. 57 n. 3: the Greek word κέντρον, Latin *centrum*. In Schwarz, *Iran im Mittelalter*, I, 16, "ein neuer Stadttheil auf der rechten Seite des Flusses"; *ibid.*, pp. 15-16, reference to Maqdisī, p. 444, concerning the *malʿab Sulaymān*, at a distance of one farsakh from Iṣṭakhr. The same author's statement there that from the *malʿab* ploughed fields and settlements extend "as far as the eye can see" (at present only a small part is covered by cultivated fields, see Tumanskii, *Ot Kaspiiskogo moria*, p. 71).

[17] Maqdisī, 436.

[18] ⟨⟨For the Sāsānid monuments in the district of Iṣṭakhr, see bibliography in Vanden Berghe, *Archéologie de l'Iran ancien*; F. Sarre, "Sasanian stone sculpture," *Survey of Persian Art*, I, 593-600; Ghirshman, *Iran. Parthes et Sasanides.*⟩⟩

[19] According to Ḥamd Allāh Mustawfī Qazwīnī, *Nuzhat al-qulūb*, Iṣṭakhr was subjected under Ṣamṣām al-Dawla (989-998) to such a destruction on the part of the Amīr Qutlumush that it could be resuscitated only as a village; it has remained a village until now: Ménant, *Les Achémenides*, p. 36. According to the *Fārs-nāma* of Ibn al-Balkhī, there were in Iṣṭakhr at the beginning of the twelfth century only some one hundred men; see Le Strange, *The Lands*, p. 276. ⟨⟨For Iṣṭakhr, see also M. Streck, *EI*[1], art. "Iṣṭakhr," and M. Streck and G. C. Miles, *EI*[2], art. "Iṣṭakhr."⟩⟩

[20] Iṣṭakhrī, p. 128.

[21] Ṭabarī, tr. Nöldeke, p. 3.

[22] ⟨⟨*xšaθra-*.⟩⟩

Sābūr, and Arrajān. The two largest ones were Iṣṭakhr, which extended northward to Yazd and Nāyin,[23] and Ardashīr-Khurra, which comprised an area from Shīrāz[24] southward to the sea, and even included the islands of the Persian Gulf from Khark[25] to Qishm. East of this district was that of Dārābjird with the towns of Dārābjird, now Dārāb, and Fasā, which has retained this name to the present. The western part of Fārs consisted of the districts of Sābūr (Shāpūr), the smallest one, with the towns of Sābūr and Kāzarūn (both still exist today) and Arrajān with its capital of the same name; the ruins of the latter are near the town of Bihbihān, which is considered part of Khūzistān; in this district was, among others, the harbor of Jannāba, now Janāwa.

The valley in which Shīrāz is located begins behind the pass of Ubarak and the gorge of Allāh Akbar, or Tang-i Qur'ān.[26] Most Arab geographers attribute the foundation of Shīrāz to the Arabs; the town, like Kūfa and Wāsiṭ, developed from a military camp. As in the case of Baghdad, here too a town founded by the Arabs received an Iranian name. In Iṣṭakhri's interpretation, Shīrāz means "lion's belly," *jawf al-asad*; the city was thus named because provisions from all the surrounding areas were brought and consumed here.[27] It is quite possible that there had been a settlement here even before the arrival of the Arabs; according to some legends, its founder, Shīrāz, was the son of Fārs son of Ṭahmūrath. The

[23] The road from Iṣfahān to Nāyin in Nāṣir-i Khusraw, *Ṣafar-nāma* (Tehran lithog.), p. 249; from Iṣfahan to Nāyin, thirty farsakhs in all.

[24] Note in connection with Shīrāz in Ṭabarī, I, 873: a native of Shīrāz was Sūkhrā, the general of King Fīrūz.

[25] Sykes, *A History of Persia*, II, 375 ff., about Dutch rule on Khārk in the seventeenth century; Mīr Muhannā from Bandar-Rīg ousted them from there; under the Dutch, a town with 12,000 inhabitants developed on this previously desolate island; after them all this disappeared.

[26] Tumanskii, *Ot Kaspiiskogo moria*, p. 72. Story in Maqdisī, p. 444, that ʿAḍud al-Dawla built between Shīrāz and Iṣṭakhr a large wall (*ḥā'iṭ*) with a base (*asās*) from lead (*bi 'l-raṣāṣ*); behind this wall flowed a river; ʿAḍud al-Dawla built on it, on both sides, ten wheels for irrigation (*dawālīb*), each of which moved a millstone; a town was built there and a canal built that irrigated 300 settlements. For this town, see *ibid.*, pp. 430-31; the name *Kurd-i fanā-Khusraw*, half a farsakh from Shīrāz (in Le Strange, *The Lands*, p. 250: to the south of Shīrāz). After ʿAḍud al-Dawla's death, the town declined. Cf. now the dam Band-i Amīr; mountains of this name delimit from the left the valley in which Shīrāz is situated. The settlement of Zargān is located at the foot of the mountain that forms a continuation of the mountains of Band-i Amīr (see Tumanskii, *Ot Kaspiiskogo moria*, p. 72); according to Sykes, *Ten Thousand Miles*, p. 324, the bridge of Band-i Amīr is six miles from Zargān ⟨⟨Sykes calls it Zargūn⟩⟩.

[27] Iṣṭakhrī, p.124.

place rose in importance only in Arab times.[28] The legend about the eponymous hero is of course without foundation; more significant are the sculptural portrayals of the Achaemenids and Sāsānids in the vicinity of the town, as well as the stronghold of Qalʿa-yi Bandar or Fāhandar, of Sāsānid origin,[29] on a mountain near the tomb of the poet Saʿdī about one mile to the northeast of the modern town. It seems to be the same citadel that the Arabs called Qalʿat Shahmūbadh;[30] this name suggests that it had been built in pre-Islamic times. The Muslims attributed the fortress of Fāhandar to the Sāsānid period; the name is encountered in the fourteenth century. The fortress was destroyed by the Arabs and restored under ʿImād al-Dawla (932-949), and again under Abū Ghānim, son of ʿAḍud al-Dawla, who for this purpose demolished the palace built by his father. Also destroyed in the Arab period was the monastery, *dayr*, that had been built there under Yazdagird III.[31] In the first half of the tenth century, Shīrāz had as yet no walls,[32] but by the end of that century, Maqdisī mentions eight gates, which suggests the existence of a wall.[33] ʿAḍud al-Dawla built for himself in Shīrāz a splendid palace, and was in general solicitous about the expansion and embellishment of the town, which after him again went into a decline.

The Buwayhid dynasty under ʿAḍud al-Dawla reached the peak of its power. The whole of Persia as far as Sind was under his rule, except for Khurāsān, which belonged to the Sāmānids; in Arabia his authority was recognized not only in ʿUmān but even in distant Yemen.[34] He maintained a large army, and he did not let religious

[28] Ibn al-Faqīh, p. 196.

[29] In Ibn al-Balkhī's *Fārs-nāma*, ed. Le Strange, pp. 133, 166, the name is Pahandiz.

[30] Iṣṭakhrī, p. 116.

[31] See extracts from the *Shīrāz-nāma* in W. Ouseley, *Travels in Various Countries of the East, More Particularly Persia* (London, 1819-1823), II, 473-74. For the *Shīrāz-nāma*, see Rieu, *Catalogue of the Persian Manuscripts in the British Museum* (London, 1897-1883), I, 294b (Add. 18185); the author is Abu ʾl-ʿAbbās Aḥmad b. Abī ʾl-Khayr al-mulaqqab bi-Muʿīn al-Mushtahir Jadduhu bi-Shaykh Zarkūb al-Shīrāzī. ⟨⟨See also Storey, *Persian Literature*, I, 351, 1,294 ⟦Storey-Bregel', II, 1028-29⟧; Wilber, "Recent Persian Contributions to the Historical Geography of Iran," *Archaeologia Orientalia . . . Herzfeld*, p. 277, no. 34; *Shīrāz-nāma*, ed. Bahman Karīmī (Tehran, 1310/1931).⟩⟩ For Shīrāz, see also Khūrmujī, *Āthār-i Jaʿfarī, Taʾrīkh-i Shīrāz.*

[32] Iṣṭakhrī, p. 125; *ibid.*: the breadth is about one farsakh. According to Nāṣir-i Khusraw, *Safar-nāma*, the wall was built by Ṣamṣām al-Dawla, son of ʿAḍud al-Dawla.

[33] Maqdisī, p. 430.

[34] *Ibid.*, p. 449. ⟦For ʿAḍud al-Dawla and his achievements, see H. Bowen, *EI*[2], s.v., and H. Busse, in *Cambridge History of Iran*, IV, 262-89.⟧

considerations hamper his efforts to keep it content; thus, according to Bīrūnī, he organized prostitution on a broad scale in order to satisfy his soldiers and protect from their excesses the wives of peaceful inhabitants.[35] He strove to embellish his capital Shīrāz, where he built for himself a grandiose palace that comprised, according to Maqdisī, 360 rooms.[36] One large hall was occupied by a library that seems to have rivaled that of the Sāmānids in Bukhārā, described in Avicenna's autobiography.[37] According to Maqdisī, ʿAḍud al-Dawla collected all the books that existed in every branch of learning. The books were kept not in boxes, as in the Bukhāran library,[38] but in special niches. These niches were built along the walls of the hall and resembled little rooms made of wood with separate doors for each. They had, according to the same author, the length of a man's body and the width of three ells.[39] The books were ranged on boards, probably shelves (*wa 'l-dafātir munaḍḍada ʿalā rufūf*). In each such niche were books pertaining to a specific branch of learning; in some cases there were several niches for one branch. Maqdisī himself fairly frequently refers to manuscripts that he used in ʿAḍud al-Dawla's library. Despite its Arab origin, Shīrāz did not have an exclusively Arab character; the *gabrs* or Zoroastrians had two temples inside the city and one at its gate; Maqdisī even scolds the inhabitants for their habit of decorating the bazaars on the holidays of the infidels.[40] The town was about one farsakh in width. Yaʿqūbī explains its spaciousness by the large number of orchards: each dwelling had an orchard (Shīrāz is still famous for

[35] *India*, tr. Sachau, II, 157.

[36] Maqdisī, p. 449.

[37] Barthold, *Soch.* I, 54.

[38] For the arrangement of conservation of books in boxes and bookcases in Old Russia, see Zarubin, "Ocherki," esp. p. 194.

[39] Concerning this library, there is also a note in Ibn al-Balkhī, *Fārs-nāma*; see Le Strange, *The Lands*, p. 250. ⟦See A. Mez, *The Renaissance of Islam*, Eng. tr. S. Khuda Bakhsh (Patna, 1937), pp. 172-73; Youssef Eche, *Les bibliothèques arabes publiques et semi-publiques en Mésopotamie, en Syrie et en Égypte au Moyen-Âge* (Damascus, 1967), pp. 332 ff.; W. Heffening and J. D. Pearson. *EI*², art. "Maktaba." For books, bookmakers, booksellers, and libraries of the time see Khalidov, "Knizhnaia kul'tura."⟧

[40] Maqdisī, p. 429. ⟦On the Zoroastrians of Shīrāz and Fārs (where the old faith was still strong in the tenth century), see Spuler, *Iran in früh-islamischer Zeit*, pp. 191-92. In Maqdisī, pp. 429, 441, we find denunciations of the Zoroastrians of Shīrāz for not wearing distinctive clothing (*ghiyār*), as prescribed for *dhimmīs*, of the general lack of respect shown in the town for the Muslim religious classes (*aṣḥāb al-ṭaylasān*), and of the low moral atmosphere of the town, which permitted the open flaunting of prostitution.⟧

its parks).[41] The city and its surroundings are watered by two small rivers, the Āb-i Mīrī and Āb-i Ruknī or Ruknābād, and a multitude of springs.[42] From among the buildings mentioned by the Arab geographers, only one exists today: the Friday mosque, according to legend, whose construction is attributed to the Ṣaffārid ʿAmr b. Layth.[43] The building, according to Maqdisī, stood in the midst of bazaars and was embellished by columns resembling those of the mosque of Jerusalem.[44] It is now dilapidated through the effect of time and earthquakes, but in the center of the courtyard stands a small cubelike stone structure with round towers on the corners and a Kūfic inscription dating from the fifteenth century; it represents an imitation of the Kaʿba. The other mosque, called "new" (*masjid-i naw*), is thought to have been built by the atabeks of the thirteenth century, the Salghurids;[b] according to Ḥamd Allāh Mustawfī Qazwīnī,[45] its builder was the atabek Saʿd b. Zangī (1195-1226).[46] The brilliance of Shīrāz, which had waned after the Buwayhids, rose again during two local dynasties, that of the Salghurids (1148-1287) and that of the Muẓaffarids (1313-1393). The latter seized control of Shīrāz in 1353. At the end of the fourteenth

[41] *Kitāb al-Buldān*, p. 362.

[42] The name of the lake into which the rivulets flow is Mahalūya in the *Fārs-nāma* of Ibn al-Balkhī and in the *Nuzhat al-qulūb* of Mustawfī, see Le Strange, *The Lands*, p. 252; now it is Mahalu; cf J.n.kan in Iṣṭakhrī, pp. 100, 122.

[43] Curzon, *Persia*, II, 101. For the mosque of ʿAmr b. Layth, see also in the *Taʾrīkh-i Shīrāz*: "The Atabek Ābish Salghurī [built] a small addition to it, and Sultan Ibrāhīm Mīrzā b. Mīrzā Shāhrukh Gurkān repaired it. Naturally, during the period of almost one thousand years that have elapsed since it was built, [the mosque] has been restored repeatedly. At present, although it [still] functions [as a mosque], earthquakes have rendered it ruined and desolate."

[44] Maqdisī, p. 430.

[b] For the Salghurids, see T. W. Haig, *EI*[1], s.v.; Zambaur, *Manuel*, p. 232; Bosworth, in *Cambridge History of Iran*, V, 172-73, cf. also 354; Erdoğan Merçil, *Fars Atabegleri Salgurlular* (Ankara, 1975).

[45] *Nuzhat al-qulūb*, University ms. no. 171, fol. 222a, ⟦ed. Le Strange, p. 115, tr. *idem*, p. 114⟧.

[46] For the mosque of Saʿd b. Zangī, see also the *Āthār-i Jaʿfarī, Taʾrīkh-i Shīrāz* (the mosque was restored under Shāh Sulṭān Ḥusayn Ṣafawī, then under Ṣādiq Khān Zand; in 1269/1852-3 it collapsed in an earthquake; Ḥājjī Mīrzā ʿAlī Akbar Qawām al-Mulk Shīrāzī restored the building in the course of five years at his own expense). There is also the Jāmiʿ-i Wakīl (of Karīm Khān-i Zand); it suffered from an earthquake under Ḥusayn ʿAlī Mīrzā, was restored, again in an earthquake; further restored on the order of Nāṣir al-Dīn Shāh. There is also a new mosque, built by Mīrzā Abu 'l-Ḥasan Khān Mushīr al-Mulk. An illustration ⟨⟨of the contemporary appearance of the mosque of Saʿd⟩⟩ is in Jackson, *Persia Past and Present*, p. 325.

century, before Tīmūr's invasion, Shīrāz was one of the greatest cities of Islam. Tīmūr took it for the first time in 1387, and again in 1393; he then founded settlements around his capital, Samarqand, and, in order to express graphically the subordination of the other places to Samarqand, he named these settlements after the largest cities of western Asia: thus alongside a Miṣr, Dimashq, Baghdād, and Sulṭāniyya, there also appeared the settlement of Shīrāz, north of Samarqand.[47] Among those places of pleasure in large centers that used to yield substantial revenues to the treasury and that Tīmūr destroyed, there is mentioned the *bayt al-luṭf* of Shīrāz.[48] Saʿdī lived there under the Salghurids, Ḥāfiẓ under the Muẓaffarids; the tombs of both these poets are located in the vicinity of Shīrāz and still bring glory to the city, although the tomb of Ḥāfiẓ in its present state dates from the eighteenth century and that of Saʿdī from the nineteenth.[49]

After the Muẓaffarids, Shīrāz never again became the capital of a local dynasty, but in Tīmūrid times it continued to be an important commercial center and one of the largest cities of Persia. Only after the unification of Persia under the Ṣafawids did Shīrāz definitively decline to the rank of a provincial town, which it has retained.[50] One exception was the brief interlude in the eighteenth century when Karīm Khān-i Zand (1750-1779), who ruled over all of Persia except Khurāsān, chose it as his capital. Karīm Khān did not assume the title of *shāh*, but even with that of *wakīl* he was a fully independent sovereign. No ruler since Shāh ʿAbbās the Great did so much to restore order and security in the country and to increase its prosperity. His special solicitude was devoted to Shīrāz, his capital, which he had again surrounded with a wall, this time from stone,[51] and which he embellished with various structures. To Karīm Khān, according to Curzon, are due all the old buildings of the town that are in any state of good repair.[52]

[47] Ibn ʿArabshāh, *ʿAjāʾib al-maqdūr*, ed. S. H. Manger, *Vitae et rerum gestarum Timuri . . . historia* (Leeuwaarden, 1767-1772, II, 856-58). According to Schiltberger, *Puteshestviia*, p. 51, Christians who wanted to practice commerce were not admitted to Shīrāz.

[48] ʿAbd al-Razzāq, *Maṭlaʿ al-saʿdayn*, ms., fol. 19a.

[49] Pictures of the tombs in Jackson, *Persia Past and Present*, pp. 332, 334 ⟦and of Ḥāfiẓ's in Lockhart, *Persian Cities*, at p. 39⟧.

[50] In the sixteenth century, Shīrāz had twelve gates.

[51] (?) According to C. Niebuhr, *Reize naar Arabië* (Amsterdam, 1779-1781), II, 107 ff., it was from unfired brick.

[52] Curzon, *Persia*, II, 102. According to the *Āthār-i Jaʿfarī, Taʾrīkh-i Shīrāz*, Āghā Muḥammad was rebuilding the fortress (with unfired bricks); in 1239/1823-4 it was

Shīrāz today cannot match, in the beauty of its buildings,[53] the northern capitals Tehran and Iṣfahān, but it does continue to be one of the cultural centers of Persia; on the coins from the end of the eighteenth century and beginning of the nineteenth, that is, prior to the centralization of the mint in Tehran, the name of Shīrāz is accompanied by the epithet *Dār al-ʿilm*. The inhabitants of Fārs, according to Curzon, take pride in the purity of their origin, the correctness of their language, and the sharpness and wit of their conversation; the warm climate of Shīrāz makes possible an animated street life. In the commercial sphere, Shīrāz appears to be the marketplace of the entire province of Fārs; some local merchants, according to Tumanskii, entertain direct relations with the merchants of Manchester.[54] The primary imports are Indian goods. The principal article of export is the locally grown opium; another, although in small quantity, is local tobacco. As for the size of the city's population, estimates range from 32,000 to 60,000.[55]

Until the Islamic conquest, the chief town of the district of Ardashīr-Khurra was a town of the same name; the Arabs called it Jūr (according to Nöldeke, the local pronunciation was Gūr),[56] a name that was eventually replaced by that of Fīrūzābād (see below). The city, built by Ardashīr, did not in the tenth century surpass Iṣṭakhr in size, and was smaller than other principal cities of the province of Fārs. It seems to have conserved especially well the traits of Sāsānid architecture, and consisted only of the *shahristān* with four gates at the four points of compass, without a *rabaḍ*. In

---

again damaged by earthquake; then Mīrzā Ḥusayn ʿAlī began to restore it; in 1269/1852-3, as a result of a fresh earthquake, the fortress was completely ruined.

53 Pictures in Jackson, *Persia Past and Present*, pp. 323-34.

54 *Ot Kaspiiskogo moria*, p. 74.

55 According to Sykes, *Ten Thousand Miles*, p. 322, there were fewer than 50,000 inhabitants. ⟨⟨For Shīrāz, its history and monuments, see also *Survey of Persian Art*, II, V; Arberry, *Shiraz. Persian City of Saints and Poets;* Aziz Hatami, *Shiraz* (Tehran, 1961); Muʿīn al-Dīn Junayd Shīrāzī, *Shadd al-izār fī khaṭṭ al-awzār ʿan zuwwār al-mazār* (Tehran, 1338/1949); Bahman Karīmī, *Rāhnamā-yi āthār-i taʾrīkhī-yi Shīrāz* (Tehran, 1327/1948); Ḥasan Imdād, *Shīrāz, dar gudhashta va-ḥāl* (Shiraz, 1339/1960); for the historical geography of Fārs see also Ḥasan Fasāʾī Shīrāzī, *Fārs-nāma-i Nāṣirī*; Muḥammad Nāṣir Furṣat, *Āthār-i ʿAjam* (Bombay, 1314/1896); Le Strange, "Description of Persia and Mesopotamia in the Year 1340 A.D. from the Nuzhat al-Ḳulūb," *JRAS* (1902); Karīmī, *Jughrāfiyā-yi taʾrīkhī-yi mufaṣṣal-i gharb-i Īrān* (Tehran, 1317/1938); Stein, *Old Routes of Western Iran*.⟩⟩ ⟦Lockhart, *Persian Cities*, pp. 42-50. The population in ca. 1950 was 129,023 (*Farhang*, VII, 148); in 1976, it was 416,408 (*Le monde iranien et l'Islam*, IV [1976-1977], 242).⟧

56 Ṭabarī, tr. Nöldeke, p. 11. Cf. also Marquart, *Ērānšahr*, p. 146.

the center of the town rose a terrace called by the Arabs *al-ṭirbāl* (a tower or prominent building), by the Persians the *aywān* or *kiyākhurra*. From its top there was a view over the whole city and its surroundings, and at the summit of this elevation stood a fire temple. Opposite the terrace, a stream was conducted from a mountain; its water fell on the terrace like a waterfall and flowed down from there in another direction. This whole structure was built from stone, which was later used by the inhabitants of the town, so that already in Iṣṭakhrī's time only insignificant remnants of it were still standing.[57] Two terraces of Sāsānid construction, named *ātashgāh*, still exist; on one of them is a tower some ninety feet high. By the gate of the town, on the bank of a pond, was a fire temple called Bārīn; it had a Pahlavi inscription saying that 30,000 dirhams had been expended on building it.[58] For a distance of one farsakh from each gate, there extended orchards and palaces. To the east of the town on a mountaintop there has been preserved a palace of Sāsānid architecture with a domelike roof; in Justi's opinion,[59] this palace had already been built in the fifth century A.D. on the site of an earlier one built by Ardashīr.[60] An article exported from Jūr was—just as it is today from modern Fīrūzābād—rose water, which was considered the best in the world.[c] According to Maqdisī, the town was named Fīrūzābād by the Buwayhid ʿAḍud al-Dawla in the tenth century. After the arrival of ʿAḍud al-Dawla in Jūr or Gūr (Persian pronunciation), the inhabitants said *malik ba-gūr raft* ⟨⟨"the king has gone into a tomb"⟩⟩; ʿAḍud al-Dawla considered this a bad omen and gave the town a new, more resonant name (that of Fīrūzābād, "abode of prosperity").[61]

[57] Iṣṭakhrī, p. 124.

[58] *Ibid.*, p. 118.

[59] *Geschichte der orientalischen Völker*, p. 457.

[60] ⟨⟨For the palace in Fīrūzābād, see O. Reuther, K. Kimball and L. C. Watelin, "Sasanian architecture," *Survey of Persian Art*, I, 493-592; Vanden Berghe, *Archéologie de l'Iran ancien*, pp. 47-51, 156.⟩⟩ ⟦Matheson, *Persia, an Archaeological Guide*, pp. 251-53; Herrmann, *The Iranian Revival*, pp. 73, 83-86, 88-89.⟧

[c] For encomia of Jūrī rose water, see Thaʿālibī, *Laṭāʾif al-maʿārif*, Eng. tr. Bosworth, *The Book of Curious and Entertaining Information* (Edinburgh, 1968), pp. 127-28; according to Maqdisī, p. 443, Fārs as a whole had a reputation for the production of perfumes and aromatic substances.

[61] Maqdisī, p. 432. Sarwistān and its pre-Islamic monuments. For Gūr and Sarwistān, see Justi, *Geschichte Irans*, p. 516 (opinion about the minaret in Sāmarrā; cf. also Yāqūt, *Muʿjam*, III, 525; IV, 658, regarding Manjashāniyya one mile from Baṣra on the road to Mecca, at one time the border between the Persians and the Arabs). Le Strange, *The Lands*, p. 256, about Fīrūzābād; the river Burāza or Barāra.

A road passed from Shīrāz through Jūr or Fīrūzābād to the port of Sīrāf, today an insignificant village.[62] In the tenth century, all the goods from India destined for Fārs were brought there: aloe wood, ebony, sandalwood, amber, camphor, precious stones, and so on; in size the town was the third in Fārs, but in terms of the opulence of its citizens it occupied the first place. The price of an individual house sometimes surpassed, according to Maqdisī, 100,000 dirhams;[63] enormous amounts of capital became concentrated in the hands of some merchants as a result of trade with India, and according to Iṣṭakhrī, the sums sometimes reached 60,000,000 dirhams.[64] The wealthy man Rāmisht, who lived in the twelfth century, was considered the richest merchant of his time. According to the continuator of Ibn Ḥawqal, Rāmisht's secretary brought back from China, where he had lived for twenty years, goods worth some 500,000 dinars.[65] From this we can make a judgment about the value brought by Rāmisht himself. The latter financed a substitution of the silver ablution basin in the Kaʿba with a gold one, and

---

⟨⟨For the Sāsānid monuments of Sarwistān, see, O. Reuther, F. Kimball, and L. C. Watelin, "Sasanian Architecture," in *Survey of Persian Art*, I, 493-592; Vanden Berghe, *Archéologie de l'Iran ancien*, pp. 47, 156.⟩⟩

[62] From Shīrāz to Sīrāf, according to Iṣṭakhrī, the distance was sixty farsakhs, from Shīrāz to Jannāba, forty-four. ⟦Concerning this route, see Aubin, "La survie de Shilau et la route du Khunj-ō-Fāl," *Iran, JBIPS*, VII (1969), 21-37, showing further that Sīrāf (Shilau is the later, dialectical form of the name) by no means lapsed into total ruin after the eleventh century, but had a modest revival of prosperity from the fourteenth to the sixteenth centuries, after the ruin of the island of Qays.⟧

[63] Maqdisī, p. 426. *Ibid.* about the decline of Sīrāf and flourishing of Ṣuḥār in the tenth century (cf. *ibid.*, p. 92); *dihlīz al-Ṣīn*; according to Maqdisī, there was an earthquake in 366 or 367 (A.D. 976-978). For Sīrāf as the chief port of the Buwayhid period, see also the *Āthār-i Jaʿfarī, Taʾrīkh-i Shīrāz*. Incorrect opinion of Welsted, *Reisen*, I, 219, that ʿUmān never had any commercial importance compared to Masqaṭ, Ṣuḥār, and Qalhāt. ⟦The site of Sīrāf has since 1966 been exhaustively examined and excavated by a team of British archaeologists under the auspices of the British Institute of Persian Studies; for interim reports, see D. Whitehouse, in *Iran, JBIPS*, VI (1968), 1-22; VII (1969), 39-62; VIII (1970), 1-18; IX (1971), 1-17, X (1972), 63-87; XI (1973), 1-30. A full account is in course of publication. See also Matheson, *Persia, an Archaeological Guide*, pp. 246-49.⟧

[64] Iṣṭakhrī, 154. ⟨⟨Cf. G. Ferrand, *Voyage du marchand arabe Sulaymân* (Paris, 1922); Krachkovskii, *Arabskaia geograficheskaia literatura*, pp. 141 ff.⟩⟩

[65] Ibn Ḥawqal, p. 198. ⟨⟨For additions to Ibn Ḥawqal's work, introduced by the editor of the Hispano-Arabic version in 1139-1184, see *BGA*, II, V; Krachkovskii, *Arabskaia geograficheskaia literatura*, p. 204.⟩⟩ ⟦Cf. A. Miquel, *La géographic humaine du monde musulman jusqu'au milieu du IIe siècle* (Paris, 1967), I, 299-309.⟧

he donated on behalf of the temple a *kiswa* made from costly Chinese fabrics.[66]

To the east of Shīrāz on the highway through Fārs to Hurmuz and the southern portion of Kirmān lay the district of Dārābjird, belonging by climate to the same middle zone; here too converged the cultivation of the products of cold and warm lands. The chief town of the district, Fasā, was second in Fārs in terms of size,[67] but the modern town has no remnants left from antiquity. No longer remarkable are the two towns, or more exactly villages, of Dārābjird, whose creation tradition ascribes to Darius I, and Furg or Furj, Arabic Burj, both also situated on the main road from Fārs to Kirmān. In the tenth century, there were fortified towns of commerce and industry here, and the main market was in Fasā. Near Dārābjird was mined, just as today, the mineral *mūmiyā'* [or mummy] a kind of bitumen used as medicine for wounds and fractures; *mūmiyā'* was exported to all countries, and its mining was then, as now, a government monopoly.[68] The same substance was used in antiquity for embalming corpses, hence the term for Egyptian mummies. A border town of Fārs was Ṭārum, now Ṭārun; the road from there to Hurmuz led, most probably, through the mountain gorge Tang-i Zag, famous, according to Tumanskii, throughout the whole south of Persia.[69] Subsequently the district of Dārābjird bore the name Shabānkāra and was ruled by a dynasty of local provenience, the Faḍlawayhids.[70] According to tradition, this dynasty's claims to legitimacy go back to pre-Islamic times, but more detailed data about its members who, like other local rulers, bore the Turkish title *atabek*, pertain only to the Mongol period.[71]

[66] The author met Rāmisht in Aden in 539/1144-5. Cf. K. Inostrantsev, "Pereselenie Parsov," p. 137 n. 2; the date 532/1138, the price of the covering was 18,000 dīnārs. In the thirteenth century, Sīrāf, according to Yāqūt, was ruined, cf. Le Strange, *The Lands*, p. 259; *ibid.*, for the destruction of Sīrāf by Rukn al-Dawla Khumārtigin, amīr of the island of Qays, according to the *Fārs-nāma*. ⟨⟨See also S. M. Stern, "Rāmisht of Sīrāf, a Merchant Millionaire of the Twelfth Century," *JRAS* (1967), pp. 10-14.⟩⟩

[67] Iṣṭakhrī, p. 128.

[68] *Ibid.*, p. 155. ⟦Dārābjird was an important town in Sāsānid times, and nearby is a celebrated Sāsānid rock relief depicting Shāpūr I, according to the traditional view, but Ardashīr I in the view of Georgina Herrmann; see her "The Dārābgird Relief—Ardashīr or Shāhpūr?" *Iran, JBIPS*, VII (1969), 63-88.⟧

[69] *Ot Kaspiiskogo moria*, p. 96.

[70] For the decline of Dārābjird in the twelfth century, according to the *Fārs-nāma*, see Le Strange, *The Lands*, p. 289.

[71] S. Lane-Poole ⟦*The Muhammadan Dynasties*, pp. 172-73⟧, Russian tr. Barthold,

The capital of the Faḍlawayhids, the fortress Īg (near the town of Zarkān), lay to the northwest of Dārābjird.[72] In the middle of the fourteenth century, this dynasty was overthrown by the Muẓaffarids. The Arab geographers give almost no information about the present district of Lāristān with the chief city of Lār and the important harbor of Linga.[73]

To the west of Shīrāz lay the district of Sābūr, the smallest [district of Fārs] in size: its chief towns were Nawbanjān and Kāzarūn. The name of the district stems from that of its former capital, the city of Shāpūr or, as Maqdisī calls it, Shahristān.[74] As the name suggests, Shāpūr was founded under the Sāsānids; in the tenth century it had already lost its former importance because of the rise of Kāzarūn. Not far from the ruins of the city one can still see in the mountains several bas-reliefs, one of which represents the victory of Shāpūr I (249-272) over the Roman emperor Valerian; there is on the same site a statue of Shāpūr I, the only extant statue from the Sāsānid period.[75] The road from Shīrāz to Kāzarūn, described

---

Musul'manskie dinastii (St. Petersburg, 1899), p. 298. ⟨⟨See also Ṣāḥib, *Daftar-i dilkushā*, ed. R. Khadi-zade (Moscow, 1965).⟩⟩ ⟦Zambaur, *Manuel de génealogie et chronologie pour l'histoire de l'Islam*, p. 233; Spuler, *Die Mongolen in Iran*, pp. 146-47; *idem*, *EI*², art. "Faḍlawayh"; Cahen, "Faḍluwayh le Shāvankāreh," *Studia Iranica*, VII (1978), 111-15. The unpublished general history of Persia, the *Majmaʿ al-ansāb fi 'l-tawārīkh* of Muḥammad b. ʿAlī Shabānkāra'ī (d. 1358), is also in large part a special history of Fārs and of the Shabānkāra'ī Kurds; see Storey, *Persian Literature*, 84-85, and Storey-Bregel', I, 334-37.⟧

72 Mustawfī, *Nuzhat al-qulūb*, University ms. no. 171, fols. 230a, 245b ⟦ed. Le Strange, pp. 138, 187, tr. *idem*, pp. 137, 178⟧. In the *Ta'rīkh-i Shīrāz*, Īk or Īj; much more correct is the form Īg in Le Strange, *The Lands*, p. 289. Cf. Yāqūt, *Muʿjam*, I, 415, for the fruits and their export to the island of Kīsh.

73 The conquest of Lāristān under Shāh ʿAbbās in 1601; succession of rulers since Kiyānid times (Iskandar Munshī, ms., fol. 119a) ⟦ed. Tehran, II, 616-18, tr. Savory, II, 805-808⟧. According to Le Strange, *The Lands*, p. 291, Lār is for the first time mentioned in the fourteenth century by Mustawfī. ⟨⟨For Lāristān, see Romaskevich, "Lar i ego dialekty" (with detailed bibliography); Aḥmad Iqtidārī, *Lāristān-i kuhan (taḥqīq dar bāra-yi Lāristān-i qadīm)* (Tehran, 1334/1955); J. Aubin, "Les sunnites du Lārestān et la chute des Ṣafavides," *REI*, XXXIII (1965), 151-71.⟩⟩ ⟦Much more, however, is known about Lāristān in post-Mongol times; see J. Calmard, *EI*², art. "Lār, Lāristān," and for the island of Linga, Bosworth, s.v.⟧

74 Maqdisī, p. 432.

75 Iṣṭakhrī, p. 150, regarding a mountain in the confines of Sābūr with portraits of Persian kings, *marzbāns* and priests (Schwarz, *Iran im Mittelalter*, II, 42). There is an error on the map (Shāpūr is to the northwest of Kāzarūn, not to the northeast). ⟨⟨For the Sāsānid monuments in the area of Shāpūr, see the bibliography in Vanden Berghe, *Archéologie de l'Iran ancien*, pp. 54-57, 158-59, 242; Ghirshman, *Iran. Parthes et Sassanides; idem, Les mosaiques sassanides* (Paris, 1956).⟩⟩ ⟦Shāpūr is more generally known today as Bīshāpūr; see also for its pre-Islamic monuments, Matheson, *Persia*,

by the Arabs,[76] coincided with the first part of the modern highway from Shīrāz to Būshahr.[77]

In Kāzarūn[78] and the modest town Tawwāj or Tawwāz, halfway between Kāzarūn and the harbor of Jannāba,[79] were woven the linen fabrics called *tawwājī* or *tawwāzī,* famous throughout the Islamic world. By Mustawfī's time (fourteenth century), Tawwāj already lay in ruins.[80] No less famous were the textiles of the town Sīnīj or Sīnīz, situated not far from the estuary of the Ṭāb on the border of Fārs and Khūzistān; the term *sīnīzī* was also borne by textiles woven in Samarqand, which shows that the crafts of Fārs influenced those of Māwarānnahr. In turn, the textile industry of Fārs developed, it would seem, under the influence of that of Egypt; flax for *sīnīzī* was first imported from that country, but later it came to be grown locally. One of the fabrics produced locally was called *dabīqī,* after the Egyptian town of Dabīq.[81]

Būshir, more exactly Būshahr, now the main port on the Persian Gulf, gained this prominence only in the eighteenth century under Nādir Shāh. The site was already inhabited, judging by archaeological finds, in pre-Islamic times. Among the finds are even inscriptions made by the inhabitants of Susiana, some dating from

an Archaeological Guide, pp. 236-40; Herrmann, *The Iranian Revival,* pp. 15-16, 23, 90, 92-94, 101-105.⟧

[76] Mention in Mustawfī, *Nuzhat al-qulūb* ⟦ed. Le Strange, pp. 185-86, tr. *idem,* p. 176⟧, of the road to Qays through Kārzīn; the latter lay, according to Iṣṭakhrī, p. 120, on the same rivulet as Kuwār. Cf. Yāqūt, *Muʿjam,* IV, 974; Le Strange, *The Lands,* pp. 257, 296. According to Iṣṭakhrī, p. 134, ten farsakhs from Fasā was Jahrum, eighteen farsakhs from it was Kārzīn.

[77] Cf. Le Strange, *The Lands,* p. 296. On the border of Shāpūr and Ardashīr-Khurra was Dasht-i Bārīn and constructions of Mihr-Narse; see Ṭabarī, tr. Nöldeke, pp. 111 ff.

[78] ⟨⟨For the history of Kāzarūn, see also ⟦the life of⟧ Abū Iṣḥāq Kāzarūnī ⟦Maḥmūd b. ʿUthmān, *Firdaws al-murshidiyya fī asrār al-ṣamadiyya*⟧, ed. F. Meier (Leipzig, 1948).⟩⟩ ⟦This work shows the continued strength of Zoroastrianism in Kāzarūn in the late tenth century, that is, under the Būyids; the governor of the town was a Zoroastrian; cf. Frye, "The New Persian Renaissance in Western Iran," *Arabic and Islamic Studies in Honor of Hamilton A. R. Gibb,* ed. G. Makdisi (Leiden, 1965), p. 227.⟧

[79] Tawwāj, according to Iṣṭakhrī, p. 120, is on the rivulet Ratīn, which flows into the Nahr Sābūr, then leaves it, passes by Tawwāj, and flows into the sea. For Tawwāj, see also Le Strange, *The Lands,* pp. 259 ff.: "its site has never been identified"; even at the beginning of the twelfth century, its greater part lay in ruins; by the fourteenth century, there was nothing but ruins.

[80] *Nuzhat al-qulūb,* University ms. no. 171, fol. 222b ⟦ed. Le Strange, p. 116, tr. *idem,* p. 115⟧.

[81] Barthold, *Turkestan,* p. 236, *Soch..* I, 296. ⟦R. B. Serjeant, *Islamic Textiles, Material for a History up to the Mongol Conquest* (Beirut, 1972), pp. 48-59.⟧

the eighth century B.C.[82] In the tenth century A.D., however, there was no harbor here that could compare with that of Jannāba, let alone Sīrāf or Hurmuz. The locality was known by the name of Sīf, "sea-coast." In the fourteenth century, Mustawfī distinguishes between Sīf Abī Rashīr[d] and Sīf ʿUmāra; here, as in other coastal areas, Arabs constituted the main element of the population.[83] In the sixteenth century the Portuguese fortification of Reshir was situated here. Some ten versts to the north of this fortress was the harbor chosen by Nādir Shāh for the construction of a fleet in the Persian Gulf.[84] The conditions for lying at anchor and especially for unloading are most unfavorable here. The harbor is not sheltered from winds, and in bad weather it is inaccessible; also, because of shallowness it is necessary to unload freight into local barges. Nonetheless, a considerable volume of trade with China, India, and Europe converges on Būshahr, which is linked with the center of the state by relatively adequate roads; this trade is almost exclusively in the hands of the British.[85]

The coastal belt, with the town of Jannāba, was usually considered a part of the district of Arrajān, although the Arab geographers do not exactly define the boundaries of the respective districts, and we find conflicting reports in their works as to the connection of the individual towns with this or that district. The town of Arrajān itself is usually identified with the ruins near the town of Bihbihān.[86]

[82] ⟨⟨For the monuments in the district of Bushīr (ancient Liyān), see bibliography in Vanden Berghe, *Archéologie de l'Iran ancien*, pp. 165-74.⟩⟩

[d] Correctly, Sīf Abī Zuhayr, as in Le Strange, *The Lands*, pp. 256-58.

[83] *Nuzhat al-qulūb*, University ms. 171, fol. 222b ⟦ed. Le Strange, p. 116, tr. *idem*, pp. 114-15⟧.

[84] For Rīshahr and Būshahr, see *Āthār-i Jaʿfarī, Taʾrīkh-i Shīrāz* (the former was supposedly founded by Luhrāsp and embellished by the constructions of the Sāsānid Ardashīr; Būshīr under Nādir Shāh, under Nāṣir al-Dīn Qājār; military clashes with the British). For Būshīr and the residence of the British agent in Sabzābād, seven miles to the south of Būshīr on the highest point of the island, for Sīf (?Shīf) to the north of Būshīr, see Sykes, *Ten Thousand Miles*, p. 313. ⟨⟨For Rīshahr and Rēshīr, see *Ḥudūd al-ʿālam*, tr. Minorsky, p. 378 and note 1.⟩⟩ ⟦Lockhart, *EI*^{2}, art. "Bū<u>sh</u>ahr (Bū<u>sh</u>īr)." In 1976, the population of Būshahr was 57,681 (*Le monde iranien et l'Islam*, IV [1976-1977], 242).⟧

[85] Rittikh, *Ocherk Persii*, pp. 190-91. ⟦It is now a base for the Iranian navy, though subordinate to Bandar ʿAbbās in the Strait of Hurmuz.⟧

[86] Arrajān as the place of residence of the governor of Fārs and Kirmān is mentioned by Balādhurī, p. 392. According to Le Strange, *The Lands*, p. 268, Bihbihān replaced Arrajān and became the chief town of the district after the end of the twelfth century. For Arrajān, see also Nāṣir-i Khusraw, *Safar-nāma* (Tehran lithog.), pp. 244-45, "twenty thousand men"; the same number in Jerusalem (Mednikov, *Palestina*, II/2, 854), in Tinnīs (in Egypt) 50,000 (Nāṣir-i Khusraw, *Safar-nāma* Teh-

In the tenth century, it lay somewhat further to the south, by the river Ṭāb, more specifically near that part of its course which is today called Khayrābād;[87] a magnificent bridge was built here with the money donated by one of the wealthy people of Fārs, and it was considered to be the boundary between Fārs and Khūzistān.[88] The foundation of Arrajān was ascribed to the Sāsānid king Qawādh who had ruled at the end of the fifth and beginning of the sixth century. In the tenth century, Arrajān was one of the large towns of Fārs but, it would seem, its importance was less industrial than commercial; this was determined by the fertility of its environs, proximity of the sea, and position of the city on the main road from Fārs to Khūzistān and from there to Mesopotamia. The road from Shīrāz to Arrajān led northwestward through the village of Guyūm or Juwaym. Its further direction is not quite clear, because the names of the villages mentioned in the Arabic itinerary no longer exist; the town of Nawbanjān lay on this road, but that of Shāpūr was situated to one side of it.[89]

Alongside the towns of commerce and industry that gained importance in the Islamic period, there were still in the tenth century remnants of earlier feudal systems exemplified by mountain castles that numbered, according to the testimony of the Arab geographers, some 5,000; among these were even such as had never been taken by assault.[90] Some of these castles were in the hands of the fire worshipers, of whom there were still many in the tenth century. They had their temples in almost every town and in each group of villages,[91] and their number exceeded that of the Christians and Jews.[92] According to Mustawfī, the ruin of towns based on commerce and crafts was caused by the inhabitants of these castles. As for the city of Arrajān, it was said to have been destroyed by the Ismāʿīlīs or Assassins.[93]

---

ran lithog., p. 97); in Nīshāpūr barely one-fifth of the number that was in Miṣr (*ibid.*, p. 143); in Jidda 5,000 (*ibid.*, p. 174); in Laḥsā the Carmathians had over 20,000 soldiers (*ibid.*, p. 220); environs of Arrajān.

[87] For the river Tāb in the Middle Ages, see Le Strange, *The Lands*, p. 270.

[88] Ibn Ḥawqal, p. 191.

[89] Iṣṭakhrī, p. 133. ⟦For the historical geography and archaeology of the region, see H. Gaube, *Die Südpersische Provinz Arraǧān/Kūh-Gīlūyeh von der arabischen Eroberung bis zur Safawidenzeit* (Vienna, 1973).⟧

[90] Iṣṭakhrī, p. 116.

[91] *Ibid.*, p. 118.

[92] Maqdisī, p. 439. *Ibid.*, for the Shīʿīs of the coastal zone and for the Ṣūfīs.

[93] *Nuzhat al-qulūb*, University ms. no. 171, fol. 227 ⟦ed. Le Strange, p. 130, tr. *idem*, p. 129⟧.

Beside the sedentary population of Fārs, there have always lived there, in the past as today, many nomads. The western edge of the Iranian plateau is formed by the same kind of parallel mountain chains with scant vegetation that we saw along its northeastern edge; the mountain chains are separated from each other by valleys and plateaus, sometimes fertile and well watered, but more often, because of their considerable altitude, suited only for pasture land. At present the nomadic peoples of Fārs and Khūzistān have various names; in their physiognomy those nomads who speak Iranian dialects differ quite sharply from the Fārsīs, and probably represent a mixture of former inhabitants with Aryan conquerors. Apart from the Iranian-speaking nomads, many groups of peoples of Turkish and Arabic origin live as nomads in the same areas.[94] The geographers of the tenth century subsume all the Iranian nomads under the name of Kurd, after that of the largest group. Similarly, corresponding to the five districts of the sedentary population, five districts of nomads were distinguished in Fārs, but the boundaries of the two types of district did not coincide. The areas of movement of each nomadic group had to cover a fairly extensive territory, because almost all the nomads spent the summers in the mountains and the winters near the seacoast. The term *zumm* (pl. *zumūm*) is used for a nomadic district; de Goeje derives this term from the Kurdish word *zume*.[95] Up to 500,000 households of nomads were accounted in Fārs; at the head of each *zumm* was a special chieftain charged with collecting taxes and insuring the security of roads.[96]

The Kurdish term *zumm* has now been replaced by its Turkish counterpart, *il*. The Persian government today pursues the same policy toward the nomads as it has in the past. According to Curzon, it has learned from experience that the only way to hold the nomads in any degree of submission is to let them keep their own chieftains: the appearance of Persian tax collectors among the nomads brought no benefit to the treasury and caused disturbances among the population.[97] At present, the Iranian nomads are counted separately

[94] ⟨⟨For the nomads of southwestern Iran, see now *Narody Perednei Azii*, pp. 276-82, 558; Ivanov, *Plemena Farsa*; Bahmanbīgī, *'Urf u 'ādāt dar 'ashā'ir-i Fārs* (Tehran, 1324/1945); C. G. Feilberg, *Les Papis, tribu persane de nomades montagnards du Sud-Ouest de l'Iran* (Copenhagen, 1952); V. Monteil, *Les tribus du Fars et la sédentarisation des nomades* (Paris and The Hague, 1956); F. Barth, *Nomads of South Persia, the Basseri Tribe of the Khamseh Confederacy* (Oslo and New York, 1961), and the bibliographies in these works.⟩⟩ ⟦For general surveys, see A.K.S. Lambton, *EI*², art. "Īlāt"; B. D. Clark, in *The Persian Gulf States*, ed. Cottrell *et al.*, pp. 503-506.⟧

[95] Ibn Khurradādhbih, tr. p. 33 (notes by de Goeje).

[96] Iṣṭakhrī, pp. 113-15.

[97] *Persia*, I, 436; II, 271.

from the tribes of Turkish[98] and Arabic origin; the latter two are combined in an artificial group, the Īlāt-i Khamsa, similar to the five *zumms* of the tenth century. Officially only 60,000 tents of nomads are counted in Fārs at present, but, in Tumanskii's opinion, this figure is below the actual one.[99] Even today the nomads spend the summers on high plateaus, whereas for the winter they descend partly to the terraces of the warm slopes turned toward the Persian Gulf (*garmsīrāt*), partly to the lowland of Arabistān—in other words, to the southern part of Khūzistān. The Persian terms *garmsīr* and *sardsīr*, used by these nomads, roughly correspond to the Turkish terms *qïshlaq* and *yaylaq*.

We have seen the district of Yazd also pertained to Fārs. The road from Shīrāz to Yazd led then, as now, through Iṣṭakhr, Dihbid, and Abarqūh. The town of Yazd also had the name Kuththa.[100] As in Kirmān, in Yazd and Abarqūh too the predominant type of building was one made from clay with a domelike roof; wood was not used because of the lack of forests. Yazd was celebrated for the fertility of its surroundings, and it was always one of the most important stations in long-distance trade. Except for the period of the Atabeks of Yazd, who ruled there from the middle of the eleventh century to the end of the thirteenth,[101] the city had no political importance; its commercial importance, however, has been maintained to this day. According to certain censuses, its inhabitants number up to 80,000 souls;[102] the number of commercial and industrial buildings, especially the spinning and weaving workshops, is also very high. In Yazd, the Zoroastrian religion still has a con-

[98] The Turks, especially the Qashqā'ī: see Tumanskii, *Ot Kaspiiskogo moria*, p. 77; article of Romaskevich, "Pesni Kashkaitsev"; their winter quarters in the southern and southwestern districts of Fārs, summer quarters in the area of Iṣfahān. ⟦See also F. Sümer, *EI*², art. "Kas̲h̲ḳāy"; P. Oberling, *The Qashqā'ī Nomads of Fars* (The Hague, 1974).⟧

[99] *Ot Kaspiiskogo moria*, p. 75.

[100] Illustrations in Sykes, *Ten Thousand Miles*, p. 420; Jackson, *Persia Past and Present*, pp. 345 ff., 374 ff.

[101] Lane-Poole, *The Muhammadan Dynasties*, pp. 172-73 tr. Barthold, *Musul'manskie dinastii*, pl. 298. ⟦See Zambaur, *Manuel*, p. 231, for the Atābeks of the thirteenth century, and for the preceding governors of Yazd and Abarqūh under the Saljuqs, the Kākūyids displaced from Iṣfahān and Hamadān, see Bosworth, "Dailamīs in Central Iran: the Kākūyids of Jibāl and Yazd," *Iran, JBIPS*, VIII (1970), 84-95.⟧

[102] The entire population of Yazd, according to Jackson, *Persia Past and Present*, p. 350, was 30,000 to 40,000, or, together with the villages, 60,000. According to Sykes, *Ten Thousand Miles*, it is 60,000. ⟦The population of the town itself in ca. 1950 was 24,959 (*Farhang*, X, 213). In 1976, it was 135,978 (*Le monde iranien et l'Islam*, IV [1976-1977], 242).⟧

siderable number of followers;[103] the Muslim population, according to Khanikoff, is noted for its fanaticism.[104] According to other reports, the population is relatively tolerant and moderate, perhaps as a result of its proximity to the *gabrs*; the explosion of fanaticism, whose victims in 1891 became the Bābīs, was deliberately provoked by the government.[105] The present town is surrounded by ruins; from among the existing buildings the most ancient—the so-called Mosque of Amīr Chaqmaq—was built, as an inscription on one of its walls shows, in 699/1299-1300 by the amīr Sunqur.[106] There is a plan of Yazd in Khanikoff's book.[107]

[103] According to Jackson, *Persia Past and Present*, pp. 354, 425, there were 8,000 *gabrs* in Yazd, and 11,000 in all of Persia; according to Sykes, *Ten Thousand Miles*, p. 423, there are 7,000 *gabrs* in Yazd, of whom only 1,000 "live in the actual city." For their rituals, Jackson, *Persia Past and Present*, p. 366: "Upon reaching the temple I found it to be a simple unpretentious building. . . . Mohammedanism allows no rivals to its beautiful mosques with turquoise domes, arabesques, arches, and slender tessellated minarets." ⟦E. G. Browne, during his stay in Iran 1887-1888, had much contact with the Zoroastrian and Bahā'ī communities of Yazd, and records of the former that "though less liable to molestation now than in former times, they often meet with ill-treatment and insult at the hands of the Muhammadans, by whom they are regarded as pagans, not equal even to Christians, Jews, and other 'people of the book,' " and mentions some of the violence and persecution that they had to suffer (*A Year amongst the Persians*, 2nd ed., pp. 404-56). The surviving Zoroastrian communities of the Yazd region, now shrinking under relentless pressures from the surrounding Muslim environment, have been recently studied at firsthand by Mary Boyce; see her "The Zoroastrian Houses of Yazd," *Iran and Islam. In Memory of the Late Vladimir Minorsky*, pp. 125-47, and *A Persian Stronghold of Zoroastrianism. Based on the Ratanbai Katrak Lectures 1976* (London, 1977).⟧

[104] *Mémoire*, p. 202.

[105] Zhukovskii, "Nedavnie kazni."

[106] Cf. Jackson, *Persia Past and Present*, p. 350; Sykes, *Ten Thousand Miles*, pp. 420-21; the mosque was built by ʿAlā' al-Dawla Garshāsp in 513/1119; it was rebuilt by Sayyid Rukn al-Dīn in 777/1375, on the mosaic there is the date of 877/1472; in that year Mīr Chaqmaq "covered it with beautiful designs." The fortress was built in 532/1137 "by Abú Jafar Sultán, Alá-u-Din, Kanjár" (Sykes, *Ten Thousand Miles*, p. 421). A fourteenth-century observatory in Yazd, according to Sykes (*ibid.*); same source for Chaqmaq. Qalʿat al-Majūs five farsakhs from Yazd, on the road to Abarqūh (Iṣṭakhrī,, p. 130). Yazd as being "extremely cold" in Maqdisī, p. 437; Cf. Jackson, *Persia Past and Present*, p. 349. In Le Strange, *The Lands*, p. 285, quotation from Mustawfī, who says that "Yazd is built with unfired bricks, which are here as durable as fired bricks in other places, for it almost never rains in Yazd."

[107] ⟨⟨*Mémoire*. For the history and monuments of Yazd, see also *Survey of Persian Art*, II, v; ʿAbd al-Ḥusayn Āyatī, *Ta'rīkh-i Yazd ya ātashkada-yi Yazdān* (Yazd, 1317/1938); Muḥammad Mufīd Bāfqī, *Jāmiʿ-i mufīdī*, III, ed. Īraj Afshār (Tehran, 1340/1961); Jaʿfar b. Muḥammad Jaʿfarī, *Ta'rīkh-i Yazd*, ed. Īraj Afshār (Tehran, 1343/1965).⟩⟩ ⟦Lockhart, *Persian Cities*, pp. 106-11.⟧

CHAPTER X

Iṣfahān, Kāshān, and Qum

THE center of Fārs is connected by several roads with the large towns of northern Persia. In the Middle Ages, the road from Shīrāz to Iṣfahān did not pass through Iṣṭakhr, as it does now; the shorter route through the town of Māyīn was considered the main road. This road joined, it would seem, the present-day one near the town of Yazdīkhwāst, situated on a cliff in the middle of a valley; this town, despite its ancient name, is not mentioned in the tenth-century itineraries. It is the fourteenth-century itinerary by Ḥamd Allāh Mustawfī Qazwīnī that mentions the chief towns along this route, Qūmish and Yazdīkhwāst;[1] the route from Yazdīkhwāst to Shīrāz through Māyīn was called the "summer [route]" (*rāh-i tābistānī*) and the present-day detour the "winter [route]" (*rāh-i zimistānī*).[2]

The town of Iṣfahān is mentioned by the classical geographers as ᾿Ασπαδάνα, but it had no importance in those days.[3] In Sāsānid times, there was here the town of Jay.[4] Its founding was attributed to Alexander of Macedonia, and the name of this town is frequently encountered even on the coins of the Arab period. There exists a work about Iṣfahān by the fourteenth-century historian Ḥusayn b. Muḥammad al-ʿAlawī; its name is *Taʾrīkh aḥwāl Iṣfahān*; the English orientalist E. G. Browne has analyzed this work in a special study.[5]

[1] *Nuzhat al-qulūb*, University ms. 171, fol. 245a ⟦ed. Le Strange, p. 185, tr. *idem*, p. 176⟧.

[2] According to Le Strange (*The Lands*, p. 283), Yazdīkhwāst is mentioned for the first time in the *Fārs-nāma*; in Maqdisī, pp. 437, 458, in the form Ikkās. The border between Fārs and Iṣfahān now passed to the north of Yazdīkhwāst (Sykes, *Ten Thousand Miles*, p. 331); for the external appearance of Yazdīkhwāst, see *ibid.*, p. 330.

[3] Cf. M.D'iakonov, *Ocherk*, pp. 288, 407.

[4] There is also a settlement called Jay one farsakh from Tehran, on the road from Karaj (Berezin, *Puteshestvie*, pt. 2, p. 141). ⟨⟨For the etymology of the name Jay, Old Iranian *Gaba-, transmitted in Greek as Γάβαι, Middle Persian Gay, Parthian Gaβ, see Henning, "Gabae," *Asia Major*, n.s., II (1952), p. 144.⟩⟩

[5] ⟨⟨"Account of a Rare Manuscript History of Isfahan," *JRAS* (1901), pp. 411-46, 661-704. For the Arabic original of this work see Barthold, *Iran, Soch.* VII, 288; for the editions of the Arabic text and Persian translation see Spuler, *Iran in früh-*

According to this source,[6] the town of Jay of the Sāsānid period was built on the model of all Sāsānid towns with four gates.[7] Among these was the "Gate of the Jews," Darvāza-i Juhūdān; obviously, a Jewish colony had sprung up here, and it subsequently gave the principal part of the city the name of Yahūdiyya.[8] In the tenth century, the old town was known by the name of Shahristān and was inferior to Yahūdiyya in size and population;[9] here the Jews were considered, just as in other places, to be descendants of Nebuchadnezzar's captives.[10] The distance between Shahristān and Yahūdiyya was two miles, that is, about four versts. There was near Shahristān a large bridge across the Zāyinda Rūd.[11] Shahristān is

---

islamischer Zeit, p. 554.⟫ ⟦This is the *Ta'rīkh Iṣfahān* of al-Mufaḍḍal b. Sa'd al-Māfarrukhī (wrote 421/1030); see on the Arabic original, Brockelmann, *GAL*, S I, p. 571, and on the Persian translation written ca. 729/1329 by Ḥusayn b. Muḥammad Ḥusaynī 'Alawī, Storey, *Persian Literature*, 349, and Storey-Bregel', II, 1,011-12. There also exists the Arabic biography of the scholars and other prominent figures of Iṣfahān by Abū Nu'aym Aḥmad al-Iṣfahānī (d. 430/1038), the *Dhikr akhbār Iṣfahān*, ed. S. Dedering (Leiden, 1931), see J. Pedersen, *EI*², s.v., and below, n. 43.⟧

[6] Browne, "Account," pp. 417-18.

[7] Description of Jay according to Ibn Rusta, pp. 160 ff.: four gates, half a farsakh in circuit (6,000 *dhirā'*s); the area 2,000 *jarībs* = 1.28 square versts. The distances between the gates and towers, according to Ibn Rusta:

Bāb Khūr (SE) to Bāb al-Yahūdiyya (SW) – 1,100 *dhirā'*s, 18 towers
Bāb al-Yahūdiyya (SW) to Bāb Ṭīra (NW) –1,200 *dhirā'*s, 23 towers
Bāb Ṭīra (NW) to Bāb Isfīj (NE) – 1,300 *dhirā'*s, 24 towers
Bāb Isfīj (NE) to Bāb Khūr (SE) – 2,400 *dhirā'*s, 35 towers

Sum total: 6,000 *dhirā'*s, 100 towers. The diameter was 320 *qaṣabas* or 1,920 *dhirā'*s. According to Browne, "Account," p. 418, the village of Ādhar-Shāpūrān is "by the gate of the Jews"; Fīrūz built here a palace with an orchard and a fire temple. For Iṣfahān, see Hamza Iṣfahānī, *Ta'rīkh sinī mulūk al-arḍ*, I, 30 (about Ṭahmūrath); pp. 35, 56 (about the order of Fīrūz son of Yazdagird to destroy the Jews of Iṣfahān). Incorrect observations regarding Jay and Yahūdiyya in Le Strange, *The Lands*, p. 204. ⟪Cf. Barthold, *ZVORAO*, XVII, 0104, *Soch.* III, 278.⟫

[8] In the Persian translation of Iṣṭakhrī, instead of Yahūdiyya we always find Jahūdistān (Iṣṭakhrī, p. 198 note t).

[9] According to *idem*, p. 199, Yahūdiyya was more than twice as large as Shahristān. According to Ibn Rusta, p. 162, there was in Shahristān an ancient fortress called, as in Hamadān, al-Sārūq. Cf. Ḥamza Iṣfahānī, I, 197; Bīrūnī, *Āthār*, ed. Sachau, p. 24. Ya'qūbī, *Kitāb al-Buldān*, p. 275, concerning the *dihqān*s and *al-luyaba* (?). About the *rustāq* Bara'ān, the inhabitants there are "cultivators [landlords/peasants], nobody else mingles with them." Error in Sykes, *A History of Persia*, II, 133, regarding the word *dihqān* as "cultivator." ⟪Cf. Barthold, "K voprosu o feodalizme v Irane," pp. 462 ff.⟫

[10] Maqdisī, p. 388. ⟪For the history of the Jewish community of Iṣfahān, see W. J. Fischel, "Isfahan. The Story of a Jewish Community in Persia," *Joshua Starr Memorial Volume* (New York, 1953), pp. 111-28.⟫

[11] Maqdisī, p. 389. In Ibn Rusta, p. 161 line 21, it is Zarrīn-rūd.

mentioned still by Chardin as a large town east of Iṣfahān with many ruins of ancient buildings.[12] According to Mustawfī, Shahristān was built by Alexander the Great and renewed under the Sāsānids.[13] From among the Arab geographers, the most detailed description of Jay, or Shahristān, is given by Ibn Rusta, himself a native of this town.[14] Maqdisī[15] describes among the individual buildings of Yahūdiyya the Friday mosque with its round columns and a minaret seventy arshins tall to the south of it;[16] this whole building was made of clay. According to the historian of Iṣfahān Ḥusayn b. Muhammad al-ʿAlawī, the Friday mosque was built by the Arabs of the Banū Tamīm tribe, and it was enlarged under the caliph Muqtadir in the tenth century; a library whose catalog alone consisted of three volumes later belonged to it.[17] This Friday mosque is still shown today; although it has retained its name, "Friday mosque" (*masjid-i jumʿa*), after the construction of the mosque of Shāh ʿAbbās I it lost its religious primacy, and as a result of the numerous reconstructions to which it was subjected it presents no architectural interest.

The plain in which Iṣfahān lies is surrounded by mountains on all sides (except on the southeast, where it is contiguous with the steppe). It is remarkable for its warm climate and plentiful water supply. According to Mustawfī, every variety of crop can grow here except the pomegranate, but even this points to the beneficial aspects of its climatic conditions, since pomegranate trees grow only in localities with an unhealthy climate.[18] The soil needs abundant fertilizing, for which pigeon manure is collected from special towers,[a] and, in addition, town refuse is used. The fields are irrigated from the small river of the Zāyinda Rūd and its canals, which are

[12] *Voyages en Perse, et autres lieux de l'Orient* (Amsterdam, 1735), II, 93-94.

[13] *Nuzhat al-qulūb*, extracts in Schefer's ed., p. 170 ⟦ed. Le Strange, p. 50, tr. *idem*, p. 57⟧.

[14] Ibn Rusta, pp. 160-63. Cf. Jackson's opinion, *Persia Past and Present*, p. 270, regarding the possibility that Julfa lies on the site of Jay.

[15] Maqdisī, pp. 388-89.

[16] According to *idem*, seventy ells long, but in Browne, "Account," p. 438, the minarets are 100 *gaz* high.

[17] *Ibid.*, pp. 437-38. For the Friday mosque of Jay, see Bundārī, *Zubdat al-nuṣra*, ed. M. T. Houtsma (Leiden, 1889), p. 181.

[18] *Nuzhat al-qulūb*, extracts in Schefer's ed., p. 168 ⟦ed. Le Strange, pp. 48-49, tr. *idem*, p. 55⟧.

[a] See E. Beazley, "The Pigeon Towers of Isfahan," *Iran, JBIPS*, IV (1966), 105-109, and *idem*, "Some Vernacular Buildings of the Iranian Plateau," *JBIPS*, XV (1977), pp. 101-102.

here called *madi*; there is also well water. The river flows out of the Zarda Kūh mountains and to the southeast of Iṣfahān it disappears in salt marshes; local inhabitants have retained to this day the belief that it surfaces again in Kirmān and flows into the sea.[19] Despite the glorification of the Zāyinda Rūd by the poets of Iṣfahān, its water was at the end of the tenth century, according to Maqdisī, so polluted with the refuse of the town that people stopped using it for drinking.[b]

In the tenth century, Iṣfahān was, after Ray, the most important town between Arab Iraq and Khurāsān;[20] some of the Buwayhid rulers chose it as their capital. After the Buwayhids several Saljuq sultans lived in Iṣfahān; one of them, Muḥammad, who died in 1118, was buried here in the madrasa that he had built. This madrasa still existed in the fourteenth century, and at the threshold of the building, just as at the doorstep of Maḥmūd's mosque in Ghazna, lay the stone sculpture of an Indian idol seized by the Muslims during one of their campaigns.[21] Thanks to its favorable

[19] Tumanskii, *Ot Kaspiiskogo moria*, p. 54.

[b] On the use of the Zāyanda-Rūd for irrigation, see Lambton, "The Regulation of the Waters of the Zāyande Rūd," BSOS, IX (1937-1939), 663-73; *idem, Landlord and Peasant in Persia*, index; *idem, The Persian Land Reform 1962-1966* (London, 1969), index.

[20] Iṣṭakhrī, p. 199. Cf. Nāṣir-i Khusraw (he was in Isfahān in 1052), *Safar-nāma* (Tehran lithog.), p. 249: "In the whole Persian-speaking area I have seen no city better, more complete, or more populous and built up than Iṣfāhān." Also Maqdisī, p. 389: the river cut through the city; twelve gates. See also the *Ta'rīkh-i aḥwāl-i Iṣfahān* (Browne, "Account," p. 676) about the construction of the town walls under 'Alā' al-Dawla; the length was 15,000 paces (*ibid.*, p. 33). Information about Iṣfahān in the time of the 'Abbāsids in Ṭabarī: about the taking of the town by Qaḥṭaba (III, 6-7); about the change of the governor under Mahdī (III, 500); about the participation in the rebellion of the Khurramiyya in 218/833 (III, 1,165); about the march of Waṣīf al-Turkī against the Kurds in 231/845-6 (III, 1,351); about the seizure of Waṣīf's possessions by Mutawakkil in 247/861 (III, 1,462); about the designation as governor, in 281/894, of Abū Dulaf's grandson (III, 2,141); events of 283/896 and 284/897 (III, 2,152, 2,155, 2,156, 2,161); about the castle (*qal'a*) of the Abū Dulafids at al-Dh.r (III, 2,180; also a fortress belonging to the family of Abū Dulaf in Dh.r); about the uprising of the Kurds (III, 1,278 ff.).

There is a description of Iṣfahān in Nāṣir-i Khusraw, *Safar-nāma* (Tehran lithog.), pp. 246-48. On the way to Iṣfahān, Nāṣir-i Khusraw passed through Khāndajān (Yāqūt, *Mu'jam*, II, 394: Khān Lanjān); Khāndajān as Firdawsī's hiding place, error in Schefer (Nāṣir-i Khusraw, *Safar-nāma*, ed. Schefer [Paris, 1881] Appendix IV, p. 298) and Le Strange (*The Lands*, p. 207 n. 1). Iṣfahān under the Saljuqs: Bundarī, pp. 82, 87, 98. Iṣfahān and the Ismā'īlīs; Shāhdiz, *ibid.*, pp. 90 ff.; Yāqūt, *Mu'jam*, III, 264. ⟦Abū Dulaf, *Travels in Iran*, tr. p. 60, #62.⟧

[21] Mustawfī, *Nuzhat al-qulūb*, extract in Schefer's ed., p. 168 ⟦ed. Le Strange, p. 49, tr. *idem*, p. 56⟧.

position, the town could rapidly recover not only from the Mongol invasion[c] but also from the more terrible devastation by Tīmūr in 1387. Iṣfahān, which at that time belonged, like Shīrāz and Yazd, to the Muẓaffarid dynasty, submitted to Tīmūr and agreed to pay a tribute, but in consequence of the exactions by those charged with the collection, a popular uprising took place. An order was then issued to launch a massacre of the population; up to 70,000 heads were harvested, the sources tell us,[22] with which towers were erected in various places.[23] Despite this, Iṣfahān was still in Tīmūr's time chosen as the residence for one of his grandsons, Rustam, when he was allotted his appanage. In the fourteenth century, the inhabitants were not yet mostly Shīʿīs as they are now, but Shāfiʿī Sunnīs. At the end of the tenth century, the people of Iṣfahān, according to Maqdisī,[24] were even filled with Sunnī fanaticism, placing Muʿāwiya on a par with the [first] four caliphs and calling all five of them "messengers," *mursalūn*.

Iṣfahān reached the peak of its glory under the Ṣafawids, when the most famous ruler of this dynasty, Shāh ʿAbbās the Great (1587-1628) chose it as his capital. He developed it into an enormous city, up to thirty-five versts in circumference,[25] although there were merely twelve gates, just as in the tenth century; only ten of these

[c] Boyle, "The Capture of Isfahan by the Mongols," *La Persia nel medievo: Atti del convegno internazionale sul tema* (Rome, 1971), pp. 331-36; J. E. Woods, "A Note on the Mongol Capture of Iṣfahān," *JNES*, XXXVI (1977), 49-52.

[22] Sharaf al-Dīn Yazdī, I, 434; ʿAbd al-Razzāq, ms., fol. 86b.

[23] Qalʿa-yi Ṭabarak as the name of the citadel of Iṣfahān under Tīmūr (Le Strange, *The Lands*, p. 205). Cf. Qalʿa-yi Tabarruk, Chardin, *Voyages*, ed. 1811, VII, 483.

[24] Maqdisī, p. 399. For the struggle between the Ḥanafīs and Shāfiʿīs in Iṣfahān, see Yāqūt, *Muʿjam*, I, 296 line 7; cf. Ibn al-Athīr, ed. Tornberg, X, 299 ff.

[25] Mustawfī, *Nuzhat al-qulūb*, extracts in Schefer's ed., p. 167 ⟦ed. Le Strange, p. 48, tr. *idem*, p. 55⟧: 21,000 paces (idea of the *shahristān* as the *shahr-i naw-i Iṣfahān*. According to Browne, "Account," p. 433: 15,000 paces. According to Olearius ⟨⟨who was in Iṣfahān in August 1637⟩⟩, the city together with the suburbs measured eight English miles in circuit. According to Raphael du Mans, *Estat de la Perse en 1660* . . . , ed. Schefer (Paris, 1890), p. 35, the diameter of Isfahan was three-quarters of the diameter of Paris ⟨⟨du Mans lived in Iṣfahān between 1656 and 1696⟩⟩. According to Chardin, *Voyages*, ed. 1735, II, 1 and *Voyages*, ed. 1811, VII, 273, it measured twelve leagues, or twenty-four miles, in circuit, but the circumference of the walls was 2,000 paces in all (*ibid.*, II, 3; VII, 284; Chardin was in Iṣfahān in 1666 and in 1671-1674). According to G. A. Olivier (*Voyage dans l'Empire Othoman, l'Egypte et la Perse fait par ordre du gouvernement, pendant les six premières années de la République* [Paris, 1807]; *Puteshestviia; Opisanie*), it measured less than two miles in diameter (Olivier was in Iṣfahān in 1788). Today, according to Dubeux, *La Perse*, p. 16, it measures two miles.

were open, according to Tavernier,[26] or eight, according to Chardin.[27]

The center of the city was—and still is—the so-called "Square of the Shah," Maydān-i Shāh, where the imperial palace, the principal mosque, and the main bazaars were located.[28] Like other large squares in Persian capitals, it was surrounded by a number of constructions with two-storied arcades; shops were located on the lower level.[29] In front of the buildings there was a continuous avenue of trees and a canal; both these features later fell into decay because of neglect, and were only partly restored in the nineteenth century. The Friday mosque, built by ʿAbbās in 1612-1613,[30] is located at the southern end of the square; in the eighteenth century it was restored several times. At the northern end was the portico (*naqqāra khāna*), whose function is evident from its name; it issues into the large bazaar (*qayṣariyya*).[31] On the eastern side is the mosque of Luṭf Allāh;[32] in the center of the square, a pole with an apple—with a golden cup at its tip on festive occasions—used to stand; it functioned as a target for shooting practice. Later there was a gibbet

[26] Tavernier, *Les six voyages*, pt. 1, p. 435.

[27] Chardin, *Voyages*, ed. 1735, II, 5.

[28] In Iskandar Munshī, it is *maydān-i naqsh-i jahān*. It is unclear what was the *naqsh-i jahān-i Isfahān* in Tīmūr's time; for example, Sharaf al-Dīn Yazdī, I. 621. According to Jackson, *Persia Past and Present*, p. 266, the square is over a quarter of a mile long (from north to south) and about an eighth of a mile from west to east (according to Olearius, the length was 700 paces, the width 250; according to della Valle, 690 and 230, and according to Chardin, 440 and 160). According to Jackson, *Persia Past and Present*, p. 266, the maydān-i Shāh is mentioned as early as Firdawsi's *Shāh-nāma*, reference to the edition of J. A. Vullers and S. Landauer (Leiden, 1877-1884), II, 746, and J. Mohl's translation (Paris, 1838-1878), II, 423, but there we only find the verse about Kay Khusraw:

sarāsar hama shahr ādhīn ba-bast
bayārast maydān wa khūd bar nashast
He adorned the whole city from end to end,
he decorated the square and seated himself on the throne.

[29] Thus according to the description by Pietro della Valle, *Viaggi*, ed. 1843, I, 454.

[30] According to Iskandar Munshī, ms., fol. 240b ff., in 1611 ⟦ed. Tehran, pp. 831-32, tr. Savory, pp. 1038-39⟧.

[31] Four bazaars of Iṣfahān; see Iskander Munshī's narrative ⟦(ed. Tehran, 1313-14/1895-7, I, 591), tr. Savory, pp. 1037-38⟧, about the events of 1611: "Naqsh-i Jahān and the Qayṣariyya and the caravanserais and the coffee-houses." See the illustrations in Sykes, *Ten Thousand Miles*, p. 332 (*masjid-i Shāh*); Jackson, *Persia Past and Present*, 266, 270. ⟦Ali Bakhtiar, "The Royal Bazaar of Isfahan," *Iranian Studies*, VII (1974), 320-47; H. Gaube and E. Wirth, *Der Bazâr von Isfahan* (Wiesbaden, 1978).⟧

[32] Shaykh Luṭf Allāh, a contemporary of Shāh ʿAbbās, d. in 1623, see Iskandar Munshī, ms. fol. 333b ⟦ed. Tehran, pp. 1007-1008, tr. Savory, pp. 1229-30⟧.

here. Two marble columns also used to stand on the square; they functioned as base-line marks for the equestrian arena during the game of polo (*chawgān*), once very popular but forgotten today. The imperial palace issued into the southwestern side of the square with its magnificent portico of the ʿAlī-kapu, which had twelve wooden pillars and a marble[-lined] pool in the center; here the shāh received ambassadors on the day of the *Nawrūz* holiday. The main facade of the palace was the portico called the Chihil Sutūn, which issued into the garden and was supported, despite its name, only by twenty wooden pillars with stone carvings of lions at their bases; the walls of the portico were covered with marble and glass. The palace consisted of several large halls, including one with small paintings that is preserved to this day. Six large scenes depict events from the lives of the shāhs: Ismāʿīl (two paintings), Ṭahmāsp, ʿAbbās the Great, and Nādir; inserted between two of them is a portrait of Nāṣir al-Dīn Shāh. During the reign of Shāh Ḥusayn (1694-1722), the portico suffered from fire and was restored. On the western side of the palace was the garden of Hasht-bihisht; that was where the avenue of Chārbāgh (Chahār bāgh) started; it continued southward to the Zāyinda Rūd and beyond, but only pitiful remnants of it exist today. Near this avenue was the madrasa of Shāh Ḥusayn, one of the finest buildings of Iṣfahān.[33] The citadel of the city is located to the southeast of the Square of the Shāh. In the city itself there was reported to stand in Ṣafawid times the tower called Kalla Minār, no longer extant.[34] It was built with skulls of the animals killed by the sovereign while hunting, although some travelers maintained that among its bones were human ones.[35]

Chārbāgh avenue goes to the bridge of Allāh Werdi Khān, named after one of the generals of Shāh ʿAbbās the Great and leading to the suburb of Julfā, where, as is well known, the Armenians forcibly

[33] More exactly, the madrasa of Shāh Ḥusayn's mother; a note about it in J. A. de Gobineau, *Trois ans en Asie (de 1855 à 1858)* (Paris, 1905), pp. 196 ff. The architect was from Tabrīz; the edifice is intact; according to Jackson (*Persia Past and Present*, p. 269), there are signs of ruin. ⟦The caravanserai attached to the Madrasa-yi Mādar-i Shāh was converted in the 1960s into a fine hotel, the Shah Abbas.⟧

[34] The tower was sixty feet high.

[35] Curzon, *Persia*, II, 23. ⟦The architecture of Iṣfahān has, not surprisingly, been much described. In addition to the references given in note 43 below, consult especially the rich bibliography to J. Sourdel-Thomine, *EI*², art. "Iṣfahān. 2. Monuments," and Wilber, *The Architecture of Islamic Iran. The Il Khānid Period*, index. See further Matheson, *Persia, an Archaeological Guide*, pp. 179-85; W. Blunt, *Isfahan, Pearl of Persia* (London, 1966); E. Galdieri, "Les palais d'Isfahan," *Iranian Studies*, VII (1974), 380-405; *Isfahan, City of Light*, Exhibition Catalogue (London, 1976).⟧

transferred by ʿAbbās lived. When the water was at low level, it was possible to ford the river on a separate covered causeway under the arches of the bridge.[36] The avenue ended in the south in the orchard of Hazār-Jarīb, which has since disappeared without trace. From among all the suburbs of the city, Julfā suffered the most during the Afghan invasion of 1722; furthermore, many Armenians emigrated from Persia after Nādir Shāh's death. At the time of Chardin's visit, there were some 30,000 inhabitants in Julfā; Curzon was told that the total population of the suburb amounted to 2,500 souls, of whom 80 percent were Armenians.[37]

Other bridges downstream from the bridge of Allāh Verdi Khan lead to other suburbs; the most remarkable among them is the magnificent Pul-i Khwājū or Pul-i Bābā-Rukn, named after the dervish Rukn al-Dīn; it leads to a suburb that used to be called Gabristān and was inhabited by the *gabr*s [Zoroastrians],[38] but that received in the seventeenth century, when Shāh ʿAbbās II (1642-1667) built a palace for himself here, the name Saʿādatābād. The name of the palace itself is Haft-Dast; there is in it the portico called Āyina-khāna, representing an imitation of the portico of Chihil Sutūn.[39] Fatḥ ʿAlī Shāh died in this palace in 1834; after his death it fell into neglect.

In the area around Iṣfahān one can observe the so-called "moving minarets," *manār-i junbān*, whose movement is usually explained as a miracle wrought by the shaykh buried here; the towers are located some eight versts to the west of the town in the settlement of Guladān. Not far from there, on a cliff, are the ruins of Ātashgāh.[40] Mustawfī mentions Ātashgāh in connection with a fortress built by the mythical third king of Persia, Ṭahmūrath; the temple of the fire worshipers would have been built there by the second mythical

[36] A picture of the bridge is in Jackson, *Persia Past and Present*, p. 263.

[37] Curzon, *Persia*, II, 53. The erroneous opinion that Julfa = Jay is in Jackson, *Persia Past and Present*, p. 270 and Justi, *Geschichte Irans*, p. 485. ⟦J. Carswell, *New Julfa, the Armenian Churches and Other Buildings* (London, 1968); *idem, EI*[2] Suppl., art. "D̲julfā," noting the population of Julfa in ca. 1975 as less than 500 families; V. Gregorian, "Minorities of Isfahan: the Armenian Community of Isfahan 1587-1722," *Iranian Studies*, VII (1974), 652-80.⟧

[38] Cf. Jackson, *Persia Past and Present*, p. 274, about the *gabr*s at the time of his visit to Iṣfahān: there were only six of them, and out of these only three were permanent residents, the others being from Yazd.

[39] A picture *ibid.*, p. 270.

[40] A picture *ibid.*, p. 254. For this monument, see also the bibliography in Vanden Berghe, *Archéologie de l'Iran ancien*, p. 198. ⟦M. Siroux, "Atesh-gâh d'Ispahân," *Iranica antiqua*, V (1965), 39-82.⟧

king, Bahman, son of Isfandiyār, who is identified with Artaxerxes I (Ardashīr-i Darāz-dast).[41] Ibn Rusta says the same thing about the origin of the temple; in his time the sacred fire was still burning.[42] Finally, to the south of Iṣfahān, at the foot of the mountain Kūh-i Ṣūfa, was Faraḥābād, Shāh Ḥusayn's country palace famous for its orchards; it was destroyed in the eighteenth century by the Afghans. On the mountain itself was the summer palace of Ḥusayn's predecessor Shāh Sulaymān (1667-1694), called Takht-i Sulaymān.[43]

The population of Iṣfahān in Ṣafawid times, by the most conservative estimates, reached 500,000 souls; except for the central square and several bazaars, however, the city resembled an enormous village, according to the impression it made on the traveler Tavernier.[44] Today only pitiful remains of Iṣfahān's former grandeur are preserved; an insignificant part of the area of the former city is inhabited, and this area is not surrounded by a wall but merges with villages and orchards. According to Tumanskii, "The houses are mostly built from unfired, square bricks; the streets are narrow and evil-smelling because of the repulsive habit of making openings on the streets into which latrines are emptied and of covering them with only a slab and sometimes leaving them uncovered altogether."[45] As in the case of other large towns of Persia, estimates of the population of Iṣfahān vary, but none exceed 90,000.[d]

[41] *Nuzhat al-qulūb*, extract in Schefer's edition, p. 170 ⟦ed. Le Strange, p. 50, tr. *idem*, p. 57⟧.

[42] Ibn Rusta, p. 153. Cf. Ḥamza Iṣfahānī, I, 30, for Ṭahmūrath and Iṣfahān.

[43] ⟨⟨For the history of Iṣfahān and its monuments, see also Cl. Huart, *EI*[1], art. "Iṣfahān"; *Survey of Persian Art*, II and V; Abū Nuʿaym, *Akhbār Iṣbahān*, ed. S. Dedering (Leiden, 1931-1934); ʿAlī b. Muḥammad Iṣfahānī, *al-Iṣfahān* (Iṣfahān, 1343/1924); Ḥusayn Nūr Ṣādiqī, *Iṣfahān*, (Tehran, 1316/1937); Luṭf Allāh Hunarfar, *Ganjīna-yi āthār-i taʾrīkhī-yi Iṣfahān* (Iṣfahān, 1344/1965); ʿAzīz Hatami, *Isfahan* (Tehran, 1962); A.K.S. Lambton and J. Sourdel-Thomine, *EI*[2], art. "Iṣfahān."⟩⟩ ⟦In addition to the Zoroastrian presence in the early Islamic period, the Ismāʿīlīs were active in the Iṣfahān countryside during Saljuq times, having seized various strongholds that threatened the town, including Shāh Diz, possibly on the top of the Kūh-i Ṣūfa, and Khān Lanjān to the south of the town; see on this last, S. M. Stern *et al.* "The Fortress of Khān Lanjān," *Iran, JBIPS*, IX (1971), 45-57, and for the former, the work cited by Stern, C. O. Minasian, *Shāh Diz of Ismāʿīlī Fame* (London, 1971). See also relevant articles in the *Studies on Isfahan: Proceedings of the Isfahan Colloquium, Harvard University, 1974 (= Iranian Studies,* 1974, vol. VII).⟧

[44] *Les six voyages . . . en Turquie, en Perse et aux Indes, etc.* (Paris, 1917).

[45] *Ot Kaspiiskogo moria*, pp. 54-55.

[d] The population in ca. 1950 was 204,598 (*Farhang*, X, 18); in 1976, it was 671,825 (*Le monde iranien et l'Islam*, IV [1976-1977], 242: Iṣfahān is the second largest city of Iran, after Tehran and before Mashhad and Tabrīz.

The city has today a great commercial importance, as well; the main articles of export are opium, tobacco, cotton, and almonds, whereas paper materials, sugar, red copper, and tea are imported.

The road from Iṣfahān to Ray, that is, to the vicinity of Tehran, has always passed through Kāshān and Qum. It follows fairly level ground except for a short distance south of Kāshān, where it cuts through a mountain chain. Here is the mountain [and village] of Kūhrūd, whose inhabitants, like those of the neighboring villages, speak a special dialect that has retained many archaic words; the dialects of Kūhrūd and of several other towns have been subjected to a special linguistic investigation by Zhukovskii.[46]

In the 10th century, Kāshān was a small but rich town. Its foundation was attributed to Zubayda, the wife of Hārūn al-Rashīd, and the town had already at that time a great manufacturing importance, and was especially renowned for its goblets. Even today, copper vessels made in Kāshān are well known. In addition, ceramics made in Kāshān are famous; such Persian words as *kāsh* "glazing"; *kāshī*, "enamel" (hence *kāshīgar*) are derived from the word Kāshān or from the abbreviation *kāsh*. Because of the mountains situated south of the city, summer is extremely hot here; moreover, all travelers, beginning with the tenth-century geographers,[47] mention the abundance of scorpions in the area. The inhabitants of Kāshān were Shīʿīs even in the fourteenth century,[48] although in the surrounding villages Sunnism was still prevalent.[49]

The inhabitants of Qum were Shīʿīs as early as the tenth century, although the Arab population of the town was larger than the Persian one;[50] in the fourteenth century, Qum was already one of

[46] *Materialy*, pt. 1. ⟦Bosworth, *EI*², art. "Ḳuhrūd"; O. Watson, "The Masjid-i ʿAlī, Quhrūd: an Architectural and Epigraphic Survey," *Iran, JBIPS*, XII (1975), 59-74.⟧

[47] Maqdisī, p. 390. There is no mention of Kāshān in Samʿānī and Yāqūt. Cf. Le Strange, *The Lands*, p. 209.

[48] And in the thirteenth century, see Rāwandī, *Rāḥat al-ṣudūr*, ed. M. Iqbāl (Leiden and London, 1921), p. 394.

[49] According to Jackson, *Persia Past and Present*, p. 410, there are in Kāshān over 70,000 inhabitants. Views of Kāshān, *ibid.*, pp. 410, 412. ⟨⟨For the history of the city, see also Huart, *EI*¹, art. "Kās͟hān"; ʿAbd al-Raḥīm Darrābī, *Ta'rīkh-i Kāshān*, ed. Īraj Afshār (Tehran, 1335/1946); *Arabskii anonim XI v.*, ed. P.A. Griaznevich, p. 144.⟩⟩ ⟦Lockhart, *Persian Cities*, pp. 120-26; J. Calmard, *EI*², art. "Kās͟hān." In 1976, the population of Kashan was 84,545 (*Le monde iranien et l'Islam*, IV [1976-1977], 242).⟧

[50] Iṣṭakhrī, p. 201. Cf. Yāqūt, *Muʿjam*, IV, 175, for Qum as a purely Muslim city without any remnants of *Aʿājim*: "[Qum] is a new Islamic city, with no trace of non-Arabs."

the centers of Shīʿī fanaticism.[51] At present, few permanent inhabitants live there (approximately 7,000),[52] but in terms of religious importance it is the second city of Persia [after Mashhad], and is visited by a great number of pilgrims.[53] The tomb of Fāṭima, sister of the imām ʿAlī b. Mūsā al-Riḍā, who is buried in Mashhad, is in Qum; the present-day structure over the grave was built in the nineteenth century by Fatḥ ʿAlī Shāh. In Qum are buried a number of Persian shāhs, beginning with those of the seventeenth century, as well as many other famous personalities and shaykhs.[54] The road from Qum to Ray used to lead from the bridge Pul-i Dallāq directly northward to the town of Kināragird; the large lake Ḥawz-i Sulṭān Kawīr was formed only in 1883, as a result of the destruction of the dam on the small river Qara-chay.[55] Curzon was told that the minister Amīn al-Sulṭān had deliberately demolished the dam in order to ruin the ancient caravan route and direct the caravans along the new road built by himself through the towns of ʿAlīābād and Manzariya.[56] A road is said to have led in the fourteenth century from Sulṭānīya, when it was the capital of Iran, through Sāwa and Āwa to Qum, and from there to Kāshān and Iṣfahān.[57]

[51] Mustawfī, *Nuzhat al-qulūb*, extract in Schefer's ed., p. 191 ⟦ed. Le Strange, p. 67, tr. *idem*, p. 71⟧.

[52] In Rittikh's opinion, *Otchet o poezdke*, pt. 1, p. 128, there are 25,000 to 30,000 inhabitants, and according to the inhabitants, twice as many. ⟦Lockhart, *Persian Cities*, pp. 127-31. The population in ca. 1950 was estimated at 83,235 (*Farhang*, I, 168), in 1976, it was 246,831 (*Le monde iranien et l'Islam*, IV [1976-1977], 242).⟧

[53] Qum and Shīʿism; the question of Zoroastrianism; Qaryat al-Majūs, according to Iṣṭakhrī, was one day's journey from Qum and two days' journey from Kāshān. The pre-Islamic fortress Dayr Kardashīr between Ray and Qum: Yāqūt, *Muʿjam*, II, 690; IV, 175, quoting Abū Dulaf.

[54] Views of Qum in Jackson, *Persia Past and Present*, p. 414; Sykes, *Ten Thousand Miles*, p. 158. For the history of Qum and its monuments, see also Ḥasan b. Muḥammad Qummī, *Ta'rīkh-i Qumm*, ed. Jalāl al-Dīn Ṭihrānī (Tehran, 1313/1934); ʿAlī Akbar Kāshif, *Rāhnamā-yi Qum dar āthār-i ta'rīkhī-yi āstāna-yi muqaddasa* (Tehran, 1317/1938). ⟦J. Calmard, *EI*², art. "Ḳumm."⟧

[55] Rittikh, *Otchet o poezdke*, pt. 1, p. 125, considers the formation of the lake to be the result of a natural spill (caused by an abundance of snow in the mountains) in 1883.

[56] *Persia*, II, 4.

[57] Mustawfī, *Nuzhat al-qulūb*, University ms. 171 fol. 245a ⟦ed. Le Strange, p. 184, tr. *idem*, p. 175⟧.

CHAPTER XI

Luristān and Khūzistān

IMMEDIATELY west of Iṣfahān begins a series of parallel mountain chains that constitute the western limit of the Iranian plateau. The Arab geographers mention two roads from Hamadān to Iṣfahān, both of which passed through the town of Burūjird and which bifurcated ten farsakhs to the south of this town, near Karaj, which no longer exists;[1] the eastern route passed through Jurbadhqān, present-day Gulpāyagān.[2] In addition, a road from Hamadān southward to Khūzistān is mentioned; it goes through Nihāwand and Gondēshāpūr, which today is a ruined site to the southeast of Dizfūl. Finally there is mention, in the fourteenth century, of a road from Baghdād to Iṣfahān through Nihāwand and Burūjird.[3]

The mountains to the south of Burūjird all the way to the Khūzistān coastal plain are inhabited by two seminomadic peoples of Aryan origin, the Lurs and the Bakhtiyārs; in antiquity there lived here a non-Aryan mountain people, the Kossai (Κοσσαῖοι, Cossaei).[4] The region of Luristān has always been divided into two main parts, the northwestern or Little Lur (Lur-i Kūchak) and the southeastern or Greater Lur (Lur-i Buzurg).[5] The border between them is considered to be the river Āb-i Diz, a tributary of the Kārūn,

[1] For Karaj, cf. Le Strange, *The Lands*, p. 197: "The exact site of this Karaj is unknown." Cf. the description of Karaj in Ibn Ḥawqal, p. 262 ⟨⟨and *Ḥudūd al-ʿālam*, tr. Minorsky, pp. 132, 201⟩⟩. ⟦*EI*², art. "al-Karadj."⟧

[2] In 1052, Nāṣir-i Khusraw traveled on the mountain road from Arrajān to Iṣfahān; cf. his *Safar-nāma* (Tehran lithog.), pp. 245-46. (The gorge Shamshīr-i Barīd; the place Lūrdaghān, forty farsakhs from Arrajān, on the border of Fārs; the town of Khān Lanjān, the name of Sultan Ṭoghrïl written on its gate; from Khān Lanjān to Iṣfahān, it is seven farsakhs.)

[3] Mustawfī, *Nuzhat al-qulūb*, University ms. no. 171, fol. 241b ⟦ed. Le Strange, pp. 171-72, tr. *idem*, pp. 166-67⟧.

[4] ⟨⟨For the Kassites (Kossai), see M. D'iakonov, *Ocherk*, pp. 39-40, 357; I. D'iakonov, *Istoriia Midii*, pp. 120-22, 125-30; *idem*, "Narody," pp. 23-26; K. Balkan, *Die Sprache der Kassiten (Kassitenstudien, I)* (New Haven, 1954).⟩⟩

[5] According to Iṣṭakhrī, p. 197, the distance from Gondēshāpūr to al-Lūr was four farsakhs, then thirty farsakhs to Shābūr Khāst (no trace of a town or settlement), twenty-two farsakhs from the latter to Nihāwand, which lies fourteen farsakhs from Hamadān. ⟨⟨For the town of Shāpūrkh(w)āst, see Le Strange, *The Lands*, pp. 201 ff.; *Ḥudūd al-ʿālam*, tr. Minorsky, p. 383.⟩⟩

according to Curzon,[6] or the snow-covered ridge of Kūh-i Garru, according to Tumanskii;[7] at the foot of the latter is situated Burūjird. Little Lur is in turn divided by the principal ridge of the Kūh-i Kabīr into Pīsh Kūh and Pusht-i Kūh. From the twelfth to the sixteenth century there ruled in Luristān a separate dynasty of atabeks,[8] under which originated, it would seem, the town of Khurramābād, which is now the administrative center of Luristān. Burūjird is the market town where in time of peace the Lurs sell the products of their herds and buy other necessities. According to Tumanskii, "the Lurs and Bakhtiyārs represent all degrees of sedentarization, from those who are wholly settled and are fully acultured to Islamic Persian civilization all the way to the vagrants who even lack the rudiments of organized nomadic life."[9] Sedentary Lurs live mostly in the northern districts around Hamadān, Burūjird, and Nihāwand. The nomadic ones are divided into a number of tribes (*keytūl*) that have their own chieftains (*tūshmāl* or *qā'id*).[10] The inhabitants of the Pusht-i Kūh, the so-called Faylī Lurs, are the ones who have best retained the original characteristics of their tribe. Their principal leader has the Arabic title of *wālī* as well as the military one of *amīr-i tūmān*, disposes of considerable forces, and is in fact almost independent of the Persian government, for he does not even pay any taxes; his homeland is shielded from the east by impassable mountains that are considered to be the highest in Persia.

The question of the origin of the Lurs and Bakhtiyārs is still uncertain. Their language, judging by the available evidence, is closer to Kurdish than to any other idiom;[11] in their physical ap-

[6] *Persia*, II, 273.

[7] *Ot Kaspiiskogo moria*, p. 38.

[8] Lane-Poole, *The Mohammadan Dynasties*, pp. 174-75.

[9] *Ot Kaspiiskogo moria*, p. 40.

[10] *Tūshmāl* or *tūshīmāl* as a court function; *tūshmāl bāshī*, see Iskandar Munshī, ms., fol. 325b ⟦ed. Tehran, II, 999; tr. Savory, II, 1223⟧. A type of Lur settlement and an example of their tents is in H. Grothe's album *Geographische Charakterbilder aus der Asiatischen Türkei und dem südlichen Mesopotamisch-Iranischen Randgebirge (Puscht-i Kûh)* (Leipzig, 1909); *ibid.*, no. 168 (pl. XCVI) includes a settlement type of Elam.

[11] ⟨⟨For the Lurs and the Bakhtiyārs, see Minorsky, *EI*[1], art. "Lur"; *Narody Perednei Azii*, pp. 261-76, 558; Trubetskoi, *Bakhtiary*; for the dialects of these two peoples, see the bibliography in Oranskii, *Vvedenie*, p. 444.⟩⟩ ⟦*Pace* what was said over eighty years ago in the *GIPh* on the close affinities of Lurī with Kurdish, it is clear that the Lurī dialects (made up, according to Morgenstierne, *HOr*, 1/4, *Iranistik*, 1. *Linguistik*, p. 175, of Bakhtiyārī, Faylī, Mamassanī, and Kūhgilūī) are quite distinct from Kurdish and are connected rather with the southwestern Iranian languages such as New Persian and the dialects of Fārs. See D.L.R. Lorimer, "The Popular Verse of the Bakhtiāri of S.W. Persia," *BSOAS*, XVI (1954), 542-55; XVII (1955), 92-110;

pearance, the Lurs, according to Tumanskii, have retained the traits of the Aryan type with greater purity than have the Persians.[12] As with all nomads, the situation of women is better among them than among the sedentary Muslims; even among sedentary Lurs, women do not veil their faces. Zhukovskii, who, during his sojourn in Persia, collected lullabies among other things, and then published an article about them, points out the sharp difference between the songs of the Persians and those of the Bakhtiyārs, as well as the difference between the attitudes of the two peoples toward their songs. Whereas the Persians discussed their poems most reluctantly, the Bakhtiyārs took unequivocal pride in them, and made no distinction between the songs of men and women, because a Bakhtiyārī wife is a faithful and devoted companion and an assiduous helpmate of her husband. "We," the Bakhtiyārs say, "are an agitated sea, and there is no end to our songs: if all the songs alive today, those that have come down to us from our ancestors, and those that keep being reborn in the mouths of the people, were collected, they would not be contained in one, or even in two *Shāh-nāmas* of an Abu 'l-Qāsim Firdawsī!"[13]

The Bakhtiyārs constitute the population of the Greater Lur and occupy a country that is delimited on the north by a road from Burūjird to Iṣfahān, on the south by that from Dizfūl to Rām Hurmuz. In their way of life and language they closely resemble the Lurs, although they consider themselves more civilized and peace-loving; a considerable number of them have become sedentarized. They are divided into two main branches, the Chahārleng and the Haftleng, and in the administrative sense into those pertaining to Burūjird and those pertaining to Iṣfahān, although they are governed by their own khans. The official heads of the nation, the *ilkhanï* and the *ilbegi*, do not have much influence, according to Tumanskii, although the *ilbegi*'s is somewhat greater.[14] The *ilkhanï* 's duty, according to Zhukovskii, consists in the delivery of taxes to the Persian government, which represents the limit of the Bakhtiyārs' dependence on Tehran.[15] Greater Luristān also had its own

---

XXVI (1963), 55-68; J. M. Unvala, *Contribution to Modern Persian Dialectology, the Lurī and Dizfulī Dialects* (Calcutta, 1959), reprinted from *Indo-Iranica*, XI-XII (Calcutta, 1958-1959).]]

[12] *Ot Kaspiiskogo moria*, p. 42.

[13] Zhukovskii, *Kolybel'nye pesni*, p. 97.

[14] *Ot Kaspiiskogo moria*, p. 45.

[15] *Kolybel'nye pesni*, p. 95. [[The Bakhtiyārī khans played a leading role in Iranian politics during the Constitutional period and its aftermath, and reached a peak of power in 1912 (see G. R. Garthwaite, "The Bakhtiyâri Khans, the Government of Iran, and the British, 1846-1915," *IJMES*, III (1972), 24-44; Lambton, *EI*², art.

local dynasty of atabeks; from the twelfth to the fifteenth centuries it was governed by the dynasty of the Hazāraspids;[16] their capital was Īdhaj, the present-day village of Māl Amīr,[17] which has extensive ruins of mostly Sāsānid date.[18] Here, archaeologists believe, was the chief town of the early inhabitants of these mountains, the Kossai. For the winter, the nomads usually descend from the mountains to the plains of ʿArabistān, the ancient Susiana.

In the geographical sense, Susiana or Khūzistān wholly belongs to the Persian Gulf basin; the principal river of the region, the Kārūn, flows into the Shaṭṭ al-ʿArab, but there are indications that even within historical times the Euphrates, the Tigris, as well as the rivers of Susiana each had its own estuary in the Gulf. The Semitic name of Susiana, Elam, appears in the Bible; the ruins and inscriptions of the area show that the region had reached a significant cultural level long before the arrival of the Aryans. The language of the population had in antiquity been as different from the Semitic tongues as from the Indo-European ones.[19] A variant of this same language is one of the three that constitute the Achaemenid inscriptions, namely, the one that used to be considered as Median.[20] H. Winkler tries to prove that the language in question

---

"Īlāt"). There was much unrest in Luristān and the Bakhtiyārī country during the First and Second World Wars, fanned by attempts of the Pahlavī shāhs after 1925 to sedentarize and disarm the tribes.⟧

[16] For the Hazāraspids see Lane-Poole, *The Mohammadan Dynasties*, pp. 174-75. ⟨⟨See also Minorsky, *EI*[1], art. "Lur-i Buzurg."⟩⟩

[17] The name Māl Amīr appears as early as Ibn Baṭṭūṭa's account (cf. Le Strange, *The Lands*, p. 245). Yāqūt, *Muʿjam*, I, 416, mentions a bridge above a deep dry wadi (in Le Strange, *The Lands*, p. 245 there is mention of a "great stone bridge over the Dujayl") and of an ancient fire temple where a fire cult had been practiced down to the time of Hārūn al-Rashīd. The dry bed, which filled with water only in floodtime, is discussed in detail by Yāqūt, *Muʿjām*, IV, 181 ff. ⟦Abū Dulaf, *Travels in Iran*, tr. Minorsky, pp. 60, 64-65, ##63, 72, comm. pp. 107-108, 116-18, was utilized by Yāqūt here.⟧

[18] ⟨⟨For the pre-Islamic monuments of Māl Amīr, see the survey and bibliography in Vanden Berghe, *Archéologie de l'Iran ancien*, pp. 60-63, 161-62. For the history of Īdhaj or Māl Amīr, see Minorsky, *EI*[1], art. "Luristān."⟩⟩ ⟦Bosworth, *EI*[2], art. "Īdhadj"; Matheson, *Persia, an Archaeological Guide*, pp. 161-63.⟧

[19] Iṣṭakhrī, p. 91, concerning the language of the inhabitants of Khūzistān in the tenth century: "and as for their language: they speak Persian and Arabic, but they also have another tongue, Khūzī, which is neither Hebrew nor Syriac nor Persian." Strabo concerning the Syriac language (Forbiger, *Handbuch*, II, 582). For the inhabitants of Khūzistān and their travels abroad for the sake of *jamʿ al-māl*, see Yāqūt, *Muʿjam*, I, 412, with a reference to Aḥmad b. Muḥammad al-Hamadhānī, that is, Ibn al-Faqīh (the passage is absent in de Goeje's edition, *BGA*, V, 51). For the language of Khūzistān, see also Yāqūt, *Muʿjam*, III, 925 line 17, and Khwārazmī, *Mafātīḥ al-ʿulūm*, ed. C. van Vloten (Leiden, 1895), p. 117.

[20] ⟨⟨Most of the monuments in the Elamite language known today are from Susa.

here is that of Anzan, a region whose king was, as we know from Babylonian inscriptions, Cyrus.[21] Anzan, in Winkler's opinion, is not identical with Susiana, as had once been assumed; in Assyrian inscriptions Anzan is mentioned separately from Elam, and Winkler places this region in Persian Kurdistān near the mountain of Bīsutūn. From there were launched the invasions into the northern part of Babylonia.[22]

The terms Khūzistān and ʿArabistān, according to Curzon, are practically synonymous, but the former is now almost entirely obsolete.[23] As early as the time of the tenth-century geographers, Khūzistān, like ʿArabistān today, was understood to be primarily the alluvial plain of the lower courses of the rivers that flow into the sea; Īdhaj and the nearby mountain chains were the only different type of terrain also included.[24] The country, protected from the north by mountains, was noted for its warm climate; according to some geographers, it did not snow in any part of Khūzistān;[25]

The oldest records written in Elamite, in a pictographic script still not fully deciphered, go back to the period around 3,000 B.C. In the middle of the third millennium, the Elamites adopted the Assyrian cuneiform script, adapting it to their own language (the oldest Elamite cuneiform document is dated to 2,250 B.C.). Ancient Elamite inscriptions from the third millennium have also been found in localities to the east of Susa, such as the districts of present-day Bandar Būshīr (ancient Lian) and Tepe Sialk near Kāshān. After the incorporation of Elam in the sixth century B.C. into the Achaemenid empire, the Elamite language ("neo-Elamite") and the Elamite written culture continued to retain their importance; this is demonstrated by the Elamite versions in the Achaemenid inscriptions and the archive of Elamite documents discovered in Persepolis. See I. D'iakonov, "Narody," pp. 18-23; G. Hüsing, *Die Sprache Elams* (Breslau, 1928); G. C. Cameron, *History of Early Iran* (Chicago, 1936); *idem, Persepolis Treasury Tablets* (Chicago, 1948); H. H. Paper, *The Phonology and Morphology of Royal Achaemenid Elamite* (Ann Arbor, 1955).⟩⟩ ⟦W. Hinz, *Das Reich Elam* (Stuttgart, 1964).⟧

[21] *Untersuchungen zur altorientalischen Geschichte* (Leipzig, 1889), p. 114.

[22] ⟨⟨The exact area denoted by Anzan (or Anchan, also Ansan, Anshan) continues to be uncertain. In late Babylonian official usage, Anzan seems to have denoted a region in eastern Elam or western Persis (present-day Fārs). Cf. I. D'iakonov, *Istoriia Midii*, pp. 294, 349-50; Dandamaev, *Iran*, pp. 102-104.⟩⟩ ⟦The conclusion of the Russian editor is substantially supported by the independently reached conclusions of J. Hansman in his detailed and convincing study "Elamites, Achaemenians and Anshan," *Iran, JBIPS*, X (1972), 101-25, that Anshan comprised *grosso modo* the western part of the modern province of Fārs and that the city of Anshan, capital of an Elamite dynasty, is probably to be identified with Maliyūn on the Bayḍāʾ plain, demonstrably, through archaeological excavations, a significant site.⟧

[23] *Persia*, II, 320.

[24] Iṣṭakhrī, pp. 89-90.

[25] *Ibid.*, pp. 90-91.

Maqdisī excepts from this Īdhaj, and adds that snow was exported from there to other towns of Khūzistān.[26] Everywhere there were palm trees, and sugar cane was grown. According to Maqdisī again, all sugar consumed in Persia, Iraq, and the Yemen was exported from Khūzistān.[27]

As for the rivers of Susiana, the Karkha, ancient Choaspes, is the westernmost one; on its banks are the ruins of Aywān-i Karkha, apparently of pre-Islamic origin, although the town of Karkha is still mentioned at the end of the tenth century by Maqdisī as a minor settlement with a market.[28] On the lower course of this river, along the banks of the old riverbed, was the town of Ḥuwayza, now in ruins but still frequently mentioned on Ṣafawid coins; even in recent times it was the chief town of the Arab shaykh who governed the region with the title of *wālī* of ʿArabistān, and was only nominally a subject of the Persian government.[29]

Between the Karkha and the next large river, the Āb-i Diz, flows a tributary of the latter, the Āb-i Shawr.[30] On the banks of this river are the ruins of ancient Susa, which Loftus and Williams began to excavate in the middle of the nineteenth century. The excavations were continued in the 1880s by Dieulafoy and in the 1890s by two expeditions of de Morgan; archaeological exploration of the site continues today.[31] As is well known, Susa was considered

[26] Maqdisī, p. 414.

[27] *Ibid.*, p. 416. ⟦It is probable that the cultivation of sugar cane was introduced into Ahwāz from India around the time of the Arab conquest; see E. Wiedemann, "Beiträge zur Geschichte der Naturwissenschaften. LII. Über den Zucker bei den Muslimen," in *Aufsätze zur arabischen Wissenschaftsgeschichte*, ed. W. Fischer (Hildesheim, 1970), II, 304-13; and "Nachträge," pp. 408-14; J. Ruska, *EI*[1], art. "Sukkar."⟧

[28] Maqdisī, p. 414. ⟨⟨For excavations of the palace-type structure of the Sāsānid period in Aywān-i Karkha, see M. D'iakonov, *Ocherk*, p. 333.⟩⟩ ⟦P. Schwarz and A. Miquel, *EI*[2], art. "Karkha."⟧

[29] Ḥuwayza, the date of its foundation and character of the town according to Yāqūt, *Muʿjam*, II, 371-72 (from a *risāla* by Abu 'l-Wafā-zād b. Khūdkām, etc.): the phrase "their nobility are [like] common people [elsewhere], and their common people are [like] the scum [elsewhere]" (*Muʿjam*, II, 372 line 11), time of the caliph al-Ṭāʾiʿ (974-991). ⟦J. Lassner, *EI*[2], art. "Ḥawīza." The *wulāt* of ʿArabistān referred to here are from the local dynasty of the Mushaʿshaʿīs ("radiant, ecstatic ones," apparently from their extremist, illuminationist Shīʿī origin in the fifteenth century), who persisted up to the early twentieth century, when their authority was subsumed into that of the Kaʿbī Shaykh Khazʿal of Muḥammara (Khurramshahr), the latter to be himself deposed in 1925. See Minorsky, *EI*[1] Suppl., art. "Mushaʿshaʿa."⟧

[30] Curzon, *Persia*, I, 309, takes this name for an abbreviation of the name Shāpūr.

[31] Susa, according to Justi, *Geschichte Irans*: three and a half English miles in circumference; three large hills; in the center a depression, on the western hill the

to be the principal city of Persia and the center of brilliance and might of the Persian kings in the Achaemenid period. Already under the Sasanids, however, the town seems to have ceded its primacy to other towns of Khūzistān; at the time of the Arab conquest, it was destroyed by the armies of ʿUmar, but was later rebuilt and is mentioned by the tenth-century geographers as al-Sūs, although at this time only its suburb, the *rabaḍ*, was inhabited.[32] Near the town, on the bottom of the river, the Arabs thought, was the tomb of the prophet Daniel; opposite this place, on the bank, was a beautiful mosque.[33] At present Daniel's tomb is shown in a building on the bank of the river somewhat further downstream from the main ruins.[34]

On the bank of the Āb-i Diz, at the border of the Bakhtiyāri region is the town of Dizfūl, named after the magnificent bridge

---

citadel, on the eastern hill lesser ruins, toward the north the palace of Darius. The area of the palace: 100 x 80 meters. Sāsānid and Parthian antiquities in the upper layers. Data in Ménant, *Les Achémenides*, pp. 136 ff.; a plan; 120 or 200 stadia (21 or 35 versts), no wall, the fortress is mentioned by Herodotus and Strabo (cf. Ṭabarī, tr. Nöldeke, p. 58, about the rebuilding of the city by Shāpūr II in the fourth century). Strabo's remarks on the ransom taken from Persian kings on their way from Susa to Persepolis (Forbiger, *Handbuch*, II, 583). According to J. de Morgan, *Mission scientifique en Perse. IV. Recherches archéologiques* (Paris, 1902), pp. 34-35), in the royal city of Susa the Achaemenid antiquities go very deep, and the Elamite ones even deeper (the trenches were five to six meters, in one place fifteen meters deep); in the acropolis, on the other hand, Elamite objects were found two meters beneath the surface under very thin layers of the Arabic, Sāsānid, Parthian, Seleucian, and Achaemenid periods. ⟨⟨For excavations in Susa one can now consult the bibliography in M. D'iakonov, *Ocherk*, pp. 8, 11, 107-109, 339, 343; S. Casson, "Achaemenid Architecture. The Aesthetic Character," in *Survey of Persian Art*, I, 330-35; R. de Mecquenem, "The Early Cultures of Susa," *ibid.*, I, 134-50; *idem*, "Achaemenid architecture. The Achaemenid and Later Remains at Susa," *ibid.*, I, 321-29; Vanden Berghe, *Archéologie de l'Iran ancien*, pp. 71-80, 83-86, 165-75; Ghirshman, *Perse*; R. Göbl, G. Le Rider, G. C. Miles, and J. Walker, *Mission de Susiane. Numismatique susienne, monnaies trouvées à Suse de 1946 ā 1956* (Paris, 1960); Ḥabib Allāh Ṣamadī, *Wirāna-hā-yi Shūsh* (Tehran, 1333/1954). For Parthian and Sāsānid monuments in Susiana, see M. D'iakonov, *Ocherk*; Koshelenko, *Kul'tura Parfii*; Vanden Berghe, *Archéologie de l'Iran ancien*, pp. 81-82, 174-75; Ghirshman, *Iran. Parthes et Sassanides.*⟩⟩ ⟦Lockhart, *Persian Cities*, pp. 132-41; Matheson, *Persia, an Archaeological Guide*, pp. 145-51.⟧

[32] Maqdisī, p. 407.

[33] *Ibid*, pp. 407-408.

[34] Mentioned as early as Mustawfī, *Nuzhat al-qulūb*, University ms. no. 171, fol. 221a ⟦ed. Le Strange, p. 112, tr. *idem*, p. 109⟧: "On the western side of the town." Daniel's body was found at the Arab conquest of the city; some people considered it to be the body of Darius, and the Persians also attributed it to Kay Khusraw (Marquart, *Ērānšahr*, p. 145).

of Sāsānid construction. The lower [older] part of the bridge is made from stone, the upper part from brick. The building of the bridge is attributed to Shāpūr II (309-379); a detailed description of the bridge is given by Sharaf al-Dīn Yazdī, the fourteenth-century historian of Tīmūr, who passed through this place in 1393.[35] According to certain reports, the same Shāpūr, but according to other more convincing ones Shāpūr I (241-272), is given credit for the foundation of the city of Gondēshāpūr, whose ruins lie to the southeast of Dizfūl.[36] According to Persian historians, Shāpūr I resettled here the prisoners whom he took at the conquest of Antioch in Syria; the new city received the Syriac name of Bēt-Lapat, from which the Persians formed the word Belābād and told a legend about the participation of a certain old man named Bela in the foundation of the city. The meaning of the Syriac word *lapat* is uncertain; *bēt*, of course, means "house, dwelling."[37] The name of Gondēshāpūr is interpreted by the Persians as derived from *bih az Andaw-i Shāpūr* ("better than the Antioch of Shapur"). Nöldeke rejects this etymology, and proposes that in the Sāsānid period the city was at first called Wandaw Shāpūr;[38] Marquart proposes the form Wandī Shāpūr[39] and believes it to be an abbreviation of the name Weh Antiyok-i Shāhpuhr, that is, "(new), better Antioch of Shāpūr."[40] The Arabs always write Jundaysābūr, the diphthong *ay* representing here the Persian long *ē*;[41] the presence of this sound, and not of the *yāy-i iḍāfat*, as well as some other linguistic features, made Nöldeke reject the etymology of Jund-i Shāpūr, that is, "army" or "camp of Shāpūr," which at first sight might seem obvious.

[35] Sharaf al-Dīn Yazdī, I, 589-90.

[36] A map of the Kārūn valley is in Sykes, *Ten Thousand Miles*, p. 240. The unnamed ruins are on the site of Gondēshāpūr ("At the present day an almost uninhabited ruin alone marks the site": Le Strange, *The Lands*, p. 238).

[37] ⟨⟨For Bet-Lapat, cf. Honigmann and Maricq, *Recherches sur les Res Gestae Divi Saporis*, p. 45.⟩⟩

[38] Ṭabarī, tr. Nöldeke, p. 42. Cf. also Huart, *EI*[1], art. "D̲jundai-Sābūr," with a reference to Yāqūt, *Muʿjam*, II, 130; ⟦Huart and A. Sayılı, *EI*[2], art. "Gondēs̲h̲āpūr."⟧

[39] *Ērānšahr*, p. 145.

[40] ⟨⟨This etymology is accepted by some scholars even today; see for example Frye, *Heritage*, p. 204; cf. Markwart, *A Catalogue*, p. 98; *Ḥudūd al-ʿālam*, tr. Minorsky, pp. 381-82; Honigmann and Maricq, *Recherchers sur les Res Gestae Divi Saporis*, p. 46 n. 3. In Shāpūr I's inscription on the "Kaʿba of Zoroaster," the name is presented in the Middle Persian form *wḥy ʾndywk šḥpwḥry*, and in the Parthian form *wḥy ʾntywk šḥypwḥr*; the Greek rendering, which is closest to the real pronunciation of the middle of the third century A.D., has in this inscription the form Γουε 'Αντιοχ Σαβωϱ.⟩⟩

[41] Cf. Ṭabarī, III, 852: "Gondēshāpūr: it is on the border between Ahwāz and Jabal."

Under the Sāsānids, Gondēshāpūr was the principal city of Khūzistān; the Nestorians had here the seat of their metropolitan as well as their principal medical school. In the ninth century, Yaʿqūb b. Layth, who had subjugated almost the whole of Persia, chose Gondēshāpūr as his capital; he died and was buried here. Maqdisī says that Gondēshāpūr had suffered a great deal from incursions by the "Kurds," that is, Aryan nomads, but the city was even in his time noted for the fertility of its environs; all sugar consumed in Khurāsān and Jibāl, the latter meaning the mountainous region to the north of Khūzistān, was exported from here.[42] The ruins are today called Shāhābād. Gondēshāpūr eventually yielded its place to Dizfūl, which was still in the nineteenth century the administrative center of Khūzistān, and has even today 16,000 inhabitants, that is, twice as many as Shushtar.[43]

The Āb-i Diz flows into the Kārūn, the main river of Khūzistān, on whose banks are situated both the city that used to be the region's capital at the time of the tenth-century geographers, Ahwāz, and the present-day regional center of Khūzistān, Shushtar, called Tustar in Arabic.[44] Shushtar stands on a cliff; as in Dizfūl, houses here are built in two levels, one stone and one brick. Shushtar has retained some of its industrial importance; even today silk and cotton textiles are manufactured here, and in the tenth century, the brocade cover for the Kaʿba [the *kiswa*] was woven in Shushtar.[45] Its population today does not exceed, according to Curzon, 8,000.[46]

[42] Maqdisī, p. 408.

[43] As late an author as Mustawfī, *Nuzhat al-qulūb*, University ms. no. 171, fol. 220b ⟦ed. Le Strange, pp. 110-11, tr. *idem*, p. 109⟧, mentions both Dizfūl and Gondēshāpūr as medium-sized towns. Cf. Streck, *EI*[1], art. "Dizfūl," and Lockhart, *EI*[2], art. "Dizfūl." The name, as Streck points out, appears for the first time in Yāqūt, *Muʿjam*, I, 372 and IV, 111; prior to that the town was called Qanṭara with the addition, in the construct state, of Andāmish (*Muʿjam*, I, 372), properly And al-Misk, whereas in *Muʿjam*, IV, 111, it is listed under the name Qaṣr Rawnāsh. ⟨⟨For Gondēshāpūr and Dizfūl, see also Le Strange, *The Lands*, pp. 238-39; *Ḥudūd al-ʿālam*, tr. Minorsky, p. 381; for their pre-Islamic monuments, see Vanden Berghe, *Archéologie de l'Iran ancien*, pp. 66, 164.⟩⟩ ⟦Lockhart, *Persian Cities*, pp. 152-56; A. A. Siassi, "L'Université de Gond-i Shâpûr et l'étendue de son rayonnement," *Mélanges d'orientalisme offerts à Henri Massé* (Tehran, 1342/1963), pp. 366-94.⟧

[44] For Tustar, see Yāqūt, *Muʿjam*, I, 847: "Today, the largest town in Khūzistān"; the same source for the quarter al-Tustariyyūn in Baghdad; Hurmuzān in Tustar (Balādhurī, p. 380; Ṭabarī, I, 2,555; a different version also in Ṭabarī, I, 2,538.

[45] Iṣṭakhrī, p. 92.

[46] For Shushtar, see V. F. Minorskii, "Turetsko-persidskoe razgranichenie," *Izvestiia Imp. Russkogo geograficheskogo obshchestva*, LII, part 5 (1916), 364; the city was

The river Kārūn here turns westward; a little further downstream from the city is the famous dam with a bridge over it that stands on forty-one arches; the whole complex was built as early as the third century by Shāpūr I, and has since then been restored several times. According to tradition it was built by Roman prisoners of war, the emperor Valerian among them;[47] for this reason, the dam and the bridge were called Band-i Qaysar and Pul-i Qaysar.[48] The tenth-century geographers used for the dam the Persian term *shādhurwān*.[49] The purpose of this and other similar constructions on the river was to raise the level of the water so as to make it possible to irrigate the fields that lay higher up; in addition the river, with its dams, brought in motion then, as now, a number of water mills.

According to Curzon, the dam of Valerian is called Band-i Mīzān, the name Band-i Qaysar being applied to another dam built

made of stone. The anarchy of recent years has been due to the antagonism of the Niʿmatī and Ḥaydarī parties, which started as religious differences but have now acquired the character of political feuds: the Niʿmatīs support the Bakhtiyārīs and the Constitution, whereas the Ḥaydarīs side with the Arabs and defend the principle of monarchic rule. ⟨⟨For the history of the city, see also Raḍī 'l-Dīn Sayyid ʿAbd Allāh Jazā'irī "Faqīr," *Ta'rīkh-i Shushtar* (Calcutta, 1343/1924).⟩⟩ ⟦Lockhart, *Persian Cities*, pp. 142-51. The population in ca. 1950 was 22,416 (*Farhang*, VI, 239-40).⟧

[47] ⟨⟨The victory over Valerian is commemorated on the Sāsānid reliefs of Nakhsh-i Rustam, Bishāpūr, and Dārābjird; see Vanden Berghe, *Archéologie de l'Iran ancien*, plates 29d, 64b,e, 77b. The event of Valerian being taken prisoner in the battle of Edessa is also mentioned in Shāpūr I's inscription on the "Kaʿba of Zoroaster" near Persepolis. According to this inscription (Parthian version, line 16), the Romans taken prisoner were settled in various parts of the Sāsānid empire, Khūzistān among them; this indirectly confirms the reports in Arabic chronicles about the participation of Romans in the construction of irrigation works in the valleys of the Kārūn, Karkha, and Āb-i Diz. Aside from the dam of Shushtar, some 550 meters long, the prisoners also built, it would seem, the bridge near Dizfūl on the Āb-i Diz, which was about 400 meters long, as well as the bridge of Pāy-i Pul on the Karkha. In all these works, the remnants of which still exist, cement was an ingredient in the masonry, a technique otherwise unknown in third-century Iran (cf. Vanden Berghe, *Archéologie de l'Iran ancien*, p. 66).⟩⟩ ⟦Matheson, *Persia, an Archaeological Guide*, p. 158; Herrmann, *The Iranian Revival*, pp. 92-93, 97-98, 104.⟧

[48] Shushtar and Valerian's dam are illustrated in Sykes, *Ten Thousand Miles*, pp. 252, 254. ⟦Streck and Lassner, *EI*², art. "Kārūn."⟧

[49] Iṣṭakhrī, p. 89. ⟦Ahwāz was the classic region for these hydraulic constructions; Abū Dulaf mentions them more than once in the account of his journeys through Ahwāz; see his *Travels in Iran*, tr. 61, 63, ##65, 70. The word *shādhurwān* has a variety of meanings; see E. Benveniste, "Le sens du mot persan shâdurvân," *Mélanges . . . Henri Massé*, pp. 31-37, and Bosworth, "Abū ʿAbdallāh al-Khwārazmī on the Technical Terms of the Secretary's Art," *JESHO*, XII (1969), 154-55.⟧

somewhat further upstream from the city for the benefit of the canal Āb-i Gargar.[50] This dam too was repaired several times; the present-day stone structure was built in the nineteenth century. Finally, the island formed by the river and the Āb-i Gargar is also irrigated by the Minaw canal; according to Curzon, this word is a contraction of *miyān-āb*. In his description, Rawlinson calls it Āb-i Miyāndāb, that is, *āb-i miyān dū āb*.[51] Several dams and the bridge Pul-i Lashkar are on this canal. In the works of the Arab geographers, the Āb-i Gargar canal is called Mashruqān; it would seem that at that time it extended somewhat further south, namely, to the city of Ahwāz. One march from Shushtar, at a point where the road from Fārs that passed through Rām Hurmuz reached the canal, was the town of ʿAskar Mukram, thus called after one of Ḥajjāj's military commanders whose camp was there. According to Ḥamd Allāh Mustawfī Qazwīnī, as early as Sāsānid times, there used to be a city called Bunj Shāpūr here.[52] There was on the canal a floating bridge built with eighteen boats. The distance from here to Ahwāz was eight farsakhs; six farsakhs, according to Iṣṭakhrī, who had personally performed this journey, were covered by boat on the canal,[53] and the rest was done on horseback along the dry bed of the canal. The ruins of ʿAskar Mukram lie, it is assumed, near the dam Band-i Qīr, which is also built from stone;[54] near this dam is the present-day confluence of the Āb-i Diz and Āb-i Gargar with the Kārūn. No trace is left of the canal mentioned by Iṣṭakhrī, according to Curzon.[55]

Ahwāz is today a minor town on the left bank of the river; its inhabitants are of Arab descent, and their number does not exceed seven hundred.[a] In the tenth century, this was the most important

[50] *Persia*, II, 372-74.

[51] *Ibid.*, II, 376.

[52] *Nuzhat al-qulūb*, University ms. no. 171, fol. 221a ⟦ed. Le Strange, p. 112, tr. *idem*, p. 110⟧.

[53] Mustawfī, pp. 89-90.

[54] The so-called ruins of the Kayānids are mentioned in Sykes, *Ten Thousand Miles*, p. 251, with a reference to A. H. Layard, *Early Adventures in Persia, Susiana, and Babylonia* (London, 1887), II, 28. See the map in Le Strange, *The Lands*, p. 25. ⟨⟨For Sāsānid monuments in this district, see Vanden Berghe, *Archéologie de l'Iran ancien*, pp. 66, 239.⟩⟩ ⟦Streck-Lockhart, *EI*², "ʿAskar Mukram." Band-i Qīr = "dam sealed with bitumen." See also Ibn al-Faqīh, *Akhbār al-buldān*, pp. 200-207, tr. pp. 77-86.⟧

[55] *Persia*, II, 358.

[a] The building of the Persian Gulf-Tehran railway, which passes through the town, but above all, the oil industry, which has brought a petrochemical installation

city of Khūzistān, straddling both banks of the dry bed of the Mashruqān. The main part of the city with the markets lay on the left, eastern bank; the part that lay on the other bank was, so to speak, on an island between the canal and the main course, with which it was contiguous on the west. The two parts of the city were connected by a brick bridge, the Qanṭarat Hinduwān; in the tenth century, ʿAḍud al-Dawla demolished this bridge and built a new one, but the inhabitants continued to use the same name for it. Considerable commerce converged upon the city, both by land and on water; boats bound for Baṣra departed from here.[56] Ahwāz was at first called Sūq al-Ahwāz, a name found in certain geographical texts but especially on coins.[57] Ahwāz is the Arabic plural of the name of a nation that in classical works is called Οὔξιοι, Uxii.[58] The large number of settlements with markets in this part of Khūzistān was a result of the growth of its trade; each had a market day once a week, and the names of the respective days, added to the word *sūq*, became the specific names of these settlements. The most celebrated one was Sūq al-Arbaʿāʾ, recorded even today on some maps; according to the tenth-century geographers, it was situated halfway between Ahwāz and the settlement Ḥiṣn Mahdī near the coastal strip where the waters of Khūzistān flow into the sea.[59]

At present the Kārūn, as is well known, flows into the Shaṭṭ al-ʿArab, the combined lower course of the Tigris and Euphrates. Information gleaned from classical authors suggests that in Alexander the Great's time the Tigris, the Choaspes (that is, the Āb-i Karkha),[60] the Pasitigris (that is, the Kārūn), and perhaps even the Euphrates flowed into a vast common estuary separated from the sea by a breakwater. The estuary was gradually silted up, at which

to the town, have transformed Ahwāz; it had a population in about 1950 of approximately 82,000 (*Farhang*, VI, 30-31); in 1976, of 329,006 (*Le monde iranien et l'Islam*, IV [1976-1977], 242).

[56] Maqdisī, pp. 411-12.

[57] The original name was Hurmuz shahr: Yāqūt, *Muʿjam*, I, 410. Article by Streck in *EI*[1], "al-Ahwāz," where the name Hurmuz Ardashīr is mentioned. ⟦See also Lockhart, *Persian Cities*, pp. 157-64; *idem, EI*[2], art. "al-Ahwāz"; Abū Dulaf, *Travels in Iran*, tr. Minorsky, pp. 61-62, #65.⟧

[58] C. F. Andreas, "Aginis," in *PW*, I, cols. 810-816.

[59] Maqdisī, p. 419.

[60] It is possible that the Choaspes corresponds to the Āb-i Shawr, and the Ἐυλαιος (Ulai) to the Āb-i Karkha (de Morgan's opinion in *Mission scientifique. III. Études géologiques*, p. 216).

point the present-day delta was formed.[61] In the Arab period the Kārūn still had its own estuary. Between the settlements of Ḥiṣn Mahdī of the Kārūn and Bayān on the Tigris was a salt marsh; ships leaving from Ahwāz and Ḥiṣn Mahdī entered the sea and from there the Tigris estuary. Only under ʿAḍud al-Dawla, that is, in the second half of the tenth century, was a navigable canal dug from the Kārūn to the Tigris.[62] It was most probably this canal, four farsakhs long, that later became the main course of the river; this origin is commonly accepted but, according to Curzon, "nobody knows when this canal was dug."[63] It seems that another, longer canal had been dug before ʿAḍud al-Dawla, in the first half of the tenth century, for it is mentioned by Qudāma, who wrote shortly after 928 and died in 337/948-9, thus beforeʿAḍud al-Dawla ascended the throne (338). Qudāma calls this canal "new" (*al-nahr al-jadīd*), and says that the distance from Ḥiṣn Mahdī to Bayān was eight farsakhs on the canal but six farsakhs by land.[64] Curzon considers Bahmashīr "the first and natural estuary of the Karun," but in the tenth century, the estuary may have been somewhat further to the east, because Maqdisī, as we have seen, defines the length of the canal as four farsakhs, whereas the canal that connects Bahmashīr with the Shaṭṭ al-ʿArab today is only three English miles long.[65] In the tenth century, the estuary of the Kārūn was most probably the channel that is recorded on Curzon's map as Kārūn el Amieh.[66] To Ḥiṣn Mahdī led a special road from the town of Arrajān, which is on the border with Fārs; half-way between Arrajān and Ḥiṣn Mahdī there is mentioned the town of Dawraq, a substantial trade center lying on the pilgrim route from Fārs and Kirmān to the holy places.[67]

[61] Andreas, "Aginis."

[62] Maqdisī, p. 419.

[63] *Persia*, II, 336.

[64] Tr., p. 152. Bayān ca. five farsakhs from Ubulla, the latter four farsakhs from Basra (Qudāma, text, p. 194, tr., p. 152).

[65] The Shaṭṭ al-ʿArab is mentioned already by Nāṣir-i Khusraw.

[66] Near the estuary of the Kārūn is Sulaymānān, so called after the governor Sulaymān b. Jābir; cf. Le Strange, *The Lands*, pp. 44, 49. ⟦Kārūn el Amieh = the Shaṭṭ al-Aʿmā, "the Blind Estuary"⟧.

[67] Iṣṭakhrī, p. 95; Maqdisī, p. 412. Dawraq is mentioned also by Iskandar Munshī. ⟨⟨For the estuary of the Kārūn as well as the villages and canals on the lower reaches of the Tigris and Euphrates, see also Le Strange, *The Lands*.⟩⟩ ⟦Abū Dulaf, *Travels in Iran*, tr. Minorsky, p. 62, #67, comm. pp. 111-12. Hansman has suggested that this Dawraq may have been the site of the Seleucia on the Hedyphon River in the

From among other manufacturing towns of Khūzistān, worthy of note was Qurqūb on the road from Arrajān to Wāsiṭ, one march west of Susa; a silk fabric called *qurqūbī* was woven there; these fabrics were [also] designated in Arabic by the term *sūsanjird*, which derives from the Persian word *sūzan* "needle." In the same area, also close to Susa, was the settlement of Baṣinnā. Veils (*sutūr*) made there were exported all over the Islamic world, and even veils produced in other places were presented under the name of Baṣinnā ones.[68] The fact that this industry was developed primarily in the western part of the region suggests that it was introduced from Egypt and western Asia.

Maritime trade was always in the hands of the Semites; today it is mostly in Arab hands. The Iranian rulers of Khūzistān have sometimes tried to benefit from this trade, as in the case of the Sāsānids or of the present-day dynasty [the Qājārs], since the time of the late Nāṣir al-Dīn Shāh; at other times, they have remained totally indifferent toward it. The historian Gutschmidt points out that the Parthians, who gained control over Iran in the second century B.C., did not show the slightest desire to reach the sea.[69] Their direct possessions would have touched the sea only at the limited coastal strip around the estuaries of the Euphrates, but they allowed here the formation of the small but rich vassal state of Μεσηνή, Maysan in Arabic, Meshan in Persian, with Χάραξ as its capital;[70] the state was sometimes also called Characene after this city. The merchant kings of this small vassal state took a far greater share of world trade than the "Great Kings" of the Parthians.[71]

The development of trade and industry in Khūzistān stimulated,

---

region of Elymais, captured by the Parthians in 139 B.C.; see "Seleucia and the Three Dauraks," *Iran, JBIPS*, XVI (1978), 154-61.⟧

[68] Iṣṭakhrī, p. 93.

[69] *Geschichte Irans*, p. 56.

[70] Brockelmann, *GAL*, I, 276: Māšān. A minor settlement (*bulayda*) not far from Baṣra, noted for its palm groves; birthplace of al-Ḥarīrī (according to Yāqūt, *Muʿjam*, IV, 536). Kaskar and Maysān in Le Strange, *The Lands*, p. 43; tomb of the prophet ʿUzayr (Ezra), according to Mustawfī, in a place inhabited only by Jews who looked after the sanctuary. Yāqūt, *Muʿjam*, IV, 714 mentions ʿUzayr's tomb as being between Baṣra and Wāsiṭ. ⟦Streck, *EI*[1], art. "Maisān"; M. G. Morony, "Continuity and Change in the Administrative Geography of Late Sasanian and Early Islamic al-ʿIrāq," *Iran, JBIPS*, XX (1982), 34 ff.⟧

[71] ⟨⟨For Mesene in Parthian and Sāsānid times see now Debevoise, *A Political History of Parthia*; U. Kahrstedt, *Artabanos III und seine Erben* (Bern, 1950); Honigmann and Maricq, *Recherches*.⟩⟩

as usual, the growth of intellectual life. The sect of the Muʿtazilīs, the most philosophical school of Islam, especially flourished in Khūzistān. One of the centers of Muʿtazilī learning was, according to Maqdisī,[72] the great library in Rām Hurmuz, which was second only to that of Baṣra in the wealth of its collection.[73]

[72] Maqdisī, p. 413.

[73] For Rām Hurmuz, see Goldziher, "Aus der Theologie des Fachr al-din al-Rāzī," *Isl.*, III (1912), 214, with a reference to the fact that according to Maqdisī, lectures were another feature of the library; ʿAskar Mukram was also a center of the Muʿtazilīs in the twelfth century (*ibid.*, p. 219). Cf. Sykes, *Ten Thousand Miles*, p. 248, regarding Ahwāz: "Free from the curse of a fanatical population." ⟨⟨For the history and monuments of Khūzistān, see also Streck, *EI*¹, art. "Kārūn"; Schwarz, *EI*¹, art. "Kerkha"; Sayyid Ahmad Kasrawī, *Ta'rīkh-i pānṣad sāla-yi Khūzistān* (Tehran, 1312/1934); Dānishjū, *Khūzistān wa Khūzistāniyān* (Tehran, 1326/1947); Muḥammad ʿAlī Imām Shushtarī, *Ta'rīkh wa jughrafiyā-yi Khūzistān* (Tehran, 1331/1952).⟩⟩ ⟦Matheson, *Persia, an Archaeological Guide*, pp. 138 ff.⟧

CHAPTER XII

Kurdistān and Mesopotamia

Both the road from Media through Hamadān and that from Fārs and Khūzistān through Susa led to Mesopotamia, the center of the most ancient civilization in Asia. The road from Hamadān to Baghdad always had great importance. In Arab times, it was part of the principal trade route from western to eastern Asia, because of which it is described by the Arab geographers in especially great detail; the most detailed description is in the work of Ibn Rusta.[1] From Hamadān, the road crossed the mountain range of Alwand, called Arwand by the Arabs and Orontes by the Greeks, and came to Asadābād or, according to some itineraries, to the village of Khūndād, which lay somewhat further south. Then, after crossing mountain gorges that were not safe from brigands, it came to the stronghold of Qaṣr al-Luṣūṣ, now the town of Kangāwar,[2] and from there to the town of Dukkān (whence—and not from Kangāwar as today—a road branched off southeastward to Nihāwand and Iṣfahān), and from Dukkān to Qirmāsīn or Qirmāshīn, present-day Kirmānshāh or, more correctly, Kirmānshāhān.[3] All along this route there were palaces and other constructions from the Sāsānid period. Those traveling this road passed between Dukkān and Qirmāsīn by the famous mountain of Bīsutūn[4] or Behistūn (Βαγίστανου ὄρος in Diodorus, probably the Persian *baghistān* from *bagh,*

[1] Ibn Rusta, pp. 163-67.

[2] Kangāwar, according to Jackson, *Persia Past and Present,* pp. 237-42: a temple of Anahita erected under the last Achaemenids; *ibid.,* p. 237, about Greek style; picture: *ibid.,* p. 243. Kangāwar, according to E. Herzfeld, is a temple of Anahita, some three hundred years more ancient than Paikuli, "the most important monument of Parthian architecture in Persia" (Herzfeld, *Paikuli. Monument and Inscription of Early History of the Sasanian Empire* [Berlin, 1924], I, 6). For the monuments of Kangāwar, see also bibliography in Vanden Berghe, *Archéologie de l'Iran ancien,* p. 108, 190; Koshelenko, *Kul'tura Parfii,* pp. 54-55. ⟦Abū Dulaf, *Travels in Iran,* tr. p. 39, #39; Savory, *EI*², art. "Kinkiwār."⟧

[3] For Kirmānshāh, see Ṭabarī, tr. Nöldeke, p. 7; Iṣṭakhrī, p. 196, note b. ⟦Also spelled Qi/armīsīn, as in Abū Dulaf, *Travels in Iran,* tr. 45, #33; it clearly represents the pre-Iranian, perhaps Assyrian name of Kirmānshāh, despite the story of its Sāsānid foundation.⟧

[4] Jabal Bihsutūn.

"deity"), on which is carved the longest extant Achaemenid inscription.[5] It tells of the enthronement of Darius and of his victories over the rebels; the bas-relief shows the king and the captive leaders of the rebels. The inscription is, as usual, trilingual; it includes a remark that molds of it had been taken and sent to the provinces so that all the people could become familiar with its content. This inscription was first copied and deciphered by Rawlinson.[6] The road here was a paved causeway overshadowed by the Bīsutūn mountain.[7]

At the western limit of the mountain, some six miles from Kirmānshāhān, was the Sāsānid relief of Ṭāq-i Bustān. It is a complex of two vaulted grottoes carved into the rock. The rear wall of the large grotto represents a Persian horseman clad in armor; on the side walls are hunting scenes, and above the entrance to the vault are portraits of goddesses of victory and of other motifs, reflecting the influence of Roman art. In the small grotto are the portraits of Shāpūr II and III with inscriptions.[8] Curzon suggests that the armored horsemen is Khusraw II, and that the whole complex deals with the enthronement of this king, with the assistance of the armies of the Byzantine emperor Maurice; this would explain the presence of classical motifs in the bas-reliefs, pointing to a participation of Roman artists.[9] The Arab authors who mention this vault by the name Shabdīz[10] saw in these portraits Khusraw II and his wife Shīrīn, to whom was attributed in some legends, albeit erroneously, a Greek origin.[11] Roman craftsmen could have been employed on

[5] The village Sāsāniyān near Bīsutūn (Iṣṭakhrī, p. 196); according to Yāqūt, *Muʿjam*, I, 769, the village of Bihsutūn = Sāsāniyān. According to Khwārazmī, *Mafātīḥ al-ʿulūm* ⟦115,⟧ *baghistān* = *bayt al-aṣnām.*

[6] ⟨⟨"The Persian Cuneiform Inscription at Behistun Decyphered and Translated," *JRAS*, X (1847), 1-349.⟩⟩

[7] The rock of Bīsutūn, picture in Jackson, *Persia Past and Present*, pp. 177, 186, 197, 211. ⟨⟨For the inscription of Behistūn, its location, and the history of its scholarship, see now Dandamaev, *Iran*, pp. 7-31.⟩⟩ ⟦Abū Dulaf, *Travels in Iran*, tr. p. 46, #35, comm., pp. 92-93, calling the mountain of Bīsutūn by its Arabic name (Sinn) Sumayra, "(Tooth of) Sumayra"; Matheson, *Persia, an Archaeological Guide*, pp. 125-29; Herrmann, *The Iranian Revival*, pp. 31, 53.⟧

[8] Other figures; question of representation of Zoroaster (Jackson, *Persia Past and Present*, pp. 216 ff.); opinion of Justi, "Geschichte Irans," pp. 219 ff., and *Geschichte der orientalischen Völker*, p. 470. Illustrations *ibid.*, p. 469; Dubeux, *La Perse*, p. 22 (after Ker Porter).

[9] *Persia*, I, 561.

[10] Ibn Rusta, p. 166.

[11] Shabdīz is the name of Khusraw II's horse (Le Strange, *The Lands*, p. 63). This

this kind of work even without such legendary associations, as prisoners of war; it is quite possible that this whole complex, as Justi surmises, pertains to the fourth century, in particular to the reigns of Shāpūr II and Shāpūr III.[12]

Kirmānshāhān, the capital of Persian Kurdistān, was, according to tradition, built by the Sāsānid Varahrān IV (388-399), who before his enthronement was governor of Kirmān and therefore bore the title of *Kirmānshāh.* The city is situated in the plain of Māhīdasht, and even today has some commercial importance, thanks to its position on the main pilgrim route to Karbalā'. Its population is about 40,000.[13] Kurds are mentioned by Xenophon in his Cyropaedia as Karduchoi, Καρδοῦχοι,[14] and in the cuneiform inscriptions, it is believed, as Kudraha.[15] They represent the westernmost branch of the Iranians; it may be that this people was formed through a fusion of Iranian conquerors with earlier inhabitants of the mountains. The Kurds never played a role in history as an independent nation,[16] but separate groups entered, as in the case of other warlike peoples, the service of various rulers; leaders of such groups would often attain outstanding positions. Saladin, the

---

is how it appears in Yāqūt; there is also the form Shudāz. Abū Dulaf's statement about the perfection of the representation. ⟨⟨Cf. *Mu'jam,* I, 534; II, 107, 393, 573, 575, 813; IV, 112.⟩⟩ ⟦Abū Dulaf, *Travels in Iran,* tr. p. 45, #34, comm. p. 92.⟧

[12] *Geschichte der orientalischen Völker,* p. 470. ⟨⟨At the present time the reliefs of Ṭāq-i Bustān are dated by the scholars to the reign of Khusraw II (590-628), see M. D'iakonov, *Ocherk,* pp. 24, 330, 354, 415; Sarre, "Sasanian Stone Sculpture" in *Survey of Persian Art,* I, 593-600; an earlier date (Pērōz, 457-83) is in Erdmann, "Das Datum des Tak-i Bustan," *Ars Islamica,* IV (1937), 79-97; cf. Vanden Berghe, *Archéologie de l'Iran ancien,* pp. 103-105.⟩⟩

[13] Present-day Kirmānshāh and the governor's palace, according to Jackson, *Persia Past and Present,* p. 231: 60,000 inhabitants; the city is some four miles in circumference. ⟦Rabino, "Kermanchah," *RMM,* XXXVIII (1920), 1-40; Lockhart, *Persian Cities,* pp. 101-105; Lambton, *EI*², s.v. The population in 1976 was 290,861 (*Le monde iranien et l'Islam,* IV [1976-1977], 242).⟧

[14] Cf. Xenophon, *Anabasis,* III, 5, 16: tradition about the destruction of the army; the country of the Kurds in Xenophon corresponds to present-day Turkish Kurdistān. ⟨⟨The identification of the ancestors of modern Kurds with the Karduchoi (or Gordioi, inhabitants of the mountains to the north of Assyria) of the classical sources is not considered as proven. Cf. Rashīd Yāsimī, *Kurd wa paywastagī-yi nizhād wa ta'rikh-i ū* (Tehran, 1319/1940); Vil'chevskii, *Kurdy.*⟩⟩

[15] Curzon, *Persia,* I, 550. ⟨⟨The word Kudraha does not occur in Old Persian inscriptions.⟩⟩

[16] ⟨⟨V. V. Bartol'd must be referring to the fact that the Kurds never succeeded in establishing an independent state.⟩⟩ ⟦One should, however, mention the short-lived Kurdish Republic of Mahābād in 1945-1946.⟧

greatest personality on the Muslim side during the epoch of the Crusades, was a Kurd.[a] Persian Kurds are mostly Shāfiʿī Sunnīs; according to Curzon, the Kurdish question in Persia is based on hatred between the Sunnīs and Shīʿīs. Some of the Kurds who came under stronger Persian influence became Shīʿīs; even the sect of the ʿAlī-Ilāhīs, which considers ʿAlī to be one of the incarnations of divinity, is prevalent among them.[17] The Kurds in the environs of Kirmānshāhān are often settled in villages, and hardly differ from the Persians; the province of Kirmānshāhān is one of the richest of Iran in terms of the cereals grown here. In the tents of the Kurdish nomads, just as in the tents of the Türkmens, are woven rugs that enjoy great demand.

From the plain of Māhīdasht, several roads lead to the small river of Ḥulwān Chay, so called after the town of Ḥulwān, which already existed under the Assyrians. The Arab geographers seem to describe the one that goes through Sar-i Pul and Karind.[18] At the western end of the pass that divides the Āb-i Karind, a tributary of the Karkha, from the plain of Māhīdasht, there was in the village of Akhurīn, settled by Kurds, a temple of fire worshipers visited by pilgrims from various countries.[19] The stretch from here to the Ḥulwān pass was considered unsafe because it was exposed to Kurdish raids. Travelers crossed the small river Ḥulwān twice, in each instance on a bridge; the town of Ḥulwān itself lay on the left side of the river, to the south of Sar-i Pul.[20] In the middle of the pass stood a stone structure of Sāsānid construction, with a marble floor;

[a] See on Saladin's ethnic background and the role of the Kurds in the Ayyūbid state, V. V. Minorsky, "The Prehistory of Saladin," in *Studies in Caucasian History* (London, 1953), pp. 107-57.

[17] Also the sect of the Yazīdiyya. See Minorskii, *Materialy*. For the Kurds and their culture, see Marr, "Eshche o slove ⟨⟨chelebi⟩⟩," pp. 120 ff. ⟨⟨See now the bibliography in Musaèlian, *Bibliografiia po kurdovedeniiu*; Vil'chevskii, *Kurdy*; Minorsky, *EI*[1], art. "Kurds"; *idem*, art. "Kurdistān"; B. Nikitine, *Les Kurdes, étude sociologique et historique* (Paris, 1956); *Narody Perednei Azii*.⟩⟩ ⟦T. Bois and Minorsky, *EI*[2], art. "Kurds, Kurdistān"; Minorsky, *EI*[2], art. "Ahl-i Ḥaḳḳ"; *idem*, "The Sect of the Ahl-i Ḥaḳḳ," *Iranica, Twenty Articles*, pp. 306-16.⟧

[18] Karind, according to Le Strange, *The Lands*, pp. 191-92, is for the first time mentioned by Mustawfī; it corresponds to the Marj al-Qalʿa of Ibn Ḥawqal.

[19] For the *bayt nār* in Akhurīn, see Ibn Rusta, p. 165.

[20] In Le Strange, *The Lands*, p. 192, a different route is described: four farsakhs from Marj al-Qalʿa is Ṭazar, the latter mentioned by Maqdisī, p. 393, probably the same as the Qaṣr Yazīd of other authors; six farsakhs further was al-Zubaydiyya, the modern village of Hārūnābād. In Ṭazar, according to Maqdisī, p. 393, were the ruins of the palace Qaṣr Kisrā, according to Yāqūt, *Muʿjam*, III, 537, a high *aywān* built by Khusrawjird ibn Shāhān.

the building still exists and is called Ṭāq-i Hirra.[21] Five farsakhs to the south of Ḥulwān, on the right bank of the river, was the village of Qaṣr-i Shīrīn, where today one can still see the ruins of a palace of Khusraw II and of a fortification from the same period. A detailed description of the palace and fortress is in the report of de Morgan's expedition.[22] Between Qaṣr-i Shīrīn and Khāniqīn, places that today are already on the Turkish [now Iraqi] side of the border, the distance was reckoned as six farsakhs; there used to be, and still is, a large arched bridge over the river at Khāniqīn. In the Middle Ages, the Ḥulwān pass to the east of the small river Ḥulwān Chay was usually considered the border of Arab Iraq; the tenth-century geographers describe the town of Ḥulwān both in the chapter dealing with Iraq and in that dealing with the province of al-Jibāl.[23] Noteworthy on the way from Khāniqīn to Baghdad are the ruins of the large Sāsānid city of Dastagird, the Daskara of the Arabs, now called Eski Baghdād, near the village of Shahrābān some sixteen farsakhs from Baghdad and fourteen from Khāniqīn. The town was destroyed by the emperor Heraclius in 627; nearby are the ruins of its citadel. In the time of Ibn Rusta, the inhabitants themselves abandoned the city for fear of the Bedouins, and moved

[21] Picture in Justi, *Geschichte*, p. 387. According to Herzfeld, *Paikuli*, I, 6, the Ṭāq-i Hirra was some three hundred years older than Paikuli, "and must have been built by an architect from Northern Mesopotamia about 600 B.C." (!) ⟨⟨Cf. Vanden Berghe, *Archéologie de l'Iran ancien*, p. 103 (the edifice in Ṭāq-i Hirra pertains to the Sāsānid period). The Sāsānid inscription in Paikuli is in Turkish ⟦that is, in modern Iraqi⟧ Kurdistān, to the west of the Diyālā, below 35° 7′ 16″ N and 45° 34′ 35″ E; Middle Persian and Parthian texts (in Herzfeld, Pahlavík and Pársík), inscription of King Narseh (293-303). A part of the text was copied by Rawlinson at a time when the inscription was in better condition (1844; he discovered it in 1836); Herzfeld found Rawlinson's notebook at the Royal Asiatic Society. The main topic of the inscription was the struggle between Narseh and Varahrān III (he ruled only for four months, thus Justi, *Geschichte Irans*, p. 520; according to Ṭabarī, tr. Nöldeke, p. 50, he ruled for four years). The text and translation are in *Paikuli*, I, 94-119; forty-seven lines with large gaps; in line 44 Kušān šāh and others are mentioned, in line 45, Xwārazmān šāh (without a name). ⟨⟨For new works devoted to the inscription in Paikuli, see W. B. Henning, "A Farewell to the Khagan of the Aq-Aqatārān," *BSOAS*, XIV (1952), 501-22; R. N. Frye, "Remarks on the Paikuli and Sar Mashad Inscriptions," *HJAS*, XX (1957), 702-706.⟩⟩ ⟦H. Humbert, *The Sassanian Inscription of Paikuli. I. Supplement to Herzfeld's Paikuli* (Wiesbaden, 1978).⟧

[22] De Morgan, *Mission*, IV, 341 ff. ⟨⟨For the Sāsānid constructions in Qaṣr-i Shīrīn, see Vanden Berghe, *Archéologie de l'Iran ancien*, pp. 98, 187.⟩⟩

[23] Cf. Iṣṭakhrī, pp. 87, 200. ⟦Lockhart, *EI*², s.v.; Morony, "Continuity and Change in the Administrative Geography of Late Sasanian and Early Islamic al-ʿIrāq," pp. 21-22. Ḥulwān was the administrative center of the early Islamic district known as Māh al-Kūfa.⟧

to the fortress on the mountaintop.[24] The prison of one of the Sāsānids was said to have been here, and even today the ruins of this fortress are called Zindān, "prison."[25]

Arab Iraq or ancient Babylonia was the furthest region in which there was a significant Iranian element in the population. As is well known, the political domination of the Iranians encompassed for a time all western Asia and Egypt, but there was never a significant number of Iranian settlers in those countries. Babylonia, on the other hand, because of its fertility and advantageous geographical position, was the center of a whole series of monarchies, and at the time when one of the capitals—sometimes the only capital—of the kings of Iran was within its territory, a considerable Iranian element must have mixed with the native population. The earliest center of the region, Babylon, became under Nebuchadnezzar in the sixth century B.C. an enormous merchant city; this monarch surrounded it with a wall eighty-four versts in circumference, so that Babylon, to use Justi's expression, resembled "a province turned into a fortress."[26] Babylon remained one of the empire's capitals under the Achaemenids; Alexander the Great wanted to make it the capital of the universal kingdom he was hoping to create. The Arab geographers mention Bābil as a minor settlement, but they also say that the ancient capital used to be here. The Persians attributed the founding of Babylon to Ḍaḥḥāk.[27] Nearby was the Muslim village of al-Jāmiʿān, on the site of which the ruler Sayf al-Dawla Ṣadaqa, of the Mazyadid dynasty, created in 1101 the town of Ḥilla. Ḥilla lay on both banks—but especially on the western bank—of the Euphrates. In the fourteenth century, Ḥamd Allāh Mustawfī Qazwīnī reports that the inhabitants spoke a corrupted Arabic, but were Shīʿī fanatics who believed that the expected Mahdī would come from their city.[28]

A new capital appeared under Seleucus I (312-280 B.C.) under the name of Seleucia, on the right bank of the Tigris, a little to the south of modern Baghdad; subsequently on the opposite bank the

[24] Ibn Rusta, p. 163. ⟦A. A. Dūrī, *EI*², art. "Daskara."⟧

[25] *Geschichte der orientalischen Völker*, p. 386.

[26] *Ibid.*, p. 363.

[27] Iṣṭakhrī, p. 86.

[28] *Nuzhat al-qulūb*, extract in Schefer's ed., p. 154 ⟦ed. Le Strange, p. 40, tr. *idem*, p. 47. For al-Jāmiʿān/Ḥilla, see G. G. Makdisī, "Notes on Ḥilla and the Mazyadids in Mediaeval Islam,"*JAOS*, LXXIV (1954), 249-62, showing that the statement that Ṣadaqa created Hilla is inaccurate and that al-Jāmiʿān was enlarged into a permanent settlement, that is, into Ḥilla, by Dubays I b. ʿAlī b. Mazyad in the early eleventh century.⟧

city of Ctesiphon (ἡ Κτησιφῶν), Ṭasafūn or Ṭisafūn in Arabic and Persian, grew. In the second century A.D. Seleucia was destroyed by the Romans, but in the third century, Ardashīr, the founder of the Sāsānid dynasty, rebuilt it under the name of Weh-Ardashīr.[29] In this manner the twin city of Seleucia-Ctesiphon remained the capital of the Parthian kings as well as of their successors the Sāsānids; in other words, it was the capital of the Persian empire down to the Islamic conquest. Isidore of Charax describes the road from Seleucia to Ekbatana or Hamadān; one can see from the stages that he mentions along this road—Χάλα or Ḥulwān, Καρίνα or Karind, and Κογκυβάρ or Kangawār—that it was identical with the road described by the Arab geographers and that exists still today.

Ctesiphon, together with Weh-Ardashir and other suburbs, bore the Arabic name al-Madā'in ("the cities").[30] Out of the ruins of al-Madā'in was later built Baghdad. Only a part of the famous palace called Ṭāq-i Kisrā[31] has remained; the construction of this palace was attributed to Khusraw Anūshirwān. The Arabs considered it to be one of the wonders of the world, and the tallest brick construction ever built.[32] There was a legend that the palace collapsed without any apparent reason on the night that the Prophet Muḥammad was born; or, according to another legend, the year when he embarked on his prophetic mission in the reign of Khusraw II. According to tradition, in the Sāsānid period the two parts of Madā'in were linked by a brick bridge, but as early as the tenth century no trace of this bridge was left.[33] On the site of the ancient city, facing the Ṭāq-i Kisrā, there was still in the fourteenth century a Muslim sanctuary, the tomb of the Prophet's barber Salmān Fārsī, which is mentioned by Maqdisī.[34] Aside from these two buildings, by the time that Mustawfī wrote, nothing was left on the eastern bank of

[29] Ṭabarī, tr. Nöldeke, p. 16.

[30] Madā'in: Iranian and Semitic quarters; Asbānbur, Yāqūt, *Mu'jam*, I, 237; Maqdisī, p. 122.

[31] Or Aywān Kisrā; cf. al-Ẓahīrī's story about the madrasa of al-Nāṣir Ḥasan (1347-1351 and 1354-1361).

[32] A contemporary view is in Sarre and Herzfeld, *Iranische Felsreliefs. Aufnahmen und Untersuchungen von Denkmälern aus Alt- und Mittelpersischer Zeit* (Berlin, 1910), atlas, pls. XXXIX and XLII; for the dimensions see Justi, *Geschichte*, p. 476 ⟨⟨for the Ṭāq-i Kisrā, see *Survey of Persian Art*, I, IV⟩⟩.

[33] Iṣṭakhrī, p. 87.

[34] Maqdisī, p. 122. Today, Salmān Pāk is a short distance to the north of Ṭāq-i Kisrā. Cf. the plan in Sarre and Herzfeld, *Felsreliefs*. ⟦For photographs of the tomb, see L. Massignon, "Nouvelles recherches sur Salmân Pāk," *A Locust's Leg, Studies in Honour of S. H. Taqizadeh*, pp. 178-81.⟧

the Tigris; on the western bank there still existed a small settlement.[35]

Nowhere were the transformations wrought by the Arabs so far-reaching as in Mesopotamia. Mustawfī remarks that in his time, all seven cities of Iraq that had existed before Islam—Madā'in, Qādisiyya, Rūmiyya, Ḥīra, Bābil, Nahrawān, and Ḥulwān—lay in ruins.[36] Among these cities, Rūmiyya was near Madā'in; just as Jundīshāpūr under Shāpūr I, so also Rūmiyya under Khusraw Anushirwān was built on the model of Antioch for the captives brought here from the latter city. Persians called it Rūmaqān, whereas in Armenian and Byzantine sources it appears also as Antioch of Khusraw.[37] Nahrawān, which still flourished in the tenth century,[38] lay four farsakhs from Baghdad by the high road to Khāniqīn, on the bank of a canal that watered the area around Baghdad. Qādisiyya, near which the famous battle between the Arabs and the Persians took place, is mentioned in the tenth century as a border point of Iraq on the west, five days' journey from Baghdad, to the southwest of Kūfa.[39] There was yet another Qādisiyya—this one on the Tigris—by the road from Baghdad to Sāmarrā, three farsakhs from the latter.[40] The city of Anbār on the Euphrates is also mentioned, on the road from Baghdad to Syria and two farsakhs from the former,[41] the ʿAbbāsid caliphs considered making Anbār their capital before the foundation of Baghdad.[b] Near Ḥīra, in the Islamic period, Kūfa was created.

All the principal cities of Iraq, that is, Kūfa, Baṣra, and Wāsiṭ as well as Baghdad, were founded only after the coming of Islam.[42]

[35] *Nuzhat al-qulūb*, extract in Schefer's ed., p. 163 ⟦ed. Le Strange, p. 45, tr. *idem*, p. 52⟧.

[36] *Ibid.*, p. 162. Parthian Hatra (al-Ḥaḍr), see Le Strange, *The Lands*, pp. 98 ff.; Justi, "*Geschichte Irans*," p. 449. ⟨⟨For Hatra and its monuments, see Koshelenko, *Kul'tura Parfii*, pp. 26-27, 137-44, 170-78, 190-98; also Maricq, "Hatra de Sanatrouq," and "Les dernières années de Hatra: l'alliance romaine," *Classica et orientalia* (Paris, 1965), pp. 1-16 and 17-26, respectively.⟩⟩ ⟦Ch. Pellat, *EI*², art, "al-Ḥaḍr"; Herrmann, *The Iranian Revival*, pp. 58-62.⟧

[37] Ṭabarī, tr. Nöldeke, pp. 165-66.

[38] Iṣṭakhrī, p. 86.

[39] *Ibid.*, p. 79. ⟦L. Veccia Vaglieri, *EI*², art. "al-Ḳādisiyya. 2."⟧

[40] Ibn Khurradādhbih, tr., p. 67; cf. Maqdisī, p. 29. ⟦Streck and Lassner, *EI*², art. "al-Ḳādisiyya. 1."⟧.

[41] Ibn Khurradādhbih, tr., p. 53. ⟨⟨See now Maricq, "Découverte aérienne d'Anbār," *Classica et orientalia*, pp. 147-56.⟩⟩ ⟦Streck and Duri, *EI*², s.v.⟧.

[b] Lassner, *The Topography of Baghdad in the Early Middle Ages* (Detroit, 1970), pp. 123-24; *idem, The Shaping of ʿAbbāsid Rule* (Princeton, 1980).

[42] The Syriac name of Kūfa is ʿAqūlā, "the crooked" (cf. W. Wright, tr. in *Kratkiy*

Kūfa lay on the Euphrates four days' journey from Baghdad and five farsakhs (fifteen miles) from Qādisiyya.[43] At a distance of one farsakh from Kūfa lay Ḥīra, the capital of the well-known dynasty of the Lakhmids, who had ruled over the limitrophic Arab tribes as vassals of the Sāsānids. The city fell to ruin after the founding of Kūfa. Two farsakhs to the southwest of Kūfa, people showed the grave of the caliph ʿAlī; near this sanctuary lay the settlement of Najaf. Even more than ʿAlī's tomb in Najaf, the Shīʿīs venerate the tomb of his son Ḥusayn at Karbalāʾ, situated to the northwest of Babylon. A legend claimed that the caliph Mutawakkil (ninth century) wanted to flood the tomb, but that the water miraculously stopped in front of the sanctuary. In the tenth century, ʿAḍud al-Dawla built here a mausoleum around which a small town developed.[44]

From Baghdad to Wāsiṭ the distance was reckoned to be eight days' journey, and from Kūfa to Wāsiṭ, through marshy territory, six days. Wāsiṭ, like Baghdad, stood on both banks of the Tigris, which were linked by a pontoon bridge.[45] Today, it is bisected not by the main course of the river but only by one of its channels. Through Wāsiṭ passed the main road from Iraq to Khūzistān. A distance of eight days' travel (or fifty farsakhs) was counted from Wāsiṭ to Baṣra, a city where in pre-Islamic times there was no settlement. "The bringing to life of dead lands" happened only under Islam, and as a result, the tax collected from cultivated plots here was not the land tax (*kharāj*) but only the tithe (*ʿushr*).[46] Baṣra, watered by a multitude of canals, still lay two days' journey from the seacoast. Four farsakhs from Baṣra was the town of Ubulla, between the main course of the Tigris and one of the channels; the harbor of Ubulla was considered very dangerous,[47] notwithstanding which its commerce grew considerably.[48] The main course

---

ocherk, p. 94 n. 4; this name was used by the Chinese (Chao Zhu-gua, *Chu-fan-chï*, tr. F. Hirth and W. W. Rockhill [St. Petersburg, 1911], p. 110). Hirra, Khawārnaq and the correct remark by Le Strange, *The Lands*, p. 76.

[43] Ibn Khurradādhbih, tr., p. 96. ⟦Hichem Djaït, *EI*², s.v.⟧.

[44] Mustawfī, *Nuzhat al-qulūb*, extract in Schefer's ed., pp. 144-45 ⟦ed. Le Strange, p. 32, tr. *idem*, p. 39. E. Honigmann, *EI*², s.v.⟧.

[45] Cf. Yāqūt, *Muʿjam*, IV, 274; II, 442, about the village of Zandaward and Dawqara; II, pp. 621, 951, Dawkar; and Wright, tr. in *Kratkii ocherk*, pp. 128, 132 n. 3. See further Yāqūt, *Muʿjam*, IV, 274; II, 442 on [the settlement of] Khusraw Sābūr.

[46] Cf. Iṣṭakhrī, p. 82.

[47] *Ibid.*, p. 81.

[48] According to Nöldeke, *Orientalische Skizzen* (Berlin, 1892), p. 157, Baṣra "weiter westlich als die heutige viel kleinere Stadt dieses Namens"; Ubulla, p. 166) "ungefähr

of the Tigris flowed into the sea near the village of ʿAbbādān on the road from Baṣra to ʿUmān, twelve farsakhs, according to Ibn Khurradādhbih, from Baṣra.[49] The landing place (*al-khashabāt*, literally, "constructions on wooden piles") of ʿAbbādān lay two farsakhs from that village, and that was where people boarded the boats. In the twelfth century, just as today, the name ʿAbbādān was applied to the island formed by the two channels of the Shaṭṭ al-ʿArab near the place where the river flows into the sea.[50]

We read in the sources that the Euphrates bifurcated below Anbār into two channels, one of which flowed toward Kūfa, whereas the other passed by Sūrā and joined the Tigris below Wāsiṭ; this second channel must clearly be identical with the present-day main course.[51] The western channel, according to Maqdisī, branched out below Kūfa into a multitude of canals; four of these reached the Tigris.[52] According to a legend, the destruction of dams in Iraq

---

an der Stelle des heutigen Basra." Cf. Nāṣir-i Khusraw, *Safar-nāma* (Tehran lithog.), pp. 228-29; about the location of Ubulla: *ibid.*, p. 238, and also Ibn Khurradādhbih, text, p. 59; Qudāma, text, p. 194; Ibn al-Faqīh, p. 191; Yāqūt, *Muʿjam*, III, 31, about the departure of the Persians in four hundred ships, at the Arab conquest, to S.b.dhān, and about the fire temples. In Baṣra there were three bazaars, see Maqdisī, p. 117 (there are other names in Nāṣir-i Khusraw). Picture of Baṣra in Sykes, *Ten Thousand Miles*, facing p. 244; in Sarre and Herzfeld, *Felsreliefs*, atlas, pl. XXXVII; text, pp. 249 ff. ⟨⟨For Baṣra in the historical geography of Iraq as a whole, see also Le Strange, "Description of Persia and Mesopotamia"; *idem, The Lands*, pp. 1-85; Markwart, *Südarmenien und die Tigrisquellen nach griechischen und arabischen Geographen* (Vienna, 1930); Streck, *Die alte Landschaft Babylonien nach den arabischen Geographen* (Leiden, 1900-1901); H. H. Schaeder, "Hasan al-Baṣrī. Studien zur Frühgeschichte des Islam," *Isl.*, XIV (1925), 4-42; Ch. Pellat and S. H. Longrigg, *EI*², art. "al-Baṣra."⟩⟩ ⟦For the early Islamic history of the *miṣr* of Baṣra, see the detailed study by Pellat, *Le milieu basrien et la formation de Ǧāḥiẓ* (Paris, 1953).⟧

[49] Text, p. 60, tr., p. 40. Kūt al-ʿAmāra, medieval Fam al-Ṣilḥ, see on it Yāqūt, *Muʿjam*, III, 917; the canal al-Ṣilḥ above; the administrative district between it and Jabbul villages, the palace of Ma'mūn's vizier al-Hasan b. Sahl, "and it ⟦that is, the palace⟧ is now ruined except for a small part." ⟦For Kūt al-ʿAmāra, see J. B. Kelly, *EI*², s.v.⟧.

[50] Ibn Ḥawqal, p. X. ʿAbbādān is the abode of the Ṣūfīs; a *ribāṭ*, with a "community of ṣufis and ascetics" in it. ʿAbbādān as an island in Nāṣir-i Khusraw, *Safar-nāma* (Tehran lithog.), p. 240; at high tide, the sea reaches the walls of ʿAbbādan, at the ebb it recedes to almost two farsakhs from it; *khashāb* (*ibid.*, p. 241, cf. *al-Khashabāt* in Ibn Khurradādhbih, tr., p. 40) as a sign marking shoals. From ʿAbbādān to Mihrūyān, Nāṣir-i Khusraw, *Safar-nāma* (Tehran lithog.), p. 242, cf. Iṣṭakhrī, p. 29. ⟦Pellat, *EI*², art. "al-Khashabāt," and Lockhart, art. "ʿAbādān"; Lockhart, *Persian Cities*, pp. 165-71. Since Barthold wrote, the town has of course enjoyed a phenomenal growth through its oil refineries and terminal; its name was Persianized to Ābādān by Riḍā Shāh Pahlavī. Its population in 1976 was 296,081 (*Le monde iranien et l'Islam*, IV [1976-1977], 242.⟧

[51] Qudāma, tr., p. 177.

[52] Maqdisī, p. 20.

and the appearance of marshlands occurred in the seventh century, shortly before the Islamic conquest. The term Shaṭṭ al-ʿArab appears as early as Mustawfī's work.[53]

From among the cities on the Tigris above Baghdad, Sāmarrā and Takrīt were noteworthy. From Baghdad to Sāmarrā the distance was reckoned to be three days' journey, and it was one more to Takrīt. Sāmarrā was built in the ninth century by the caliph Muʿtaṣim (833-842), and finished in the reign of Mutawakkil (847-861), under the name of Surra man ra'ā or, according to Maqdisī, Surūr man ra'ā, which was also shortened to Surmarā.[54] It stood on the eastern bank of the Tigris at the edge of the desert; the nearby settlements, orchards, and fields were all on the western bank. Here lived the caliph surrounded by his guard; according to Maqdisī,[55] here was also built a Kaʿba, and places called "the valley of Minā" and "the mountain of ʿArafāt," so that the captains of the guard could not leave the caliph even under the pretext of going on pilgrimage.[56] Nevertheless, the city did not last much more than one hundred years; Muʿtamid (870-892) moved his residence back to Baghdad, and Sāmarrā began to fall into neglect. The name itself was changed, according to Maqdisī, into Sā'a man ra'ā, which then became Sāmarrā;[57] the latter form is already employed, however, by Iṣṭakhrī.[58]

The city of Takrīt was in the tenth century and even later one of the Christian centers of Iraq; even in the thirteenth century, at the time of the Mongol conquest of Baghdad, Christians constituted a significant part of Takrīt's population.[59] In the Mongol period,

[53] *Nuzhat al-qulūb*, University ms. 171, fol. 254 ⟦ed. Le Strange, p. 215, tr. *idem*, p. 207⟧. It appears as early as the account of Nāṣir-i Khusraw, who was there on 20 Shaʿbān 443/27 December 1051, see *Safar-nāma* (Tehran lithog.), p. 228. Cf. Quatremère's opinion (Rashīd al-Dīn, *Histoire des Mongols de la Perse*, note 58) that the name Shaṭṭ al-ʿArab refers to the whole course of the Tigris.

[54] Maqdisī, p. 122.

[55] *Ibid.*

[56] Doubtfulness of this story; Yaʿqūbī.

[57] Maqdisī, p. 123.

[58] Iṣṭakhrī, pp. 79, 85. ⟨⟨For the history and monuments of Sāmarrā, see Herzfeld, *Geschichte der Stadt Samarra* (Hamburg-Berlin, 1948).⟩⟩ ⟦For the buildings of Sāmarrā, see K.A.C. Creswell, *Early Muslim Architecture: Umayyads, Early ʿAbbāsids and Tulūnids*, II (London, 1950); for its site and planning, J. M. Rogers, "Sāmarrā, a Study in Medieval Town-Planning," *The Islamic City*, ed. A. H. Hourani and S. M. Stern (London, 1970), pp. 118-55.⟧

[59] C. d'Ohsson, *Histoire des Mongols*, III, 270-71. ⟦Takrīt was the center of the pre-Islamic district of Ṭīrhān, a Monophysite Christian metropolitanate that from 629 onward exercised authority over the whole Monophysite Church in the East; it further possessed a Nestorian bishopric. See J.-M. Fiey, "Tagrit," *L'Orient syrien*,

the city, situated on the western bank of the Tigris, enjoyed the reputation of being a solid stronghold, and it was believed to have been built by the Sāsānids. In 1393, Takrīt was taken and demolished by Tīmūr. The garrison, for its stubborn resistance, was exterminated; at the demolition of the fortress one wall was left standing as a warning to posterity.[60]

The Shīʿī rulers of Persia were of course reluctant to leave a region that harbored the principal Shīʿī sanctuaries, and where the Shīʿīs constituted the major part of the population, in the hands of the Sunnī sulṭāns of Turkey. Already in the middle of the thirteenth century, when the Mongols marched on Baghdad, the Shīʿīs of Ḥilla and other places on the Euphrates defected from the ʿAbbāsids and assisted the Mongols.[61] In the seventeenth century, Shāh ʿAbbās the Great took Baghdad from the Turks for some time, but in 1638 the latter city reverted to the Ottoman empire.[62]

VIII (1963), 292 ff.; *idem, Assyrie chrétienne* (Beirut, 1968), II, 329; III, 18, 105-106; Morony, "Continuity and Change," pp. 15-16.⟧

[60] Sharaf al-Dīn Yazdī, I, 647-56.

[61] C. d'Ohsson, *Histoire des Mongols*, III, 255.

[62] A. A. Adamov's book *Irak Arabskii*. The dynasty of the Afrāsiyābids, amīrs of Baṣra in the sixteenth century, in R. Hartmann, *EI*[1], art. "al-Baṣra": descendants of Afrāsiyāb; the *firmān* of 1616 that confirmed Afrāsiyāb as governor of Baṣra; end of these governors in 1668 ⟨⟨Adamov, *Irak Arabskii*, pp. 332-42⟩⟩. Information about Baṣra and Muḥammara in Sykes, *Ten Thousand Miles*, pp. 243-48. Muḥammara's cession to Persia in accordance with the treaty of Erzurum of 1846 ⟨⟨Adamov, *Irak Arabskii* p. 450⟩⟩. Muḥammara, according to Le Strange, *The Lands*, p. 48, on the place of Bayān (for it, see *ibid.*); concerning the fortress of Fao: cf. Yāqūt, *Muʿjam*, III, 849, s.v. "Fāw." ⟦H.A.R. Gibb, *EI*[2], art. "Afrāsiyāb."⟧

CHAPTER XIII

The Mountains North of Hamadān

THE Arab geographers also included in the province of al-Jibāl, which comprised Ray, Iṣfahān, Hamadān, and other cities, the mountains to the north of Hamadān up to the border of Azerbaijan. The main component of the population there was constituted, then as now, by Kurds; the region between Kirmānshāhān and Azerbaijan bears today the name of Ardalān; its chief city is Sinna, or, more exactly, Senna [Modern Sanandaj].[a] In the nineteenth century, the Kurdish *wālī* of this city was still in fact independent of the Persian government; only in the reign of Nāṣir al-Dīn Shāh, who sent as governor to Senna his uncle (who was later himself succeeded by his son), could this region be brought under control. In the Middle Ages, the chief city of the region was Dīnawar, four farsakhs west of the village of Saḥna or Siḥna.[1] The road to Dīnawar branched off from the high road between Hamadān and Baghdād at the village of Mādarān, four farsakhs from Qaṣr al-Luṣūṣ or Kangāwar and the same distance from Siḥna. The ruins of Dīnawar lie on the banks of a small river that flows into the Jamas Āb near the mountain of Bīsutūn, and that is still called Āb-i Dīnawar. From Dīnawar it was four days' march to Shahrazūr, the latter situated to the southeast of present-day Sulaymāniyya, not far from the modern border between Turkey and Persia. The same distance was reckoned from Dīnawar southward to Sīrawān, whose ruins can still be seen in the mountains; one day's march farther lay the town of Ṣaymara. From Shahrazūr it was also four days' journey to Ḥul-

[a] See Minorsky, *EI*[1], art. "Senna."

[1] According to Le Strange, *The Lands*, p. 189, in the tenth century Dīnawar was the capital of the Ḥasanwayhids. According to Ibn Ḥawqal, p. 260, the dimensions of Dīnawar were two-thirds those of Hamadān, and the level of education of its citizens was higher. Cf. Iṣṭakhrī, p. 198; *Ḥudūd al-ʿālam*, fol. 29a; the Friday mosque was a construction of Ḥasanwayh (cf. Maqdisī, p. 394, about the dome above the *minbar* and the attractive *maqṣūra*, whose floor was higher than that of the mosque). The town was still inhabited in the fourteenth century, and was probably ruined after Tīmūr. Samʿānī, facs. ed. Margoliouth, fol. 299a, s.v. "Sufyānī" about the school of Sufyān al-Thawrī, which was still dominant in Dīnawar in his time. For Dīnawar, see Samʿānī's remark, fol. 238a: "one of the towns of Jabal near Qirmīsīn." ⟦Lockhart, *EI*[2], art. "Dīnawar."⟧.

wān; according to Ibn Rusta, the road to Shahrazūr branched off from the high road at Qaṣr-i Shīrīn.[2] Shahrazūr was also called by the Persians Nīmrāh, because it lay half way between Madā'in, the ancient capital, and Shīz, the principal temple of the fire worshipers in the southern part of Azerbaijan, where there are today the ruins of Takht-i Sulaymān.[3] Ardalān, together with Nihāwand, constituted in Sāsānid times the province of Māh;[4] the revenues from this province were subsequently apportioned between the Arab military establishments at Kūfa and Baṣra, so that its northern part, with Dīnawar, received the appellation Māh al-Kūfa, and the southern part Māh al-Baṣra.

There was not a single city to the northeast of Hamadān before Qazwīn. A road went to the north of Hamadān toward Zanjān, passing through the town of Suhraward; the latter was the birthplace of the illustrious twelfth-century mystic, the shaykh Suhrawardī, who was executed in 1191 at Aleppo.[5] This more direct road, however, was not always safe from the Kurds who usually controlled Suhraward; this would then make a detour necessary through Qazwīn.[6] At Zanjān, the road from Jibāl merged with the high road from Ray to Azerbaijan.

The first important town on this road was Qazwīn.[7] This city remained for a long time, even during the ʿAbbāsids, one of the border posts of the Islamic empire, because Daylam—the mountainous part of modern Gīlān—remained unconquered by the Arabs. The propagation of Islam in Daylam was carried out at the beginning of the fourth century of the Hijra by one of the ʿAlid missionaries; and it was from this region that the dynasty of the

[2] Ibn Rusta, p. 164.

[3] A description of the ruins is in Jackson, *Persia Past and Present*, pp. 124-43. ⟨⟨For the excavations, see R. Naumann *et al.*, "Takht-i Suleiman und Zendan-i Suleiman. Vorläufiger Bericht über die Grabungen in Jahre 1962," *AA*, III (1964), 1-76; *idem*, "Takht-i Suleiman . . . die Ausgrabungen in den Jahren 1963 und 1964," *AA*, IV (1965), 619-801.⟩⟩ ⟦D. Huff, "Takht-i Suleiman," *Iran, JBIPS*, VII (1969), 192-93; VIII (1970), 194-97; IX (1971), 181-82; Matheson, *Persia, an Archaeological Guide*, pp. 102-104; Herrmann, *The Iranian Revival*, pp. 113-18.⟧

[4] ⟨⟨*Māh* is from Old Iranian *māda-* "Media."⟩⟩

[5] There are several mystics by the name of Suhrawardī; see Brockelmann, *GAL*, I, 436 ff., 440. ⟦The shaykh intended here is Shihāb al-Dīn Yaḥyā b. Ḥabash b. Amīrak, called, because of his martyrdom, al-Maqtūl, and the proponent of *ishrāq*, "illuminative wisdom" in his *Kitāb Ḥikmat al-ishrāq*. See S. Van den Bergh, *EI*[1], s.v.; Brockelmann, *GAL*, I[2], 564-66, S I, pp. 781-83.⟧

[6] Iṣṭakhrī, p. 196.

[7] Nāṣir-i Khusraw was in Qazwīn in the summer of 1046 (Muḥarram 438), *Safarnāma* (Tehran lithog.), p. 9. Description of the city.

Buwayhids emerged in the tenth century. Tradition attributed the creation of Qazwīn to Shāpūr, son of Ardashīr, the founder of the Sāsānid dynasty. We have relatively detailed information about the city's history and topography, because it was the home town of the fourteenth-century historian and geographer Ḥamd Allāh Mustawfī.[8] The inhabitants were still in the fourteenth century mostly Shāfiʿī Sunnīs and, according to Mustawfī, never submitted to the heretical Ismāʿīlīs, even though the principal strongholds of this sect were situated immediately north of the city in Rudbār, a district that lay only six farsakhs from Qazwīn.[9] Up to fifty solidly-built strongholds were in this district; the two principal ones were Alamūt and Maymūn Diz. In Alamūt, destroyed by the Mongols, lived the head of the sect of the Ismāʿīlīs or Assassins.[10] The name of the castle meant, according to Mustawfī, "eagle's nest," *āl amūt*, obviously in the local dialect.[11] We still have no single even moderately detailed study of the Ismāʿīlī sect, and in general the eleventh and twelfth centuries are the least researched periods of Islamic history. It would be most worthwhile to investigate the reasons for the success of this sect, which brought under its control a whole series of strong castles over a vast area all the way to Qūhistān in the east, and which dispatched in secret assassins of predetermined victims all over Muslim Asia. As is known, the French word *assassin* goes back to the name of this sect, al-Ḥashīshiyyūn.[12] At the same

[8] *Nuzhat al-qulūb*, extract in Schefer's ed., pp. 178-81. ⟨⟨Cf. C. Barbier de Maynard, "Description historique de la ville de Kazvîn, extrait du Tarikhé guzidèh de Hamd Allah Mustôfî Kazvînî," *JA*, sér. 5, vol. X (1857), 257-308⟩⟩ ⟦ed. Le Strange, pp. 56-59, tr. *idem*, pp. 62-64.⟧

[9] Rittikh, *Otchet o poezdke*, pt. 1, p. 108, about the beauty of Shāh ʿAbbās's mosque in Qazwīn. Cf. Jackson, *Persia Past and Present*, p. 444 (according to Yāqūt, *Muʿjam*, IV, 89) about the old mosque as a building of Hārūn al-Rashīd. *Ibid.* for the "tax of the town" and 10,000 dirhams. According to Yāqūt, *Muʿjam*, IV, 455, Madīnat Mūsā opposite Qazwīn, a construction of the caliph Hādī in Mahdī's lifetime (cf. Samʿānī, facs. ed. Margoliouth, fol. 516b below: Madīnat al-Mubārak bi-Qazwīn; the village of Rustamābād. For Rustamābād, see also Yāqūt, *Muʿjam*, II, 778, s.v., where it is said that "Mūsā established it as a waqf for the benefit of the city of Qazwīn and of its ghazis" (Rustamābād does not appear in Samʿānī). ⟦On Shāfiʿism in Qazwīn, see H. Halm, *Die Ausbreitung der šāfiʿitischen Rechtsschule von den Anfängen bis zum 8./14. Jahrhundert* (Wiesbaden, 1974),p. 144.⟧

[10] Nasawī's narrative about his mission to Alamūt in 1230, in d'Ohsson, *Histoire des Mongols*, III, 180 ff. ⟦W. Iwanow, *Alamut and Lamassar, Two Mediaeval Ismaili Strongholds in Iran. An Archaeological Study* (Tehran, 1960); P.J.E. Willey, *The Castles of the Assassins* (London, 1963).⟧

[11] *Nuzhat al-qulūb*, extract in Schefer's ed., p. 183 ⟦ed. Le Strange, p. 61, tr. *idem*, p. 66⟧.

[12] ⟨⟨For the Ismāʿīlīs, see I. P. Petrushevskii, *Islam v Irane v VII-XV vekakh (kurs*

time, the leaders of the sect were not averse to cultural aspirations: a great library of wide renown was assembled in Alamūt. Before the destruction of the stronghold by the Mongols in 1256, the historian Juwaynī, who accompanied Hülegü, drew the khan's attention to the value of this library; Hülegü ordered that all the books be delivered to Juwaynī, who then conserved those works and astronomical instruments that he considered valuable, and had the books that contained the heretical Ismāʿīlī doctrine burned.[13] According to Chardin, Alamūt was subsequently restored, and served under the Ṣafawids as a government prison; persons whom the authorities wanted to get rid of were hurled from the cliff on which the fortress stood.[14] Among the border fortresses around Qazwīn, also mentioned is Ṭālaqān, situated to the east of that city and closer to the mountain; at the end of the tenth century it was a considerable town.[15] In the sixteenth century, under Shāh Ṭahmāsp, Qazwīn was for some time the capital of Persia; the impression of seventeenth-century travelers was that it did not yield, in terms of brilliance, to any city of Persia except Iṣfahān. Even today, on account of its position on the main road from the Caspian seaport of Rasht to the capital of the country, Tehran, Qazwīn continues to be a vigorous merchant city. It is the first large town that those arriving in Persia along that route encounter. Its population is estimated to be as much as 40,000, although Curzon finds this number exaggerated.[16]

The road from Qazwīn to Zanjān passed through the town of Abhar, which still exists today, although it lies off the high road; in the tenth century, Abhar, like Qazwīn, suffered much from the Kurds and Daylamīs.[17] Between Abhar and Zanjān, some nine far-

---

lektsii) (Leningrad, 1966), pp. 276-310 (and bibliography on pp. 386-88).⟫ ⟦M.G.S. Hodgson, *The Order of Assassins. The Struggle of the Early Nizârî Ismāʿīlīs against the Islamic World* (The Hague, 1955); B. Lewis, *The Assassins, a Radical Sect in Islam* (London, 1967); W. Madelung, *EI*², art. "Ismāʿīliyya."⟧

[13] C. d'Ohsson, *Histoire des Mongols,* III, 198.

[14] *Voyages,* ed. 1735, II, 267.

[15] Maqdisī, p. 360. ⟦Cl. Huart, *EI*¹, art. "Ṭālakān."⟧

[16] Curzon, *Persia,* I, 35. According to Jackson, *Persia Past and Present,* p. 443, there were 50,000 to 100,000 inhabitants, and according to his *From Constantinople to the Home of Omar Khayyam,* p. 93, there were 60,000 inhabitants or more. ⟪For the history of Qazwīn and its monuments, see also Huart, *EI*¹, art. "Kazwīn"; Gulrīz Sayyid Muḥammad ʿAlī, *Mīnūdar yā Bāb al-Janna Qazwīn* (Tehran, 1337/1958).⟫ ⟦A.K.S. Lambton and R. L. Hillenbrand, *EI*², art. "Ḳazwīn." The population in 1976 was 138,527 (*Le monde iranien et l'Islam,* IV [1976-1977], 242).⟧

[17] Ibn Ḥawqal, p. 258. ⟦Minorsky, *EI*², s.v.⟧.

sakhs from the former and five farsakhs from the latter, the Mongols created the new capital of Iran, Sulṭāniyya. Its construction began in the thirteenth century under the il-khan Arghun, and it was completed in the fourteenth century under Öljeytü. The latter sovereign wanted to surround the city with an extensive wall 30,000 paces in circuit, but, according to Mustawfī, he never managed to finish this project.[18] Clavijo, who saw it at the beginning of the fifteenth century, says that the city lay in a plain and was not surrounded by a wall, but that it had a fortification with thick walls and beautiful towers.[19] This citadel was built with hewn stones. According to Clavijo, Sulṭāniyya remained behind Tabrīz in terms of size, but had an even greater commercial importance.[20] Here was brought silk from Gīlān (where sericulture flourished in the Middle Ages and declined only recently) and from Shamākhī, and also silken and other fabrics and carpets from southern Persia, and finally Indian goods via Hurmuz. Sixty days' journey was reckoned from Sulṭāniyya to Hurmuz, but only six days' to the Caspian sea through Gīlān. Mustawfī makes all the itineraries that he describes converge at Sulṭāniyya, the hub of the political and commercial life of Persia:

1. *Shāhrāh-i janūbī,* the road to Hamadān and from there to Baghdad and Mecca;
2. *Shāhrāh-i sharqī,* the road to Qazwīn, Warāmīn, and Khurāsān;
3. *Shāhrāh-i shimālī,* the road through Zanjān to Ardabīl and the regions of Transcaucasia;
4. *Shāhrāh-i gharbī,* the road from Zanjān to Tabrīz and Asia Minor; and
5. *Shāhrāh bayna 'l-sharq wa 'l-janūb,* the road through Sāwa to Qum and from there to Iṣfahān, Shīrāz, and the ports on the Persian Gulf.[21]

After Tīmūr, Sulṭāniyya began to decline, and by the end of the sixteenth century it had lost its former grandeur. In the seventeenth century, its population was some 6,000 in all; in the nineteenth century, when Ker Porter visited it, Fatḥ ʿAlī Shāh had built here his

[18] *Nuzhat al-qulūb,* extract in Schefer's ed., p. 177 ⟦ed. Le Strange, p. 55, tr. *idem,* p. 61⟧.

[19] Clavijo, ed. Sreznevskii, p. 176 ⟦tr. Le Strange, pp. 158-59⟧.

[20] *Ibid.,* pp. 177-79 ⟦tr. pp. 158-61⟧.

[21] *Nuzhat al-qulūb,* University ms. 171, fols. 239a-245b ⟦ed. Le Strange, pp. 164 ff., tr. *idem,* pp. 161 ff.⟧.

summer palace with a citadel, and had dreamed of restoring the city under the name of Sulṭānābād; some three hundred families lived in it at the time. After the Russo-Persian war of 1826-1828, however, Fatḥ ʿAlī's plan was abandoned. At present Sulṭāniyya is remarkable only for its ruins of buildings from the fourteenth century, in particular those of the two large mosques. In the great mosque, which was seriously damaged by an earthquake early in the nineteenth century, is the tomb of Sulṭān Öljeytü, who is better known by his Muslim name of Khudābanda.[22] The building, according to Mustawfī, stood within the citadel. Of the latter, as one can see from illustrations in Ker Porter's book,[23] only an insignificant part of the wall with a tower on the northwestern side remains. The dimensions of the citadel are indicated by a square ditch: each side measures 300 yards or 900 feet, so that the circumference of the citadel would thus be just under one verst, a size that approximately corresponds to that given by Mustawfī of 2,000 paces.[24] Best preserved is the so-called "outer mosque" with a 120-foot-high dome, four minarets, and two entrance arches. Historical sources

[22] Verse about Khudābanda in Browne, *A Year amongst the Persians*, p. 75:

Ay Shāh Khudābanda,
Ẓulm kunanda,
Iki ṭawuq bir kanda!

⟦Browne's translation:
Oh Shāh Khudābanda,
Practiser of tyranny,
Two fowls to one village!⟧

The height of Khudābanda's tomb, according to Dieulafoy, *La Perse*, p. 91, is 51 meters above the platform of the parvis. Cf. Sykes, *A History of Persia*, II, 235, about the dome: 84 feet in diameter, "the largest in Persia"; the whole mausoleum was "certainly the first building of this kind erected under the Mongols"; according to Barbaro, *Viaggi*, the dome was larger than that of San Joanni Paulo in Venice; it was built ostensibly for a translation of the remains of ʿAlī and Ḥusayn from Najaf and Karbalāʾ. Data in C.F.M. Texier, *Description de l'Arménie, la Perse et la Mésopotamie* (Paris, 1839-1852), pt. 2, pp. 76-77: an octagon, 26 meters in diameter inside, the inner height to the cornice equals the diameter; a round gallery of 24 arcades to the height of 15 meters; from among its eight minarets, only one has been preserved. It is the only building in which the inner, spherical, dome is not covered by an egg-shaped external one; all the other large mosques of Persia, which are also later, have a double dome. The other, more recent travelers in their description always mean the large mosque and not the "outer" one. ⟨⟨For the history and monuments of Sulṭāniyya, see also Minorsky, *EI*[1], art. "Sulṭānīya"; *Survey of Persian Art*, II, V; Wilber, *The Architecture of Islamic Iran. The Il Khanid Period* (Princeton, 1955).⟩⟩

[23] *Travels*, I, 278.

[24] *Nuzhat al-qulūb*, extract in Schefer's ed., p. 178 ⟦ed. Le Strange, p. 55, tr. *idem*, p. 61⟧.

also mention a madrasa, with sixteen teachers and two hundred students, built by Khudābanda alongside the large mosque, as well as numerous buildings by the sulṭān's vizier ʿAlī Shāh.[25]

To the east of Sulṭāniyya was a district with a settlement that even today bears the half-Mongol name Ṣāyin Qalʿa (*sāyin* means "good" in Mongolian); the pre-Mongol name of this village was Quhūd.[26] The road from Sulṭāniyya to Zanjān passes along the valley of the Zanjān Rūd, an affluent of the Isfīd Rūd (now Safīd Rūd), a river that was of considerable length but not navigable; alongside this Persian name mentioned even by the Arab geographers, the Safīd Rūd also bears the Turco-Mongol name of Qïzïl Uzun.[b] To the south of Sulṭāniyya and of this valley stretched the mountains of Sujās, where in 1291 was buried one of the Mongol rulers of Persia, Arghūn.[27]

The town of Zanjān had little importance in the Middle Ages; at present its population may reach some 20,000 souls. In the nineteenth century, it attracted attention as one of the bases of the Bābīs; in 1850 it was stormed by government troops and the Bābī uprising was crushed after fierce resistance. Just as in the time of the tenth-century geographers and during the Mongol period, two roads led from Zanjān to Azerbaijan; one northeastward across the Safīd Rūd to Ardabīl, the other to Tabrīz and Marāgha.[c]

[25] C. d'Ohsson, *Histoire des Mongols*, IV, 542, 545-46.

[26] Mustawfī, *Nuzhat al-qulūb*, extracts in Schefer's ed., p. 187 ⟦ed. Le Strange, pp. 64-65, tr. *idem*, p. 69⟧.

[b] Huart, *EI*², art. "Ḳizil-Üzen."

[27] Mustawfī, *Nuzhat al-qulūb*, extracts in Schefer's ed., p. 186 ⟦ed. Le Strange, p. 64, tr. *idem*, p. 69; Mustawfī says that, according to Mongol custom, the area around the grave was made into a *qurugh* or sanctuary.⟧

[c] On Zanjān (which Abū Dulaf, *Travels in Iran*, tr. p. 34, #11, comm. p. 71 archaically spells Zhanjān), see Browne, *A Year amongst the Persians*, 2nd ed., pp. 79-81; Le Strange, *The Lands*, p. 222. The population in ⟨⟨ca. 1950 was approximately 48,000 (*Farhang*, II, 141)⟩⟩ ⟦and in 1976 was 99,967 (*Le monde et iranien et l'Islam*, IV [1976-1977], p. 242)⟧.

CHAPTER XIV

Azerbaijan and Armenia

AZERBAIJAN or more exactly Ādharbāyjān, constituted in antiquity the northwestern part of Media; it acquired an importance of its own only after the death of Alexander of Macedonia, when the Persian Atropates, sent by Alexander in 328 B.C. as a satrap to Media, asserted himself there. Atropates succeeded in establishing a modest kingdom that received his name (Atropatene in Greek, Atrpatakan in Armenian, whence Azerbaijan); this small state is noteworthy as the first manifestation of the reaction of the Iranian element against the Greek conquest and against the irruption of Greek civilization. The capital of the region, Γάζα or Γάζακα in classical sources, Gandzak or Ganzak in the Armenian and Syriac ones, that is, Persian Ganjak, in Arabic sources Gaznā (with a metathesis) or Janza,[1] was at that time the main religious center; the town or its surrounding area was called by the Arabs also al-Shīz. There was a temple of the fire worshipers there, to which, according to tradition, the Persian kings of the Sāsānid dynasty had, on their accession, to perform a pilgrimage on foot from Madā'in.[2] The location of the town is indicated by the ruins of Takht-i Sulaymān, southeast of Marāgha. The Arab geographers mention, as the former capital and military camp of the region, only this latter town, located south of the high mountain of Sahand on the bank of a stream that flows from this mountain into Lake Urmiya. The town became a military camp with the arrival of the Arabs, and received its name from them. Yāqūt mentions the old Persian name of the town: Afrāzah-Rūdh;[3] the Arabic word *marāgha* from the root *m-*

[1] Marquart, *Ērānšahr*, p. 108. V. V. Minorsky, "New Light on the Shaddādids of Ganja," in *Studies in Caucasian History*, pp. 1-77.

[2] Ibn Khurradādhbih, tr. p. 91, cf. Yāqūt, *Muʿjam*, III, 353 ff. s.v. "Shīz." Legend about Jesus; cf. Barthold, "K voprosu o polumesiatse," pp. 476 ff. ⟨⟨*Soch.* VI, 490 ff.⟩⟩ and also Ibn Rusta, p. 74 line 18. For Shīz, cf. also Le Strange, *The Lands*, p. 224, after Ḥamd Allāh Mustawfī Qazwīnī—construction by Abaqa and legend about the constructions of Kay Khusraw. Abū Dulaf, *Travels in Iran*, tr. pp. 32-33, ##5-7, comm. pp. 68-70; Barthold and Boyle, *EI*², art. "Gandja."

[3] In Ibn al-Faqīh, p. 284; tr. p. 341. Afrāh-rūdh and likewise Balādhurī, p. 330 n. 2.

r-gh (in the Vth form, *tamarragha*, "to graze") means "pastureland for horses" (lit. "place where horses wallow on the ground").[4] Here was the headquarters of the Arab governor of Azerbaijan and Armenia. Mountains protect Marāgha from northern winds, as a result of which agriculture and especially horticulture became quite well developed, but the climate was considered unhealthy. In the Mongol period an observatory for the famous astronomer Naṣīr al-Dīn Ṭūsī, who compiled here his tables, the *Zīj-i Ilkhānī*, was built on the hill north of the town; the observatory was joined by a library that contained most of the books seized after the taking of Baghdad. The instruments of the observatory cost 20,000 dinars; in addition to Persian astronomers, Chinese ones also worked here, from whom Naṣīr al-Dīn obtained information about Chinese year reckoning.[5] Already in the time of Ḥamd Allāh Mustawfī Qazwīnī, who wrote in 1339, the observatory lay in ruins,[6] although in 1300 the il-khān Ghazan had visited and inspected it.[7]

At the time of the Arab geographers the administrative and military center of the region was Ardabīl. The town was located in a well-watered plain, not far east of the snowy mountain Sawalān, called Sabalān by the Arabs, the highest mountain in Azerbaijan and one of the highest mountains of Persia. Roads to Azerbaijan branched out at the town of Zanjān,[8] but there was yet another road to Ardabīl, just as today, through Miyāna, Miyānaj in medieval sources;[9] the town may have received this name because of its equal distance (about twenty farsakhs) from the two principal towns of

[4] Yāqūt, *Muʿjam*, IV, 476. *Ibid.*, for the founding of the town by Marwān II (at the time of his pilgrimage); cf. Ibn al-Faqīh, p. 284.

[5] C. d'Ohsson, *Histoire des Mongols*, III, 264-66.

[6] *Nuzhat al-qulūb*, extract in Schefer's ed., p. 219 ⟦ed. Le Strange, p. 87, tr. *idem*, p. 88⟧.

[7] C. d'Ohsson, *Histoire des Mongols*, IV, 271. Barthold's marginal note: in 1304 Öljeytü, *ibid.*, IV, 483. According to de Morgan (*Mission*, I, 337) the ruins of the observatory have disappeared, the bricks having been used for construction. ⟨⟨See also Minorsky, *EI*[1], art. "Marāgha."⟩⟩ ⟦Lockhart, *Persian Cities*, pp. 58-64. There are several tomb towers still standing in Marāgha. See A. Godard, *Les monuments de Marāgha* (Paris, 1934); *idem*, "Notes complémentaires sur les tombeaux de Marāgha," *AI*, I (1936), 125-60; Matheson, *Persia, an Archaeological Guide*, pp. 97-99. Examination of the site of Naṣīr al-Dīn's observatory, indeed situated on a hill some 1,600 feet/500 meters above the surrounding plain and to the north of the town, was begun in 1972; see Parviz Vardjavand, "Rapport préliminaire sur les fouilles de l'observatoire de Marâqe," *Le monde iranien et l'Islam*, III (1975), 119-24.⟧

[8] The bridge in Dubeux, *La Perse*, fig. 27.

[9] The form Miyāna is already found, however, in Maqdisī, p. 378.

Azerbaijan, Ardabīl and Marāgha.[10] Ardabīl is mentioned as the residence of the region's governor as early as the account of the Arab conquest. As a result of the abundance of irrigation, travelers as late as the seventeenth century compare Ardabīl with Venice; for the same reason, however, the mud of the streets of Ardabīl became proverbial as early as the tenth century.[11] As late as the fourteenth century, at the time of Mustawfī, the inhabitants considered themselves Shāfiʿīs,[12] but at the end of the fifteenth century the Shīʿī movement originated from here, a movement that led to the establishment of the new Persian state in which Shīʿī Islam became the dominant religion. The ancestor of the Ṣafawid dynasty, Shaykh Ṣafī al-Dīn, was probably not a Shīʿī, since Mustawfī says about the inhabitants of Ardabīl that they were "Shāfiʿīs and *murīds* of Shaykh Ṣafī al-Dīn"; it may be that only the descendant of this shaykh, Ismāʿīl, founder of the Ṣafawid dynasty, declared himself and his ancestor to be descendants of ʿAlī, and raised the banner of Shīʿī Islam.[13] Shāh Ismāʿīl, who died in 1524, was also buried in Ardabīl;[14] as a result of this, the city retained under his descend-

10 According to Yāqūt, *Muʿjam*, IV, 716, between Marāgha and Tabrīz.

11 Cf. Barthold, *Turkestan*, p. 145, *Soch.* I, 200. Ardabīl, according to Iṣṭakhrī, p. 181, is two-thirds of a farsakh long and wide.

12 *Nuzhat al-qulūb*, extract in Schefer, p. 210 ⟦ed. Le Strange, p. 81, tr. *idem*, p. 84. H. Halm, *Die Ausbreitung der šāfiʿitischen Rechtsschule von den Anfängen bis zum 8/14 Jahrhundert* (1974), pp. 138-39.⟧

13 For Ismāʿīl the Ṣafawid, see also P. Horn, "Geschichte Irans in islamischer Zeit," *GIPh*, II, 586, after a legendary biography; the epic motif about the "playing being a king." See also Barthold, "Khalif i sultan," *Soch.* VI, 54, 72 ff. Account told by Olearius (512) about the Ṣafawid court; the octet (Grand Marshall, after the banquet):

ṣofra ḥaqqïna	For the sake of [this] repast,
shāh dewletine	For the shah's good fortune,
ghāzīler quwwetine	For the *ghāzīs*' strength,
Allāh diyelim Allāh Allāh	Let us say "Allāh Allāh"!

Cf. Barthold, "Khalif i sultan," *Soch.* VI, 54 n. 177. Remarks of Olearius about the tomb of Burle-Khatun in Urmiya, the tomb of Qazan-bek near Tabrīz; the tomb of Qorqud near Darband. Already Shaykh Khwāja ʿAlī (d. 1426 or 1429) was a Shīʿī, see Petrushevskii, *Islam*, pp. 364-66. ⟦On the origin of the Ṣafawids, see W. Hinz, *Irans Aufstieg zum Nationalstaat im fünfzehnten Jahrhundert* (Berlin and Leipzig, 1936); M. M. Mazzaoui, *The Origins of the Ṣafawids. Šīʿism, Ṣūfism, and the Gulāt* (Wiesbaden, 1972); Savory, *History of the Safavids* (Cambridge, 1981).⟧

14 Information about the mausoleum in de Morgan, *Mission*, I, quoting Lebrun; according to Berezin, *Puteshestvie*, pt. 2, there were four gates and courtyards of the mosque, gilding tiles, designs on a dark blue background with gold. Streck, *EI*[1], art. "Ardabīl." ⟦Frye, *EI*[2], s.v. For the buildings making up the shrine complex of Shaykh Ṣafī al-Dīn Isḥāq, see F. Sarre *et al.*, *Denkmäler persischer Baukunst. Geschichtliche Untersuchung und Aufnahme muhammedanischer Backsteinbauten in Vorderasien und Per-*

ants a certain importance.[15] Thus Shāh ʿAbbās bestowed upon it, as *waqf*, a rich library.[16] Ardabīl was taken by [General] Paskevich at the beginning of 1828, and the greater part of the library was sent as military booty to St. Petersburg, where it is today in the public library; among these manuscripts there are many rare and precious works.

The town of Tabrīz, the present-day capital of Azerbaijan, is believed to have been founded only in the Islamic period, namely, at the end of the eighth century, by Zubayda, wife of the caliph Hārūn al-Rashīd. In the initial period after its foundation, Tabrīz remained a village; only under the caliph Mutawakkil (847-861) did it become a fortified town, when it was the residence of the rebellious general al-Rawwād al-Azdī and his successor.[17] In the tenth century, it was still an insignificant town;[18] by the time of the

---

sien (Berlin, 1901-1910); F. Sarre, *Ardabil, Grabmoschee des Scheich Safis* (Berlin, 1924); A. H. Morton, "The Ardabīl Shrine in the Reign of Shah Ṭahmāsp I," *Iran, JBIPS*, XII (1974), 31-64; XIII (1975), 39-58.⟧

[15] At the beginning of the nineteenth century, there were 4,000 inhabitants in all, later 16,000 to 18,000. ⟦Lockhart, *Persian Cities*, pp. 51-57. The population in 1976 was 147,404 (*Le monde iranien et l'Islam*, IV [1976-1977], 242).⟧

[16] Shāh ʿAbbās donated Persian books to Ardabīl, see Iskandar Munshī, ms. fol. 202b ⟦ed. Tehran, p. 761, tr. Savory, pp. 954-55.⟧ ⟨⟨Cf. Petrushevskii,, "Vakfnye imeniia."⟩⟩

[17] Yāqūt, *Muʿjam*, I, 822. However, according to Yaʿqūbī, *Taʾrīkh*, II, 446, this was under Manṣūr; al-Rawwād b. al-Muthannā al-Azdī and Yemeni Arabs. In Ṭabarī, III, 1,172, there is mention of al-Wajnāʾ b. al-Rawwād, who was served by al-Baʿīth (under Muʿtaṣim). Cf. Le Strange, *The Lands*, p. 161.

[18] The dynasty of the Sallārids, tenth to eleventh centuries. Al-Marzubān b. Muḥammad b. Musāfir al-Sallār, a Shīʿī, born in the Caspian regions, conquered Azerbaijan in 330/941-2. In 337 his march on Ray against the Būyid Rukn al-Dawla. Marzubān taken prisoner, his father mounts the throne in Ardabīl, then his brother Wahsūdān, who invites the Kurd Ḍaysam b. Ibrāhīm, the latter is defeated by Muḥammad b. ʿAbd al-Razzāq sent by Rukn al-Dawla, who takes control of Azerbaijan, then returns to Ray and from there to Khurāsān. Ḍaysam is driven out of Azerbaijan in 342; the region passes back to Marzubān. The death of Marzubān in Ramaḍān 346/December 957; struggle between Wahsūdān and Marzubān's sons Justān, Ibrāhīm, and Nāṣir. Victory of Wahsūdān in 349; struggle between Ibrāhīm and Wahsūdān in the following years. Ultimately, toward 355/966, Ibrāhīm returned to Azerbaijan and took possession of it. After the death of Fakhr al-Dawla (387/997), Wahsūdān's descendant Ibrāhīm b. Marzubān b. Ismāʿīl b. Wahsūdān extended his domains to Zanjān and Shahrazūr. The defeat of Ibrāhīm in the battle with Masʿūd of Ghazna in 420/1029. In this same year Wahsūdān b. Mahlān (?) ⟦read Mamlān⟧ became ruler. In 432 he beat off an attack by the Ghuzz in Tabrīz. ⟨⟨For the Sal(l)ārid (or Musāfirid) dynasty, see Sayyid Aḥmad Kasrawī, *Shahriyārān-i gumnām-i Īrān* (Tehran, 1307-8/1928-9); Minorsky, *La domination des Dailamites* (Paris, 1932).⟩⟩ ⟦Also in *Iranica, Twenty Articles*, pp. 12-30.⟧

Mongol invasion, it is already mentioned as the capital of the local dynasty of atabeks.[a] Yāqūt, who was there in 1213, speaks of Tabrīz as a large manufacturing center; the textiles made here were exported to every country.[19]

Tabrīz gained still greater importance in the thirteenth century under Mongol rule, when it became the capital of Persia. This was due partly to the necessity of concentrating here the military forces of the country in order to repulse the invasions constantly threatening from the north, partly to natural conditions of the region, which always attracted nomads. The latter found here for their herds both elevated pasturelands and winter quarters sheltered from the winds. The winter quarters of the Mongol khans was the valley of a stream called Jaghatu, which flows into Lake Urmiya near Marāgha, and especially the Mūqān plain on the lower course of the Kur. As summer quarters, the mountains Siyāh-Kūh, that is, Qaradagh in Azerbaijan and Alatagh in Armenia, were used; near Alatagh was the summer court of the khan Arghun.[20] The burial place of the first Mongol khans, Hülegü and Abaqa, was the mountain Shāhī or Telia, which is today on a peninsula,[21] but at that time Lake Urmiya occupied a larger area than now, and the mountain was on an island in the midst of the lake. The Hülegids had to defend their rule in Azerbaijan constantly against the khans of the Golden Horde. The Caspian regions and Azerbaijan were already ravaged by the Mongols under Chingiz Khan and, together

[a] These atabeks were the Ildegizids or Ildeñizids or Eldigüzids, a powerful force on northwestern Iran, including Arrān, Jibāl, and most of Azerbaijan (except for the area round Marāgha held by the parallel Atabek line of the Aḥmadīlīs). See Mirza Bala, *EI*², art. "Ildeñiz," and Bosworth, art. "Ildeñizids"; Bosworth in *Cambridge History of Iran*, V, 169-71, 176 ff.

[19] For Tabrīz in Nāṣir-i Khusraw, see *Safar-nāma* (Tehran lithog.), p. 13: "The city is the capital of Azerbaijan—a populous city. I measured its length and width by ⟦walking around it and counting⟧ my paces: each ⟦side⟧ was one thousand and four hundred ⟦paces⟧. The name of the ruler of the province of Azerbaijan is mentioned in the *khuṭba* in this form: the Great Prince Sayf al-Dawla and Sharaf al-Milla, Abū Manṣūr Wahṣūdān b. Muḥammad, vassal of the Commander of the Faithful." He submitted to Ṭoghrïl Beg in 446/1054. The walls of the city were in Yāqūt's time made of brick (*Muʿjam*, I, 822); in general "[its] buildings are from red carved bricks and stucco, extremely solid." ⟦Serjeant, *Islamic Textiles*, pp. 68-69⟧.

[20] Mustawfī, *Nuzhat al-qulūb*, extr. in Schefer, p. 232 ⟦ed. Le Strange, p. 101, tr. *idem*, p. 100⟧.

[21] According to some data, now an island again. See Maqdisī, p. 381, for the mountain: "There are in Lake Urmiya inhabited mountains [that is, a mountainous island; its inhabitants] bind children's feet with chains and ropes lest they roll down into the lake." ⟦Barthold and Boyle, *EI*², art. "Hūlāgū."⟧

with all the western parts of the empire, they were supposed to form part of Jochi's appanage. But when in the middle of the thirteenth century, Möngke khan sent to Persia his brother Hülegü, and the latter founded there an independent Mongol state, its rulers, the Il-Khanids, also occupied Azerbaijan and refused to recognize the rights of the family of Jochi to this region; for their part, the Jochids claimed their rights by force of arms several times. All these factors combined to make the Mongol khans live primarily in Azerbaijan; they continued here their nomadic way of life, and they genuinely wished to concentrate the government organs as close to their encampments as possible. For this purpose, Tabrīz, a town that had suffered relatively little in Chingiz Khan's time, was chosen. The Mongols approached the town three times, but each time the inhabitants succeeded in buying themselves off. This fact shows how extensive the material means of the inhabitants were, thanks to the development of industry.

Already at the time of the il-khan Arghun (1284-1291), the Persian Mongols started displaying a penchant for building. Arghun erected several structures in the village of Shanab,[22] in the western environs of Tabrīz; the village received from him the name of Arghuniyya.[23] Arghun had not yet adopted Islam, and the principal building erected by him was a temple of idol worshipers; on the walls there was a portrait of Arghun himself.[24] This temple was torn down under Arghun's son, Ghazan (1295-1304), a fervent Muslim, one of the most remarkable medieval rulers of Persia. While remaining a Mongol and appreciative of Mongol antiquities, Ghazan acquired at the same time, to a higher degree than his predecessors, the elements of Persian culture, was able to debate about astronomical instruments with the learned men of the Marāgha observatory, and wanted to give Persia the kind of governmental structure and laws that would satisfy equally the interests of the sedentary and of the nomadic population of the country.

Under Ghazan, Tabrīz expanded to the dimensions of the capital of an extensive state. Previously, the walls of the city measured only 6,000 paces in circumference. Ghazan ordered the city, together with the neighboring villages, to be surrounded by a new wall whose circumference equalled 25,000 paces,[25] or according to another

[22] *Shanab* apparently meant "cemetery" in Mongolian.

[23] C. d'Ohsson, *Histoire des Mongols*, IV, 58.

[24] *Ibid.*, IV, 282.

[25] Mustawfī, *Nuzhat al-qulūb*, extr. in Schefer, p. 204 ⟦ed. Le Strange, p. 76, tr. *idem*, p. 79⟧.

definition four and one half farsakhs, that is, a little under thirty versts;[26] as a result of his death this construction was not finished. Like his father, he took a liking to the village of Shanab, which under him received the name Ghāzāniyya; most often it was called Shanab-i Ghāzān Khān.[27] Here Ghazan erected for himself a mausoleum that surpassed that of Sulṭān Sanjar in Marw, which had until then been considered by the Muslims to be the tallest building;[28] also a mosque; two madrasas, one of these for Ḥanafīs and one for the Shāfiʿīs; and a whole number of other buildings. His vizier, the historian Rashīd al-Dīn, erected buildings in one of the quarters, which received after him the name Rabʿ-i Rashīdī or Rashīdiyya, in the eastern part of the city.[29] To the other vizier, Tāj al-Dīn ʿAlī-Shāh, the person responsible for Rashīd al-Dīn's death, is due the building of a mosque that is still partly standing in the citadel in the southwestern part of the city.[30] A detailed description of the buildings, owed to the fifteenth-century Arab historian al-ʿAynī, was published by the late Baron V. Tiesenhausen.[31] According to Mustawfī,[32] "an immeasurable quantity of marble" was used for this construction.[33] By the seventeenth century, only the cupola was intact. In the nineteenth century, the remainders of the buildings were turned into a military depot and an observation tower, and in 1850 the Bāb, founder of the sect of the Bābīs, was executed here.

Mustawfī affirms in 1339 that all of the rest of Iran did not have

[26] C. d'Ohsson, *Histoire des Mongols*, IV, 276. Ten gates down to the time of the Mongols, six gates in the fourteenth century, eight gates today (after Berezin, *Puteshestvie*, pt. 2). The gate Waliyān, where the Rabʿ-i Rashīdī was situated, lay, according to Mustawfī, inside the walls built under Ghazan Khan.

[27] According to Minorsky (personal communication), Shamghāzān is now the northwestern quarter of the Tabrīz.

[28] See above, p. 42. For Ghazan Khan's mausoleum, see Wilber, *The Architecture of Islamic Iran. The Il Khanid Period*, pp. 124-26.

[29] Rashīd al-Dīn, ed. Quatremère, p. LVII. ⟨⟨For the Rabʿ-i Rashīdī, see information in Rashīd al-Dīn's *Mukātabāt.*⟩⟩

[30] Under Shāh ʿAbbās in 1610, the old citadel, easily flooded from the river, was destroyed, and a new one was built in the Rabʿ-i Rashīdī (Iskandar Munshī, ms., fol. 238b) ⟦ed. Tehran, p. 826, tr. Savory, pp. 1,032-33⟧. According to Chardin, this fortress too was abandoned under ʿAbbās's successors.

[31] ⟨⟨"O mecheti Alishakha."⟩⟩

[32] *Nuzhat al-qulūb*, extr. in Schefer, p. 205 ⟦ed. Le Strange, p. 77, tr. *idem*, p. 80⟧. The mosque of ʿAlī-Shāh was built at the gate called Kharbanda (Tiesenhausen, "O mecheti Alishakha," p. 116); *ibid.*, for the Turkish sacking in 1635. However, according to Chardin, the lower part of the mosque was subsequently rebuilt and in his time was used for worship.

[33] For marble quarries near Tabrīz, see Sharaf al-Dīn Yazdī, I, 802; marble was used for the construction of the palace called Bāgh-i Shimāl in 1397.

as many high and beautiful buildings as Tabrīz. After the fall of the Mongol dynasty of Persia, the city became the capital of the dynasty of the Jalāyirids, then of the Türkmens of the Black Sheep (Qara Qoyunlu), and finally of those of the White Sheep (Aq Qoyunlu), and it retained its importance in the fifteenth century despite the calamities that befell it at the end of the fourteenth century. In 1385 Toqtamïsh plundered it, and in 1386 Tīmūr. How quickly the city managed to recover is seen from the report of Clavijo, who passed through it in 1404. Tabriz made on him the impression of an enormous and rich city with 200,000 inhabitants; a vast amount of goods passed through it every day. He describes the huge house built by Sulṭān Uways (1356-1374) of the Jalāyirid dynasty: it comprised 20,000 rooms and had the name of Dawlat-khāna. The city had no walls at the time.[34]

To the fifteenth century, namely, to the time of Jahānshāh, khan of the Qara Qoyunlu Türkmens (1437-1467), pertains the best of those buildings of Tabrīz, the remainders of which are preserved to this day, namely, the so-called "blue mosque," Masjid-i Kabūd, which received its name from the color of the magnificent glazed tiles that had once adorned it. An illustration of the ruins of this mosque is to be found in Curzon's book.[35] The building suffered a great deal from the earthquakes that frequently afflict Tabrīz.[36] Mustawfī asserts[37] that after the earthquake of 434/1042,[38] measures were taken during the reconstruction of the city, upon the

[34] Clavijo, tr. Sreznevskii, pp. 167-70; tr. Le Strange, pp. 153-54.

[35] *Persia*, I, 520.

[36] "The blue mosque" is in a still more westerly location than the citadel. The mosque is a Sunnī one, with a Sunnī cemetery nearby. The plan and description appear in Texier, *Description*, II, 48-50. Chardin, *Voyages*, ed. 1811, II, 330 ff., atlas, pl. XI, and Tavernier, *Les six voyages*, I, 58-59, saw the building in its entirety; it suffered from the earthquake of 1776. The colors are blue, white, gold, black, and green. Texier, *Description*, about the simplicity and at the same time impressiveness of the plan; the entrance arch was 15 meters high, the first hall 16 meters square, the second 11 meters square; the extant base of the minaret is 2 meters 60 centimeters in diameter, the cupola some 30 meters high (estimate). The Masjid-i Kabūd is also in Dubeux, *La Perse*, p. 25; Jackson, *Persia Past and Present*, p. 42. ⟨⟨For the date of the mosque's construction, see Minorsky, "Geographical Factors in Persian Art," *BSOS*, IX (1938), 633.⟩⟩ ⟦Also in *Iranica, Twenty Articles*, p. 50 n. 1. For earthquakes in the district, see C. Melville, "Historical Monuments and Earthquakes in Tabriz," *Iran, JBIPS*, XX (1981), 159-77.⟧

[37] *Nuzhat al-qulūb*, extr. in Schefer, p. 204 ⟦ed. Le Strange, pp. 75-76, tr. *idem*, p. 79⟧.

[38] The earthquake of 434 is also mentioned in Nāṣir-i Khusraw (Thursday, Rabīʿ I/4 November 1042); one part of the town was destroyed, the other did not suffer; up to 40,000 people perished.

advice of an astrologer, in order to prevent a repetition of the catastrophe. The astrologer maintained that the danger of earthquakes was thenceforward removed, and, indeed, none took place after then until the author's time, that is, for three hundred years.[39] On the other hand, the city was stricken by terrible earthquakes in 1721 and 1780; in the former, 80,000 people, perished, in the latter, 40,000.[40] Despite all this, the city did not lose its importance, although in the sixteenth century it ceased to be the country's capital. In the seventeenth century Chardin[41] stated that it had 550,000 inhabitants, and that its area was larger than that of any other city he saw, far surpassing that of Iṣfahān.[42] At the beginning of the nineteenth century, there were in Tabrīz 50,000 inhabitants in all, and according to some reports only 30,000; since then, however, it has become again a lively commercial place and, according to some statements, the most populous city of Persia: up to 240,000 inhabitants are estimated to live there, that is, somewhat more than in Tehran.[43] In the nineteenth century, the city was usually the

[39] For Tabrīz ⟨⟨at the end of the fourteenth and the beginning of the fifteenth century⟩⟩, see Schiltberger, *Puteshestvie*, p. 44. The center of an enormous volume of trading; it provides the King of Persia with an income which surpasses that of even the most powerful Christian monarch.

[40] Curzon, *Persia*, I, 518.

[41] *Voyages*, ed. 1735, I, 256-57.

[42] According to Chardin, there are nine quarters in the city; according to Jackson, twenty-four. Division in Chardin's time into Ḥaydarīs and Niʿmatallāhīs, as in other towns. Minorsky's observations in 1914 in Shushtar and Dizfūl (*Materialy*, p. 271).

[43] According to de Morgan, *Mission*, I, 322, there were in Tabrīz about 100,000 inhabitants; the bazaar was large and good, but the number of its shops was well below the 15,000 of Chardin's time. The wall in the nineteenth century under ʿAbbās Mīrzā; according to Ker-Porter, it was 6,000 yards in circumference; according to other sources, three and a half and three and a quarter miles; according to Berezin, *Puteshestvie*, pt. 2, p. 55, four and a half versts. Jackson, *Persia Past and Present*, p. 44, is of the opinion that the old wall surrounded the most ancient part of the city; in Dieulafoy's opinion, the city in the course of 600 years moved over a distance of 12 kilometers and is still moving in the direction of the river. Verses about the people of Tabrīz in Browne, *A Year amongst the Persians*, p. 77 ⟦2nd edition, p. 84⟧:

zi Tabrīzī bi-juz ḥīzī [?khīzī] na-bīnī
hamān bihtar ki Tabrīzī na-bīnī

⟦Browne's translation:
From a Tabrīzī thou wilt see naught but rascality:
Even this is best, that thou shouldst not see a Tabrīzī.⟧

The population in ⟦1976 was 598,576; it is now the fourth largest city in modern Iran, after Tehran, Isfahan, and Mashhad (*Le monde iranien et l'Islam*, IV [1976-1977]), 242⟧.

residence of the heir apparent.[44] In Tabrīz is the juncture of the road from Russia across Transcaucasia with that from western Europe and Turkey through Trebizond. The latter road was restored in the nineteenth century by ʿAbbās Mīrzā, but it is already mentioned by the tenth-century geographers; the greater part of Greek wares brought to Muslim countries went through Trebizond.[45]

Under the Mongols, yet another town, Ūjān, was founded or rebuilt in Azerbaijan; it was situated eight farsakhs from Tabrīz on the way to Miyāna. The rebuilding of this town was also the work of Ghazan Khan, who called it Shahr-i Islām; revenues from it and from the surrounding villages were reserved for Ghazan's pious foundations. In Ūjān there was still situated in the nineteenth century one of the summer palaces of the shāh; the little town was considered to be one of the coolest places of Persia.[46] In the fourteenth century a Christian community, among other things, was here.[47] Further on the road to Miyāna is the village of Turkmānchay, where peace was concluded in 1828.[b] As early as the fourteenth century there was here the village of Dih-i Turkmānān, six farsakhs from Miyāna; Clavijo mentions here the Türkmen village of Tucelar (Tuzlar).[48] The Turks constitute today, as is well known, the majority of the population of Azerbaijan, not only of the nomadic part but also of the sedentary;[49] the language of the sedentary Azerbaijanis, which has a literature, belongs, together with the language of the Türkmens and that of the Ottomans, to the

[44] ⟨⟨For the history of Tabrīz and its monuments, see also V. Minorsky, *EI*[1], art. "Tabrīz"; *Survey of Persian Art*, II, V; Wilber, *The Architecture of Islamic Iran*.⟩⟩ ⟦Lockhart, *Persian Cities*, pp. 10-17. One should note the prominent part that Tabrīz and its citizens played in the Constitutionalist movement in the first decade of the century.⟧

[45] Ibn Ḥawqal, p. 246. ⟦C. Issawi, "The Tabriz-Trabzon Trade, 1830-1900; Rise and Decline of a Route," *IJMES*, I (1970), 18-27.⟧

[46] Later in ruins, described in W. Ouseley, *Travels in Various Countries of the East* (London, 1819-1823), III, 394, Chaman-i Ūjān.

[47] Mustawfī, *Nuzhat al-qulūb*, extr. in Schefer, p. 209 ⟦ed. Le Strange, p. 80, tr. *idem*, p. 83⟧.

[b] That is, the peace made between Russia and Iran after the war of 1826. Clavijo passed through the village, calling it Tunglar and Tucelar (? Türkler), both on the way to Samarqand and on his return; see his travel narrative, ed. Sreznevskii, pp. 172, 354, tr. Le Strange, pp. 155, 309, and V. Minorsky, *EI*[1], art. "Türkmän-čai."

[48] Tr. Sreznevskii, p. 172; tr. Le Strange, p. 309.

[49] The Turkish character of the population; the first village where the Persian language predominates is Kirishkīn, before Qazwīn (Browne, *A Year amongst the Persians*, p. 77). Even in Qazwīn almost everybody also knows Turkish (*ibid.*, p. 78, 2nd ed., pp. 85-86.

so-called South Turkic group.[c] With respect to religion, Azerbaijani Turks are as zealously Shīʿī as the Persians.

Among the towns and villages situated in the basin of Lake Urmiya, those that have retained their medieval names are, besides Tabrīz and Marāgha, Dih-Kharraqān, Khōy, Marand, Salmās, Urmiya, and others. No fish can live in the water of the lake on account of its extremely high salinity, and even bathing is impossible; we have already mentioned the change in the level of the lake. It used to be called by pre-Islamic Persians Chīchasht,[50] a name still encountered in the fourteenth century;[51] now it is known by the name Daryā-yi Shāhī. On its shore, especially in Dih-Kharraqān, excellent marble is quarried, which the khans and viziers of the Mongol period used for their construction; its quarrying is allowed only by the express permission of the shāh. The town of Urmiya is also noteworthy as the center of Persian Nestorians, who, as is known, have recently joined the Orthodox faith.[52]

The mountains of the northeastern part of Azerbaijan are called Qaradagh. Here took place in the ninth century the last struggle of the heretic Bābak with the armies of the ʿAbbāsid government under Afshīn. The latter's base of operation was the town of Barzand, fourteen farsakhs from Ardabīl on the road to the Kur;[53] from there it was two farsakhs to each of the defensive trenches dug by Afshīn, and from the last trench it was still one farsakh to Bābak's capital, called by the Arabs al-Badhdh.[54] The followers of Bābak, the so-called Khurramiyya or Khurramdīniyya, in the tenth century still lived south of Azerbaijan in inaccessible mountains. In their villages, according to Maqdisī, there were no mosques, and the inhabitants did not observe the religious duties of Islam;[55] to

[c] For the Azeri language and its literature, see A. Caferoğlu, *EI*², art. "Ādharī"; *idem* and G. Doerfer, in *Philologiae turcicae fundamenta*, I (Wiesbaden, 1959), 280-307 (Azeri language), and Caferoğlu, in II (Wiesbaden, 1964), 635-99 (Azeri literature).

[50] Cf. Marquart, *Ērānšahr*, p. 108. ⟦In the period of the Pahlavī shāhs, Lake Urmiya and the nearby town of that name were renamed Riḍā'iyya (Rezaieh) after the founder of the line; since 1979, they have reverted to the old designation.⟧

[51] Mustawfī, *Nuzhat al-qulūb*, extr. in Schefer, pp. 217 ff. ⟦ed. Le Strange, p. 85, tr. *idem*, p. 87⟧.

[52] The church of St. Mary and its picture in Jackson ⟨⟨*Persia Past and Present*⟩⟩, p. 101; legend about ⟨⟨the burial of⟩⟩ the Magi.

[53] According to Iṣṭakhrī, about fifteen farsakhs.

[54] Ibn Khurradādhbih, tr. p. 92. Al-Badhdh madīnat Bābak on the river Kalān Rūdh, Yāqūt, *Muʿjam*, IV, 297. ⟦C. E. Bosworth, *EI*² Suppl., s.v.⟧.

[55] Maqdisī, pp. 398-99.

Maqdisī's question of why the Muslims left them in peace, they answered that they recognized one God and that, besides, every year they brought a considerable sum of money to the government's treasury.[56]

Azerbaijan constitutes at present a border region of Persia, which approximately corresponds to the ethnic borders of the Iranian population in antiquity.[57] The cultural influence of the Iranians, however, and sometimes even the political rule of Persia spread over the neighboring areas of Armenia, Albania (Arrān among the Muslims), Iberia (Georgia), and present-day Dāghistān, with the famous Darband pass. All of these regions were originally inhabited by populations of non-Aryan stock, which in some respects reached a considerable cultural level well before the arrival of the Aryans, and which subsequently came under, for longer than Iran, the influence of Greek and Christian civilizations; at the time of tenth-century Arab geographers, the towns of Armenia and Transcaucasia still surpassed in their commercial and industrial evolution the towns of Azerbaijan.[d] The question of the ethnic origin of the Armenians has not yet been fully solved; some scholars, such as Hübschmann, consider the Armenians to be a special branch of the Indo-Europeans, others believe that the inhabitants of Armenia together with the ancient Hittites and the inhabitants of Albania and Georgia constituted a special, so-called Alarod group that had no connection with the Aryans. The Alarods are mentioned by Herodotus (Ἀλαρόδιοι); in Assyrian inscriptions there is mention of the kingdom of Urartu, whose center, as we know from this kingdom's own inscriptions, was situated near Lake Van.[58] Con-

[56] Muḥammad b. al-Baʿīth, associate, then enemy of Bābak. Ṭabarī, III, 1,388, about his Persian verses. Tabrīz and the island of Shāhī; for the latter, see Ṭabarī, III, 1,380. ⟦On the Khurramiyya, see Gh. H. Sadighi, *Les mouvements religieux iraniens au IIe et au IIIe siècle de l'hégire* (Paris, 1938), pp. 187-280; B. S. Amoretti, "Sects and Heresies," in *Cambridge History of Iran*, IV, 503-509; W. Madelung, *EI*², s.v.⟧.

[57] ⟨⟨For the historical geography and history of Azerbaijan, see also: *Ḥudūd al-ʿālam*, tr. Minorsky, pp. 394-411; Miklukho-Maklai, "Geograficheskoe sochinenie"; Petrushevskii, "Khamdallakh Kazvini"; *idem*, "Gosudarstva Azerbaidzhana v XV veke"; *idem, Ocherki*; A. Ali-zade, *Ist. Azerbaidzhana*; Minorsky, *Studies in Caucasian History* (London, 1953); also the literature indicated in Spuler, *Iran in früh-islamischer Zeit*, pp. 576-77, and in Barthold, *Soch.* II/1, 651 n. 1; p. 766 n. 1; III, 335, 352, 373.⟩⟩ ⟦V. Minorsky, *EI*², art. "Ādharbāydjān."⟧.

[d] See on these regions the *EI*² arts. "Armīniya," "Arrān," "Dāghistān," and "al-Ḳabḳ."

[58] ⟨⟨For the kingdom of Urartu, see now B. B. Piotrovskii, *Vanskoe tsarstvo, Urartu* (Moscow, 1959); for the ethnogenesis of the Armenians, see I. D'iakonov, *Proiskhozhdenie*.⟩⟩ ⟦There now exists an English translation of Piotrovskii's book by P. S.

nected with the name of this kingdom is also the word Ararat, which the Armenians always used as the name of an area, not of a mountain; the latter was called Masis. Tenth-century Arab geographers called Mount Ararat al-Ḥārith and Lesser Ararat al-Ḥuwayrith.

Not far from Ararat, on the Araxes, were both Artaksata, capital of the Armenian kings at the time of Parthian rule, and Dwīn, the Dabīl of the Arabs, capital of Muslim amīrs of Armenia. The town was larger than Ardabīl; the textiles made there were famous. Armenian rugs are mentioned among the gifts sent by Maḥmūd of Ghazna to Qadïr Khan of Kāshghar.[59] Through Dwīn passed the trade route from Trebizond;[60] subsequently, an attempt was made to reroute it more directly through Ānī, on the Arpa-chay, a tributary of the Araxes. The tenth-century kings of the Bagratid dynasty lived in Ānī, to be succeeded in 1044 by Byzantine governors, in 1072 by Muslim amīrs of the Shaddādid dynasty, and in the twelfth century again by Armenian princes, under the suzerainty first of the Georgian kings and then of the Mongol khans. The ruins of Ānī have been studied in detail by N. Ia. Marr, according to whom they constitute "a whole museum of Armenian art."[61]

That part of Armenia which now constitutes the province of Erivan and the region of Kars was in the modern period, especially in the sixteenth and seventeenth centuries, still the object of a struggle between the Ottoman sulṭāns and the Persian shāhs. Thus in 1590 the Persians were obliged by an agreement to cede to the Turks all the Transcaucasian regions and even Azerbaijan. In 1603 and 1604, however, Shāh ʿAbbās recovered all these areas and even took Kars. The province of Erivan, which had previously been divided into the khanates of Erivan and Nakhchiwān, was annexed [by Russia] in 1828 from the Persians, and the region of Kars was annexed from the Turks in 1878. Nakhchiwān and Kars are frequently mentioned in the Middle Ages.[62] Erivan originated as a village in Tīmūr's time, and became a town only in the sixteenth

Gelling, *Urartu—The Kingdom of Van and Its Art* (London, 1967); see also R. Grousset, *Histoire de l'Arménie des origines à 1071* (Paris, 1947); C. A. Burney and D. M. Lang, *Peoples of the Hills, Ancient Ararat and Caucasus* (London, 1971), pp. 127-82.⟧

[59] Barthold, *Turkestan*, p. 284, *Soch.* I, p. 345.

[60] ⟨⟨For Dwīn, see Minorsky, "Le nom de Dvin en Arménie," *JA*, CCXIX (1930), 41-52.⟩⟩ ⟦Also in *Iranica, Twenty Articles*, pp. 1-11; M. Canard, *EI*², art. "Dwīn."⟧.

[61] ⟨⟨Marr, "Ani, stolitsa drevnei Armenii." See also *idem, Ani*; Orbeli, "Razvaliny Ani"; *idem*, "Kratkii putevoditel' "; Barthold, *EI*¹, art. "Ānī," *Soch.* III, 327-30; Barthold and Minorsky, *EI*², art. "Ānī."⟩⟩

[62] ⟨⟨See Barthold, *EI*¹, art. "Kars."⟩⟩

century under Shāh Ismāʿīl, when it also received its present-day name.[63] The strong fortress of Beyazit southwest of Ararat remained in Turkish hands and in the nineteenth century was still the capital of a semi-independent Kurdish state.

The Araxes river, which used to have an estuary separate from that of the Kur, also constituted the border between Azerbaijan and Arrān, ancient Albania. The present-day province of Elisavetpol' and a portion of that of Bākū used to be parts of Arrān; Arrān in the narrow sense of the word was understood to include the area between the Araxes and the Kur. Like Armenia, Arrān too was originally inhabited by a population of non-Aryan stock. Tenth-century Arab geographers still speak of a distinct Arrān language, and according to Armenian reports, a special alphabet was invented for this language in the fifth century.[64] The chief town of Arrān was Partav, the Bardhaʿa or Bardaʿ of the Arabs, and the site is today marked by ruins near the village of Barda not far from the estuary of the Terter into the Kur; the Arabs reckoned the distance from Bardhaʿa to the banks of the Kur to be two or three farsakhs. In the tenth century, it surpassed in size all the other towns of Transcaucasia and Azerbaijan, and covered an area one farsakh long and somewhat less wide; from among the towns between Iraq[65] and Khurāsān, only Ray and Iṣfahān were larger. Near the gate there was a huge bazaar held on holidays; the silk produced there was exported to Fārs and Khūzistān.[66] According to Maqdisī's definition, the city was, as it were, the "Baghdad" of this country.[67] The riches of the town must have been the cause of its being plundered by the Rūs at the time of the 943 campaign.[68]

[63] ⟨⟨For the ancient Urartian settlement of Erebuni (eighth to seventh centuries B.C.), see Oganesian, *Arin-berd*. For the historical geography of Armenia, see also Markwart, *Südarmenien*; Manandian, *O torgovle i gorodakh; idem, Goroda Armenii*; K. V. Trever, *Kul'tura drevnei Armenii*; M. Canard, *EI*², art. "Armīniya."⟩⟩

[64] Marquart, *Ērānšahr*, p. 117. ⟨⟨For Arrān, see also Barthold, *EI*¹, art. "Arrān," *Soch.* III, 334-35; *Ḥudūd al-ʿālam*, tr. Minorsky, pp. 398-411; V. Minorsky, "Caucasica IV," *BSOAS*, XV (1953), 504-29. For monuments of ancient Albanian literature, see now Trever, *Kavkazskaia Albaniia*, pp. 335-53; Klimov, "K sostoianiiu deshifrovki."⟩⟩

[65] ⟨⟨In the text there is a misprint; correction to "Iranom" by Barthold's hand.⟩⟩

[66] Iṣṭakhrī, p. 183. ⟦Serjeant, *Islamic Textiles*, p. 69.⟧.

[67] Maqdisī, p. 375. See Barthold, *EI*¹, art. "Bardhaʿa," ⟨⟨*Soch.* III, 372-73.⟩⟩ ⟦D. M. Dunlop, *EI*², s.v.⟧ Silk production and export. The tower in Dorn's time, from the fourteenth century. (Khanikoff concerning the date 722/1322); destruction of the town in Nādir Shāh's time.

[68] ⟨⟨Cf. A. Iakubovskii, "Ibn-Miskaveikh o pokhode Rusov v Berdaa v 332 g. = 943/44 g.," *Vizantiiskii Vremennik*, XXIV (1926), 63-92. For the history of the town,

Bardhaʿa was the point of departure of all the trade routes across Transcaucasia used by the Arabs. These routes comprised the following:

1. The road eastward through Shamākhī to Shīrwān, a region that constitutes a part of the present-day province of Bākū, a region ruled in the Middle Ages by the dynasty of the Shīrwānshāhs.[69] From there it proceeded along the Caspian coast to Darband, the Bāb al-Abwāb of the Arabs and the capital of those parts at the time;[70] the town was larger than Tiflis and was exceeded in size only by Bardhaʿa.[71] The port of Bākū (Bākūh, later Bākūya) is also mentioned, but it did not have a great importance at that time; its rise occurred only after the Mongol invasion, when European travelers often called the Caspian sea the Sea of Bākū.[72]

2. The road southeastward to Baylaqān, located not far from the confluence of the Araxes and the Kur, from there southward to Ardabīl across the so-called Mūqān steppe,[73] and to Vart, the border town of Azerbaijan, seven farsakhs south of Baylaqān. The town of Baylaqān was destroyed in 1221 by the Mongols and no longer exists, although it was rebuilt under Tīmūr in 1403. Already in the year of Clavijo's journey, that is, in 1405, there were up to 20,000 houses in this town.[74]

3. The northwestern road through Ganja, the Janza of the Arabs, now Elisavetpol',[75] to Tiflis. By the thirteenth century, the town had reached such a level of industrial development that it was able to buy off the Mongols with its textiles.[76]

---

see also the literature given in Barthold, *Soch.* III, 373.⟩⟩ ⟦D. S. Margoliouth, "The Russian Seizure of Bardhaʿah in 943 A.D.," *BSOS*, III (1918), 82-95; W. Madelung, in *Cambridge History of Iran*, IV, 233-34.⟧

[69] ⟨⟨Cf. Barthold, *EI*[1], art. "Shīrwān"; Petrushevskii, "Iz istorii Shirvana"; V. Minorsky, *A History of Sharvān and Darband in the 10th and 11th centuries* (Cambridge, (1953); Russian tr., Minorskii, *Ist. Shirvana.*⟩⟩

[70] Iṣṭakhrī, p. 184.⟩⟩

[71] Barthold, *EI*[1], art. "Derbend," *Soch.* III, 419-30. ⟦H. Carrère d'Encausse, *EI*[2], art. "Derbend."⟧ Importance of the town and its harbor; a review in *ZVORAO*, XXI ⟨⟨(Barthold, "Novoe izvestie o stenakh Derbenta"); see also *idem*, "K istorii Derbenta"; and for new literature about the history of the town, see *idem, Soch.* II/1, 786-88; III, 430⟩⟩.

[72] Barthold, *EI*[1], art. "Bākū," *Soch.* III, 350-52. ⟦A. Bennigsen, *EI*[2], art. "Bākū."⟧ The mosque with an inscription from 471/1078. ⟨⟨Information in Mustawfī about a village where the "chief of the priests," *buzurg-i kashīshān*, called Marjāthiyā, refers not to Bākū, as Barthold thought (cf. *Soch.* III, 350-51) but to Mākū. See Petrushevskii, "Khamdallakh Kazvini," p. 910.⟩⟩

[73] ⟨⟨Cf. Minorsky, *EI*[1], art. "Mūḳān."⟩⟩

[74] Tr. Sreznevskii, p. 358 ⟦tr. Le Strange, p. 312; *idem, The Lands*, p. 178⟧.

[75] ⟨⟨Now the city of Kirovabad in the Azerbaijan SSR.⟩⟩

[76] C. d'Ohsson, *Histoire des Mongols*, 1, 334. Barthold, *EI*[1], "Gandja" ⟨⟨*Soch.* III, 405-

4. The road southeastward to the Armenian capital Dwīn.

Under the Sāsānids, all these regions belonged to the Persians, who protected from the nomads' raids the two main roads across the Caucasus mountain chain, namely, the Caspian Gate, that is, the Darband pass, and the Alan Gate, that is, the Daryal Gorge. In the latter half of the Middle Ages as well as today, the Turco-Persian term Qarabāgh instead of the term Arrān has been in use. Mustawfī mentions instead of the above-mentioned roads only the road from Ardabīl to the town of Qarabāgh, which should roughly correspond to the location of Baylaqān, and from there through Ganja to Tiflis.[77] Moreover, a road from Qarabāgh southwestward to Tabrīz through Ahar is mentioned.

407)) ⟦and Barthold-Boyle, *EI*², s.v.⟧. The Arab (in terms of the period of its foundation) town was still small in Iṣṭakhrī's time; account about the earthquake of 533/1138-9; sacked by the Georgians; the gate that had been carried off is in the monastery of Gelata, the inscription has the date 455/1063; Qara Sonqor, d. 535/1140-1. The mausoleum of the poet Niẓāmī; for it see *ZVORAO*, XXI ((Barthold, "Mogila poeta Niẓāmī," *Soch.* II/1, 784-85)). Picture in Jackson, *Persia Past and Present*, p. 3. ((For the history of Ganja, see also Al'tman, *Istoricheskii ocherk*.))

[77] *Nuzhat al-qulūb*, University ms. no. 171, fol. 244 ⟦ed. Le Strange, pp. 181-82, tr. *idem*, pp. 173-74⟧. ((See also Barthold, *EI*¹, arts. "Arrān" and "Dāghestān," *Soch.* III, 334-35, 408-18.)) ⟦R. N. Frye, *EI*², art. "Arrān"; Barthold and A. Bennigsen, art. "Dāghistān"; C. E. Bosworth, art. "Ḳarā Bāgh."⟧

CHAPTER XV

Gīlān and Māzandarān

THE region along the southern coast of the Caspian sea differs radically, in nature and climate, from all the other regions of Iran. Gīlān and Māzandarān, which occupy the narrow belt between the mountains and the sea, suffer not from lack, but from excess of moisture. A multitude of rivers flow from the mountains; most form at their estuaries the so-called *murdābs,* lagoons with stagnant water that emit exhalations of decomposition and are separated by shoals from the sea. There is not a single navigable river on this whole littoral, a feature remarked upon even by the tenth-century geographers.[1] South of this marshy coastal belt extends a zone of thick shrubland; mountains rise further south, their lower slopes covered with dense forests; still higher up are alpine pastures. Amid the overgrowth of shrubs and forests are scattered patches of land cleared of shrubs and trees in order to permit agriculture and human settlement.

In antiquity, the population of Gīlān consisted of the Cadusians, who were independent of the Achaemenid government; this same people, or a part of it, was also called Geloi (Γῆλαι, Γέλαι, Γέλοι), an appellation then transferred to the region itself.[2] Further east lived the Anariachs, Mardoi or Amardoi (a name that was then applied to the river Safīd Rūd as Amardos), and the Tapurs (Τάπυροι or Τάπουροι), whose name the Persians then applied, as Tapuristān, to present-day Māzandarān; this name, later modified by the Arabs as Ṭabaristān, still appears on the coins of the Sāsānid period and of the early Islamic period, just after the Islamic conquest. The eastern part of Māzandarān was reckoned as part of

[1] Iṣṭakhrī, p. 212.

[2] Caspii; Caspiana as part of Albania (Strabo, #502); according to Eratosthenes, the local name of the Caucasus (*ibid.,* #497). The Cadusii among the nations independent of Alexander, to the south of the Geloi (cf. map of Alexander's empire in Sykes, *A History of Persia,* I, 252). The order of succession in Strabo, #510: Γῆλαι καὶ Καδούσιοι καὶ Ἄμαρδοι. The Cadusii were infantry warriors fighting with spears. According to Strabo, #514, the Tapuroi were between the Arioi and the Hyrcanians, the Amardoi were behind the Hyrcanians along the seacoast, cf. Gutschmid, *Geschichte Irans,* pp. 49, 71, and Forbiger, *Handbuch,* II, 567, 589.

Hyrcania. All these peoples, with the exception of the Hyrcanians, were of non-Aryan stock. The Tapurs, who originally lived in the southeastern part of the area, were subjugated early by the Achaemenids; the Mardoi were defeated by Alexander the Great and later by the Parthians, who in the second century B.C. resettled them in the environs of Ray. The former territory of the Mardoi was occupied by the Tapurs; Ptolemy mentions in the area east of Daylam (Δελυμαῖς) on the coast of the Caspian only the Tapurs. Daylam was the mountainous part of Gīlān.

A separate principality was formed in Ṭabaristān, according to some reports, toward the end of the Arsacid period, and maintained itself under the Sāsānids; after the fall of the latter dynasty, the rulers of Ṭabaristān assumed the title of Ispahbads of Khurāsān. One modern scholar, Marquart,[3] points out the fact that alongside the Ispahbad dynasty[4] there was in Ṭabaristān also the dynasty of Pādūspānids[5] (civilian governors), and postulates that at a certain moment, probably at the time when Fīrūz, grandson of Yazdigird III, tried to restore the Iranian state, an entire system of government after the pattern of the Sāsānid state was formed in Ṭabaristān. The Arabs never conquered Gīlān.[6] Ṭabaristān fully submitted to them only under the ʿAbbāsid caliph Manṣūr, although even after that, coins with Pahlavi inscriptions continued to be struck in Ṭabaristān.[7]

Iṣṭakhrī states that in Ṭabaristān the distance between the mountains and the sea nowhere exceeded one day's journey; in some places it reached the foot of the mountains. In Gīlān this distance grew to two days or more.[8] The level of the sea was in the tenth

[3] *Ērānšahr*, p. 133.

[4] The question of the Ispahbads; the ruler of Ṭabaristān called himself Ispahbad, see Yaʿqūbī, *Kitāb al-Buldān*, p. 277. For the Ispahbads, see Ṭabarī, II, 1,206 line 4. ⟦Bosworth, *EI*², art. "Ispahbadh," M. Rekaya, art. "Ḳārinids."⟧

[5] ⟨⟨Persian *padōspān* from the Middle Persian title *patkōspān*.⟩⟩ ⟦F. Justi, *Iranisches Namenbuch* (Marburg, 1895), pp. 245-46; B. Nikitine, *EI*², art. "Bādūsbānids."⟧

[6] For the Daylamites and their relations with the Sāsānids, see Ṭabarī, tr. Nöldeke, pp. 167, 479 (about Persian garrisons; cf. Balādhurī, p. 321).

[7] ⟨⟨Cf. R. Vasmer, "Die Eroberung Ṭabaristāns durch die Araber zur Zeit des Chalifen al-Manṣūr," *Islamica*, III (1927), 86-150; H. L. Rabino, "Les dynasties du Māzandarān de l'an 50 avant l'hégire à l'an 1066 de l'hégire (572 à 1597-1598), d'après les chroniques locales," *JA*, CCXXVIII (1936), 397-474; *idem*, L'histoire du Mâzandarân," *JA*, CCXXXIV (1943-1945), 211-43. For the dynasty of the Ispahbads of Ṭabaristān, see also the bibliography in *Arabskii anonim XI v.*, p. 191.⟩⟩ ⟦R. Vasmer, *EI*¹, art. "Māzandarān, the coins of"; W. Madelung, in *Cambridge History of Iran*, IV, 198 ff.⟧

[8] Iṣṭakhrī, p. 206.

century somewhat higher than today; this can be deduced from the fact that the distance between the town of Sārī and the sea was, according to Ibn al-Faqīh, three farsakhs in all.[9] The staple food of the population was fish; rice predominated among the cereals, as a result of the warm and humid climate. The eastern border of Ṭabaristān passed between Ṭamīs [Tamīsha] and Astarābād, one day's journey east of Ṭamīs. The border city of Ṭabaristān on the west was Shālūs, which lay twenty farsakhs from Āmul and on the seacoast, probably at the estuary of the Chalas. Thus only one part of present-day Māzandarān entered into the structure of Ṭabaristān; its western districts were counted as part of Gīlān, and its eastern ones, together with the city of Astarābād, of Jurjān.[10] As for the province of Gīlān, it appears in the sources as Jīlān or al-Daylam, and was divided into two parts, that of the plains and that of the mountains. In the coastal plain lived the Geloi, al-Jīl, in the mountains "the real Daylams," *al-Daylam al-maḥḍ*. The Geloi constituted the greater part of the population in the littoral and along the border of Ṭabaristān; they spoke a distinct language that differed from Persian, Arranian, and Armenian.[11] Political domination was in the hands of the Daylamīs, from whom there sprang the dynasty of the Justānids, Āl-i Justān, who lived in the town of Ṭārum.[12] This same name (Ṭārum) is still applied to the district along the middle course of the Safīd Rūd. According to other data,[13] the residence of the Justānids was Rūdbār on the Safīd Rūd.[14] In Maqdisī's time, Barwān was considered the chief town of the Daylamīs.[15] It was a minor town whose location is not indicated; nearby was a place called Shahristān, where at the bottom of an excavated well the rulers' treasures were kept. The principal

[9] Ibn al-Faqīh, p. 303, tr. p. 359; see also Ibn al-Faqīh's data in the new edition of the chapter on Ṭabaristān based on the Mashhad ms. in ⟦Ibn al-Faqīh, Russian:⟧ *As-Savad i Ṭabaristān.*

[10] Important for the Muslims of the border ⟨⟨illegible⟩⟩; for Qazwīn in Yāqūt. Remarks about the Ahl Jurjān and about the roads to Khurāsān in Ṭabarī, I, 2,839.

[11] Ibn Ḥawqal, p. 268.

[12] *Ibid.*

[13] Iṣṭakhrī, p. 204.

[14] ⟨⟨For the Justānid dynasty, see also Kasrawī, *Shahriyārān-i gumnām*, I; Minorsky, "La domination des Dailamites," in Minorsky, *Iranica*, pp. 12-30; H. L. Rabino, "Rulers of Gilan," *JRAS* (1920), 277-96; *idem*, "Les dynasties locales du Gîlân et du Daylam," *JA*, CCXXXVII (1949), 301-50.⟩⟩ ⟦W. Madelung, in *Cambridge History of Iran*, IV, 223-26.⟧

[15] Maqdisī, p. 360.

towns of the Geloi are listed only by Maqdisī;[16] from among these the most important one was Dūlāb, a mercantile center not far from the sea, seemingly in the western part of Gīlān, because five days' journey was reckoned from it to Mūghān, and eleven days' journey to Shālūs.[17] According to Iṣṭakhrī, there lived in the mountains yet another people, who spoke a language different from that of the Geloi and the Daylamīs.[18]

Also as a part of Daylam was originally counted the mountainous region of Rūyān or Rūyānij, which occupied the area immediately north of Ray on both slopes of the mountain range; the town of Shālūs was ascribed to this region, but the chief city was called Kajja. Rūyān was annexed to Ṭabaristān only under the governor ʿUmar b. al-ʿAlāʾ, whose coins begin with the year 770 A.D. Four farsakhs from Shālūs lay the "new town," *madīna muḥaddatha*, where ʿUmar b. al-ʿAlāʾ settled the Daylamīs who had adopted Islam and submitted to him; further on lived the Daylamīs who had not acknowledged him.[19] That part of the region which lay on the southern slopes of the mountain range was governed from Ray, the northern part was governed from Ṭabaristān.[20] Mention is also made of the following additional mountain regions: 1). Damāwand and its environs, administered by a special governor whose title was Mas-i Mūghān, that is, the chief of the Magi;[21] this district was conquered by the Arabs under the caliph Manṣūr;[22] 2). the mountains of Sarwīn or "Mountains of Ibn Qārin," further east; here was the town of Sihmār and the fortress of Firrīm, residence of the local rulers; the Arabs subjugated these mountain dwellers in the ninth century, but then they allowed the rise of the local dynasty of the Qārinids;[23] 3). "the mountains of Pādūspān," Jabal Fādūsbān,

[16] *Ibid.*, p., 355, 360. ⟨⟨Cf. Barthold, "Gilian po rukopisi Tumanskogo," *Soch.* VII, 453-55; *Ḥudūd al-ʿālam*, tr. Minorsky, pp. 136-37, 391.⟩⟩

[17] Maqdisī, p. 373.

[18] Iṣṭakhrī, p. 205.

[19] Ibn al-Faqīh, p. 305; tr. p. 361.

[20] Iṣṭakhrī, p. 206. ⟨⟨For the history and historical geography of Rūyān, see Awliyāʾ Allāh Muḥammad b. Ḥasan Āmulī, *Taʾrīkh-i Rūyān* (Tehran, 1313/1934); *Ḥudūd al-ʿālam*, tr. Minorsky, p. 387 and the bibliography there.⟩⟩

[21] Cf. Marquart, *Ērānšahr*, p. 127. ⟨⟨See also *Ḥudūd al-ʿālam*, tr. Minorsky, p. 391; Spuler, *Ivkan in früh-islamischer Zeit,* p. 310, and the bibliography there.⟩⟩ ⟦V. Minorsky, *EI*[1], art. "al-Maṣmughān"; M. Streck, *EI*[2], art. "Damāwand."⟧

[22] Ibn al-Faqīh, pp. 276, 314; tr. pp. 330 ff., 372 ff.

[23] ⟨⟨For Sihmār, Firrīm, and the Qārinid dynasty, see *Ḥudūd al-ʿālam*, tr. Minorsky, p. 387, and the bibliography there.⟩⟩ ⟦M. Rekaya, *EI*[2], art. "Ḳārinids"; C. E. Bosworth, *EI*[2] Suppl. art. "Firrīm."⟧

where there was not a single Friday mosque; the main settlement was called Uram. Like Sihmār, Uram too lay at a distance of one day's journey from Sārī.[24]

In that part of Daylam which retained its independence, the spread of Islam was connected with a popular movement.[25] According to Iṣṭakhrī, the first propagator of Islam in Daylam was the ʿAlid imām Ḥasan b. Zayd; in 864 he led the people of Shalūs and of another border town, Kalār, in their uprising against the Ṭāhirids.[26] This uprising was provoked by an attempt on the part of the Ṭāhirids to seize for their own benefit the lands that were in common use and did not belong to any specific owner.[27] Ḥasan b. Zayd and his successor Muḥammad were obliged to wage ceaseless war for Ṭabaristān and Ray, first with the Ṭāhirids, then with the Ṣaffārids and Sāmānids;[28] the chief support of their rule came from Daylam, where they won to their side the dynasty of the Justānids. Muḥammad b. Zayd fell in 900 in a battle with the Sāmānid troops; in 902 the Justānid ruler of Daylam was pushed out of Ṭabaristān, but managed to maintain himself in his original possessions.[29]

[24] Evidence of Nāṣir-i Khusraw (*Safar-nāma* [Tehran lithog.], pp. 10 ff.) who traveled from Qazwīn to Tabrīz through Gīlān in the summer of 1046. *Ibid.*, pp. 12-13, from Shamīrān (*qaṣaba-yi wilāyat-i Ṭārum*) on 26 Muḥarram; for its ruler: "And this prince writes his name in documents in the following manner: Marzbān of Daylam, Jīl of Jīlān, Abū Ṣāliḥ, client of the Commander of the Faithful; his name is Justān Ibrāhīm." ⟨⟨Cf. Barthold, "K istorii krest'ianskikh dvizhenii," p. 60 n. 1, *Soch.* VII, 446 n. 48); for the title of the ruler, see Spuler, *Iran in früh-islamischer Zeit*, p. 357.⟩⟩ On 14 Ṣafar he arrived in the city of Sarāb, from there on the 16th he passed through Saʿīdābād, on the 26th he arrived in Tabrīz. For Shamīrān, see Le Strange, *The Lands*, p. 226.

[25] The uprising of Māzyār b. Qārin also had a popular character; see Ṭabarī, III, 1,268 ff. ⟨⟨For Māzyār's rebellion, see Barthold," K istorii krest'ianskikh dvizhenii," pp. 57-58, *Soch.* VII, 443-44; Rabino, *Mázandarán and Astarábád*, pp. 408 ff.: V. Minorsky, *EI*[1], art. "Māzyār"; B. Spuler, *Iran in früh-islamischer Zeit*, pp. 65-67 and the bibliography there, pp. 136, 195, 235.⟩⟩ ⟦Sadighi, *Les mouvements religieux iraniens*, pp. 290 ff.⟧

[26] Iṣṭakhrī, p. 205.

[27] Ṭabarī, III, 1,524. ⟦W. Madelung, in *Cambridge History of Iran*, IV, 206-12; Bosworth, *ibid.*, pp. 99-100.⟧

[28] ⟨⟨For Ḥasan b. Zayd, see also Barthold, *Turkestan, Soch.* I, 272; H. L. Rabino, "Les dynasties alaouides du Mazandéran," *JA*, CCX (1927), 253-77; Spuler, *Iran in früh-islamischer Zeit*, pp. 71, 75, 79, 170-71, 221 n. 8, 310.⟩⟩

[29] Gīlān belonged to the ʿAlids in the tenth century; the Justānids existed still in the eleventh century, according to Nāṣir-i Khusraw; from Gīlān there also issued in the tenth century the dynasty of Mārzbān b. Sallār in Azerbaijan ⟨⟨see above, p. 217, n. 18⟩⟩.

The Shīʿī movement was renewed in 914; this time the imām Ḥasan b. ʿAlī al-Uṭrūsh, according to Ibn al-Athīr,[30] called upon the population of Daylam and Gīlān to rise against the Justānids and to accept Islam, while at the same time he promised them freedom from the tithe. The democratic nature of the uprising comes out even more clearly in the words of the eleventh-century historian Bīrūnī, who accuses Ḥasan al-Uṭrūsh of destroying the structure of the clan whose founder was considered to be the mythical hero Farīdūn.[31] Only from this time onward were the Daylamīs officially recognized as Muslims, and as a sign of this Ḥasan ordered the border fortress in Shālūs to be dismantled. Ḥasan died as early as 917; the strong impression made by his reforms is conveyed in the words of the historians, who state that never before had there been such a just ruler.[32] In the same century there issued from among the Daylamī mountain dwellers the Shīʿī dynasty of the Buwayhids, whose members at first served the Ṭabaristān dynasty of the Ziyārids and then became rulers of all Iran except Khurāsān.[a]

The principal cities of present-day Gīlān, Lāhijān and Rasht, are mentioned for the first time in the Mongol period.[33] The development of towns and of crafts in Gīlān began, it would seem, only after the tenth century. The geographers of that century speak of silk production and the manufacture of silk fabrics only in Ṭabaristān, especially Āmul, whither the seeds of mulberry trees were

[30] Ed. Tornberg, VIII, 61.

[31] Barthold, *Turkestan, Soch.* I, 273.

[32] Ṭabarī, III, 2,292. ⟨⟨For Ḥasan Uṭrūsh's rebellion, see also Barthold, "K istorii krest'ianskikh dvizhenii," pp. 58-60, *Soch.* VII, 444-46; Spuler, *Iran in früh-islamischer Zeit,* p. 86 and note 2 with bibliography, pp. 89, 462.⟩⟩ ⟦W. Madelung in *Cambridge History of Iran,* IV, 208-10; R. Strothmann, *EI*², art. "Ḥasan b. Uṭrūsh"; W. Madelung, *EI*² Suppl., art. "al-Ḥasan b. Ḳāsim."⟧

[a] For the Buwayhids, or Būyids, see Cl. Cahen, *EI*², art. "Buwayhids"; H. Busse, *Chalif und Grosskönig, die Buyiden im Iraq (945-1055)* (Beirut-Wiesbaden, 1969); *idem,* "Iran under the Būyids," in *Cambridge History of Iran,* IV, 250-304.

[33] For Rasht, see Le Strange, *The Lands,* p. 174, first mentioned by Mustawfī ("Mustawfî is one of the earliest authorities to describe Rasht, now the capital of Gîlân, but none of the Arab geographers appear even to name it"). Ṭāq-i Gabr in Lāhijān, see Jackson, *From Constantinople to the Home of Omar Khayyam,* p. 89; illustration of the site in the same work, pp. 83-92. Minorsky's remarks in his "Kelyashin," p. 182, that the town of Lāhijān in Gīlān was called Lārjān. In Yāqūt, *Muʿjam,* IV, 340, Lārjān is between Ray and Āmul, eighteen farsakhs from either town. ⟨⟨The districts of Lāhijān (in the form Lāfjān) and Rasht are mentioned in *Ḥudūd al-ʿālam,* fol. 30b; see Barthold, "Gilian po rukopisi Tumanskogo," *Soch.* VII, 454; *Ḥudūd al-ʿālam,* tr. Minorsky, pp. 137, 384, 388, 390, 410 n. 1. For the history of Lāhijān, see H. L. Rabino, "Rulers of Lāhijān and Fūman in Gīlān, Persia," *JRAS* (1918), pp. 85-100.⟩⟩ ⟦Bosworth, *EI*², art. "Lāhīdjān."⟧

brought from Gurgān.[34] In the thirteenth century and later, it was Gīlān silk that enjoyed the greatest renown. Yāqūt, at the beginning of the same century, mentions the silk of a place called Lāhij in Gīlān, that is, from the district of Lāhijān, as being of poor quality.[35] By the end of that same century, the silk of Gīlān, according to Marco Polo, was a commodity coveted by the Genoese merchants whose ships made their appearance on the Caspian shortly before Marco Polo wrote his book.[36] Gīlān was conquered by the Mongols only in 1307, thus much later than the rest of Iran. It was by that time divided up into twelve small principalities and the chief town was Lāhijān. The Mongols penetrated the region from several directions: from Ardabīl, Khalkhāl, Qazwīn, and Sulṭāniyya via Ṭārum.[37] Subsequently, from the end of the fourteenth century and throughout the fifteenth and sixteenth centuries, two small dynasties reigned in Gīlān: the Kiyā dynasty of Lāhijān and the Isḥāqids of Rasht. Both ceased to exist at the close of the sixteenth century.[38] A part of Gīlān with the town of Rasht was conquered by Peter the Great in 1723; according to an agreement concluded in that same year, Iran also ceded to Russia Māzandarān and Astarābād, but neither region was really occupied; even the occupation of Lāhijān in 1725 was realized only through force of arms. In 1729, Russia officially renounced Māzandarān and Astarābād, in 1732 it returned Gīlān and the whole territory south of the Kur, and in 1735 even Bākū and Darband, which were, however, reconquered at the beginning of the nineteenth century.

At the present time, the chief town of Gīlān is Rasht, one of the important commercial centers of Persia; it is situated on the rivulet Shāh Rūdbar (the left-hand channel of the Safīd Rūd), which forms at its estuary the bay of Enzeli, a *murdāb* or lagoon of the abovementioned type; on the spit of land that separates the bay from the sea lies the port of Enzeli. Rasht is the main import and export

[34] Iṣṭakhrī, p. 213. ⟨⟨Cf. *Ḥudūd al-ʿālam*, fols. 29b-30a.⟩⟩

[35] *Muʿjam*, IV, 344.

[36] Tr. Minaev, p. 31 ⟦tr. Yule, I, 51, 56⟧. ⟨⟨For sericulture in Gīlān in the thirteenth, fourteenth, and subsequent centuries, see Petrushevskii, *Zemledelie*, pp. 166-70.⟩⟩ ⟦Serjeant, Islamic Textiles, pp. 71, 75-76.⟧

[37] D'Ohsson, *Histoire des Mongols*, IV, 488-94.

[38] Lane Poole, tr. Barthold, *Musul'manskie dinastii*, pp. 293-94. J. von Hammer-Purgstall, *Geschichte des Osmanischen Reiches* (Pest, 1827-1835), II, 562, concerning an embassy of the Khan of Gīlān Aḥmad in 1588. Cf. Iskandar Munshī, ms., fol. 39a, ed. Tehran, p. 112, tr. Savory, pp. 185-86, concerning a journey to Lāhijān and Qazwīn. The harbor of Lankrūd, on which see Rittikh, *Ocherk Persii*, p. 14 n. 2.

center in the trade with Russia; its importance as the mart of Gīlān has fluctuated with the ups and downs in the main source of the province's wealth, sericulture.[39] A decline in sericulture occurred during the political upheavals at the beginning of the eighteenth century. At the beginning of the nineteenth century, following the reestablishment of order, this branch of industry again showed considerable growth. Rasht had at that time, according to Ferrier, between 60,000 and 80,000 inhabitants,[40] whereas at present the number does not exceed 30,000.[41] Sericulture in Gīlān suffered much from the plague among the silkworms in 1866; measures for a rehabilitation of this industry began to be taken only in 1890. Another product of the environs of Rasht is tobacco. The streets of the city are narrow and dirty, and it has no walls or gates; its environs, like the whole southern coast of the Caspian sea, are conspicuous for their fertility. According to Tumanskii's observations, the people of Gīlān differ even today in their physiognomy from the rest of the Persians and resemble rather the inhabitants of southern Europe;[42] also characteristic are the distinctive peculiarities in their clothes and the type of their dwellings.[43] Tumanskii explains the low standard of living among the peasant population by its almost serflike dependence on the landlords. From Rasht the main road led through the pass of Kharzān to Qazwīn, and from there to Tehran. Of the other cities of Gīlān, only Lāhijān deserves to be mentioned. To the east of it, beyond the mountain of Dulfaq, was the hilly region of Tunkābun with a narrow coastal belt that bordered on Māzandarān; the chief town of Tunkābun was Khurramābād.[44]

[39] Regarding the commerce of Gīlān in 1907, there is an article by S. Olfer'ev, superintendent of the consulate in Rasht, "Torgovlia Giliana." Renaissance of sericulture; tobacco growing, unknown forty years ago, now provides a secure income for the population. Rice began to be grown because of the disease of silkworms; in the past, the wealth of the Gīlānīs was based on sericulture, just as the wealth of the Māzandarānīs was based on rice and cotton. Wheat and barley are almost never sown in the Caspian regions. Cf. Iṣṭakhrī's statement (p. 212) about Māzandarān: "and their bread is mostly [baked] from rice [flour]."

[40] *Travels and Adventures*, p. 151.

[41] Curzon, *Persia*, I, 385; Jackson, *Persia Past and Present*, p. 445: "possibly 100,000." ⟦Lockhart, *Persian Cities*, pp. 73-79. The population in 1976 was 187,203 (*Le monde iranien et l'Islam*, IV [1976-1977], 242).⟧

[42] *Ot Kaspiiskogo moria*, p. 6.

[43] Schiltberger, *Puteshestviia*, pp. 49-50, singles out as a speciality of the Gīlānīs "woven shoes."

[44] ⟨⟨For the historical geography and history of Gīlān, see in addition to the works mentioned above, Barthold, "Mesto prikaspiiskikh oblastei," *Soch.* II/1; Cl. Huart,

As for Māzandarān, both the origin and the time of appearance of this name are unclear. Yāqūt (thirteenth century A.D.) remarks that this name was of recent date, for he did not find it in written sources.[45] Persian authors offer several explanations for this appellation; one claims that it meant "land inside the mountains of Māz," mountains that were said to extend from the border of Gīlān to Jājarm; according to another etymology, Māz was the name of a wall stretching from Gīlān to Jājarm, allegedly built by the local ninth-century ruler Mazyār b. Qārin.[46] Some, however, consider this name to be much older, and interpret the words of the Avesta regarding the "dīws of Māzān" as referring to Māzandarān.[47]

The tenth-century geographers knew Māzandarān, as we have seen, only under the name Ṭabaristān. Its ancient capital was Sārī on the river Tejen,[48] three farsakhs from the sea;[49] today the coast is farther from the town. The rulers of the region, the Ispahbads, lived in the city of Ispahbadān slightly further north, only two miles, that is, about four versts, from the sea. Mention is also made of a place named Tāq in the mountains where, according to tradition, were kept the treasures of the Persian kings from the time of the mythical Manūchihr.[50]

After the Arab conquest, the Ispahbads continued to live in Sārī. Āmul became the residence of the Arab governors; it lay on the left bank of the Haraz, a stream on which there is still a bridge of ancient construction.[51] Āmul soon became the foremost town of

---

EI[1], art. "Gīlān"; H. L. Rabino, "Les provinces caspiennes de la Perse. Le Guîlân," *RMM*, XXXII (1915-1916), 1-499; ʿAbbās Kadīwar, *Taʾrīkh-i Gīlān* (Tehran, 1319/1940); *Ḥudūd al-ʿālam*, tr. Minorsky, pp. 384-91.⟫

45 *Muʿjam*, IV, 392. According to Minorsky, *EI*[1], art. "Māzandarān," the name, known in pre-Islamic Iran, reappears in the Saljuq period, soon supplanting the earlier Islamic name of Ṭabaristān.

46 Ẓahīr al-Dīn Marʿashī, ed. Dorn, p. 21. ⟪Cf. V. Minorsky, *EI*[1], art. "Māzyār."⟫

47 Justi, *Geschichte der orientalischen Völker*, p. 335. ⟪Cf. Jackson, *Persia Past and Present*, pp. 12, 445.⟫

48 In Ẓahīr al-Dīn Marʿashī it is Tījna Rūd or Tajīna Rūd.

49 Approaching from Gurgān, the first town of Ṭabaristān is Ṭāmis between Sārī and Astarābād; concerning the walls, see Ibn Rusta, p. 150. ⟪In the Arab geographers also, Ṭamīsa, in *Ḥudūd al-ʿālam*, fol. 29b, Tamīsha; cf. Le Strange, *The Lands*, p. 375; *Ḥudūd al-ʿālam*, tr. Minorsky, p. 386.⟫ ⟦On these walls and the excavations there, see A.D.H. Bivar and G. Fehérvári, "The Walls of Tammīsha," *Iran, JBIPS*, IV (1966), 35-50. The Tammīsha walls seem to have been a second line of defense after the first line in Gurgān, the so-called "Wall of Alexander," in Türkmen terminology, Qïzïl Yïlan, see R. N. Frye, "The Sasanian System of Walls for Defense," pp. 12-14 in M. Rosen-Ayalon (ed.), *Studies in memory of Gaston Wiet* (Jerusalem, 1977), pp. 7-15.⟧

50 Ibn al-Faqīh, p. 310; tr. p. 368.

51 In Ẓahīr al-Dīn Marʿashī, it is Harhaz.

Ṭabaristān in terms of its population and of the development of its industry; it retained that importance even though the Ṭāhirids and ʿAlids moved the region's capital temporarily back to Sārī. The population of Āmul in the tenth century surpassed that of Qazwīn;[52] the silk fabrics for which Ṭabaristān was famous were manufactured chiefly in Āmul.[53] From Āmul originated the greater part of the historians and scholars whose *nisba* was al-Ṭabarī, among them the famous Muḥammad b. Jarīr, author of the first historical compilation and of the first voluminous Qur'ān commentary. The Arab geographers mention only one road that went from the south through the mountains to Ṭabaristān: from Ray past Mount Damāwand to Āmul.[54]

Besides the dynasties of the Ziyārids and Buwayhids, which gained importance throughout the whole of Persia, there also ruled in Māzandarān during the Middle Ages the local dynasties of the Bāwandids and, in the mountain areas of Rūyān and Rustamdār, the Bādūspānids (Rustamdār is an area along the Shāh Rūd, an affluent of the Safīd Rūd).[55] Also mentioned as a separate political unit is the district of Kabūd-Jāma; according to Ḥamd Allāh Mustawfī Qazwīnī,[56] it was "an island with a large population, whither head the ships from Gīlān and Māzandarān, from which it derives great income; it lies some three farsakhs from Astarābād."[57] At the present time, the distance between Astarābād and the sea is greater, almost thirty versts; the island of Ashur-Ada, which in the nineteenth century became a Russian naval station, lies some ten versts

[52] Iṣṭakhrī, p. 212.

[53] Ibn al-Faqīh, p. 304; tr. p. 361. ⟨⟨For sericulture in Māzandarān, see Petrushevskii, *Zemledelie*, pp. 166, 169-70.⟩⟩ ⟦L. Lockhart, *EI*², s.v.; Serjeant, *Islamic Textiles*, pp. 76-79.⟧

[54] Sykes, *Ten Thousand Miles*, p. 8, regarding the contentment of the Māzandarānīs with their country. For literature on this subject, see W. Geiger, "Kleinere Dialekte und Dialektgruppen," *GIPh*, I, 346; Amīr Pāzwār or Pāzwārī: it is not known when he lived. S. F. Ol'denburg's remarks ("Valentin Alekseevich Zhukovskii," p. 2,044) regarding Amīr Pāzwārī. ⟨⟨For Amīr Pāzwārī and other early medieval poets who wrote in the dialects of Māzandarān and Gīlān, see now J. Rypka, *Dějiny novoperské literatury* (Prague, 1963), pp. 60, 76 ⟦enlarged Eng. tr. (Dordrecht, 1968), pp. 74, 92⟧; Spuler, *Iran in früh-islamischer Zeit*, p. 240 n. 4.⟩⟩

[55] In Rustamdār there are strongholds of the Ismāʿīlīs, Le Strange, *The Lands*, p. 374; the chief fortress, Kalām, was destroyed by the Saljuq sulṭān Muḥammad (Yāqūt, *Muʿjam*, IV, 297).

[56] *Nuzhat al-qulūb*, University ms. 171, fol. 238a ⟦ed. Le Strange, p. 160, tr. *idem*, p. 157⟧.

[57] For Kabūd-Jāma, see Le Strange, *The Lands*, p. 375. The town of Rawʿad or Rawghad measured ⟨⟨according to Mustawfī⟩⟩ 4,000 paces in circuit.

further off the eastern coast.[58] The Bāwandid dynasty ruled, with brief interruptions, until the middle of the fourteenth century; that of the Bādūspānids, as vassal rulers, lasted until the second half of the sixteenth century. The names of most members of both these dynasties (Shahriyār, Rustam, Yazdigird, Ardashīr, and so on), like those of the Ziyārids and Buwayhids, show how long were retained, despite Islam, the traditions of the Sāsānid epoch in these regions.[59] We also know that the inhabitants of the Caspian regions still wore long hair in the fourteenth century, in contrast with the rest of the Muslims.[60]

The Mongols did not encounter much resistance in Māzandarān; Astarābād and the capital of Māzandarān, Āmul, suffered the most in the invasion. Under the Il-Khanids, Astarābād and its environs had some importance as winter quarters of certain khans and princes, the latter being primarily the governors of Khurāsān. Here ruled the last member of the Mongols of Persia, Tuga Tīmūr, who was killed in 1353. Afterwards, Astarābād and the eastern part of Māzandarān were acquired by the amīr Walī, who was defeated by Tīmūr in 1384.[61] In the fourteenth century, a dynasty of Shīʿī imāms, who united temporal and spiritual rule, arose in Māzandarān. In 1392 the province was subjected to Tīmūr's invasion; his soldiers laboriously and with axes hacked their way from Astarābād to Sārī through thick growths of vegetation (*jangal*). The Sayyids fled to the fortress of Māhāna Sar, some four farsakhs from Āmul, near the seacoast on a high hill.[62] Today the distance between Āmul and the coast is reckoned to be only twelve English miles, so that

[58] The occupation of Ashur-Ada by the Russians in 1838. Sykes, *Ten Thousand Miles*, p. 6, Bandar Gaz is to the south of it.

[59] Cf. Lane-Poole, tr. Barthold, *Musul'manskie dinastii*, pp. 290-93. ⟨⟨For the Bāwandids and Bādūspānids, see also Kasrawī, *Shahriyārān-i gumnām*; Rabino, *Mázandarán and Astarábád; idem*, "Les dynasties du Māzanderān."⟩⟩ ⟦Zambaur, *Manuel*, pp. 186 ff.; R. N. Frye, *EI²*, art. "Bāwand."⟧

[60] Ẓahīr al-Dīn Marʿashī, p. 341.

[61] The bay of Nīm-Murdān near the island of Ashur-Ada is mentioned by Mustawfī ⟨⟨cf. Le Strange, *The Lands*, p. 375⟩⟩. Astarābād is mentioned by Isfizārī, Asiatic Museum ms., 574 agh, fols. 80b-81a, regarding silk and other items; revenue: "the *zakāt* revenue from there amounts to eighty *kebekī* tūmāns," that is, somewhat more than all of Kirmān. According to Sykes, *Ten Thousand Miles*, p. 11, about one-half of the territory of Astarābād is inhabited, and the population does not exceed 10,000; according to Dubeux, *La Perse*, the number is 30,000. ⟨⟨For the history of Astarābād, see also the literature mentioned on p. 117, n. 29.⟩⟩

[62] Sharaf al-Dīn Yazdī, I, 570-71. ⟦This dynasty is that of the Ḥusaynid Marʿashī Sayyids, see Zambaur, *Manuel*, p. 193; Rabino, *Mázandarán and Astarábád*, pp. 142-43; Mīr Taymūr Marʿashī, *Taʾrīkh-i Khāndān-i Marʿashī-yi Māzandarān*, ed. Manūchihr Sutūda (Tehran, 2536 *shāhānshāhī*/1336 A.S.H./1967).⟧

little seems to have changed in this part of littoral (in contrast to places further east). The fortress was taken by Tīmūr with the help of a fleet put together by the boatmen of the Āmū Daryā; after its fall, Tīmūr returned to Sārī, where the Sayyids were put on a ship and, according to Ẓahīr al-Dīn, were shipped on the sea and then on the Jayḥūn [that is, the Āmū Daryā] to a destination whence they were sent to Khwārazm, Samarqand, and Tashkent, places of assigned residence for the members of the fallen dynasty.[63] This account of events that took place in 1392 is significant as one of the weightiest arguments for the theory that the course of the Āmū Daryā again changed direction, after Mongol invasion, toward the Caspian, and maintained it down to the second half of the sixteenth century. The historians, Ẓahīr al-Dīn among them,[64] also report the discussions between Tīmūr and the Sayyids, whom he reproached for their hostile behavior toward the Companions of the Prophet. The subsequent ferocious slaughter of the inhabitants of Sārī, Āmul, and other places was explained as punishment of Shīʿī heretics. We know that in Damascus Tīmūr presented himself as an avenger of the insults perpetrated by the Umayyads on the family of the Prophet; this led not only the Arab historians of the time, such as Ibn ʿArabshāh,[65] but even many European scholars (such as Müller, the author of a well-known history of Islam) to consider Tīmūr a protector of the Shīʿīs.[66] But a comparison of Tīmūr's actions in Syria and in the Caspian regions provides the best proof that to him—just as to Chingiz Khan and most other conquerors—religion was only a tool for the attainment of political goals.

After Tīmūr's death, the Sayyids received permission to return to Māzandarān, and they reigned there as vassal rulers to the end of the sixteenth century; from then onward, Māzandarān no longer had any separate political importance. Among the Persian shāhs, ʿAbbās the Great (1587-1628) was the one who paid the most attention to this province.[67] In his reign, a paved road was built from Astarābād to Sārī and Āmul; it made Māzandarān accessible in any season of the year.[68] Khanikoff, who was there in 1858, says that

[63] Ẓahīr al-Dīn, p. 436.

[64] *Ibid.*, pp. 430 ff.

[65] Ed. Manger, I, 632.

[66] A. Müller, *Der Islam im Morgen- und Abendland* (Berlin, 1885-1887), II, 316.

[67] The conquest of Māzandarān in 1596 by way of Āmul (Iskandar Munshī, ms. fols. 77a ff.) ⟦ed. Tehran, pp. 518-20, tr. Savory, pp. 693-98⟧.

[68] The road was laid down in 1622, cf. *ibid.*, fol. 324a-b ⟦ed. Tehran, p. 990, tr. Savory, pp. 1060-61⟧. The road "from the region of Khwār and H.b.lrūd and

the road does not seem to have been repaired since Shāh ʿAbbās's time, and that in many places the paving stones had been removed by peasants.[69] ʿAbbās built for himself palaces in the town of Ashraf, on the road from Astarābād to Sārī seven versts south of the coast, and in that of Faraḥābād, four and one half versts from the estuary of the Tejen, the same river on which Sārī lies; Faraḥābād was the place where Shāh ʿAbbās died. His constructions in both these cities lie in ruins today.

Under Shāh ʿAbbās was created the town of Bārfurūsh, on the small river Bābil[70] along the road from Sārī to Āmul; it too had a palace of Shāh ʿAbbās. As a settlement, however, Bārfurūsh is already mentioned by Ẓahīr al-Dīn; its ancient name was Mamṭīr.[71] Bārfurūsh became at the beginning of the nineteenth century, under Fatḥ ʿAlī Shāh, the foremost city of Māzandarān in terms of trade and population; the latter includes today, according to certain accounts, up to 50,000 souls.[72] At the mouth of the same river, twenty miles from Bārfurūsh, is the anchorage of Mashhad-i Sar, visited by Russian steamers; its name is due to the tradition that the head of the imām al-Riḍā's brother was cut off and buried here. This anchorage is plagued by the same shallowness and other drawbacks that exist in the other harbors of the southern coast of the Caspian. Under Nāṣir al-Dīn Shāh, the Austrian engineer Gasteiger Khan built a road from Tehran to Āmul, and one of the wealthy Persian merchants, Ḥājjī Muḥammad Ḥasan, built a railroad from Āmul to the coast with the help of Belgian engineers; this railroad, however, then fell into neglect.[73]

Fīrūzkūh to Faraḥābād ⟦the distance is⟧ close to eight-nine marches, approximately forty-five farsakhs or perhaps more."

[69] *Mémoire*, p. 71.

[70] In Ẓahīr al-Din Marʿashī, it is Bāwil.

[71] *Ibid.*, p. 80. Mamṭīr or Mamāṭīr in Le Strange, *The Lands*, pp. 374-75, reference to Yāqūt, *Muʿjam*. Incorrect remark on Bārfurūsh, *ibid.*, p. 375 n. 1. In Yāqūt, *Muʿjam*, IV, 642, Mamṭīr is the second largest town of Ṭabaristān; reference to Ibn al-Faqīh, cf. pp. 302, 304.

[72] Also 50,000 in Bārfurūsh, according to Geiger, "Geographie von Iran," *GIPh*, II, 384, and 10,000 in Āmul.

[73] ⟨⟨For the historical geography and history of Māzandarān, see in addition to the works cited above also Barthold, "Mesto prikaspiiskikh provintsii," *Soch.* II/I, 649-772; Ibn Isfandiyār, ed. ʿAbbās Iqbāl (Tehran, 1330-1 /1941-2) and tr. by E. G. Browne (Leiden and London, 1905); ʿAbbās Shāyān, *Māzandarān (awḍāʿ jughrafiyā'ī wa ta'rīkhī)* (Tehran, 1326-7/1937-8); Ahmad Barīmānī, *Daryā-yi Khazar yā Daryā-yi Māzandarān* (Tehran, 1326/1947); Ismāʿīl Māhjūy, *Ta'rīkh-i Māzandarān* (Tehran, 1343/1964); Vanden Berghe, *Archéologie de l'Iran ancien*, pp. 3-7, 140-42.⟩⟩

BIBLIOGRAPHY

Oriental Sources and Texts

Abū Dulaf, see al-Khazrajī.

Abu 'l-Ḥasan b. Muḥammad Amīn Gulistāna. *Mujmal al-ta'rīkh-i ba'd Nādiriyya*. Ed. O. Mann. 2 vols. Leiden, 1891-1896.

Āmulī, Awliyā' Allāh Muḥammad b. Ḥasan. *Ta'rīkh-i Rūyān*. Tehran, 1313/1934.

Astarābādī, Muḥammad Mahdī Khān b. Muḥammad. *Ta'rīkh-i Nādirī*. Tabrīz, 1265/1849.

Bābur, Ẓahīr al-Dīn Muḥammad b. 'Umar. *Bābur-nāma*. Ed. A. S. Beveridge. GMS. I. Leiden and London, 1905. Tr. Beveridge, *The Bābur-nāma in English (Memoirs of Bābur)*. London, 1922.

al-Balādhurī, Aḥmad b. Yaḥyā. *Futūḥ al-buldān*. Ed. M. J. de Goeje. *Liber expugnationis regionum*. Leiden, 1866. Tr. P. K. Hitti and F. C. Murgotten, *The Origins of the Islamic State*, 2 vols. New York, 1916-1924.

Bayhaqī, Abu 'l-Faḍl Muḥammad b. Ḥusayn. *Ta'rīkh-i Mas'ūdī*. Ed. Qāsim Ghanī and 'Alī Akbar Fayyāḍ. Tehran, 1324/1945. Tr. A. K. Arends, *Istoriya Mas'uda 1030-1041*, 2nd ed. Moscow, 1969.

Bayhaqī, see Ibn Funduq.

al-Bīrūnī, Abu 'l-Rayḥān Muḥammad b. Aḥmad. *Taḥqīq mā li 'l-Hind*. Ed. E. Sachau. *Alberuni's India*. London, 1887. Tr. Sachau, Alberuni's India . . . an English Edition. 2 vols. London, 1888.

Ḥāfiẓ-i Abrū, 'Abd Allāh b. Luṭf Allāh. *Dhayl-i Jāmi' al-tawārīkh*. Part 1. Ed. Khānbābā Bayānī. Tehran, 1317/1938. Tr. Bayānī, *Chronique des rois mongols en Iran*. Paris, 1936.

———. *Jughrāfiyā*. Ms. India Office 3874, London.

[Hamza Isfahānī] Ḥasan Fasā'ī Shīrāzī. *Fārs-nāma-yi Nāṣirī*. 2 vols. Tehran, 1313/1895-6. Partial tr. H. Busse, *History of Persia under Qājār Rule*. New York and London, 1972.

Ḥudūd al-'ālam. Tr. and comm. V. Minorsky. *The Regions of the World, a Persian Geography 372 A.H. - 982 A.D.* GMS N. S. XI. London, 1937.

Ibn al-Athīr, 'Izz al-Dīn 'Alī b. Muḥammad. *al-Kāmil fi 'l-ta'rīkh.*

Ed. C. J. Tornberg. *Chronicon quod perfectissimum inscribitur.* 14 vols. Leiden, 1851-1876.

Ibn al-Balkhī. *Fārs-nāma.* Ed. G. Le Strange and R. A. Nicholson. GMS N. S. I. London, 1921. Tr. G. Le Strange, *Description of the Province of Fars in Persia.* London, 1912.

Ibn Baṭṭūṭa, Muḥammad b. ʿAbd Allāh. *Riḥla.* Ed. and tr. C. Defrémery and B. R. Sanguinetti. 4 vols. Paris, 1853-1859. Tr. H.A.R. Gibb, *The Travels of Ibn Battuta.* Hakluyt Society. 3 vols. Cambridge, 1958-1971.

Ibn al-Faqīh, Aḥmad b. Ibrāhīm al-Hamadhānī. *Mukhtaṣar Kitāb al-Buldān.* Ed. M. J. de Goeje. BGA V. Leiden, 1885.

Ibn Funduq, ʿAlī b. Zayd Bayhaqī. *Ta'rīkh-i Bayhaq.* Ed. Aḥmad Bahmanyār. Tehran, 1317/1938.

Ibn Ḥawqal, Abu 'l-Qāsim b. ʿAlī. *Kitāb Ṣūrat al-arḍ.* Ed. M. J. de Goeje. BGA II. Leiden, 1873. Ed. J. H. Kramers. 2 vols. Leiden, 1938. Tr. de Goeje and G. Wiet, *Configuration de la terre.* 2 vols. Paris, 1964.

Ibn Isfandiyār, Muḥammad b. Ḥasan. *Ta'rīkh-i Ṭabaristān.* Ed. ʿAbbās Iqbāl. 2 vols. Tehran, 1330-1/1941-2. Abridged tr. E. G. Browne. *History of Ṭabaristán.* GMS I. Leiden and London, 1905.

Ibn Khurradādhbih, ʿAbd Allāh b. ʿAbd Allāh. *Kitāb al-Masālik wa 'l-mamālik.* Ed. and tr. M. J. de Goeje. BGA VI. Leiden, 1889.

Ibn Rusta, Aḥmad b. ʿUmar. *Kitāb al-Aʿlāq al-nafīsa.* Ed. M. J. de Goeje. BGA VII. Leiden, 1892. Tr. G. Wiet, *Les atours précieux.* Cairo, 1955.

Ibn Zarkūb Shīrāzī, Aḥmad b. Abi 'l-Khayr. *Shīrāz-nāma.* Ed. Bahman Karīmī. Tehran, 1310/1931-2.

Isfizārī, Muʿīn al-Dīn Muḥammad Zamchī. *Rawḍāt al-jannāt fī awṣāf madīnat Harāt.* Ed. Sayyid Muḥammad Kāẓim Imām. 2 vols. Tehran, 1338-9/1959-60. Partial tr. A. C. Barbier de Meynard. "Extraits de la chronique persane d'Herat." *JA*, ser. 5, vol. XVI (1860), 461-520; XVII (1861), 438-57, 473-522; XX (1862), 268-319.

Iskandar Beg Munshī. *Ta'rīkh-i ʿĀlam-ārā-yi ʿAbbāsī.* 3 vols. Tehran, 1313-4/1895-7. Tr. R. M. Savory, *The History of Shah ʿAbbas the Great.* 2 vols. Boulder, Col., 1978.

al-Iṣṭakhrī, Ibrāhīm b. Muḥammad. *Kitāb al-Masālik wa 'l-mamālik.* Ed. M. J. de Goeje. BGA I. 2nd ed. Leiden, 1927.

Jaʿfarī, Jaʿfar b. Muḥammad. *Ta'rīkh-i Yazd.* Ed. Īraj Afshār. Tehran, 1343/1965.

Jūzjānī, Minhāj al-Dīn b. Sirāj. *Ṭabaqāt-i Nāṣirī.* Ed. W. Nassau Lees.

Calcutta, 1863. Ed. ʿAbd al-Ḥayy Ḥabībī. 2nd ed. 2 vols. Kabul, 1342-3/1963-4. Tr. H. G. Raverty. *Ṭabaḳát-i-Náṣirí. A General History of the Muhammadan Dynasties of Asia, including Hindustan.* 2 vols. London, 1881-1899.

al-Khazrajī, Abū Dulaf Misʿar b. Muhalhil. *al-Risāla al-Thāniya.* Ed., tr., and comm. V. Minorsky, *Abū-Dulaf Misʿar ibn Muhalhil's Travels in Iran (circa A.D. 950).* Cairo, 1955.

Khurmūjī, Muḥammad Jaʿfar Husaynī. *Ta'rīkh-i Shīrāz* or *Āthār-i Jaʿfarī.* Tehran, 1276/1860.

Kirmānī, Aḥmad ʿAlī Khān Wazīrī. *Ta'rīkh-i Kirmān (Sālāriyya).* Ed. Muḥammad Ibrāhīm Bāstān-Pārīzī. Tehran, 1340/1961.

al-Māfarrukhī, al-Mufaḍḍal b. Saʿd. *Maḥāsin Iṣfahān.* Ed. Jalāl al-Dīn Ṭihrānī. Tehran, 1312/1933. Enlarged Persian tr. Ḥusayn b. Muhammad Ḥusaynī, *Tarjama-yi Maḥāsin-i Iṣfahān.* Ed. ʿAbbās Iqbāl. Tehran, 1328/1949.

al-Maqdisī, Muḥammad b. Aḥmad. *Aḥsan al-taqāsīm fī maʿrifat al-aqālīm.* Ed. M. J. de Goeje. *Descriptio imperii moslemici.* BGA III. Leiden, 1877.

Marʿashī, Ẓahīr al-Dīn b. Naṣīr al-Dīn. *Ta'rīkh-i Ṭabaristān u Rūyān u Māzandarān.* Ed. B. Dorn. *Muhammedanische Quellen zur Geschichte der südlichen Küstenländer des Kaspischen Meeres,* I. St. Petersburg, 1850. Ed. ʿAbbās Shāyān. Tehran, 1333/1954.

al-Muqaddasī, see al-Maqdisī.

Mustawfī Qazwīnī, Ḥamd Allāh b. Abī Bakr. *Nuzhat al-qulūb.* Partial ed. and tr. G. Le Strange. *The Geographical Part of the Nuzhat-al-qulūb.* 2 vols. GMS XXIII/1-2. London, 1915-1919.

Nāṣir-i Khusraw. *Safar-nāma.* Ed. and tr. Ch. Schefer. Paris, 1881, Ed. Muḥammad Dabīr-Siyāqī. Tehran, 1335/1956.

Nāṣir al-Dīn Shāh Qājār. *Safar-nāma-yi Nāṣir al-Dīn Shāh Qājār ba-Khurāsān (safar-i duwwum).* Tehran, 1306/1889.

Qudāma b. Jaʿfar. *Kitāb al-Kharāj.* Ed. M. J. de Goeje. BGA VI. Leiden, 1889.

Qummī, Ḥasan b. Muḥammad. *Ta'rīkh-i Qum.* Ed. Jalāl al-Dīn Ṭihrānī. Tehran, 1313/1934.

Rashīd al-Dīn Faḍl Allāh Hamadānī. *Jāmiʿ al-tawārikh.* Vol. I, ed. and tr. E. Quatremère, *Histoire de Mongols de la Perse,* Paris, 1836. Vol. II, ed. E. Blochet, *Histoire des empereurs mongols successeurs de Tchinkkiz Khaghan,* GMS XVIII/2, London, 1911. Vol. III, ed. A. A. Alizade, tr. A. K. Arends, Baku, 1957. Vol. I Part 2, tr. O. I. Smirnova, Moscow-Leningrad, 1952. Vol. II, tr. Iu. P. Verkhovskii, Moscow-Leningrad, 1960.

———. *Mukātabāt.* Ed. Muḥammad Shafīʿ. Lahore, 1364/1945.

al-Samʿānī, ʿAbd al-Karīm b. Muḥammad. *Kitāb al-Ansāb*. Facs. ed. D. S. Margoliouth. GMS XX. London, 1912. Ed. ʿAbd al-Raḥmān b. Yaḥyā al-Yamānī *et al.* II vols. Hyderabad, Dcn., 1382-1400/1962-80.

Samarqandī, ʿAbd al-Razzāq b. Isḥāq. *Maṭlaʿ al-saʿdayn wa-majmaʿ al-baḥrayn*. Ed. Muḥammad Shafīʿ. 2 vols. Lahore, 1360-8/1941-9.

Ṣanīʿ al-Dawla Muḥammad Ḥasan Khān Wazīr. *Maṭlaʿ al-shams-i Nāṣirī*. 3 vols. Tehran, 1301-3/1384-6.

al-Ṭabarī, Muḥammad b. Jarīr. *Taʾrīkh al-Rusul wa ʾl-mulūk*. Ed. M. J. de Goeje *et al. Annales*. 14 vols. Leiden, 1879-1901. Partial tr. Th. Nöldeke, *Geschichte der Perser und Araber zur Zeit der Sasaniden*. Leiden, 1879.

Waṣṣāf, ʿAbd Allāh Sharaf b. Faḍl Allāh Shīrāzī. *Taʾrīkh-i Waṣṣāf*. Vol. I. Ed. Bombay, 1269/1853. Ed. and tr. J. von Hammer-Purgstall. Vienna, 1856.

al-Yaʿqūbī, Aḥmad b. Abī Yaʿqūb, Ibn Wāḍiḥ. *Kitāb al-buldān*. Ed. M. J. de Goeje. BGA VIII. Leiden, 1892. Tr. G. Wiet, *Les pays*. Cairo, 1937.

Yāqūt, Yaʿqūb b. ʿAbd Allāh al-Ḥamawī. *Muʿjam al-buldān*. Ed. F. Wüstenfeld. *Yacuts geographisches Wörterbuch*. 6 vols. Leipzig, 1866-1873.

Yazdī, Sharaf al-Dīn ʿAlī. *Ẓafar-nāma*. Ed. Maulawí Muḥammad Ilahdád. 2 vols. Calcutta, 1887-1888. Ed. Muḥammad ʿAbbāsī. 2 vols. Tehran, 1336/1957.

Western and Modern Oriental Studies (other than Russian)

Arberry, A. J. *Shiraz, Persian City of Saints and Poets*. Norman, Okla., 1960.

Balsan, F. *Au Registan inexploré (Sud-Afghan)*. Paris, 1972.

———. *Étrange Baloutchistan*. Paris, 1969.

Barthold, W. *Mīr ʿAlī-Shīr*. Tr. V. and T. Minorsky. *Four Studies on the History of Central Asia*, III. Leiden, 1962.

———. *Turkestan down to the Mongol Invasion*. GMS N.S. V. London, 1928. 3rd. ed. with an additional chapter hitherto unpublished. Ed. C. E. Bosworth. London, 1968.

———. *Ulugh-Beg*. Tr. V. and T. Minorsky. *Four Studies on the History of Central Asia*, II. Leiden, 1958.

Bosworth, C. E. *The Ghaznavids, their Empire in Afghanistan and Eastern Iran 994-1040*. Edinburgh, 1963. 2nd ed. Beirut, 1973.

———. *The Islamic Dynasties, a Chronological and Genealogical Handbook*. Edinburgh, 1965.

———. *Sīstān under the Arabs, from the Islamic Conquest to the Rise of the Ṣaffārids (30-250/651-864)*. Rome, 1968.

Boyce, M. *A History of Zoroastrianism*. Handbuch der Orientalistik. Leiden and Cologne, 1975.

———. *A Persian Stronghold of Zoroastrianism. Based on the Ratanbai Katrak Lectures 1976*. Oxford, 1977.

Brockelmann, C. *Geschichte der arabischen Litereatur*. 2nd ed. 2 vols. and Supplement 3 vols. Leiden, 1937-1949.

Browne, E. G. *A Year amongst the Persians. Impressions as to the Life, Character, and Thought of the People of Persia received during Twelve Months' Residence in that Country in the Years 1887-1888*. London, 1893. 2nd ed. Cambridge, 1926.

The Cambridge History of Iran. I. *The Land of Iran*. Ed. W. B. Fisher. Cambridge, 1968. IV. *From the Arab Invasion to the Saljuqs*. Ed. R. N. Frye. Cambridge, 1975. V. *The Saljuq and Mongol Periods*. Ed. J. A. Boyle. Cambridge, 1968.

Cameron, G. C. *History of Early Iran*. Chicago, 1936.

Caroe, Sir Olaf. *The Pathans 550 B.C. - A.D. 1957*. London, 1958.

Carswell, J. *New Julfa, the Armenian Churches and Other Buildings*. Oxford, 1968.

Chardin, J. *Voyages du Chevalier Chardin, en Perse, et autres lieux de l'Orient*. 4 vols. Amsterdam, 1735. Ed. L. Langlès, 10 vols. and Atlas. Paris, 1811.

Christensen, A. *L'Iran sous les Sassanides*. 2nd ed. Copenhagen, 1944.

Clavijo, Don Ruy Gonzalez de. *Embassy to Tamerlane, 1403-1406*. Tr. G. Le Strange. London, 1928.

Cottrell, A. J., *et al.*, eds. *The Persian Gulf States, a General Survey*. Baltimore and London, 1980.

Curzon, the Hon. G. N. *Persia and the Persian Question*. 2 vols. London, 1892.

Debevoise, N. C. *A Political History of Parthia*. Chicago, 1938.

Dieulafoy, J. *La Perse, la Chaldée et la Susiane*. Paris, 1887.

Diez, E. *Churasanische Baudenkmäler*. Berlin, 1918.

Dorn, B. *Muhammedanische Quellen zur Geschichte der südlichen Küstenländer des Kaspischen Meeres*. 4 vols. St. Petersburg, 1850-1852.

Dubeux, L. *La Perse*. Paris, 1841. 2nd ed. Paris, 1881.

Dupree, L. *Afghanistan*. Princeton, 1973.

Ferrier, J. P. *Caravan Journeys and Wanderings in Persia, Afghanistan, Turkistan, and Baluchistan*. London, 1857. French tr., *Voyages et aventures en Perse, dans l'Afghanistan, le Beloutschistan et le Turkestan.* 2 vols. Paris, 1870.

Fiey, J.-M. *Assyrie chrétienne.* Beirut, 1968.

Fischer, K. "Zur Lage von Kandahar an Landverbindungen zwischen Iran und Indien." *Bonner Jahrbucher des Rheinischen Landmuseum in Bonn,* CLXVII (1967), 129-232.

———; Morgenstern, D. and Thewalt, V. *Nimruz. Geländebegehungen in Sistan 1955-1973 und die Aufnahme von Dewal-i Khodaydad 1970.* 2 vols. Bonn, 1974-1976.

Floyer, E. A. *Unexplored Baluchistán.* London, 1882.

Forbiger, A. *Handbuch der alten Geographie aus den Quellen bearbeitet.* 2nd ed. 2 vols. Hamburg, 1876-1877.

Fraser, J. B. *Narrative of a Journey into Khorasan, in the Years 1821 and 1822, including some Account of the Countries to the North-east of Persia . . .* London, 1825.

———. *Travels and Adventures in the Persian Provinces on the Southern Banks of the Caspian Sea.* London, 1826.

Fraser-Tytler, W. K. *Afghanistan, a Study of Political Developments in Central and Southern Asia.* 3rd ed. revised by M. C. Gillett. London, 1967.

Frye, R. N. *The Golden Age of Persia, the Arabs in the East.* London, 1975.

———. *The Heritage of Persia.* London, 1962.

Gabriel, A. *Durch Persiens Wüsten.* Stuttgart, 1935.

———. *Die Erforschung Persiens. Die Entwicklung der abendländischen Kenntnis der Geographie Persiens.* Vienna, 1952.

Gaube, H. *Die südpersische Provinz Arrağān/Kūh-Gīlūyeh von der arabischen Eroberung bis zur Safawidenzeit. Analyse und Auswertung literarischer und archäologischer Quellen zur historischen Topographie.* Vienna, 1973.

Geiger, W. *Ostīrānische Kultur im Alterthum.* Erlangen, 1882.

——— and Kuhn, E., eds. *Grundriss der iranischen Philologie.* 2 vols. Strassburg, 1895-1904.

Ghirshman, R. *Les Chionites-Hephthalites.* Cairo, 1948.

———. *Iran. Parthes et Sassanides.* Paris, 1962.

———. *Perse. Proto-iraniens, Mèdes, Achéménides.* Paris, 1963.

von Gutschmid, A. *Geschichte Irans und seiner Nachbarländer von Alexander dem Grossen bis zum Untergang der Arsaciden.* Tübingen, 1888.

Henning, W. B. *Zoroaster, Politician or Witch-doctor?* London, 1951.

Herrmann, G. *The Iranian Revival.* Oxford, 1977.

Herzfeld, E. *Iran in the Ancient East.* London and New York, 1941.

———. "Khorasan. Denkmalsgeographische Studien zur Kulturgeschichte des Islam in Iran." *Isl.*, XI (1921), 107-74.

———. *Paikuli. Monument and Inscription of Early History of the Sasanian Empire.* 2 vols. Berlin, 1924.

———. *Zoroaster and His World.* 2 vols. Princeton, 1947.

Holdich, Sir Thomas H. "Afghan Boundary Commission: Geographical Notes." *PRGS*, N. S. VII (1885), 39-44, 160-66, 273-92.

———. *The Gates of India.* London, 1910.

———. *The Indian Borderland 1880-1900.* London, 1901.

Huart, Cl. *La Perse antique et la civilisation iranienne.* Paris, 1925.

Hughes, T. P. *The Country of Balochistan.* London, 1877.

Humlum, J. *et al. La géographie de l'Afghanistan, étude d'un pays aride.* Copenhagen, 1959.

Imperial Gazetteer of India. New ed. 26 vols. Oxford, 1907-1909.

Ivanow, W. *Alamut and Lamasar, Two Mediaeval Ismaili Strongholds in Iran, an Archaeological Study.* Tehran, 1960.

Jackson, A. V. Williams. *From Constantinople to the Home of Omar Khayyam, Travels in Transcaucasia and Northern Persia for Historic and Literary Research.* New York, 1911.

———. *Persia Past and Present, a Book of Travel and Research.* New York, 1906.

———. *Zoroaster, the Prophet of Ancient Iran.* New York, 1899.

Justi, F. *Geschichte des alten Persiens.* Berlin, 1879.

———. *Geschichte der orientalischen Völker im Altertum.* Berlin, 1884.

———. "Geschichte Irans von den ältesten Zeiten bis zum Ausgang der Sāsāniden." *GIPh*, II, 395-551.

Kasrawī, Sayyid Aḥmad. *Shahriyārān-i gum-nām.* 3 vols. Tehran, 1307-8/1928-9.

———. *Ta'rīkh-i pānṣad sāla-yi Khūzistān.* Tehran, 1312/1934.

Kent, R. *Old Persian, Grammar. Texts, Lexicon.* 2nd ed. New Haven, 1953.

Khanikoff, N. *Mémoire sur la partie méridionale de l'Asie Centrale.* Paris, 1861.

———. *Mémoire sur l'ethnographie de la Perse.* Paris, 1866.

Krawulsky, D. *Īrān, das Reich der Īlḫāne, eine topographisch-historische Studie.* Wiesbaden, 1978.

Lambton, A.K.S. *Landlord and Peasant in Persia, a Study of Land Tenure and Land Revenue Administration.* London, 1953.

Lane-Poole, S. *The Mohammadan Dynasties, Chronological and Genealogical Tables with Historical Introductions.* London, 1894.

Layard, A. H. *Early Adventures in Persia, Susiana, and Babylonia*. 2 vols. London, 1887.

Le Strange, G. "Description of Persia and Mesopotamia in the Year 1340 A.D. from the Nuzhat al-Ḳulūb of Ḥamd-Allāh Mustawfī, with a Summary of the Contents of that Work." *JRAS* (1902), 49-74, 237-66, 509-36, 733-84.

———. *The Lands of the Eastern Caliphate, Mesopotamia, Persia, and Central Asia from the Moslem Conquest to the Time of Timur*. Cambridge, 1905.

Lewis, B. *The Assassins, a Radical Sect in Islam*. London, 1967.

Lockhart, L. *Famous Cities of Iran*. London, 1939.

———. *Nadir Shah, a Critical Study Based Mainly upon Contemporary Sources*. London, 1938.

———. *Persian Cities*. London, 1960.

MacGregor, C. M. *Narrative of a Journey through the Province of Khorasan and on the North-West Frontier of Afghanistan in 1875*. 2 vols.

du Mans, R. *Estat de la Perse en 1660, par le P. Raphael du Mans, Supérieur de la Mission des Capucins d'Isfahan*. Ed. Ch. Schefer. Paris, 1890.

Maricq, A. *Classica et Orientalia*. Paris, 1965.

——— and Wiet, G. *Le minaret de Djam, la découverte de la capitale des Sultans Ghorides (XIIe-XIIIe siècles)*. Paris, 1959.

Markwart, J. *A Catalogue of the Provincial Capitals of Ērānshahr*. Ed. G. Messina. Rome, 1931.

———. *Südarmenien und die Tigrisquellen nach griechischen und arabischen Geographen*. Vienna, 1930.

———. *Wehrot und Arang, Untersuchungen zur mythischen und geschichtlichen Landeskunde von Ostiran*. Ed. H. H. Schaeder. Leiden, 1938.

Marquart, J. "Beiträge zur Geschichte und Sage von Erān." *ZDMG*, XLIX (1895), 628-72.

———. *Ērānšahr nach der Geographie des Ps. Moses Xorenacʿi, AGWG*, N. S. III/2. Berlin, 1901.

———. *Untersuchungen zur Geschichte von Eran*. 2 vols. Göttingen and Leipzig, 1896-1905.

Maspero, G. *Histoire ancienne des peuples de l'Orient classique*. 3 vols. Paris, 1895-1899.

Matheson, S. A., *Persia, an Archaeological Guide*. London, 1972.

Melgunof, G. *Das südliche Ufer des Kaspischen Meeres oder die Nordprovinzen Persiens*. Leipzig, 1868.

Ménant, J. *Les Achéménides et les inscriptions de la Perse*. Paris, 1872.

Minorsky, V. "Addenda to the Ḥudūd al-ʿĀlam." *BSOAS*, XVII (1955), 250-70.

———. *Iranica, Twenty Articles/Bīst maqāla-yi Mīnūrskī.* Tehran, 1964.

———. *Studies in Caucasian History.* I. *New Light on the Shaddādids of Ganja.* II. *The Shaddādids of Ani.* III. *Prehistory of Saladin.* London, 1953.

Mordtmann, A. D. "Hekatompylos, ein Beitrag zur vergleichenden Geographie Persiens." *SB Bayr. AW*, I (1869), 497-536.

de Morgan, J. *Mission scientifique en Perse.* I-II. *Études géographiques.* III. *Études géologiques.* IV. *Recherches archéologiques.* V. *Études linguistiques.* 5 vols. Paris, 1894-1904.

Morony, M. G. "Continuity and Change in the Administrative Geography of Late Sasanian and Early Islamic al-ʿIrāq." *Iran, JBIPS*, XX (1982), 1-49.

Naval Intelligence Division, British Admiralty. *Persia.* Geographical Handbook Series. London, 1945.

Nāẓim, Muḥammad. *The Life and Times of Sulṭān Maḥmūd of Ghazna.* Cambridge, 1931.

von Niedermayer, O. *Afghanistan.* Leipzig, 1924.

Nikitine, B. *Les Kurdes, étude sociologique et historique.* Paris, 1956.

Nöldeke, Th. "Das iranische Nationalepos." *GIPh*, II, 130-211. 2nd ed. Berlin and Leipzig, 1920.

d'Ohsson, C. *Histoire des Mongols, depuis Tchinguiz Khan jusqu'à Timour bey ou Tamerlan.* 4 vols. The Hague and Amsterdam, 1834-1835.

Polo, Marco. *The Book of Ser Marco Polo, the Venetian, Concerning the Kingdoms and Marvels of the East.* Tr. Colonel H. Yule. 2 vols. London, 1871. 3rd ed. revised by H. Cordier. 2 vols. London, 1903.

Pope, A. U., and Ackermann, P. A., eds. *A Survey of Persian Art from Prehistoric Times to the Present.* 6 vols. London and New York, 1938-1939.

Rabino di Borgomale, H. L. *Mázandarán and Astarábád.* GMS N.S. VII. London, 1928.

Razmārā, ʿAlī. *Farhang-i jughrāfiyā-yi Irān.* 10 vols. Tehran, 1328-32/1949-53.

Sadighi, Gh. H. *Les mouvements religieux iraniens au IIᵉ et au IIIᵉ siècle de l'hégire.* Paris, 1938.

Sarre, F. *et al. Denkmäler persischer Baukunst. Geschichtliche Untersuchung und Aufnahme muhammedanischer Backsteinbauten in Vorderasien und Persien.* 2 vols. Berlin, 1901-1910.

——— and Herzfeld, E. *Iranische Felsreliefs. Aufnahmen und unter-*

suchungen von Denkmälern aus Alt- und Mittelpersicher Zeit. 2 vols. Berlin, 1910.

Savory, R. M. *History of the Safavids.* Cambridge, 1981.

Schiltberger, Hans. *Reisebuch.* Ed. V. Langmantel. Tübingen, 1885.

Schmidt, E. F. *Persepolis.* I. *Structures, Reliefs, Inscriptions.* II. *Contents of the Treasury and other Discoveries.* 2 vols. Chicago, 1953-1957.

Schurmann, H. F. *The Mongols of Afghanistan, an Ethnography of the Moghôls and Related Peoples of Afghanistan.* The Hague, 1962.

Schwarz, P. *Iran im Mittelalter nach den arabischen Geographen.* 9 vols. Leipzig, Zwickau, Stuttgart, Berlin, 1896-1936.

Serjeant, R. B. *Islamic Textiles, Material for a History up to the Mongol Conquest.* Beirut, 1972.

Spuler, B. *Iran in früh-islamischer Zeit. Politik, Kultur, Verwaltung und öffentliches Leben zwischen der arabischen und der seldschukischen Eroberung 633 bis 1055.* Wiesbaden, 1952.

———. *Die Mongolen in Iran. Politik, Verwaltung und Kultur der Ilchanzeit 1220-1350.* Leipzig, 1939. 2nd ed. Berlin, 1955.

Stein, Sir Aurel. *Archaeological Reconnaissances in North-Western India and Southern Iran.* London, 1937.

———. *An Archaeological Tour in Gedrosia.* Calcutta, 1931.

———. *Old Routes of Western Iran.* London, 1940.

Storey, C. A. *Persian Literature, a Bio-Bibliographical Survey.* I. *Qur'ānic Literature, History and Biography.* II. *Mathematics, Weights and Measures, Astronomy and Astrology, Geography, Medicine, Encyclopaedias and Miscellanies, Arts and Crafts, Science and Occult Arts.* 2 vols. London, 1927-1977.

Streck, M. *Die alte Landschaft Babylonien nach den arabischen Geographen.* 2 vols. Leiden, 1900-1901.

Stronach, D. *Pasargadae, a Report on the Excavations of the British Institute of Persian Studies.* Oxford, 1978.

Sykes, P. M. "Historical Notes on Khurasan." *JRAS* (1910), 1113-54.

———. *A History of Persia.* 2 vols. London, 1915. 3rd ed. London, 1930.

———. *Ten Thousand Miles in Persia or Eight Years in Irán.* London, 1902.

[Taqizadeh, S. H.] *A Locust's Leg, Studies in Honour of S. H. Taqizadeh.* Ed. W. B. Henning and E. Yarshater. London, 1962.

Tarn, W. W. *The Greeks in Bactria and India.* 2nd ed. Cambridge, 1951.

Tate, G. P. *Seistan, a Memoir on the History, Topography, Ruins, and People.* 4 vols. Calcutta, 1910-1912.

Tavernier, J.-B. *Les six voyages de Jean Bapt. Tavernier . . . en Turquie, en Perse, et aux Indes, etc.* 3 vols. Paris, 1712.

Texier, C.F.M. *Description de l'Arménie, la Perse et la Mésopotamie.* 2 vols. Paris, 1839-1852.

Tomaschek, W. "Kritik der ältesten Nachrichten über den skythischen Norden." *SBWAW,* CXVII (1888), 1-70.

———. "Über die ältesten Nachrichten über den skythischen Norden." *SBWAW,* CXVI (1888), 715-80.

———. "Zur historischen Topographie von Persien." *SBWAW,* CII (1883), 145-231; CVIII (1885), 561-66.

della Valle, Pietro. *Viaggi di P. della Valle il pellegrino. . . . Divisi in tre parti cioè, la Turchia, la Persia e l'India. . . .* 3 vols. Venice, 1667. French tr., *Voyages de pietro della Vallé, gentilhomme romain, dans la Turquie, l'Égypte, la Palestine, la Perse, les Indes Orientales, et autres lieux.* 8 vols. Paris, 1745.

Vanden Berghe, L. *Archéologie de l'Irān ancien.* Leiden, 1959.

Wilber, D. N. *Annotated Bibliography of Afghanistan.* New Haven, 1956.

———. *The Architecture of Islamic Iran. The Il Khānid Period.* Princeton, 1955.

Willey, P.J.E. *The Castles of the Assassins.* London, 1963.

Wilson, Sir Arnold T. *The Persian Gulf, an Historical Sketch from the Earliest Times to the Beginning of the Twentieth Century.* London, 1928.

Winckler, H. *Untersuchungen zur altorientalischen Geschichte.* Leipzig, 1889.

Wulff, H. E. *The Traditional Crafts of Persia.* Cambridge, Mass., 1966.

Yate, C. E. *Khurasan and Sistan.* Edinburgh and London, 1900.

———. *Northern Afghanistan or Letters from the Afghan Boundary Commission.* Edinburgh and London, 1888.

de Zambaur, E. *Manuel de généalogie et de chronologie pour l'histoire de l'Islam.* Hanover, 1927.

Works in Russian

Adamov, *Irak Arabskii* – A. A. Adamov. *Irak Arabskii: Bassorskii vilaièt v ego proshlom i nastoiashchem.* Saint Petersburg, 1912.

Adykov, "Doroga" – K. A. Adykov. "Torgovo-pochtovaia doroga iz Merva na Merverrud: K istorii izucheniia srednevekovykh torgovykh putei Turkmenistana." *Izvestiia AN TurkmSSR, SON,* 3 (1962), 50-63.

———, "Glavnye stantsii" – "Glavnye stantsii na srednevekovom torgovom puti iz Serakhsa v Merv (po arkheologicheskim dannym)." *SA*, 4 (1959), 212-27.

Ali-zade, *Ist. Azerbaidzhana* – A. Ali-zade. *Sotsial'no-èkonomicheskaia i politicheskaia istoriia Azerbaidzhana XIII-XIV vv.* Baku, 1956.

Al'tman, *Istoricheskii ocherk* – M. M. Al'tman. *Istoricheskii ocherk goroda Giandzhi.* Chast' I. Baku, 1949.

Arabskii anonim XI v. – *Arabskii anonim XI veka.* Izdanie teksta, perevod, vvedenie v izuchenie pamiatnika i kommentarii P.A. Griaznevicha. Moscow, 1960. (*Pamiatniki literatury narodov Vostoka.* Teksty. Bol'shaia seriia VI.)

Ardatov, *Poslednee politicheskoe dvizhenie* – [M. Ardatov]. *Poslednee politicheskoe dvizhenie v Persii.* 2 parts. Saint Petersburg, 1906-1907.

Aristov, "Anglo-indiiskii 'Kavkaz' " – N. A. Aristov. "Anglo-indiiskii 'Kavkaz.' Stolknoveniia Anglii s avganskimi pogranichnymi plemenami. Ètniko-istoricheskii i politicheskii ètiud. III. Obzor stolknovenii Anglo-Indii s vostochnymi avganskimi plemenami." *Zhivaia starina,* Year X (1900), I-II, 3-150.

Bagrov, *Materialy* – L. S. Bagrov. *Materialy k istoricheskomu obzoru kart Kaspiiskogo moria.* Saint Petersburg, 1912.

Barthold, "Bashnia Kabusa" – V. V. Bartol'd. "Bashnia Kabusa kak pervyi datirovannyi pamiatnik musul'manskoi persidskoi arkhitektury." *Ezhegodnik Rossiiskogo instituta istorii iskusstv.* Petrograd, I, part 2 (1921), 121-25 = *Soch.*, IV, 262-66.

———, "Gilian po rukopisi Tumanskogo" – "Gilian po rukopisi Tumanskogo." *Izvestiia Kavkazskogo Istoriko-arkheologicheskogo instituta v Tiflise,* VI (1928), d63-65 = *Soch.*, VII, 453-55.

———, "Greko-Baktriiskoe gosudarstvo" – "Greko-baktriiskoe gosudarstvo i ego rasprostranenie na severo-vostok." *Izvestiia Imperatorskoi Akademii Nauk,* ser. VI, X (1916), 823-28 = *Soch.*, II/2, 455-60.

———, *Islam* – Islam. Petrograd, 1918 = *Soch.*, VI, 79-139.

———, *Ist. kul'turnoi zhizni Turkestana* – *Istoriia kul'turnoi zhizni Turkestana.* Leningrad, 1927 = *Soch.*, II/1, 167-433.

———, *Istoriko-geograficheskii obzor Irana* – *Istoriko-geograficheskii obzor Irana.* Saint Petersburg, 1903 = *Soch.*, VII, 29-225.

———, "K istorii Derbenta" – "K istorii Derbenta." *ZVORAO*, XIX (1919) xi-xii – *Soch.*, II/1, 786-87.

———, "K istorii krest'ianskikh dvizhenii" – "K istorii krest'ianskikh dvizhenii v Persii." *Iz dalekogo i blizkogo proshlogo; Sbornik ètiudov iz vseobshchei istorii v chest' 50-letiia nauchnoi zhizni N.I. Kareeva.*

———, "K istorii Merva" – "K istorii Merva." *ZVORAO*, XIX (1910), 115-38 = *Soch.*, IV, 172-95.

———, "K istorii persidskogo èposa" – "K istorii persidskogo èposa." *ZVORAO*, XXII (1915), 257-82 = *Soch.*, VII, 383-408.

———, "K voprosu o feodalizme v Irane" – "K voprosu o feodalizme v Irane." *Novyi Vostok*, XXVIII (1930), 108-116 = *Soch.*, VII, 459-68.

———, "K voprosu o iazykakh" – "K voprosu o iazykakh sogdiiskom i tokharskom." *Iran*, I. Leningrad, 1927, pp. 29-41 = *Soch.*, II/2, 461-70.

———, "K voprosu o kaitakakh" – "K voprosu o proiskhozhdenii kaitakov." *Ètnograficheskoe obozrenie*, Year 22, books LXXXIV-LXXXV (1910), 1-2, pp. 37-45 = *Soch.*, V, 369-75.

———, "K voprosu o polumesiatse" – "K voprosu o polumesiatse, kak simvole islama." *Izvestiia Rossiiskoi Akademii nauk*, ser. VI, XII (1918), 475-77 = *Soch.*, VI, 489-91.

———, "Kafiristan v XVI v." – "Kafiristan v XVI v." *Sredne-Aziatskii vestnik*. Tashkent, July 1896, pp. 1-3 = *Soch.*, VIII, 21-22.

———, "Merverrud" – "Merverrud." *ZVORAO*, XIV (1902), 28-32 = *Soch.*, III, 252-56.

———, *Mesto prikaspiiskikh oblastei* – *Mesto prikaspiiskikh oblastei v istorii musul'manskogo mira*. Baku, 1925 = *Soch.*, II/1, 649-772.

———, "Mir-Ali-Shir" – "Mir-Ali-Shir i politicheskaia zhizn'." *Mir-Ali-Shir. Sbornik k piatisotletiiu so dnia rozhdeniia*. Leningrad, 1928, pp. 100-64 = *Soch.*, II/2, 197-260.

———, "Mogila poèta Nizami" – "Mogila poèta Nizami." *ZVORAO*, XXI (1913), 34-36 = *Soch.*, II/1, 784-85.

———, "Novoe izvestie o stenakh Derbenta" – "Novoe izvestie o stenakh Derbenta." *ZVORAO*, XXI (1913), pp. iv-v = *Soch.*, II/1, 788.

———, "O nekotorykh vostochnykh rukopisiakh" – "O nekotorykh vostochnykh rukopisiakh." *Izvestiia Rossiiskoi Akademii nauk*, ser. VI, XIII (1919), 923-30 = *Soch.*, VIII, 340-49.

———, *Oroshenie* – *K istorii orosheniia Turkestana*. Saint Petersburg, 1914 = *Soch.*, III, 97-233.

———, "Ocherk istorii turkmenskogo naroda" – "Ocherk istorii turkmenskogo naroda." *Turkmeniia*. vol. I. Leningrad, 1929, pp. 1-69 = *Soch.*, II/1, 545-623.

———, "Persidskoe ark" – "Persidskoe ark 'krepost', tsitadel'." *Izvestiia Rossiiskoi Akademii istorii material'noi kul'tury*. Petrograd T. I, V, (1920), pp. 29-32 = *Soch.*, VII, 413-16.

Barthold, "Po povodu" – "Po povodu arkheologicheskikh rabot v. Turkestane v 1924 g." *Soobshcheniia Gosudarstvennoi Akademii istorii material'noi kul'tury*, I (1926), 207-16 = *Soch.*, IV, 282-90.

———, "Popravka" – "Popravka k stat'e o proiskhozhdenii kaitakov." *Ètnograficheskoe obozrenie*, Year 22, book LXXXVI-LXXXVII (1911), 3-4, pp. 283-284 = *Soch.*, V, 376.

———, *Soch.* – *Sochineniia*. 9 vols. Moscow, 1963-1976.

———, "Šuʿūbīja" – "Die persische Šuʿūbīja und die moderne Wissenschaft." *ZA*, XXVI (Festschrift für Ignaz Goldziher) (1912), 249-66 = "Persidskaia shuʿubiia i sovremennaia nauka." *Soch.*, VII, 359-70.

———, "Tadzhiki" – "Tadzhiki: istoricheskii ocherk." *Tadzhikistan*. Sbornik statei pod redaktsiei N. L. Korzhenevskogo. Tashkent, 1925, pp. 93-111 = *Soch.*, II/1, 449-68.

———, *Turkestan* – *Turkestan v èpokhu mongol'skogo nashestviia*. 2 vols. Saint Petersburg, 1898-1900 = *Soch.*, I (only ch. II).

———, *Ulugbek* – *Ulugbek i ego vremia*. Petrograd, 1918 = *Soch.*, II/2, 25-196.

———, "Zur Geschichte der Ṣaffāriden" – "Zur Geschichte der Ṣaffāriden." *Orientalische Studien Theodor Nöldeke zum siebzigsten Geburtstag (2. März 1906) gewidmet von Freunden and Schülern und in ihrem Auftrag hrsg. von C. Bezold.* Book I. Giessen, 1906, 171-91 = "K isktorii Saffaridov." *Soch.*, VII, 337-53.

Belenitskii, "Istoricheskaia topografiia Gerata" – A. M. Belenitskii, "Istoricheskaia topografiia Gerata XV v." *Alisher Navoi*: sbornik statei pod redaktsiei A. K. Borovkova. Moscow and Leningrad, 1946, pp. 175-202.

———, "Zoomorfnye trony" – A. M. Belenitskii. "Zoomorfnye trony v izobrazitel'nom iskusstve Srednei Azii." *Izvestiia AN TadzhSSR, OON*, 1, 28 (1962), 14-27.

Beliaev, *Otchet* – D. D. Beliaev. *Otchet o poezdke iz Kermana v Bender-Abbas cherez Gouk, Bam, Dzhiruft i Teng-i-Nivergu v iune i iiule 1906 g.* 2 vols. Tiflis, 1908.

Berezin, *Puteshestvie* – I. N. Berezin. *Puteshestvie po Vostoku*. 2 vols. 2nd ed. Kazan, 1850-1852.

Bertel's, "Baba Kukhi" – E. È. Bertel's. "Baba Kukhi. Predislovie k izdaniiu 'Divana.' " *Izbrannye trudy*. [vol. III]. *Sufizm i sufiiskaia literatura*. Moscow, 1965, pp. 285-99.

———, "Proiskhozhdenie sufizma" – "Proiskhozhdenie sufizma i zarozhdenie sufiiskoi literatury." *Ibid.*, pp. 13-54.

Bodianskii, *Bakhrein* – V. L. Bodianskii. *Bakhrein: K istorii stran Persidskogo zaliva*. Moscow, 1962.

Bogdanov, *Persia* – L. F. Bogdanov, *Persiia v geograficheskom, religioznom, bytovom, torgovo-promyshlennom i administrativnom otnoshenii.* Posobie dlia slushatelei Kursov vostokovedeniia. Saint Petersburg, 1909.

Boldyrev, "Memuary Vosifi" – A. N. Boldyrev, "Memuary Zain-ad-dina Vosifi kak istochnik dlia izucheniia kul'turnoi zhizni Srednei Azii i Khorasana na rubezhe XV-XVI vekov." *Trudy Otdela istorii kul'tury i iskusstva Vostoka Gosudarstvennogo Èrmitazha,* II (1940), 203-74.

———, "Ocherki" – "Ocherki iz zhizni geratskogo obshchestva na rubezhe XV-XVI vv." *Ibid.*, IV (1947), 313-422.

———, *Zainaddin Vasifi* – *Zainaddin Vasifi - tadzhikskii pisatel' XVI v.; Opyt tvorcheskoi biografii.* Stalinabad, 1957.

Bulgakov, "Iz arabskikh istochnikov o Merve" – P. G. Bulgakov. "Iz arabskikh istochnikov o Merve." *Trudy IUTAKÈ*, XII (1963), 213-24.

Bushev, *Gerat i anglo-iranskaia voina* – P. P. Bushev. *Gerat i anglo-iranskaia voina 1856-1857 gg.* Moscow, 1959.

Clavijo, ed. Sreznevskii – Riui Gonzales de Klavikho. *Dnevnik puteshestkviia ko dvoru Timura v Samarkand v 1403-1406 gg.* Podlinnyi tekst s perevodom i primechaniiami, sostavlennymi pod redaktsiei I. I. Sreznevskogo. Saint Petersburg, 1881.

Dandamaev, *Iran* – M. A. Dandamaev. *Iran pri pervykh Akhemenidakh (VI v. do n.è.).* Moscow, 1963.

I. D'iakonov, "Assiro-vavilonskie istochniki" – I. M. D'iakonov. "Assiro-vavilonskie istochniki po istorii Urartu." *Vestnik drevnei istorii* (1951), 2, pp. 255-356; 3, pp. 205-52.

———, *Istoriia Midii* – *Istoriia Midii ot drevneishikh vremen do kontsa IV veka do n.è.* Moscow and Leningrad, 1956.

———, "Narody" – "Narody drevnei Perednei Azii." *Peredneaziatskii ètnograficheskii sbornik,* I. Moscow, 1958, pp. 5-72.

———, *Proiskhozhdenie* – *Proiskhozhdenie armianskogo naroda.* Erivan, 1967.

M. D'iakonov, *Ocherk* – M. M. D'iakonov. *Ocherk istorii drevnego Irana.* Moscow, 1961.

———, "Slozhenie klassovogo obshchestva" – "Slozhenie klassovogo obshchestva v Severnoi Baktrii." *SA*, XIX (1954), 121-40.

Dvoriankov, *Iazyk pushtu* – N. A. Dvoriankov. *Iazyk pushtu.* Moscow, 1960.

Edel'man, *Dardskie iazyki* – D. I. Edel'man. *Dardskie iazyki.* Moscow, 1965.

Efimov, *Iazyk afganskikh khazara* – V. A. Efimov. *Iazyk afganskikh khazara*. Moscow, 1965.

Farmakovskii, *Khudozhestvennyi ideal* – B. V. Farmakovskii. *Khudozhestvennyi ideal demokraticheskikh Afin: obshchii ocherk*. Petrograd, 1918.

Freiman, "Tokharskii vopros" – A. A. Freiman. "Tokharskii vopros i ego razreshenie v otechestvennoi nauke." *Uchenye zapiski LGU*, 128, ser. vostokoved. nauk, III (1952), 123-35.

Frolova, *Beludzhskii iazyk* – V. A. Frolova. *Beludzhskii iazyk*. Moscow, 1960.

Gankovskii, *Imperiia Durrani* – Iu. V. Gankovskii. *Imperiia Durrani: ocherki administrativnoi i voennoi sistemy*. Moscow, 1958.

———, *Narody Pakistana* – *Narody Pakistana: osnovnye ètapy ètnicheskoi istorii*. Moscow, 1964.

———, "Nezavisimoe Afganskoe gosudarstvo" – "Nezavisimoe Afganskoe gosudarstvo Akhmed-shakha Durrani i ego preemnikov (1747-1819)." *Nezavisimyi Afganistan*. Moscow, 1958, pp. 164-79.

Geier, *Putevoditel* – I. I. Geier. *Putevoditel' po Turkestanu*. Tashkent, 1901.

Grantovskii, *Iranoiazychnye plemena Perednei Azii* – È. A. Grantovskii. *Iranoiazychnye plemena Perednei Azii v IX-VIII vv. do n.è.* Avtoreferat dissertatsii na soiskanie uchenoi stepeni kandidata istoricheskikh nauk. Moscow, 1964.

———, "Iranskie imena" – "Iranskie imena iz Priurmiiskogo raiona v IX-VIII vv. do n.è." *Drevnii mir*. Moscow, 1962, pp. 250-65.

Griunberg, "Seistanskii dialekt" – A. L. Griunberg. "Seistanskii dialekt v Serakhse." *Kratkie soobshcheniia Instituta narodov Azii*, LXVII (1963), 76-86.

Grodekov, "Poezdka" – "Poezdka gen. sht. polkovnika Grodekova iz Samarkanda cherez Gerat v Afganistan (v 1878 godu)." *Sbornik geograficheskikh, topograficheskikh i statisticheskikh materialov po Azii*. Saint Petersburgh, V. 1883, pp. 58-107.

Ibn al-Fakikh, *Akhbar al-buldan* – [Ibn al-Faqīh] Ibn al-Fakikh, *Akhbar al-buldan: izvestiia o stranakh*. Vvedenie, perevod s. arabskogo, izdanie teksta i kommentarii A. S. Zhamkochiana. Erivan, 1979.

———, *As-Savad i Tabaristan* – *As-Savad i Tabaristan po mashkhadskoi rukopisi truda Ibn al-Fakikha al-Khamadani*. Izdanie arabskogo teksta, perevod i primechaniia O. V. Tskitishvili. Tbilisi, 1977.

Inostrantsev, "O do-musul'manskoi kul'ture" – K. A. Inostrantsev, "O do-musul'manskoi kul'ture Khivinskogo oazisa." *Zhurnal Ministerstva narodnogo prosveshcheniia,* n.s. XXXI (1911, fevral'), otd. 2, pp. 284-318.

———, "Pereselenie Parsov" – "Pereselenie Parsov v Indiiu i musul'manskii mir v polovine VIII veka." *ZVORAO,* XXIII (1915), pp. 133-66.

———, "Reka Īrān-Vīdzha" – "Reka Īrān-Vīdzha v parsiiskoi traditsii." *Izvestiia Akademii nauk,* ser. VI, XI (1917), 12, pp. 891-95.

Ist. tadzhikskogo naroda – *Istoriia tadzhikskogo naroda.* 2 vols. Moscow, 1963-1964.

Ist. Turkmenskoi SSR – *Istoriia Turkmenskoi SSR.* 2 vols. Ashkhabad, 1957.

Ivanov, *Plemena Farsa* – M. S. Ivanov. *Plemena Farsa: kashkaiskie, khamse, kukhgiluie, mamasani.* Moscow, 1961.

Khalidov, "Knizhnaia kul'tura" – A. B. Khalidov. "Knizhnaia kul'tura." *Ocherki istorii arabskoi kul'tury V–XV vv.* Moscow, 1982, pp. 215-310.

Klimov, "K sostoianiiu deshifrovki" – G. A. Klimov. "K sostoianiiu deshifrovki agvanskoi (kavkazsko-albanskoi) pis'mennosti." *Voprosy iazykoznaniia,* 1967, 3, 68-80.

Klimov-Edel'man, *Iazyk burushaski* – G. A. Klimov and D. I. Edel'man, *Iazyk burushaski,* Moscow, 1970.

Konshin, *Raz"iasnenie* – A. M. Konshin. *Raz"iasnenie voprosa o drevnem techenii Amu-Dar'i po sovremennym geologicheskim i fizikogeograficheskim dannym.* Saint Petersburg, 1897.

Koshelenko, *Kul'tura Parfii* – G. A. Koshelenko. *Kul'tura Parfii.* Moscow, 1966.

Kostenko, *Turkestanskii krai* – L. F. Kostenko, *Turkestanskii krai: Opyt voenno-statisticheskogo obozreniia Turkestanskogo voennogo okruga.* 3 vols. Saint Petersburg, 1880.

Krachkovskii, *Arabskaia geograficheskaia literatura* – I. Iu. Krachkovskii, *Arabskaia geograficheskaia literatura* = *Izbrannye sochineniia.* IV. Moscow and Leningrad, 1957.

Kushkaki – Burkhan-ud-Din-khan-i-Kushkeki. *Kattagan i Badakhshan: Dannye po geografii strany, estestvenno-istoricheskim usloviiam, naseleniiu, èkonomike i putiam soobshcheniia.* Perevod s persidskogo P. P. Vvedenskogo, B. I. Dolgopolova i E. V. Levkievskogo, pod redaktsiei, s predisloviem i primechaniiami A. A. Semenova. Tashkent, 1926.

Lane-Poole, *Musul'manskie dinastii* – S. Lèn-Pul'. *Musul'manskie dinastii: Khronologicheskie i genealogicheskie tablitsy s istoricheskimi vvedeniiami.* Perevel s angliiskogo s primechaniiami i dopolneniiami V. Bartol'd. Saint Petersburg, 1899.

Logofet, *Na granitsakh Srednei Azii* – D. N. Logofet. *Na granitsakh Srednei Azii.* 3 vols. Saint Petersburg, 1909.

Manandian, *Goroda Armenii* – Ia. A. Manandian. *Goroda Armenii* v X-XI vv. Erivan, 1944.

———, *O torgovle i gorodakh* – *O torgovle i gorodakh Armenii v sviazi s torgovlei drevneishikh vremen (V v.* do n.è.-XV v. n.è.). Izd. 2. Erivan, 1954.

Mandel'shtam, "O nekotorykh rezul'tatakh" – A. M. Mandel'shtam. "O nekotorykh rezul'tatakh rabot frantsuzskoi arkheologicheskoi missii v Afganistane." *SA*, XIX (1954), 415-29.

Marr, *Ani* – N. Ia. Marr. *Ani.* Erivan, 1939.

———, "Ani, stolitsa drevnei Armenii" – "Ani, stolitsa drevnei Armenii: Istoriko-geograficheskii nabrosok." *Bratskaia pomoshch' armianam, postradavshim v Turtsii.* Izd. 2. Moscow, 1898, pp. 196-222.

———, "Eshche o slove 'chelebi' " – "Eshche o slove 'chelebi.' " *ZVORAO*, XX (1911), 99-151.

Masal'skii, *Turkestanskii krai* – V. I. Masal'skii. *Turkestanskii krai.* Saint Petersburg, 1913.

M. Masson, "Gorodishcha Nisy" – M. E. Masson. "Gorodishcha Nisy v selenii Bagir i ikh izuchenie." *Trudy IUTAKÈ*, I (1949), 16-105.

———, "K izucheniiu proshlogo Starogo Merva" – "K izucheniiu proshlogo Starogo Merva: Ot redaktora." *Trudy IUTAKÈ*, XII (1963), 7-19.

———, "K istoricheskoi topografii Gerata" – "K istoricheskoi topografii Gerata XV veka." *Velikii uzbekskii poèt.* Sbornik statei pod red. M. T. Aibeka. Tashkent, 1948, pp. 120-45.

———, "Kratkaia khronika" – "Kratkaia khronika polevykh rabot IUTAKÈ za 1948-1952 gg." *Trudy IUTAKÈ*, V (1955), 197-249.

———, "Novye dannye" – "Novye dannye po drevnei istorii Merva: Iz rabot IUTAKÈ." *Vestnik drevnei istorii* (1951), 4, pp. 89-101.

V. Masson, "Arkheologicheskie raboty" – V. M. Masson. "Arkheologicheskie raboty na Misrianskoi ravnine." *Kratkie soobshcheniia Instituta istorii mirovoi kul'tury*, LXIX (1957), 66-71.

———, *Margiana* – *Drevnezemledel'cheskaia kul'tura Margiany.* Moscow and Leningrad, 1959.

———, "Problema drevnei Baktrii" – "Problema drevnei Baktrii i novyi arkheologicheskii material." *SA* (1958), 2, pp. 49-65.

Masson-Romodin – V. M. Masson and V. A. Romodin. *Istoriia Afganistana.* 2 vols. Moscow, 1964-1965.

Materialy po zemle-vodopol'zovaniiu – *Materialy po zemle-vodopol'zovaniiu v Zakaspiiskoi oblasti, sobrannye i izdannye po prikazaniiu Nachal'nika Zakaspiiskoi oblasti, general-leitenanta D. I. Subbotina.* Askhabad, 1903.

Mednikov, *Palestina* – N. A. Mednikov. *Palestina ot zavoevaniia ee arabami do krestovykh pokhodov po arabskim istochnikam.* 2 vols. Saint Petersburg, 1897-1903 = *Pravoslavnyi Palestinskii sbornik,* part 50 (= Vol. XVII, part 2).

Mikhailova, "Novye èpigraficheskie dannye" – A. I. Mikhailova. "Novye èpigraficheskie dannye dlia istorii Srednei Azii IX v." *Èpigrafika Vostoka,* V (1951), 10-20.

Miklukho-Maklai, "Geograficheskoe sochinenie" – N. D. Miklukho-Maklai, "Geograficheskoe sochinenie XIII veka na persidskom iazyke: Novyi istochnik po istoricheskoi geografii Azerbaidzhana i Armenii," *Uchenye zapiski Instituta vostokovedeniia AN,* IX, 1954, pp. 175-219.

A. Miller, "Proshloe i nastoiashchee Seistana" – A. A. Miller, "Proshloe i nastoiashchee Seistana: ocherk," *Zhivaia starina,* XV, 1906, III, pp. 237-48; IV, pp. 297-307.

Minaev, *Svedeniia* – I. Minaev, *Svedeniia o stranakh po verkhov'iam Amu-Dar'i.* SPb., 1879.

Minorskii, *Ist. Shirvana* – V. F. Minorskii, *Istoriia Shirvana i Derbenda X-XI vekov.* M., 1963.

———, "Keliashin" – "Keliashin, stela u Topuzava i drevneishie pamiatniki vbliz Urmiiskogo ozera." *ZVORAO,* XXIV (1917), 145-93.

———, *Materialy* – *Materialy dlia izucheniia persidskoi sekty "Liudi Istiny" ili Ali-Ilakhi.* Moscow, 1911.

Mukhammed Ali, *Afganistan* – Mukhammed Ali, *Afganistan: novyi putevoditel'.* Moscow, 1957.

Musaèlian, *Bibliografiia po kurdovedeniiu* – Zh. S. Musaèlian, *Bibliografia po kurdovedeniiu.* Moscow, 1963.

Narody Perednei Azii – *Narody Perednei Azii.* Pod redaktsiei N. A. Kisliakova i A. I. Pershitsa. Moscow, 1957.

Oganesian, *Arin-berd* – K. L. Oganesian. *Arin-berd: arkhitektura Èrebuni.* Erivan, 1961.

Olivier, "Opisanie" – "Opisanie goroda Ispagani: Otryvok iz puteshestviia g-na F. Oliv'e v Persiiu." *Vostochnye izvestiia*. Astrakhan, 1813, 4, pp. 33-35; 5, pp. 46-48; 6, pp. 52-55.

———, "Puteshestviia" – "Puteshestviia Oliviera v Persiiu i Maluiu Aziiu v 1796 g." *Zhurnal noveishikh puteshestvii*. Saint Petersburg, 1809, I, pp. 3-29; 2, pp. 189-208; 3, pp. 242-88.

Ol'denburg, "Valentin Alekseevich Zhukovskii" – S. F. Ol'denburg. "Valentin Alekseevich Zhukovskii (1858-1918): Popytka kharakteristiki deiatel'nosti uchenogo." *Izvestiia Rossiiskoi AN*, ser. VI, XII (1918), 2039-68.

Olfer'ev, "Torgovlia Giliana" – S. Olfer'ev. "Torgovlia Giliana v 1906-1907 godu: Donesenie upravliaiushchego konsul'stvom v Reshte." *Sbornik konsul'skikh donesenii*, Year XI, I (1908), 60-77.

Oranskii, "Neskol'ko zamechanii" – I. M. Oranskii. "Neskol'ko zamechanii k voprosu o vremeni vvedeniia drevnepersidskoi klinopisi." *Vestnik drevnei istorii* (1966), 2, pp. 107-16.

———, *Vvedenie* – *Vvedenie v iranskuiu filologiiu*. Moscow, 1960.

Orbeli, "Kratkii putevoditel' " – I. A. Orbeli. "Kratkii putevoditel' po gorodishchu Ani." *Izbrannye trudy*. I. Erivan, 1963, pp. 103-32.

———, "Razvaliny Ani" – "Razvaliny Ani." *Ibid*., pp. 1-23.

P'iankov, *Vostochnye satrapii* – I. V. P'iankov. *Vostochnye satrapii derzhavy Akhemenidov v sochineniiakh Ktesiia*. Avtoreferat dissertatsii na soiskanie uchenoi stepeni kandidata istoricheskikh nauk. Moscow, 1966.

Petrushevskii, "Gosudarstva Azerbaidzhana v XV veke" – I. P. Petrushevskii. "Gosudarstva Azerbaidzhana v XV veke." *Izvestiia Azerbaidzhanskogo Filiala AN*, Baku, 1944, 2-3, pp. 85-108.

———, "Iz istorii Shirvana" – "Iz istorii Shirvana (konets XV veka)." *Istoricheskii zhurnal* (1944), 1, pp. 87-91.

———, "Khamdallakh Kazvini" – "Khamdallakh Kazvini kak istochnik po sotsial'no-èkonomicheskoi istorii vostochnogo Zakavkaz'ia." *Izvestiia AN SSSR, OON* (1937), 4, pp. 873-920.

———, *Ocherki* – *Ocherki po istorii feodal'nykh otnoshenii v. Azerbaidzkhane i Armenii v. XVI-nachale XIX vv.* Leningrad, 1949.

———, "Trud Seifi" – Trud Seifi kak istochnik po istorii Vostochnogo Khorasana." *Trudy IUTAKÈ*, V (1955), 130-62.

———, "Vakfnye imeniia" – "Vakfnye imeniia Ardebil'skogo mazara v XVII veke." *Trudy Instituta istorii im. A. Bakikhanova AN AzerbSSR*, I (1947), 24-39.

———, *Zemledelie* – *Zemledelie i agrarnye otnosheniia v Irane XIII-XIV vekov*. Moscow and Leningrad, 1960.

Radlov, *K voprosu ob uigurakh* – V. V. Radlov. *K voprosu ob uigurakh: iz predisloviia k izdaniiu Kudatku-Bilika.* Saint Petersburgh, 1893.

Ramstedt, "Otchet" – "Otchet d-ra G.I. Ramstedta za 1903 god." *Izvestiia Russkogo komiteta dlia izucheniia Srednei i Vostochnoi Azzi v istoricheskom, arkheologicheskom, lingvisticheskom i ètnograficheskom otnosheniiakh,* II (1904), 11-14

Rittikh, *Ocherk Persii* – P. A. Rittikh. *Politiko-statisticheskii ocherk Persii.* Saint Petersburg, 1896.

———, *Otchet o poezdke* – *Otchet o poezdke v Persiiu i persidskii Beludzhistan v 1900 godu.* 2 vols. Saint Petersburg, 1901.

Robertson, *Kafiry Gindukusha* – Sèr Dzh.S. Robertson. *Kafiry Gindukusha: izvlechenie.* Tashkent, 1906.

Romaskevich, "Lar i ego dialekty" – A. A. Romaskevich. "Lar i ego dialekty." *Iranskie iazyki,* I (= *Iranica,* III) (1945), 31-86.

———, "Pesni kashkaitsev" – "Pesni kashkaitsev." *Sbornik Muzeia antropologii i ètnografii,* V, 2 (1925), pp. 573-610.

Rossiia i Turkmeniia v XIX veke – *Rossiia i Turkmeniia v XIX veke: K vkhozhdeniiu Turkmenii v sostav Rossii.* I. Ashkhabad, 1946.

Samoilovich, "Novoe o turkmenakh" – A. N. Samoilovich. "Novoe o turkmenakh." *Zhivaia starina,* XIX (1910), II-III, pp. 297-98.

Semenov, *Musul'manskii mistik* – A. A. Semenov. *Musul'manskii mistik i iskatel' Boga X-XI vv. po R.Kh.: Stranichka iz velikogo proshlogo Zakaspiiskogo kraia.* Askhabad, 1905.

———, "Nadpisi na portale" – "Nadpisi na portale mecheti v Meshed-i-Misrian." *ZVORAO,* XVIII (1908), 154-57.

———, *Ocherki* – *Ocherki iz istorii prisoedineniia vol'noi Turkmenii (1881-1885): po arkhivnym dannym.* Tashkent, 1909.

———, "Razvaliny Abiverda" – "Razvaliny g. Abiverda i pamiatniki stariny vblizi ego." *Trudy Sredne-Aziatskogo GU,* ser. II, *Orientalia,* 3 (1931), 7-27.

Shtal', "Khamadan" – A. F. Shtal'. "Gorod Khamadan i ego okrestnosti." *Izvestiia Imperatorskogo Russkogo geograficheskogo obshchestva,* LII (1916), 3, pp. 395-401.

Staviskii, *Kushanskaia Baktriia* – B. Ia. Staviskii. *Kushanskaia Baktriia: problemy istorii i kul'tury.* Moscow, 1977.

Storey-Bregel' – C. A. Storey. *Persian Literature, a Bio-Bibliographical Survey . . . translated into Russian, edited and expanded by Iu. E. Bregel'.* 3 vols. Moscow, 1972. (Russian title-page: Ch. A. Stori. *Persidskaia literatura, bio-bibliograficheskii obzor.*)

Tizengauzen, "O mecheti Alishakha" – V. Tizengauzen. "O mecheti Alishakha v Tebrize." *ZVORAO,* I (1887), 115-18.

Tokharskie iazyki – *Tokharskie iazyki*. Sbornik statei pod redaktsiei i s vstupitel'noi stat'ei Viach. V. Ivanova. Moscow, 1959.

Trever, *Kavkazskaia Albaniia* – K. V. Trever. *Ocherki po istorii i kul'ture Kavkazskoi Albanii IV v. do n.è.-VII v.n.è.* Moscow and Leningrad, 1959.

———, *Kul'tura drevnei Armenii* – *Ocherki po istorii kul'tury drevnei Armenii (II v. do n.è.-V v.n.è).* Moscow and Leningrad, 1953.

Trubetskoi, *Bakhtiary* – V. V. Trubetskoi. *Bakhtiary: Osedlo-kochevye plemena Irana.* Moscow, 1966.

Tumanskii, *Ot Kaspiiskogo morio* – A. G. Tumanskii. *Ot Kaspiiskogo moria k. Khormuzskomu prolivu i obratno. 1894 g.: Populnye topograficheskie i statisticheskie materialy po Persii.* Saint Petersburg, 1896.

Umniakov-Tumanovich – I. I. Umniakov. *Annotirovannaia bibliografiia trudov akademika V. V. Bartol'da;* N. N. Tumanovich, *Opisanie arkhiva akademika V. V. Bartol'da.* Moscow, 1976.

Usmanova, "Èrk-kala" – Z. I. Usmanova. "Èrk-kala: po materialam IUTAKÈ 1955-1959 gg." *Trudy IUTAKÈ*, XII (1963), 20-94.

Vavilov-Bukinich, *Zemledel'cheskii Afganistan* – N. I. Vavilov and D. D. Bukinich, *Zemledel'cheskii Afganistan.* Leningrad, 1929.

Viazigin, "Stena Antiokha Sotera" – S. A. Viazigin. "Stena Antiokha Sotera vokrug drevnei Margiany." *Trudy IUTAKÈ*, I (1949), 260-75.

Vil'chevskii, *Kurdy* – O. L. Vil'chevskii. *Kurdy: Vvedenie v ètnicheskuiu istoriiu kurdskogo naroda.* Moscow and Leningrad, 1961.

Wright, *Kratkii ocherk* – V. Rait. *Kratkii ocherk istorii siriiskoi literatury.* Perevod s angliiskogo K. A. Turaevoi. Pod redaktsiei i s dopolneniiami prof. P. K. Kokovtsova. Saint Petersburg, 1902.

Zarubin, "K kharakteristike" – I. I. Zarubin. "K kharakteristike mundzhanskogo iazyka." *Iran.* I. Leningrad, 1927, pp. 111-99.

———, "N. Ia. Marr i kandzhutskii iazyk" – "N. Ia. Marr i kandzhutskii (burishsko-vershikskii) iazyk." *Iazyk i myshlenie.* VIII. Moscow and Leningrad, 1937, pp. 165-70.

———, "Vershikskoe narechie" – "Vershikskoe narechie kandzhutskogo iazyka." *Zapiski Kollegii vostokovedov* II/2 (1927), 275-364.

N. Zarubin, "Ocherki" – N. N. Zarubin. "Ocherki po istorii bibliotechnogo dela v drevnei Rusi. I. Primenenie formatnogo printsipa k rasstanovke knig v drevnerusskikh bibliotekakh i ego vozniknovenie." *Sbornik Rossiiskoi Publichnoi biblioteki.* II.

Materialy i issledovaniia. I. Petrograd, 1924, pp. 190-229.

Zarudnyi, "Otchet" – N. Zarudnyi. "Predvaritel'nyi kratkii otchet o poezdke v Persiiu v 1900-1901 gg." *Izvestiia Imperatorskogo Rossiiskogo geograficheskogo obshchestva,* XXXVIII (1902), 2, pp. 127-70.

Zhukovskii, *Materialy* – V. A. Zhukovskii. *Materialy dlia izucheniia persidskikh narechii.* 1-3. Saint Petersburg-Petrograd, 1888-1922.

———, "Mogila Firdousi" – "Mogila Firdousi: Iz poezdki v Khorasan letom 1890 g." *ZVORAO,* VI (1892), pp. 308-14.

———, "Nedavnie kazni" – "Nedavnie kazni babidov v gorode Ezde." *Ibid.,* pp. 321-27.

———, *Razvaliny Starogo Merva* – *Drevnosti Zakaspiiskogo kraia. Razvaliny Starogo Merva.* Saint Petersburg, 1894.

INDEX

Yüeh-chih, 17-19, 68n. *See also* Hayṭal

Zābulistān, 33n
Za'farānlū, 92n
Zagros, 133
Zāhidān, 68, 68n
Zamān Khān, 74n
Zamīndāwar, 72, 74
Zamm, 19
Zanjān, 208, 210, 211, 213, 215, 217n
Zanjān Rūd, 213
Zarafshān, 38
Zarah, 67
Zarand, 128, 129, 137
Zaranj, 50n, 67, 68, 70, 71, 73, 133
Zarda Kūh, 172
Zargān, 153n
Zarkān, 162
Zarq, 41
Zarūn, 144
Zawzān, 135n
Zāyinda Rūd, 170, 171, 175
Zīj-i Ilkhānī, 215
Zindān-i Sulaymān, 149n
Ziyārids, 116, 235, 239, 240
Zoroaster, 8-11, 15, 196n; Zoroastrian, Zoroastrians, 16, 155, 163n, 167, 168n, 179n
Zubayda, 178, 217
al-Zubaydiyya, 198n
Zulfikār, 61
zume, 166
al-Zuṭṭ, 146

Library of Congress Cataloging in Pubication Data
Bartol'd, V. V. (Vasiliĭ Vladimirovich), 1869-1930.
An historical geography of Iran.
(Modern classics in Near Eastern studies)
Translation of: Istoriko-geograficheskiĭ obzor Irana.
Bibliography: p. Includes index.
1. Iran—Historical geography. 2. Soviet Central Asia—Historical Geography. 3. Afghanistan—Historical geography. I. Bosworth, Clifford Edmund. II. Title. III. Series.
DS254.8.B3713 1984 911'.55 83-24548
ISBN 0-691-05418-5